Psychological Anthropology

*An Introduction
to Human Nature
and Cultural Differences*

Erika Bourguignon
The Ohio State University

Holt, Rinehart and Winston
New York   Chicago   San Francisco   Dallas
Montreal   Toronto   London   Sydney

To My Husband
Paul H. Bourguignon

Acknowledgments

All photographs by permission of Paul H. Bourguignon.
Figure 1—Whiting, B. B. & Whiting, J. W. M. *Children in Six Cultures*. Copyright ©1976 by the President and Fellows of Harvard College.
Figures 2 and 3—Bourguignon, E. "World Distribution and Patterns of Possession States." In R. Prince, ed., *Trance and Possession States*. Montreal: R. M. Bucke Memorial Society.
Figure 4—Spindler, G. & Spindler, L. *Dreamers Without Power: The Menomini Indians*. Copyright©1971 by Holt, Rinehart and Winston. Reprinted by permission of Holt, Rinehart and Winston.

Library of Congress Cataloging in Publication Data.

Bourguignon, Erika, 1924–
Psychological anthropology.

1. Ethnopsychology. I. Title.
GN502.B68 301.2 78-27125

ISBN 0-03-034921-4

Printed in the United States of America
9 0 1 2 038 9 8 7 6 5 4 3 2 1

Preface

This book is the product of many years of teaching psychological anthropology to undergraduate and graduate students. In the course of these years, the field has undergone important transformations. We once talked about an anthropological specialty called culture and personality and sought to describe personality patterns, modal or basic, that were thought to characterize specific cultures. The range of possible variations was held to be very great, and personality almost infinitely plastic, to be molded by the great diversity of cultural conditions. The relativity of culture was the key; the modal personality of each society reflected its central themes and configurations.

We now speak of a much broader field, named psychological anthropology. The range of questions asked is far wider, as reflected in the coverage of this book. There is a renewed interest, as in anthropology in general, in a common human nature that underlies the great variations in behavior and attitudes that we have documented. We are concerned with new questions, with more rigorous methods of study, and with practical applications of our findings. In part, too, anthropology has "come home": we are beginning to consider aspects of modern industrial societies, as well as the increasingly changing tribal and peasant societies that were once our primary concern.

To understand our present situation in psychological anthropology, it is helpful to look back at our beginnings and to trace the sources of our orientations. This book, therefore, considers the development of the field wherever it sheds light on current concerns. No one chapter treats the historic background by itself, but historical material is provided throughout the book for each of the subject areas in turn.

Although psychological anthropology is an interdisciplinary field, and we have drawn heavily from personality psychology, child psychology, social psychology, psychiatry, and psychoanalysis, the emphasis in this volume is on the contributions anthropologists have made and on the special orientations they have developed. The principal exception to this practice is Chapter 6, which deals with perception and cognition. Here, the work of cross-cultural psychologists is drawn on heavily.

In this large field, I have attempted to cast a wide net, indeed somewhat wider than has been customary so far. I have defined a series of issues to be dealt with and have drawn on a broad literature to review them. The notes at the end of each chapter offer leads for further explorations.

I have attempted to make the best possible use of materials cited by referring to some of the same important studies at more than one point in the text, since a given report may be relevant to several topics, both with regard to its substantive contribution and the methods it employs. Such cross-references provide an opportunity to recall what has been said in a different context and to relate ideas from different parts of the book to each other. A number of topics also return in several different contexts, and all the topics are set in a historical framework.

Among the themes that recur and are given major attention are the concept of a common human nature and the diversity of the worlds that cultures structure and in terms of which people live. Cultural change and its psychological implications is another such theme.

A note ón the illustrations: the photographs that illustrate this book were taken by my husband, Paul H. Bourguignon. They come, principally, from Haiti and the highlands of Peru. Using pictures of landscapes and people from these two societies throughout makes it possible to provide continuity by means of the scenes that illustrate various topics. At the same time, the striking contrasts between these two societies are worth exploring: Haiti and highland Peru differ importantly in ecology and history and consequently, in race and such visible elements of culture as economy, child training, clothing, and architecture.

A great number of people have contributed to the process of which this book is the current end product. There are, first of all, the students who took my courses in culture and personality, psychological anthropology, and ethnopsychiatry over a period of thirty years. I have learned much from their questions, from their criticisms of course materials, and from the changing orientations and life experiences that they shared with the classes. A number of colleagues read the manuscript and offered helpful comments and criticisms. Among them I especially wish to mention R. Clyde McCone, David Spain, Allen L. Tan, and Richard Thompson. George D. Spindler was particularly generous with his time and thoughtful advice. Semra Somersan and Susan McCabe read the manuscript and provided comments and assistance with various chores. For their work on the production of this manuscript I owe special thanks to Madge Sanders, Sue Griffith, Marge Wedge, Meg Stemple, and Caryl Young.

I wish to thank my editors, James F. Bergin for suggesting that I undertake the writing of this book and David P. Boynton of Holt, Rinehart and Winston for his encouragement and faith in the final product. I am grateful to Arlene Katz, who has given unstintingly of her time and effort in the production of this volume.

My greatest debt is to my husband, Paul H. Bourguignon, whose patience and unfailing support saw me through the bad days, and whose sense of humor helps me to keep a sense of what really matters in this world.

Columbus, Ohio   E.B.
February 18, 1979

Contents

CHAPTER 1

What is Psychological Anthropology?

INTRODUCTION: WHEN ONE CHILD HITS ANOTHER

Children pass in front of our house on their way to and from school. On occasion, some of them fight. We hear voices raised in anger and complaint; one child is hitting another. Two children are chasing each other. One falls, then runs again. The group moves on and the street is quiet until the next few children come along.

Could this scene occur anywhere in the world where children walk to school? If it happens to take place on a residential street in a middle-sized city in the midwestern United States in the late 1970s what is peculiar about it? How does it reflect this particular time and place? How is it part of U.S. culture? And how does it interest the psychological anthropologist?

We can answer these questions best by contrasting our scene with one observed in another part of the world. In Peyrane, a village in southern France, two boys are quarreling. They insult and threaten each other fiercely. Finally one of them strikes the other with his fist. Then he runs away. The other boy makes a brief pretense of chasing him, then goes off.

Here is one more scene, from a third culture. In the mountains of Haiti, two children are walking along a path. They are a girl of seven or eight and a boy of about six. She is hitting him vigorously as they walk along, berating him, and calling him names. He is wailing and complaining loudly, trying to shield himself against her blows, but making no attempt to hit back.

What are the differences between these scenes, and how are they related to the differences in culture and in personality in these three societies?

Let us start with our last example first: what is going on here? Why, for example, does the boy not hit back? When we inquire about this scene, we find that the girl is the boy's older sister, and their mother has put her in charge. He has been disobedient and she is punishing him, as their mother might. They are not equals. She is older, and he, therefore, owes her respect and obedience. She may strike him with full authority to discipline him; he must not strike back. Hitting an older sister is almost as wicked as hitting one's mother, and, informants say, it is a sin to be repented, one to be admitted in confession to the Catholic priest.

What about the French children? Laurence Wylie, who studied the village of Peyrane, tells us:

> If two children start to fight they are immediately separated by any adult who may happen to witness the scene . . . If it is relatives who separate fighting children, both children are punished. No inquiry is made into the question of which child started the fight or which was in the right. They are both fighting and consequently they are both guilty (Wylie 1974:49–50).

This attitude is expressed in the proverbial saying *"jeu de mains, jeu de vilains,"* which greets youngsters observed in rough-and-tumble play. It says that those engaged in rough physical contact play will come to no good.

Wylie goes on to note that adults in Peyrane "will never punish a child for insulting another child." When the children he observed quarreled, "threats of violence were fierce, and the violence rarely occurred." A boy who was struck might chase after the attacker, but he might also cry and run away to seek adult help. Wylie remarks that he never observed a fight that got beyond "the one-blow stage."

Clearly, French parents discourage physical aggression in their children, but allow verbal aggression as an outlet for anger. The behavior of the adults is a model in this regard, for they themselves may on occasion make a great public show of anger in words and threats, but physical fighting is said to be rare.

What of the first example, children in the United States? Physical fighting is engaged in freely. Unlike the French children, they do not run away to seek adult help, and I have never seen an adult intervene. Boys fight among themselves, and at times also boys and girls will hit each other. Traditionally, there are differences in fighting styles between the sexes, but more recently I have seen little girls swing their fists, as boys do.

These observations relate to other aspects of each culture: the first example illustrated an emphasis on self-reliance and independence in children. Adults do not interfere. Aggression is expressed physically among children, as it is frequently in the adult society. School is coeducational and so is social interaction, including fighting. Sex differences are increasingly deemphasized, and little girls and boys learn to fight, as well as to play, alike.

In the United States we strongly value self-reliance and independence and consider that physical fighting, in the form of appropriate self-defense, represents important training. This attitude is illustrated forcefully in yet another scene. In this case, a family from the United States living abroad is anxious to train its children in the traditional patterns of the home culture. The family lives in a residential suburb of Lima, the capital of Peru. Their neighbors are upper-class Peruvians and some Europeans. Johnny, age seven, runs home crying, fleeing once again from some Peruvian street urchins. This time his father does not let him in. Seeing that Johnny is trying to get away from a fight, he calls the two boys, who at that point are themselves fleeing. He explains that he wants each of them to fight with Johnny. To encourage the reluctant youngsters he gives them a few coins. Although the father acts as referee, Johnny is quickly trounced. The neighbors and the Peruvian servants are shocked. Among Johnny's friends are Peruvian upper-class youngsters and several European children. They have been taught not only that physical fighting is wrong, but that it is behavior characteristic of slum children. Accordingly, violence is typical of the poor and uneducated, and self-control and verbal skills distinguish "better" people. They see Johnny's father as cruel and unreasonable, and suspect that in spite of his money, he is of lower-class origins. His behavior shows him to lack proper breeding.[1]

The Haitian example, in spite of first appearances, belongs to a different type of social interaction. We are dealing here with an example of child socialization. Children are beaten to enforce obedience toward elders, a central concern in this society. The little girl who is punishing her brother by striking and berating him is herself obedient to her mother's orders to watch him. Haitian society is based on a hierarchy of age as well as of class. It places less stress on differences in sex, so that the girl may lord it over the younger boy. We would not find an analogous situation in Japan, for example, where hierarchy is also important. There a young

Two children in the Haitian countryside.

boy striking his mother will be thought to be manly! In the Haitian case, furthermore, the age hierarchy is reinforced by religious sanctions: hitting your older sister is a sin. This is a system in which there are no equals. Everyone is either above you or below you in rank.

The French examples, too, show a stress on obedience: "you must not fight" is a fixed injunction. "Who is right" and "who started it" are irrelevant questions. At the same time, value is placed on verbal skills, on the ability to express feelings in dramatic and colorful language. The same value appears in the farming village of Peyrane and among more highly educated people of the large towns and cities. As Martha Wolfenstein points out, in the context of observations in Paris:

> What French children learn is not the prized Anglo-Saxon art of self-defense or the rules that determine a fair fight. What they learn is that their own aggression is not permissible. A consequence of the prohibition against physical aggression is that verbal disputes are substituted for it (Wolfenstein 1963:105).

In small scenes of aggressive interaction among children in four settings we have found a series of striking differences. Not only is the behavior of the children different, but the action sequences are embedded in larger contexts. They are linked, in other words, to important differences in the total cultures. Furthermore, by the age of six or seven, these children already express their own cultures. Children in the United States do not seek adult help; they fight their own fights. This is both a descriptive statement and a normative one. Johnny in Peru is exposed to contradictory pressures. His father, living in a foreign country, seems to feel the need for strong measures not only to impress the traditional values on his son but also to teach him to defend himself in an unfriendly environment. French children know that if they strike and are caught they will be punished; the aggressor therefore runs away. The Haitian child knows that if she—more rarely he—is assigned child-care duties, they involve both the responsibilities and the right to enforce rules. At seven, these children act differently in roughly comparable situations.

We also find that they feel differently about themselves and others. Youngsters in the United States might feel satisfaction at having stood up for their, rights. They have been encouraged by parents not to let others "push them around,"[2] not to be a "crybaby" or a "sissy." They may brag at having taken on the class bully or a youngster who was older or bigger. They have been told to fight their own battles and cannot run to adults for help. A child that does may not only be ridiculed by peers but rebuffed by adults as well. Fighting, then, is part of gaining mastery. Besides, adults see it as a normal part of emotional release, as implied in the quotation from Wolfenstein, an observer from the United States looking at French children.

The French child might feel guilty about having broken the rule against fighting; this child has learned, on the whole, to control physical aggressivity and instead to give vent to emotions in forceful words. One child in Peyrane explained how it feels to be teased at school:

> It makes me want to run after him and show him what's what, but what I really do is to go off into a corner and yell at him, "you wait and see after school. You'll see what happens. You won't go home with your nose in the right place." It's all right to get angry when someone teases you, but there is no excuse for fighting . . . (Wylie 1974:199).[3]

The Haitian child has learned that anger is best vented against someone younger or lower in the social hierarchy, a dog, if need be. Haitian society is organized along lines of hierarchy, so that, at least in theory, an adult man may be beaten by his father. Since overt aggression can be legitimately directed only against inferiors, hostility against others must be expressed by more subtle means, which range from gossip to sorcery.

F. L. K. Hsu has written:

> What we in anthropology need is to deduce premises or postulates about the human condition from the characteristic patterns of affect of each society and culture. . . . Human beings do not feel the same in diverse societies about their fellow humans, their gods, and objects, and in the long run such differences will find expression in their individual and group behavior (Hsu 1978a:7).

As we have seen in our brief examples, such differences in how people feel about each other and about themselves are established early in life, as are the differences in ways of expressing feelings in behavior. Indeed, we started out with examples of behavior and saw that they can be understood only in larger contexts. Culture is a system; it is a puzzle that consists of many interlocking pieces. We can, apparently, start virtually anywhere, with any piece of the puzzle, and if we seek to understand it fully, we will have worked our way through the whole system before we are through.

That group differences in behavior exist is a commonsense observation. Psychological anthropology attempts to discover how such differences come about, and how they are related to other aspects of social life. It also explores basic, underlying similarities among human beings, which set limits to the range of differences and variations that we observe. Both these differences and the underlying unity will be the subject of this book. A great deal has been written about these matters in the past fifty years. We shall see how these and related problems have been approached by anthropologists, and in some instances, by other students of human behavior. We shall try to learn what has been discovered, what methods of research have proven fruitful, and what new questions have emerged in the process.

Our frame of reference throughout will be *cross-cultural,* that is, we shall keep in mind that our society is only one of many and our way of life a special, local phenomenon. U.S. culture and psychological types do not provide us with more than one group of examples of the larger human spectrum. It will help us in understanding ourselves to see how other peoples, at other times and other places, have developed along different lines. Since physical aggression plays such an important part in the United States, it is only fitting that we should have started with a look at aggressive behavior in children.

A WIDER FRAMEWORK

As members of a single species all human beings past and present share a common human nature; yet this common humanity of billions of unique individuals finds its expression in a great range of diverse cultures. The fascination of anthropology resides in the apparent paradox: such a great variety of traditional patterns solves a common set of problems by utilizing common human capacities. A shared human nature has given rise to, is expressed in, and is filtered through a multitude of unique and divergent cultures.

For psychological anthropology, with its emphasis on human behavior and dispositions toward behavior, some aspects of this paradox have been of particular interest. As we take a brief look at the historical background of our subdiscipline we shall see that emphases and concerns have varied over time, and that different paths have been taken by individual investigators. As a result, to assess the field as a whole, we shall have to review a sizable number of approaches and areas of subject matter; yet all point to a small number of key discoveries.

Some of these discoveries are so well established now that it comes as a surprise to realize how recent their acceptance has been. For example, it is generally agreed that the human capacity for culture evolved over time, and that we can see its roots in the animal species that are most closely akin to our own, the living great apes. There are continuities in needs, behaviors, and capacities between ourselves and related life forms. Yet, with its fully developed cultural mode of existence, *Homo sapiens* is unique. Similarities and differences must both be understood, if we are to gain a balanced view of our species. We are not "naked apes," nor are we the product of a separate and special creation. We are, rather, the result of an evolutionary process in which we share distant, but common ancestors with the great apes. What is unique about humanity evolved among species that are now extinct, and of which we have only fragmentary evidence.

We have also learned that the cultural mode of life must be studied not only to make an inventory of objects and customs, nor to evaluate the success of an adaptive response. Such approaches are surely valid in their own right, but they cannot tell the whole story. Differences among human groups are to be found not only in the utilization of the environment, in the objects they make and employ, and in the things they do, but also in what they say and think and feel. There may even be differences in *how* they think and how they perceive the world about them. As a result, we come to see that culture is not merely an external factor or the "man-made part of the human environment," but part and parcel of people's personalities and of their very selves. From birth, indeed from conception, a series of interacting processes takes place: physiological development, growth, and maturation; and language acquisition, cognitive development, personality development, and the learning of cultural ways, often termed socialization. They are all aspects of a single continuous process, which we separate for purposes of analysis only. In the course of this process, culture is "built into" us —it cannot be put on and taken off like a suit of clothes—and we learn much that we are not aware of learning. Moreover, although as individuals we may know some of our own habits or preferences, we often are not able to articulate the regularities that observers refer to as the "culture" of our group.

Culture is learned, or more accurately, in Edward Sapir's phrase, "gradually and gropingly discovered" by each individual in the process of growing up (Sapir 1949 [orig. 1934]:596). It is not handed down complete and fully shaped from generation to generation. It is constantly reworked and reformulated. This fact is true of all human groups, however traditional and conservative.

One of the major discoveries of anthropology in the course of the last century has been precisely the importance of learning in the development of culture, and hence the potential for transformation of individuals and groups. Culture is acquired through learning and experience; it is not inherited in the individual's genetic makeup. The migrations of millions of people to the Americas and the radical transformations that have taken place all over the globe since the end of World War II, for example, all show that cultural changes are a great deal faster than genetic changes. Indeed, the fastest biological changes result from inter-breeding among peoples of different ancestral stocks, itself a by-product of social and cultural processes, such as wars and migrations.

Race and Culture

The emphasis on distinctions between culture and learning, on the one hand, and "race" and biology, on the other, is one of the major achievements of twentieth century anthropology, and of U.S. anthropology in particular. A confusion between the two often arises, as M. J. Herskovits pointed out long ago in his epoch-making discussions of the importance of the African background of Afro-Americans, as a result of the fact that we learn certain aspects of behavior without our being aware of them. They are not consciously taught, but we pick them up through imitation and identification with models. Herskovits (1966 [orig. 1945]: 59) speaks of *cultural imponderables* that are "carried below the level of consciousness." Among them he includes linguistic patterns, musical style, motor habits, systems of values, and codes of etiquette. We might add control or freedom of emotional expression within a cultural style, voice quality and speech rhythms, gesture patterns and dance styles, and so on. Often such features of behavior are ascribed to "race" in popular usage, whether by members of the groups themselves, or by outsiders. Sometimes these racially tagged behaviors are praised and positively valued; sometimes they are part of a low evaluation of a given group.

During the 1930s David Efron (1941) studied differences in gesture patterns among several so-called "racial" groups in New York City: traditional East European Jews, traditional Italians, and Americanized East European Jews and Italians. The gesture patterns of the two traditional groups differed dramatically, although both punctuated their conversations with the active use of their hands. The acculturated groups gestured much less and approximated the U.S. nongesture norm. These findings were interpreted as showing that specific patterns of gestures were part of the cultural heritage of each of the traditional groups. As a different cultural pattern came to be accepted by certain members of these groups, gestures changed, as did language, clothing, and other items of the cultural inventory. The differences in gesture patterns were not part of a "racial" or biological difference between these two ethnic groups, nor between them and older Americans.

Culture, including gesture patterns and speech habits, may change rapidly under appropriate circumstances, without having to wait for slow biological changes to take place. In making such a remark, we generally have in mind that people who, as the phrase has it, were "living in the Stone Age" only a few years ago, are now driving cars or working in factories, while their children are attending universities. However, rapid cultural borrowing and acquisition may be illustrated by other cases as well. For example, when the Spaniards lost their hold on their South American Empire in 1824, many Spanish soldiers remained behind. Some historians have it that these soldiers had sided with the colonists, and others claim that Spain simply did not repatriate a major portion of its army. Whatever the truth may be, in the Peruvian highlands, about the town of Ayacucho, there

"White Indian" in the Peruvian highlands. His features, beard, and moustache show his Spanish ancestry; his clothes indicate his ethnic affiliation.

still live so-called "white Indians": people whose features give evidence of their Spanish ancestry, but whose clothes, speech, and general patterns of behavior make them indistinguishable from their "pure" Indian neighbors.

The notion of "race" that is used when people attribute behavioral characteristics of groups to their biological identity also deserves closer scrutiny. Let us compare the race classification in use in Latin America with that which holds sway in the United States. For example, in this country, even in government guidelines for affirmative action programs, only a small number of terms are used: white, black, oriental, Native American. In Latin America, on the other hand, the list includes a large number of labels for intermediate groups, such as *mestizos, mulatos,* and *zambos.* Marvin Harris (1970) found that Brazilians use more than a dozen different terms, many of which have no North American equivalents. Furthermore, there is little agreement among individuals in assigning these labels, and a variety of social factors are used in placing people into what purport to be "racial" categories.

These striking differences in the classification of "races" among modern societies has an important implication: when people talk about "racial" differences in ability, aptitude, or personality, they are, in fact, not talking about biologically distinct groups at all. Rather, the terms they use are labels for social groupings recognized in the society.

Terms for Our Field

Interest in the interrelations between culture and personality began to develop in the United States in the 1920s and 1930s. In the years just before and during World War II, research in this field grew into a scientific fad. Since then, other fads and trends have come and gone, but culture-and-personality studies have become a standard part of the anthropology curriculum in U.S. colleges and universities. As the faddish aspect of this research area waned, approaches have diversified and the scope of interest in the psychological ramifications of anthropology has increased. Because of these innovations, it has, at times, been claimed that "culture and personality" is dead. However, as George Spindler (1978a) has noted, various "dismal diagnoses" of the field were unwarranted and numerous "obituaries" were premature. Instead, he points to the great current vitality of what he calls "psychologizing anthropology," that is, the application of psychological approaches to anthropological problems and data.

Reference is now most often made to "psychological anthropology" as a subfield of cultural anthropology. At least two of the original concerns of culture-and-personality research have acquired the status of independent specializations and now often are treated as separate areas of study: the comparative, cross-cultural study of mental health and mental illness and the comparative, cross-cultural study of child rearing. The former is, at present, frequently a part of programs of medical anthropology or of transcultural psychiatry; the latter is sometimes linked to training in educational anthropology.

The terms "culture and personality" and "psychological anthropology" will both be used in this book. The first will refer to the somewhat narrower range of concerns that were the principal subject of the original field of study bearing that label. The second will cover a much larger area that includes, among other topics, such current interests of anthropologists as studies in perception and cognition. This subject has concerned social psychologists for a long time. We shall see, however, that there are important differences in the ways in which the two disciplines approach topics in which they appear to have common interests.

In this book, we shall cast a wide net, to provide the reader with a broad view of our field. Our perspective will be cross-temporal as well as cross-cultural. That is, we shall deal with behavioral evolution, cultural evolution, and the psychological relevance of culture change, as well as with comparative, cross-cultural investigations. We shall be concerned primarily with work that has been carried out by anthropologists, but at times we shall refer to the research and writing of colleagues in neighboring fields. Our emphasis will be on research among peoples of diverse traditions yet occasionally we shall find examples closer to home. Since the aim of examples is to reveal principles, readers may well find other examples, from their own experiences, to enlarge on the issues raised in these pages.

PSYCHOLOGY VERSUS PSYCHOLOGICAL ANTHROPOLOGY

Since both psychology and psychological anthropology study human behavior, we might expect a great deal of overlap between these two disciplines. What, then, makes psychological anthropology, and the narrower field of culture and personality, different? How does our approach as anthropologists differ from that of our colleagues in social psychology or, let us say, child psychology?

One difference is obvious: the sociologist and the psychologist in the United States are most likely to study behavior here, although this generalization is certainly much less true today than it was twenty or twenty-five years ago. So-called "primitive," "tribal," or "traditional" societies are to a large extent still left for the anthropologist to investigate.

Nowadays some students of the behavioral sciences are emulating European and Third World scholars who are increasingly engaged in social psychological research in Third World areas. How lively this interest is at present is shown, for example, by the multivolume *Handbook of Cross-Cultural Psychology* (Triandis, Brislin, and Draguns 1979). We shall consider this area of research in some detail in Chapter 6. On the other hand, anthropologists in the United States are slowly beginning to address themselves to studies of their own society, or segments of that society, so that they too are reducing what has traditionally been one of the distinctive features of their discipline. As a result, the difference between the anthropologist and other social and behavioral scientists no longer lies primarily in the choice of the people among whom they carry on their research. It is at best only a superficial distinction. More important differences between cultural anthropology and psychology in the United States today lie in the formulation of research problems and in the methods used to investigate them.

It is true that the choice of location for their research no longer distinguishes anthropologists as clearly from their academic neighbors as it once did. Yet, historically, this choice played an important role. It had a significant impact on the development of the several disciplines, on the problems they investigate, and the methods they employ. As a result, the anthropologist keeps a characteristic basic orientation, implicit if not explicit: a concern with *comparison*. In asking what life is like among Haitian peasants, Ojibwa Indians, or U.S. college students, there is, for the anthropologist, an implicit comparison with other peoples studied at first hand or through the reports of others. This is one reason why fieldwork, particularly in an unfamiliar setting, is such an important part of the training of the cultural anthropologist. The comparisons, then, are *cross-cultural;* the study of any given group, however interesting it·may be, is not an end in itself but a contribution to our knowledge of humanity throughout its history. We ask how the universal human problems are dealt with by a given group, within a given historical and ecological context.

Variations among societies and cultures, great as they may be, fall within limits set by the human psychobiological equipment, the constraints of social life, and the relations between human societies and their environmental settings that we call cultural ecology. Culture, then, may be seen as a variable system of solving constant problems. It is not a random aggregate of traits and complexes fortuitously acquired by a given human society, but a more or less flexible and changing system or structure of more or less congruent elements.

Such a comparative view of culture is directly related to the anthropologist's second orientation, which is also comparative: toward discovering what is generically and specifically human. This concern involves a comparison among species within the framework of *behavioral evolution*. Rather than asking how behavior among the Navajo is different from behavior among the Trobriand Islanders, we ask: how is behavior in groups of a given primate species, say the chimpanzee (*Pan troglodytes*) different from behavior among groups of *Homo sapiens?* And how do we account for these differences?

Although psychologists also study the behavior of other animal species as well as of humans, they do not as a rule address themselves to the problem of the evolution of behavior. They are more likely to be concerned with *similarities* in the behavior they study rather than with differences; for example, with regard to principles of learning, they work as readily with dogs or pigeons as with monkeys or college freshmen.

Similarly, cross-cultural comparisons are not basic to the orientation of most psychologists in the United States who study human social behavior; indeed, the presence of cultural factors is likely to be given scant attention, and the psychologist's approach is likely to be focused much more narrowly. To cite an example at random: a textbook edited by two social psychologists carries the broad title *Human Behavior.* But this topic is narrowed by a more specific subtitle, *A*

Contemporary View of Experimental Research (Baron and Liebert, 1971). The editors might have further added: by U.S. social psychologists working with U.S. subjects. When we look at typical papers in this collection, we find that the subjects were small numbers of Americans, identified as forty-eight undergraduates in a psychology course, forty-eight children between the ages of three and five, sixty-six high school males, and so on. We are told very little about them. Specific hypotheses about human social behavior are formulated and tested with these subjects. No consideration is given to the possibility that U.S. culture, or some aspects of it, or some specific cultural attributes of this or that particular group of subjects might be relevant to their performance in the test situation. The anthropologist might ask: would the expectation expressed in the hypothesis be equally probable for a different cultural group—Eskimos or Tungus? Mbuti pygmies or Haitian peasants? Even in the United States, would it hold equally true of a different age group? Of people at a different educational or class level? Is ethnic membership relevant? In other words, how broadly can the results of these experiments be generalized to human social behavior? Writing in a different context, the psychologist W. K. Estes has described this situation in the following terms: "The main harvest of psychological research has been a vast collection of facts and local principles that are largely specific to particular types of people in particular situations." (Estes 1975:649).

A second difference between psychological anthropology and psychology involves methodology. The research of the psychologist is, as a rule, experimental and statistical, involving the formulation and testing of hypotheses, the building of experimental apparatus, the contriving of situations in the laboratory, and the setting up of specifically predefined, controlled conditions. A good deal of effort and imagination goes into the development of such experiments. The work of the anthropologist, by contrast, is most typically concerned with natural situations, with "field research." These are situations over which the investigator is likely to have only minimal control, although—in personality assessment in particular —various psychological experimental and testing procedures often have been attempted. This anthropological emphasis on comparative field research holds whether we deal with studies in cultural anthropology, where participant observation and interviewing play a prominent role, or with primate studies, where ethological research—the observation of animal behavior in the animals' natural habitat—is of key importance. In either case the field rather than the laboratory is the anthropologist's primary workshop.

Thus, whereas psychologists tend to look for regularities that cut across differences among groups, even among species, anthropologists tend to compare. They look for *both* similarities and differences. And rather than utilizing experimental procedures, anthropologists are likely to attempt to understand a specific set of behaviors within the larger context of the culture. This search for a context, this claim that behavior can be understood only when we know how it fits into the larger cultural and social situation, has been called "holism." Holism, too, distinguishes the anthropological from the psychological approach. In part, too, holism is related to fieldwork, for in the anthropologist's experience there is the field-worker's total immersion in an alien culture. By contrast, the psychologist's laboratory provides a contrived situation, part of whose artificiality resides precisely in the fact that it is not related to a larger sociocultural context, except that of the research itself.

Anthropologists, then, carry on much of their research by doing fieldwork in alien societies, approaching these societies holistically. Generally, they do not carry on experiments, but seek to understand the behavior they observe from the point of view of the people observed; and they view their own research within a comparative framework. Psychologists, on the other hand, typically look for regularities, and carry on experiments to test hypotheses. They work in carefully controlled, contrived situations. As a result, when anthropologists and psychologists claim to be dealing with the same problem, they may actually be talking past each other, addressing different matters. In recent years, as we shall see in Chapter 6, there has been some recognition of these differences, and small beginnings have been made in improving communication between the two disciplines and in removing the obstacles to interdisciplinary research.

Cultural Relativism Versus Ethnocentrism

One important aspect of the comparativist perspective is often spoken of as "cultural relativism." As a point of view, it must be opposed to "ethnocentrism." In field research, cultural relativism means not assuming, wittingly or unwittingly, the superiority of one's own society and culture. It also means that one must expect that the behavior of people in an alien society—particularly one previously unstudied—will be full of surprises, of attitudes and behaviors not to be readily predicted or anticipated. Fieldworkers experience culture shock; they may commit serious errors in interpersonal relationships, thus risking the whole research enterprise, and, on rare occasions, even their lives.

Methodologically, this element of the unanticipated has additional implications. It means that the best-laid research plans may turn out to be faulty and need to be modified as the study progresses. It means that only rarely is enough background information available prior to fieldwork to construct the types of experiments, interview schedules, and other devices readily used by psychologists and sociologists in their home societies. The anthropologist, then, must ever be alert to the need to deviate from a preestablished research plan, to take advantage of unanticipated opportunities in the field situation, and to improvise in the face of unanticipated complexities. The behavior of the people studied must be understood in its own terms, in the context of the institutions, values, and meanings of their particular culture.

In culture-and-personality studies, cultural relativism is a subject to which we shall have frequent occasion to return. It strikes, among other things, directly at the question, "what behavior is normal?" It has bearing on such issues as deviancy and psychopathology, norms of child development, perception and cognition, and many more.

"Psychologizing Anthropology"

Much, if not all, social and cultural anthropology is, in Spindler's terms, "psychologizing" anthropology. This fact has been pointed out most emphatically by critics of psychological anthropology, such as Marvin Harris (1968:395–396) who see a lurking mentalistic cast in most ethnographic monographs, even in the work of the most antipsychological, usually the British social anthropologists.

Some British social anthropologists have themselves been aware of this tendency to bootleg psychological concepts into their analyses of ethnographic data. One of them, I. M. Lewis, has commented on this trend in the work of A. R. Radcliffe-Brown and his intellectual descendants, noting their "phobic reaction to psychoanalysis and psychology" (Lewis 1977:2). At the same time, he himself vigorously attacks "the American Culture and Personality school, with its prostitution of anthropological ideas and materials" (1977:5), ridiculing what he calls the "excesses" of this school. Having thus paid his dues to his fraternity, he goes on to present a most spirited defense of the need for a psychological approach to anthropological investigations:

> It is simply no longer good enough to pretend that the protective posture of blissful ignorance ... still entitles us to ignore what our colleagues in these adjacent fields have to say about the emotions and the motives we so carelessly impute to our informants ... When we assert that customs and institutions significantly modify people's feelings or expect significant effects on their emotions we must be prepared to seek the best possible independent evidence [that is, from psychological research]. ... We must also be much more explicitly aware of the psychological status of our own interpretative assumptions and so be better equipped to assess their value and plausibility (Lewis 1977:14).

Although one must assume that Lewis would not call himself a psychological anthropologist, he makes it clear that he thinks it better to utilize an acknowledged, explicit psychological frame of reference than a covert, "commonsense" approach.

THE HISTORICAL BACKGROUND

The study of culture and personality grew up in the context of U.S. cultural anthropology in the second quarter of this century, when psychoanalysis was becoming increasingly influential in the United States. Psychoanalysis, in more or less modified form, had for a long time the principal psychological influence in this field of anthropology.

Hallowell (1954) has shown common origins for psychology and anthropology about one hundred years earlier, in the first half of the nineteenth century. A full development of common interests, however, only came later under the impact of Darwin's work. For example, much of the earliest German anthropology, such as that of T. Waitz and A. Bastian, was psychologically oriented. This early psychology was a *social* psychology. In this sense E. B. Tylor's (1871:1) famous definition of culture is eminently both social and psychological: "culture," it states, is "that complex whole which includes knowledge, belief, art, law, custom and any other capabilities and habits acquired by man as a member of society." It is social, for it deals with "man as a member of society," not as a unique or isolated individual. It is psychological, because it involves the acquisition (or learning) of patterns of behavior, such as customs, capabilities, and habits, and because it includes cognitive orientations such as knowledge, belief, art (both a set of skills and a body of aesthetic values), and law (values and methods of social control).

Darwin's theory of evolution dealt not only with the evolution of anatomical structures, but also with the evolution of behavior, as shown in his *Descent of Man* (1871) and in the *Expression of Emotion in Man and Animals* (1872). This dimension of Darwinian anthropology had to wait for another three-quarters of a century to be developed.

Another area of early development of psychological anthropology was the work of W. H. R. Rivers, the British psychologist, who participated in the Torres Straits Expedition in 1898, studying the psychology of vision (visual acuity, color vision, color vocabulary, reactions to visual illusions) among the native populations. Similar interests were being developed at the turn of the century in Germany as well by the psychologist Wilhelm Stern and the anthropologist Richard Thurnwald, who worked in what were then the German South Seas colonies. These early comparative studies in perception and cognition also had to wait until the second half of the twentieth century to be taken up again systematically.

One of the most famous early attempts to link psychology and anthropology is W. Wundt's monumental *Völkerpsychologie* (1900–1920). This study was a massive undertaking, seeking to work out a psychological history of humankind in the context of cultural differences. ("Folk psychology," incidentally, is rather an inadequate and unfortunate translation of the title which may be better expressed as ethnic psychology). It is interesting that Wundt, the father of "scientific" (laboratory) psychology, spent the last twenty years of his life on this essentially historical, ethnographic, and philosophical enterprise.

Hallowell (1954:168) has noted that G. Stanley Hall, an American student of Wundt's, "was a key figure in the early promotion in the United States of anthropology and child psychology as well as psychoanalysis." In 1888, he brought Franz Boas to Clark University, where he began his long career of teaching anthropology. Hall was also the author of a book on adolescence, and in accord with the intellectual climate of the day, he saw adolescence as one stage in the development of the individual, which, like other such stages, recapitulates the evolutionary development of mankind. We shall have occasion to return to this evolutionary recapitulation theory in Chapter 2. Here it is interesting to note, that almost forty years after Boas came to Clark University, he wanted Margaret Mead to study the adolescence of girls in Samoa. Writing to her in 1925, before her departure, he said

> One question that interests me very much is how the young girls react to the restraint of custom . . . I am not at all clear in my mind in how far similar conditions [various expressions of rebelliousness] may occur in primitive society and in how far the desire for independence may be simply due to our modern conditions and to a more strongly developed individualism (Mead 1972:138).

The publication in 1928 of Mead's study, *Coming of Age in Samoa: A psychological study of primitive youth for Western Civilization,* is generally cited as marking the beginning of the field of culture and personality. The book is also a fine example of what A. F. C. Wallace (1963:42) has called "the anecdotal veto," for Mead found that, contrary to the theory then generally popular in this country, the universal biological changes of adolescence are not everywhere associated with social and psychological storm and stress. The universal rule is disproved by a single negative instance.

Aside from the substance of Mead's findings and the landmark character of the publication, a number of other points concerning this study deserve mention. Mead herself has discussed in some detail how she came to make the study and her preparation (or rather lack of preparation) for it, from the perspective of many later field trips and close to fifty years as an anthropologist (Mead 1972). These important pages should now be read together with the earlier book that they so greatly illuminate. We know that the cross-cultural test of a Western psychological hypothesis was Boas' idea, and this fits well with remarks he made at Clark University, in 1909, on the historical occasion of the visit there by Freud and Jung:

> We [anthropologists] are endeavoring to elucidate the events which have led to the formation of human types, past and present . . . We are also trying to determine the psychological laws which control the mind of man everywhere, and that may differ in various racial and social groups (Boas 1911, cited in Hallowell 1954:188).

A second notable feature of this first of Mead's many studies is the influence on her methods and approach of contemporary psychology, such as her attempt to use modified intelligence tests (Mead 1928, Appendix V), and an absence of any influence of psychoanalysis at that time, in spite of the fact that there is a good deal of talk of sex and sexual experimentation in descriptions of Samoan adolescence. Finally, another important feature was that, by emphasizing the lesson to be drawn for her home society from this study, Mead laid the groundwork for the popularization of anthropology and indeed for the later development of applied anthropology.

Mead concludes that rebelliousness and psychological stress is absent in Samoan girls not only because there is no conflict over sex, but also because there is a lack of emphasis on achievement, a lack of choices to be made, and a general shallowness of affect. V. Barnouw (1973:132) has pointed out that others have found evidence of unconscious conflict in other South Sea cultures and has criticized Mead for not using personality tests, but rather relying on intuitive, descriptive presentation. Needless to say, the tests were not available in 1925. Moreover, although absence of overt rebellion and conflict does not deny the possible presence of unconscious conflict and hostility, it is also true that the Western hypothesis of the relation between physiological adolescence and storm and stress was based on gross evidence of such disturbances, not on subtle studies of individual adjustment. It would be interesting to test Mead's findings by seeking out other societies where there is a lack of competitiveness or a lack of choices to be made by adolescents, and making a systematic comparison of adolescent adjustment with modern methods of research. The principal difficulty, however, is that nowadays a society of such relative stability and tranquility as the Samoa of the 1920s will be hard to find! It is, of course, always easy to look back after the passage of fifty years and to suggest how work could have been improved. Undoubtedly the same will be said in the future of the work of present-day anthropologists! We shall have to keep this caution in mind as we review studies that have been instrumental in bringing about the present state of our science.[4]

In her 1928 study Mead dealt with a specific, rather narrow question: the relationship between cultural factors and the psychological aspects of female adolescence. The problem quickly came to be broadened in Mead's own work, in that of Ruth Benedict, and of others, to become a general question about the relationship between culture and the psychological characteristics of people who live according to the ways of that culture.

Group Differences

Underlying this formulation is a much older question: what are the differences between the people of one society and those of another, and how can we account for them? Salvador de Madariaga (1928) had treated this subject brilliantly in his book *Englishmen, Frenchmen, Spaniards* (1969 [orig. 1928]). Ruth Benedict, a little later, compared Zuni, Kwakiutl, and Dobuans in *Patterns of Culture* (1961 [orig. 1934]). Over the centuries, in fact, much has been written about the differences in the "temperament," the "genius," the *Zeitgeist* or the "national character" of various peoples, societies, or civilizations. The famous handwriting expert, Klara Roman, observed:

Just as national flavor marks gait and voice, speech and gesture among the people of a given nation, so national characteristics appear also in writing style. The differences between the emotional expressiveness of Latins, the rigid, disciplined behavior of Germans, and the traditional restraint of Englishmen, are universally recognized. We find corroboration of these differences in examining the school copy books of the respective nations or ethnic groups (Roman 1952:92).

That they differ, in some significant ways, appears to be a commonsense observation. Yet are claims of such differences more than mere ethnocentric judgments of one group by another, more than stereotypes?

Whatever the differences may be, how are they to be explained? By what factors are they caused? By climate, as Montesquieu had thought? By differences in their cultures, as Mead, Benedict, and the culture-and-personality anthropologists came to argue? But, and this was a major difficulty to which we shall have to return, how do we account for the differences in culture in the first place? Furthermore, if the differences are indeed not innate (or "racial") but cultural and learned, we must ask, how are they learned?

Thus culture and personality inherited its central problem, the identification of distinctive personality patterns of different societies with different cultures, from a long tradition of social philosophers and world travelers, from Herodotus on. In the culture-and-personality literature these differences have been termed variously temperament or modal or basic personality structure. Some sociologists, and some anthropologists as well, have spoken of national or social character. Yet a survey of the anthropological literature will reveal that relatively few studies have sought to establish such overall patterns for individual cultures and societies, and these studies, it must be admitted, have as a whole not been particularly successful. As we shall see in Chapter 3, these studies have suffered from a variety of methodological difficulties and have drawn much critical fire.

The vast bulk of the literature, quite to the contrary, has been primarily concerned with either a broader or a narrower scope. The broader scope involves the evolutionary trends that have brought about the development of a generic and distinctive human personality structure. Hallowell, in particular, saw such a personality structure as the result of behavioral evolution and as characteristic of a distinctively human mode of existence. Although these concerns go back to Darwin, research in this area has been quickening in recent years and has been producing interesting results. We shall deal with these matters in Chapter 2.

Individual Differences

Studies of narrower scope have dealt with more limited problems than the assessment of the basic personality structure exhibited by an entire society, however small. From the beginning, some specialists in culture and personality have shown a considerable interest in the unique individual. The importance of the study of the individual and of individual differences is brilliantly spelled out in Sapir's pathbreaking paper "Why Cultural Anthropology Needs the Psychiatrist" (1938).

This concern with the individual and with individual differences was at least in part a reaction against the many anthropological descriptions of tribal societies in which we read that "The Eskimo believe ..." or "the Ganda do ...," as if individual differences did not exist and as if normative statements actually did describe social and cultural reality. This pattern of reporting in the early years of anthropological fieldwork developed from the frequent need to reconstruct partly vanished ways of life by using a small number of informants who reported on what have come to be termed "memory cultures." When emphasis came to be placed on direct observation and on the collection of information from a *range* of persons, then variations among those interviewed and observed began to stand out.

Concern with the individual has led to the collection of a large number of personal documents and life histories.[5] These documents often provide startling insights into the experience of life and of the world as seen by a member of a society whose ways are strange and unfamiliar to us. However, because of the fact that they are about unique individuals, with their idiosyncracies and personal perceptions, it is often difficult to know what part of these perceptions and experiences are shared by other members of their societies. We receive a glimpse into an alien world, but may not be sure just what we see. The task is generally complicated by the fact that those whose biographies and autobiographies we read are likely to be exceptional individuals in their own societies. It remains for us to discover in what ways they are representative.

The problem may be illustrated by autobiographical writings from the United States, which we read while assuming—only in part correctly—that we know all about the cultural and social elements, looking as we read primarily for the particular and unique. Margaret Mead's autobiography, *Blackberry Winter* (1972), is a case in point. It tells us a great deal about U.S. culture and society in the twentieth century while focusing on the life of one exceptional woman. Like most other life histories, it tells us not what is typical in a given society, but rather what is possible. However unusual a given life may be, however atypical in a statistical sense, still it could and did take place in this particular society, at that particular period in time. Would it be conceivable in some other society or in the same society at a different moment of its history? Cultures make possible and facilitate; they set obstacles and establish limits. They do not fully determine personal character, choices, actions, or experiences. As L. L. Langness (1965b) points out, although many life histories have been published, they remain a rich and generally untapped vein for cultural analysis.[6]

The anthropologist, as a student of culture, is interested in individual differences not as ends in themselves but as raw material for the construction of cultural patterns. Culture, after all, is an abstraction that cannot be observed. We observe human behavior; we collect information on the experiences, attitudes, and perceptions of human individuals. We then analyze this information in a search for regularities, patterns, or themes. In short, we look at the information we collect as a basis for predicting behavior. I do not mean the kind of prediction in which political pollsters or market researchers engage. Rather, if I have figured out how a given pattern of interaction works, I should have a reasonable chance of predicting what the response to a given bit of behavior will be.

Let me give two very small examples. The rules that govern the use of the handshake in greeting differ in the United States and France, a difference that is greater among women than among men. Until the Frenchwoman visiting the United States has mastered the American pattern, she will not be able to predict the response to her proffered hand, and a series of comic or embarrassing mistimings will result. Another example: While I was conducting fieldwork in a rural region of Haiti, I had learned something about behavior attributed to spirits. One night I heard a neighbor speak in his sleep, and half asleep myself, I guessed this behavior would be interpreted as the speech of spirits rather than as human sleep talk. I was gratified to discover the following morning that this view was indeed the subject of excited comments in the hamlet. Until we discover such regularities, we find it difficult to survive in a human group, for smooth interactions with others depend to a large extent on our ability to predict their responses to our words and actions.

Yet the implicit and explicit rules that govern behavior in a given society vary in degree of stringency. The discovery of the *range* of permissible individual differences is as important as the discovery of central tendencies. It is this range of variation that the personal documents help us to see. Ideally, a series of such documents would be required for each culture that we wish to examine in this light. Other differences in the behavior and the attitudes among actors have to do, not with personal variations and individual uniqueness, but rather with the place of the given individual in the society and in the network of relations with others. Behavior appropriate for men and women, for adults and children, for specialists in a given activity, among brothers or brothers-in-law, for kin and nonkin: all of these illustrate patterns of diversity.

THE SPECIAL PERSPECTIVE OF PSYCHOLOGICAL ANTHROPOLOGY

The study of how prescribed or normative behavior contrasts to actual and variable behavior is not unique to psychological anthropology. It may be carried on by students of social structure, role analysts, political anthropologists, and a host of other social and behavioral scientists outside of anthropology. Psychological anthropology deals to a considerable extent with the same data as other divisions of social and cultural anthropology, and several neighboring disciplines as well.

The difference between psychological anthropology and other specialized divisions of our discipline is one of perspective, not, initially, one of data. First of all, we address the psychological and psychodynamic elements in human behavior explicitly, not merely as afterthoughts. Second, we start from the observation that the behavior we deal with is learned, taught, invented, or modified by individuals. We must therefore ask what we can discover about these processes of learning, teaching, inventing, and modifying *as they occur in particular cultural contexts.*

This perspective has drawn anthropologists into the study of socialization and child development, and hence into questions of cross-cultural differences as well as regularities.

As we noted earlier, psychological interests were deeply rooted in the Boasian tradition and, even earlier, in most of the anthropology of the nineteenth century. However, how one approaches these and related questions depends to a considerable extent on one's views of personality and personality processes on the one hand, and on one's view of culture on the other. A. I. Hallowell, for example, deals first of all with a generic human nature, a human "personality structure whose genesis lies in social interaction." In this view,

> the individual functions as a psychobiological whole, a total personality. Behavior has a structural basis, but this structuralization has arisen out of experience and cannot, therefore, be reduced to an inherited organic structure . . . the distinctive psychological organization of the human being . . . is just as much a function of his membership in a social group as it is a function of his inherited organic equipment (Hallowell 1974 [orig. 1950]:8).

If we take this statement as our starting point, we must then speak, first of all, of the generic human personality structure, shared by all members of our species. Second, we must look at the differences in the types of experiences provided to individuals by different cultural groups, and how they lead to personality patterns that vary from group to group. However, since experiences as well as genetic endowment are never alike for any two individuals, we find that groups are, indeed, made up of unique personalities. We shall keep returning to this point: What is the range of variations tolerated by given cultures?

ABOUT THIS BOOK

Psychological anthropology is a broad field that includes a variety of topics, and individual specialists have tended to seek out and develop their own particular areas of interest within it. This book is designed to survey this field, and to introduce the student to its diverse subjects and research problems. In doing so, we shall be covering some well-trodden territory and also approach certain frontiers that are treated more rarely in books of this type, but which increasingly have made claims on our attention. We shall find that some topics that were central to the field in its beginnings, such as attempts to identify and describe the normative personality types of individual societies, have tended to recede somewhat into the background, as other interests have moved to the fore. Among these new interests are altered states of consciousness.

We shall begin quite literally at the beginning, by dealing with evolution (Chapter 2). Since the term "evolution" is used in several different senses by anthropologists, we shall need to examine three that have important implications for our field: behavioral evolution, classical theory of cultural evolution, and contemporary approaches to cultural evolution. However, we shall not review the fossil record and the evidence of human paleontology, which are more properly treated by physical anthropologists. A review of the various meanings of "evolution" will help us to establish a framework for the analysis of both our common human nature and of the factors that lead to group differences.

We shall then move to a discussion of group differences and of the principal studies that have dealt with this broad subject (Chapter 3). Because it has been claimed often that group differences in personality are the outcome of the child-training practices that characterize particular cultures, we next turn to this topic (Chapter 4). As mentioned earlier, over the years cross-cultural studies of child training have become one major focus of psychological anthropology. Such research is also of great interest to anthropologists of education, students of child development, and workers in a number of other fields. Nowadays studies of child training are often pursued without any attempts at linking what happens in childhood to personality characteristics that are said to be typical of a given society. Instead, child training may be related to the subsistence economy of the society, the family structure, the religious beliefs, or other cultural features. Often, too, knowledge about child training is seen as important and valuable enough in itself to merit special attention.

In order to be able to discuss the relationship between personality and culture as separate variables, many researchers have felt it necessary to make use of methods and techniques by which personality could be assessed. A variety of such methods have been used in cross-cultural studies, and they will be our next concern (Chapter 5). We shall see that some methods used in earlier years are now less popular, whereas some newer approaches are still in experimental stages. Because there are differences in what researchers are looking for when they speak of "personality," it is not surprising that they have employed different methods of assessing it.

The tool kit of the psychological anthropologist has long contained items borrowed from clinical psychology. The psychologists themselves have entered the cross-cultural field more recently. Since World War II, however, and increasingly as time goes on, a field of cross-cultural psychology has grown up. We shall look at what has been going on there under the heading of "Perception and Cognition" (Chapter 6). These are topics that psychologists have long treated in the laboratory, and that anthropologists have approached in their fieldwork, but they have done so quite differently. The contrasts between the two disciplines have to do both with methods of research and with the formulation of the problems under investigation.

We next turn to an area of human experience that generally has been neglected by psychological anthropology—altered states of consciousness. Chapter 7 attempts to fill a major gap in the literature of psychological anthropology. We shall discover that altered states of consciousness play a major role in the operation of human societies, as well as in the functioning of individuals. They provide a source for the perception of certain aspects of the world and for how people think about themselves and others. We shall be looking at ethnographic data here, and not at neurophysiology. Although a good deal has been published on these subjects, the neurophysiology of altered states is still poorly understood. We know something about the actions of certain drugs, but little about other types of states. Instead, we have been offered speculations based on limited laboratory research on matters such as differences in the operations of the right and left hemispheres of the brain. At present, the speculations are by far more extensive than the research by which they are inspired.[7]

In part because the theories of culture and personality initially drew heavily on psychoanalysis and clinical psychology, the language in which the earliest studies in this field were couched often appeared to carry clinical connotations. At the same time, the work was often set in the context of a debate about cultural relativity. As a result, it frequently involved questions about the quality of personality functioning, normalcy and deviancy, and health and adjustment. In this setting, much information was collected on deviant individuals and how various societies dealt with them. In more recent years, some psychiatrists have taken a lively interest in certain aspects of these questions, and have raised some issues of their own. For example, they have asked whether mental illnesses exist that are specific to certain cultures. We have also witnessed the development of a field of medical anthropology. In this area, as well as in transcultural psychiatry, there has been much interest in the theories of illness and the methods of treatment to be found in traditional cultures. These and related subjects will be our concerns in Chapter 8.

A theme that runs through much of this volume is culture change and its psychological implications. In Chapter 9 we address this topic directly. It brings us full circle to the beginning, because our first concern, evolution, represents a theoretical approach to certain kinds of change. Although change is indeed ever present in human affairs, modernization and Westernization involve particular psychological issues of motivation and adaptation for Third World peoples.

Rapid change is central to life in our own society. It appears wherever we may turn, in virtually all social and cultural contexts. It is therefore appropriate that, in looking at psychological anthropology, we note how it, too, has changed and developed over time. In various parts of this book a place is reserved for the history of the discipline, as it is revealed in the development of approaches to given problems. Science is a continous self-correcting enterprise, and answers are never final. Therefore, it we were to limit ourselves to an assessment of the field as it is "now" (meaning, say, during the five years prior to this writing) we would be limiting and handicapping our understanding. It is only by looking back over a longer period of time, and charting the course of developments, that we can hope to make sense of the changes that have occurred in the field.

Students in the United States may be reluctant to look at the past, preferring to ask, "What do we know now? Where do we go from here? Never mind how we got here." This attitude reflects a long antihistorical tradition in this country.

It constitutes a rejection of the past in favor of the present and, even more, of the future. It has often been said that the United States is a nation of immigrants, who left the Old World behind in order to build a new life here for the tomorrow of their children. In the consumer society of the 1960s and early 1970s, we often lived the new life today at the expense of tomorrow. Yet in the late 1970s some changes seem to have taken place in outlook. The interest stirred by the bicentennial observances in 1975–1976, the growth of concern for ethnic identities and ethnic heritage, the fascination with family histories and genealogies in the wake of the fabulous success of Alex Haley's *Roots* (as a book and as a TV dramatization), the sustained interest in folklife and folk traditions sparked by the *Foxfire Books*—these and a hundred other items are all signs of a change in our attitude toward the past. This change also appears to be related to a reevaluation of earlier, optimistic projections of a science-fiction type of future. Certainly the energy crisis has helped to bring about a startled recognition of the finite nature of world resources, and it has been one significant factor in changing attitudes toward the past as well as the future.

As A. I. Hallowell (1976 [orig. 1965]) remarked, the history of anthropology is itself an anthropological problem. We may ask, for example, in what social and cultural context culture and personality, and later psychological anthropology, developed. What are the social factors to which these intellectual developments constituted a response? We cannot hope to answer such questions fully, but we need to be alert to them. Our concern is with the past not as an end in itself, but only as it helps us to answer questions concerning the development of ideas and research approaches.

Culture and personality, as a subfield of cultural anthropology, had its beginnings in the 1920s, and gained momentum in the 1930s and 1940s, when it reached its peak of popularity. Since then it has undergone a variety of changes and ramifications. Its earliest successes must surely be seen in the light of the crises of the larger society within which it developed: the years of the Great Depression and the social problems of the 1930s, the rise of fascism abroad, and then the upheaval of World War II. In more recent years, interest in altered states of consciousness, which was an oddity in 1960, has grown as a result of the timeliness of this subject in our own society. After all, scientific disciplines do not develop in a social and cultural vacuum; they respond to the challenges of their society.

At present, psychological anthropology is a mature part of our discipline. Yet considering this field simply as a subject matter area would be a serious error. Rather, we will gain in understanding if we view it as an *integrating orientation* that allows us to pull together data from a broad variety of sources. In this sense, the work of the psychological anthropologist complements that of other specialists, such as those whose primary concern is with primatology, human evolution, or cultural ecology. We must seek out these connections, for our emphasis is placed explicitly on a holistic view of culture, one that seeks to understand culture as a system of interrelated parts.

The history of psychological anthropology teaches us another point as well. As we look back, we see that it, like other branches of science, does not provide timeless, fixed answers to our questions. It does not resolve problems "once and for all." We shall see that many of the questions posed in the beginning of our study have not been answered in the form in which they were stated originally. Rather, as work proceeded, the questions were reformulated over and over again. Instead of answers, in fact, we have achieved better questions. Science, moreover, has a curious spiral character. We come back again and again to old questions in new dress. Often enough, the investigators themselves are only dimly aware that they are "discovering" a problem that was, in fact, dealt with a long time ago, albeit in a different context and through different methods and approaches. What appears new and original is often quite old.

With these remarks in mind, we may now begin our study of psychological anthropology by starting at the beginning, with a look at evolution, the many meanings of that word, and the significance of the several types of evolutionary theory for psychological anthropology.

NOTES

1. The observations in the United States and Haiti are my own. For the Peruvian observation I am indebted to my husband, Paul H. Bourguignon.

2. Note the comment made by President Carter in Texas (June 23, 1978) that he would "not let the Soviet Union push us around."

3. Wylie's original study of Peyrane was first published in 1957. He has since returned to the village twice after lapses of 10 and of 25 years. In epilogues to later editions of his book he reports on the transformations that had taken place during the intervening years, as well as on the continuities. He notes that child training is among the most stable aspects of culture in this French village.

4. For a critical review of the research design used by Mead in this study, see Brim and Spain (1974).

5. See Langness (1965b) for an impressive bibliography, which provides chronological groupings of publications. See also Mandelbaum (1973). For some specific examples, see Jones (1972), Lame Deer and Erdoes (1972), and P. J. Wilson (1975). The use of the life history in psychological anthropology is treated in Chapter 5, which deals with methods of assessing personality.

6. See Mandelbaum (1973) for some methodological suggestions.

7. Students wishing to pursue these matters further may turn to the work of psychologists such as Robert Ornstein (1972) and Charles Tart (1972).

CHAPTER 2

Evolution: Behavior and Culture

INTRODUCTION

> An adult female . . . will unerringly interfere in an infant play group if her friend's
> child is, in her opinion, being treated roughly . . . An infant that is known to have
> influential protectors will be treated with great respect, at least if any of its protectors
> are in sight. An adult male . . . will carefully avoid walking directly up to an infant
> because if one happens to scream at his approach a pack of females will instantly
> attack him, assuming him to have harmed it . . . In this way an infant learns its own
> status including its rank, which is basically that of its mother . . . (Rowell 1976:26).

Could this passage be a discription of a group of people at a beach or on a
playground in the United States? Or does it refer to some matrilineal group, in
some far distant place? Does the phrase "a pack of females" indicate that the
author is a male chauvinist?

In fact, this passage is taken from a paper by Thelma E. Rowell, a zoologist,
who writes about "Growing Up in a Monkey Group." The observations deal with
various species of monkeys studied in captivity. At least part of the human
atmosphere of the quotation is due to a use of words that conjure up specific
human relationships: "her friend's child," "influential protectors," "status," and
"rank." Also, various attitudes and cognitive processes are attributed to individual animals: they are said to hold opinions, to show great respect, and to assume
information not directly in evidence.

The fact that this paper appeared in a volume dedicated to Margaret Mead and
entitled *Socialization as Communication* (Schwartz 1976a) indicates that studies
of the development of primate infants are nowadays considered relevant to the

26

understanding of human childhood. It is one small bit of evidence showing the importance of the concept of evolution to modern anthropology, cultural as well as physical.

Evolutionary theory has been called "the unifying paradigm of all the biological sciences, from biochemistry to ecology" (Freeman 1970:5). However, among the behavioral sciences, as D. A. Hamburg (1963:300) has pointed out, "anthropology alone . . . has taken evolution seriously and has made it a major focus of research." He goes on to add that "this neglect applies also to the emotional aspects of behavior which is remarkable . . . since Darwin was so strongly interested in emotions and pointed the way to future investigators."

"Evolution" has meant different things in the course of time to investigators in the several fields of anthropology. Anthropologists have used the term in three different contexts. It is important to identify them and to make the distinctions between them explicit.

First, the term refers to the biological evolution of the species *Homo sapiens.* Here, our basic information comes from physical anthropology, specifically, human paleontology. The data consist of the fossilized remains of early hominids: skulls, teeth, and bones that reveal changes in size and shape of the brain, changes in posture, and so on. Related evidence comes from the archaeological record in the form of tools and from the ecological contexts of the finds. Together with zoologists and psychologists, some physical anthropologists have also turned to the observation of living nonhuman primates. They do so, in part, to shed light on human behavior.

Concerning biological evolution, the psychological anthropologist asks three questions: 1) What is the relationship between skulls, teeth, bones and behavior? 2) What changes in capacity are reflected in the paleontological and archaeological record? 3) What changes were necessary to make culture, as we know it, possible?

To deal with these questions, following A. I. Hallowell, we shall speak of *"behavioral evolution."*

A second context is the classical concept of *unlineal cultural evolution.* Most of the major figures of nineteenth century anthropology and sociology, such as Comte, Spencer, Tylor, Morgan, and Frazer, as well as Marx, believed in the idea of *progress,* propelling cultures from "primitive" to "advanced" stages. Freud incorporated it into his writings on anthropological subjects. This concept of cultural evolution was rejected by most anthropologists of the first half of the twentieth century. As a result, culture-and-personality studies emerged in an intellectual climate that was hostile to evolutionary thought.

A third context is the *contemporary theories of cultural evolution,* developed principally by two groups of U.S. scholars, centering about Leslie White on the one hand and Julian Steward on the other. These approaches redefine earlier ideas, incorporating such concerns as cultural ecology and adaptation. Such investigations offer a variety of research opportunities for psychological anthropology. To cite only one example, we may investigate the relationship between child training and levels of subsistence economy. Do societies with different economies make different kinds of demands of their children?

Let us now deal one by one with these three divergent and yet overlapping approaches. All of them speak to the issue of "evolution."

BEHAVIORAL EVOLUTION

In his 1949 presidential address to the American Anthropological Association, A. I. Hallowell noted that a central problem of nineteenth century anthropology had been the evolution of man. Darwin's opponents, by contrast, had stressed the discontinuity between humans and other animals. Evolution had gained the day in physical anthropology, where stress was placed on fossil remains of early human forms and on tools showing evidence of the activity of ancient types of man. Yet, as Hallowell points out, anthropologists of the twentieth century (that is, the group he was addressing),

> while giving lip service to organic evolution have, by the special emphasis laid upon culture as the prime human differential, once again implied an unbridged gap between ourselves and our animal forebears . . . (Hallowell 1974:2).

Because the biological evolution evident in the organic transformations of animal species is only part of a larger process, Hallowell proposes the study of *behavioral evolution.* He argues that "the achievement of a human status in the evolutionary process . . . is . . . to be conceived of . . . as a total *psychobiological* adjustment" (Hallowell 1974 [orig. 1950]:6; italics in original). He calls the outcome of this evolutionary process "man's novel personality structure."

What is this structure, and how can we discover it? Hallowell is speaking of a human nature that underlies "the range and variation of personality structures" that have been reported in the culture-and-personality literature, which describes a great variety of contemporary cultures. In other words, just as we can speak about culture in the generic sense by identifying the universal features that appear in the many specific cultures that have been studied, so also we can speak of a generic human personality structure on the basis of comparative research.

Over a period of almost two decades following his presidential address, Hallowell refined and elaborated these ideas.[1] He stressed the *continuity* as well as the *differences* between our species, its precursors (earlier species of the genus *Homo*), and its relatives among the infrahuman primates. During the same period, research in two directions had filled out our knowledge of these related species. One direction has been the rapid growth of research dealing with primate (and other animal) behavior in the animals' natural habitats. The other is a great increase in the variety and intensity of experimental research with primates. Both of these types of studies by zoologists, psychologists, and anthropologists have greatly enriched our understanding of the behavior and the capacities of primates.

We can now speak with some confidence about the difference between monkeys and apes in the laboratory, in the zoo, and in their native habitats. We have learned about differences between arboreal and ground-dwelling species. We have information about the relationship between ecology and such variables as group size, troop organization, relations between the sexes, and a host of other matters.[2]

More than a quarter of a century has passed since Hallowell's initial call to action. A great many questions remain, yet on the whole they are better questions, based on better data. Issues that had virtually disappeared from view have moved back emphatically to the center of attention. In some respects the abundance of information available to us now might make it appear that Hallowell's appeal for research in behavioral evolution has indeed been heeded. Yet a note of caution must be added: knowing about contemporary infrahuman primates is not the same as knowing about the behavior of extinct species of primates or of early humans. We must not be misled into reading too easily and carelessly from one to the other. Also, it is largely students of fossil man and primatologists who have carried on this research, rather than cultural anthropologists, or specialists in culture and personality.

Continuity and Differences: The Concept of Protoculture

Hallowell proposed a new concept for the study of the evolution of the human mode of cultural adaptation. He spoke of *protoculture,* a preadaptive stage involving six elements: "simple forms of learning, some socialization of the individual, a social structure based on role differentiation in organized social groups, the transmission of some group habits and perhaps tool using and a 'non-syntactic' form of communication" (Hallowell 1960:359–60). The novel psychological factor by means of which these preadaptive conditions were transformed into culture is, in Hallowell's view, a "psychological restructuralization." This factor is expressed, among other things, in the capacity for language development and other forms of symbolic communication. This new capacity transformed the previously existing conditions not only of communication but also of social life, of tool using, of learning, and so on. As we shall see, it also made possible the creation of a uniquely human behavioral environment. We shall briefly consider the six features of protoculture in Hallowell's definition.

Learning of some sort exists at all levels of the animal kingdom, and psychologists have long studied learning in a broad variety of animals species. However, since cultural behavior is consistently—and by definition—learned behavior, a capacity for complex learning is a prime prerequisite for the development and acquisition of culture. It is, however, not the only such prerequisite.

Socialization involves an early period in life in which learning takes place that is required for the adaptation of the individual to the group. This learning occurs in particular in relation to mature adults, especially, but not exclusively, in the relationship between mothers and their young. Therefore the duration of a period of socialization and the amount and complexity of what is learned is directly related to the length of the period of immaturity and dependency characteristic of a particular species. It is also related to the *need* for learned behavior, in contrast to unlearned responses, for the survival of the individual. In human beings the length of this period is enormously increased beyond that of all other species, as is the amount and complexity of learning.

The existence of socialization is necessarily dependent on the third feature of protoculture, the presence of *organized social groups.* Again, we find social animals on many levels of the evolutionary scale. However, in contrast to the complex social organizations of insects that are determined by structural differentiations among the members, say, of a termite hill or a beehive, the organization of a primate group and the role differentiation within it are based on learning, socialization, and experience, as well as on differences in sex and age. For instance, dominance gradients in troops of monkeys such as baboons, or apes such as chimpanzees, are established through encounters among individuals, that is, through experience. Moreover, in contrast to the organically based social hierarchies among insects, they are both impermanent and reversible.

Social groups among infrahuman primates are composed of adults of both sexes and young of varying ages, as well as individuals in different positions within the social hierarchy. Socialization therefore takes place within highly differentiated groups and involves the learning of relationships with individuals occupying a variety of social statuses. Because of the similarities of some of these patterns to human social organization, a prefiguring as it were, of some human patterns, writers on primate behavior are sometimes tempted into the use of an anthropomorphic, and thus misleading, terminology. Our introductory quote illustrates this point.

The fourth aspect of protoculture, the *transmission of some group habits,* is of particular interest, for it is sometimes considered to be virtually synonymous with culture. For example, Jolly says: "A great deal of the behavior of primates can be called cultural, *in the sense that it is transmitted by learning from generation to generation*" (Jolly 1972:350; italics added). B. Campbell (1974), the British biologist, insists that the transmission of learned behavior defines culture, and chides anthropologists for refusing to recognize the existence of culture, so defined, among primates. However, transmission of learned behavior is not limited to primates either. It has been shown, for example, to occur among birds. To cite only one instance, W. H. Thorpe (1961) reports that birds of the same species share a basic song pattern, but the elaborations of these patterns vary among local groups. Birds such as chaffinches who have been reared in isolation produce only the simplest form of this typical song, whereas those reared in groups produce a unique local variation of the song.

In primates, the socially transmitted behaviors are often innovations initiated by individuals. Among Japanese macaques, animals that have been studied intensively, we know of innovations such as learning to eat, and even to unwrap, sweets offered by tourists, washing and eating sweet potatoes, and even swimming. According to D. Miyadi (1967) the innovations were usually made by infants and transmitted through imitation to their mothers. When these mothers were dominant females, the innovation would be observed by and transmitted to other animals lower in the dominance hierarchy and would spread in this way. Older, dominant males in many cases were the most conservative, the slowest to accept innovations.

As Hallowell (1960:338) points out, in infrahuman primates, social transmission of learned habits does not, however, become cumulative either over time, from generation to generation, or in space, that is, among large numbers of animals. He suggests that the high degree of territoriality among primates causing the virtual isolation of rather small groups from others of the same species, sets up barriers to the formation of larger and more complex social groups, and thus to the transmission and accumulation of learned habits. This observation leads to the further question of how the development of such larger and more complex social groups did in fact become possible. Whatever the ecological reasons might have been, factors of a psychological order must have been involved also: "The social integration of groups larger in size, distributed more widely in space, and characterized by greater diversity in roles required a transformation in psychological structure" (Hallowell 1960:338).

The presence of *tools* in association with fossil bones long has been used as a criterion for assigning human status to remains. The extended debate over the status of the australopithecines and of the modified bones of other animals found with them is a dramatic case in point (Dart 1959, Le Gros Clark 1967). The use of sticks, leaves, and stones by primates in the wild is well known, as is their extraordinary ability to manipulate human tools in captivity.[3] The extensive observations on wild chimpanzees by Jane van Lawick-Goodall (1968, 1971), moreover, dramatically document the fact that chimpanzees *fashion* rudimentary tools, for example by modifying grasses or sticks before using them to draw termites out of their hills.

By contrast, human tool-making is not only much more complex; it also involves the existence of traditions, that is, of *shared patterns* of working materials. Here again we find the accumulation of learned patterns over space and time. Humans also use *secondary tools,* or tools to make tools; moreover, there is always among humans an extensive and far-reaching *dependence* on tools.

Among these tools there are generally the means of *making fire.* The controlled use of fire is universal among human populations and appears to go back at least to Peking Man, half a million years ago. Fire may indeed be said to be the most important human tool, one that radically transformed ecology: it made various otherwise inedible root crops digestible and so extended and survival base; it assisted in the making of other tools; it provided light and warmth; it frightened away predators. The psychological transformation of early human beings from animals fearful of fire to ones able to control and use it is one of the truly remarkable parts of the story, although it has left us no specific clues. The great significance many societies attach to the conquest of fire, however, is recorded amply in the myth of Prometheus and in similar myths throughout the world.

The last feature of protoculture identified by Hallowell is a *form of communication*. Communication of some sort is basic to the existence of social life and is universal among social animals. Most simply, it may be defined as the stimulation by one animal of behavior in another; there is no need to infer *intention* on the part of the organism producing the stimulus, thus sending a message. Such stimuli may consist of evidence of physiological changes, chemical discharges, motion, gestures, touch, sound, and so on. In some animals, such as bees, complex systems of communication have been studied. These systems involve information about the location of nectar and utilize patterns of motion—the "dance of the bees"—as well as chemical exchanges (von Frisch 1950). Indeed, complex social organizations, such as that of bees, could not function without communication to maintain cooperation and interaction among members.

How Language Differs. If communication is so widespread among animals, how is human language distinctive? The linguist Charles Hockett (Hockett 1960, Hockett and Ascher 1964, Hockett 1973) has identified a series of "design features" of language, most of which exist in other communication systems as well. For instance, language employs a vocal-auditory channel; the messages are composed of sounds produced by the voice and received by the ear. The same channel is used for the singing of birds or the barking of dogs. In some animals, other channels are utilized: for example, motion serves in the dance of the bees mentioned earlier. In human beings, too, there are many types of nonvocal communication. They may be secondary elaborations of spoken language, such as writing, or even tertiary elaborations based in their turn on writing, such as the Morse code. On the other hand, human beings also use bodily forms of communication that are independent of language, and that are sometimes used to accompany it, such as gestures or various other expressive movements or postures. The latter have occasionally been called "body language." It is also true that not all elements of human communication that do use the vocal-auditory channel are language; some examples of these nonlanguage sounds are laughing, giggling, yawning, hissing, hemming and hawing, and so on. Language, in other words, is not our only type of communication. It is, however, a separate system and can be analyzed as such. Nor is all communication language. Also, as we shall see, communication is not the only function of language, although it is, of course, a vital one.

Which design features are distinctive of language, according to Hockett's analysis? There are three: openness or productivity, displacement, and duality of patterning. Let us take a closer look at each.

An *open* or *productive* system is one in which new messages are possible. As Hockett and Ascher put it, "we freely emit utterances that we have never said nor heard before, and are usually understood, neither speaker nor hearer being aware of the novelty" (Hockett and Ascher 1964:139). By contrast, a *closed* system, such as the call system of gibbons, consists of a limited repertory of signals, each of which is associated with a specific set of stimuli, such as food, danger, or sex.

Displacement refers to the fact that human beings can and do produce utterances that refer to other times and other places. We may speak of food in its absence; gibbons utter food calls only in its presence.[4] Displacement is crucial for the human capacity to learn from the experience of others, which makes possible the growth of culture over time; to formulate collective memories in myth and history, providing human beings with a past; to develop goals and devise utopias, that is, to think and speak about the future and the potential; to tell lies and to speak nonsense; to develop mathematics and science.

Duality of patterning means order or structure at two different levels. On the one hand, there is the patterning of the sound system, which is made up of a small number of elementary signaling units. These units, by themselves, are without meaning. On the other hand, there is the order or structure of larger, meaningful forms. This order is quite independent of the first, A combination of two such systems makes language extremely flexible and economical. By contrast, the units of a call system cannot be broken down into smaller significant elements, nor are they grouped into larger sequences according to a set of rules or a grammar.

Can Apes Learn Language?   Over the years, a number of experimenters have been intrigued by the possibility that young apes might be taught human language.[5] Several such attempts have been carried out with important results. The first of these attempts was the effort of two psychologists, Keith and Catherine Hayes, who raised a young female chimpanzee, named Viki, in their home from shortly after birth to the age of six and one-half. In spite of being treated like a human infant and child, and in spite of enormous efforts on the part of Catherine Hayes, Viki never learned to utter more than three or four words. Yet she learned to respond to a large vocabulary, acted in many ways like a human child, and even appeared to play with an imaginary pull-toy (Hayes 1951). However much she was able to learn of human ways, it was clear that vocal, articulated language was beyond her capacity.

A more successful experiment was carried out by R. A. and B. T. Gardner, who brought up an infant female chimpanzee whom they called Washoe (Gardner and Gardner 1975). Rather than seek to teach Washoe spoken language, they used the American Sign Language for the Deaf (ASL or Ameslan). This language is not a manual version of English. Rather, it consists of conventional representational signs. (Deaf children, having mastered Ameslan, must learn English when they learn to read and write, or lip read and produce vocal speech, or even use the manual alphabet.) The Dutch primatologist, A. Kortlandt, who, himself, has carried on extensive studies of chimpanzees in the wild, has made some interesting comments on Washoe's accomplishments that are worth quoting. Having observed her when she had already acquired a vocabulary of more than one hundred signs, he writes:

I was very deeply impressed by what I saw. Perhaps the most convincing of all was to watch Washoe "reading" an illustrated magazine. When, for example, a vermouth advertisement appeared, she spontaneously made the gesture for "drink"; when, on the next page, a picture of a tiger appeared, she signed "cat." It was fascinating to see a chimpanzee "think aloud" in gestural language, but in perfect silence, and without being rewarded for her performance (Kortlandt 1973:14).

He goes on to remark: "In situations when Washoe was not rewarded, she tended much more often to think aloud in silence than to talk to the Gardners and their assistants. This suggests that these apes have a lot more to think than to say," a remark which, he says, also fits well his observations of chimpanzees in the wild (Kortlandt 1973:14).

Another approach has been that of Premack (1976a, 1976b), who uses plastic chips of different colors and sizes to represent words, while at the same time also speaking to his chimpanzees. The animals in time have acquired large vocabularies and are able to arrange the chips so as to form phrases. In various tests, they have demonstrated their ability to establish relationships among items, to abstract characteristics such as color, and to handle "displacement," that is, to understand statements about things that are not present.

A fourth study (Rumbaugh 1977, Rumbaugh and Gill 1976) at the Yerkes Primate Center involves a chimpanzee by the name of Lana, who has been taught a specially designed "language" called Yerkish; in this system, Lana constructs sentences by punching buttons on a computer to select among a limited number of signs.

As a result of these experiments we now know that it is possible to teach elements of a human communications code to young apes, and that their learning capacity is greater than inferred from previous observations. However, we need to be cautious in drawing conclusions, as H. J. Jerison has noted:

One often underestimates the capacity of animals to learn and to perform complex tasks. The effect of the study of animal language, in my judgment, is to force linguists to define language more precisely, rather than to demonstrate "language" in chimpanzees. We must, after all, know what it is we are trying to demonstrate (Jerison 1975a:421).

Have we learned anything more specific from these studies, anything that might shed light on the development of language, with its distinctive features, from some other types of communication? Hockett (1973) thinks so. In Washoe's use of Ameslan, he finds a pattern that is frequent in child language, called "pivot grammar." In English baby talk, the pivots are words such as *allgone, nightnight, more,* and various objectives, such as *big* and *little.* A pivot is combined with a noun or name to produce new utterances, such as *nightnight Jimmy,* or *candy allgone.* Although Hockett notes that there is no evidence of such grammar in the communication of chimpanzees in the wild, he concludes:

In pivot grammar, thus, we seem to have found a limited variety of openness much older than human language, an inherited kernel on which our cousins the chimpanzees may never have built, but on which all human languages have elaborated and with which each human individual begins his linguistic life history (Hockett 1973:117).

Concerning Washoe, we must note that Ameslan lacks two of the distinctive features of language: the vocal-auditory channel and duality of patterning. Neither Washoe nor the other chimps in these various studies have shown evidence of being able to handle these features. We have seen the failure of the Hayes' attempt to teach Viki spoken language. The signs that Washoe, Premack's Sarah, and Rumbaugh's Lana have been taught are complete units and cannot be further broken down into constituent parts, as are human words, or morphemes. Premack, as we saw, says that chimps can handle displacement.

In spite of the claims by Premack, Rumbaugh, and their associates, not all linguists and students of primate behavior agree with their assessments. Harry F. Harlow, a pioneer of experimental work with primates, notes Premack's description of "serialized complex learning problems" as "language." In contrast to abstract (human-type) learning, he argues, "Premack's and Rumbaugh's chimpanzee performances required only 'concrete' (animal-type) learning" (H. F. Harlow, 1977:640). He also stresses that, by contrast, the Gardners came to understand complex, unlearned gestural "language" responses made spontaneously by Washoe. That is, they made a first step toward learning the communication system of chimpanzees. The other types of research involve training in concrete, artificial situations. This fact has led scholars (Mounin 1976) to point to numerous other problems involved in evaluation of these experiments. To mention only one difficulty: what Washoe "says" is translated into English by her trainers, so that her "utterances" are made to appear to conform to English language patterns. They might appear quite different if translated into another human language.

It will take time to sort out the significant contributions of these studies and to consider their full implications. For now, it is important to distinguish between an animal's *potential* for behavior, exhibited in these types of learning in a human environment, and the behavior that is learned or released in the animal's own native ecological and social setting. For example, Washoe was able to learn Ameslan when taught by her human associates. However, in that setting she did not develop her capacity for supplying her own subsistence, as chimpanzees do in the wild.

Language and the Construction of Reality.   These experiments with apes focused on the animals' learning capacities and stressed the use of language to communicate. They also have implications for our understanding of the evolution of language. In view of the importance of gestures in primate communication both in the wild and in the experimental situations of the Hayes and the Gardeners, G. W. Hewes (1973) has suggested a gestural origin of language.

A different approach is taken by Jerison, who considers the development of language from the point of view of the evolution of the vertebrate brain and intelligence. For him, the first and original function of language may have been as a tool for perceiving the world and ordering these perceptions. Language, for Jerison, facilitates "the construction of reality" for our species. The fact that language is also a system of communication means that "reality" can be shared.

"Construction of reality" requires some explanation. Jerison (1973, 1975a, 1975b, 1976) defines intelligence as a species' capacity to process information that comes to it through the sense organs, such as those of smell, touch, sight, hearing, and so on, and to connect this information with its sources. To do so involves basic cognitive capacities that vary from species to species. Consequently the "perceptual world," as Jerison terms it, that is experienced by a given species, including *Homo sapiens,* depends on how its brain works. For example, color variation is an attribute of the environment only for species with color vision— for humans, but not for dogs. On the other hand, ultra high frequency sounds are part of the perceptual world of dogs, whose sense of hearing can register and process information of that kind, whereas humans are not biologically equipped to do so. As a result, the image of the world constructed by the nervous system of the dog, its "perceptual world," is different from that of the people with whom the dog shares a home.

"From this perspective," Jerison (1975a:403) notes, "language is better understood as having first evolved because it enhances the image-construction capacity of the nervous system, rather than because of its facilitation of communication." Consequently, in order to understand the evolution of language, it becomes more important to understand the evolution of the brain than the evolution of modes and methods of communication in infrahuman primates.

The concept of a species-specific "perceptual world" is of crucial importance in recognizing a uniquely human mode of adaptation. It is similar to the concept of a "behavioral environment" used by the Gestalt psychologist Kurt Koffka. Hallowell adds a further dimension to this concept by noting that in humans the behavioral environment made possible by a common organic equipment is made variable by the fact that it is also culturally constituted. Such within-species variation of the construction of reality and its modification by largely linguistically formulated images is uniquely human. This is an important topic, and we shall return to it a number of times in the course of this book.

Language and Human Evolution.   At present 4000 to 5000 languages are spoken throughout the world. For such a diversity to have arisen, linguists such as Hockett believe that it is likely that language in the full sense of the word must have been in existence not much less than 50,000 years. Hockett suggests that it was preceded by a "pre-language," and he speculates (Hockett 1973) on what that might have been like. During that period when language might have been developing to its full characteristic form, say some 100,000 years, the human brain increased greatly; then, 50,000 years ago, it ceased to grow in size. Once the brain had reached its present size and form and once language had developed fully, an enormous increase in cultural development can be observed. The significance of the relationship among the three factors—brain, language, and culture—must not be underestimated.

Among the transformations that are associated with the full development of language and of culture are changes in the organization of local groups and, we may assume, in the rules that are associated with that organization. Let us examine one important example of such change.

Breaking Out of the Local Group: The Incest Taboo. We have already referred to the territoriality and relative isolation of individual primate groups, and we have related it to the lack of any significant accumulation of socially transmitted learned behavior among them. When we look at human groups, even the smallest among the hunting and gathering societies, such as various bands of Australian aborigines, Bushmen, or Pygmies, we never find similarly self-contained units. For example, Lauriston Sharp (1974:417) says of the North Australian Yir Yoront that the stone they used for their axe heads came "from quarries 400 miles to the south, reaching the Yir Yoront through long lines of male trading partners." Lorna Marshall deals with !Kung-speaking Bushmen in a region of southwest Africa (Namibia), who live in twenty-seven intermarrying autonomous bands. She notes: "The !Kung have intermarried within the Nyae Nyae region to such an extent that . . . the people of the whole region are what we call name relatives, applying kinship terms to each other" (Marshall 1965:259).

How did human groups (or protohuman groups) cease to be self-contained units? Leslie White (1949) argues that the incest taboo created interdependent groups by requiring members of each individual family and social group to marry out. Although we may agree that the incest taboo—the prohibition on marriage or mating between parents and children and between siblings—does indeed create networks of relationships among families and social groups, this fact does not tell us *how* such a prohibition came about. The universality of the incest taboo, often noted, suggests its great age. Anthropologists and others have often speculated on its origins; Freud offered his own "myth"—as he called it—of the origin of the incest prohibition in his book *Totem and Taboo* (1912–1913).

Over the years a number of reports have shown a lack of inbreeding (or "incest avoidance," in anthropomorphic terms) among diverse species of mammals and birds. However, although such a lack is widespread, it is by no means universal. According to Aberle et al. (1963:261) "on a cross-species basis, restriction on inbreeding . . . is found among larger, long-lived, slower-maturing and more intelligent animals." They suggest a genetic basis for this behavior, and they go on to note: "in the perspective of population genetics, close inbreeding of an animal like man has definite biological disadvantages, and the disadvantages are far more evident as respects the mating of primary relatives than as respects other matings" (Aberle et al. 1963:257).

When we speak of the incest prohibition in human societies, it is clear that we are dealing with a *social rule.* There may well be an underlying biological factor at work, but if that is so, this factor has been reworked in cultural terms by means of language, and set up as a rule, the infraction of which is punished by human institutions. To note that such a rule has a biological grounding is not the same as to reduce an analysis of the incest taboo to that starting point. This important consideration must be kept in mind.

Seymour Parker (1976) has sought to formulate a psychobiological theory of incest avoidance. In addition to the materials cited above, he also refers to studies of the deleterious genetic effects of human incestuous unions, which confirm the conclusions arrived at on the basis of population genetics. The implication from both of these approaches is that for human beings and for animals that are like them in the respects noted above, incest avoidance has important survival value. The question that remains, and to which Parker addresses himself, is what psychobiological mechanisms might produce incest avoidance in certain animal species, including humans.

Parker suggests two such mechanisms. First, Parker suggests a psychological and physiological link between sexual and agonistic (aggressive) responses. Prolonged association among individuals during socialization reduces the agonistic responses, and as a result, also reduces the sexual ones. Second, he suggests a link between an exploratory tendency—a search for novelty—and the sexual response. This tendency, too, is reduced during the long association and habituation among individuals during socialization. Parker finds support for both of these propositions in studies of animals and humans. Much of his human evidence for the argument that childhood association leads to a reduction in sexual attraction is drawn from two societies, the Israeli kibbutz and the Chinese.

The Chinese data come from a Taiwanese village where A. Wolf (1966) studied traditional marriage patterns. In one pattern a small girl is adopted into her future husband's family. Among the younger people this form of marriage is strongly disliked, and there is evidence that such marriages in the past have often been unsuccessful, either not resulting in conjugal unions, or, in an earlier generation, involving a higher degree of adultery. Informants talked about marriages with housemates as being "embarrassing" or "uninteresting."

In the Israeli case, a number of researchers have found that in the kibbutz young people consistently "marry out" although there are no rules requiring them to do so. In the collective education pattern of the kibbutz all the children of the community are brought up in the children's house. For example, in his study of the kibbutz Kiryat Yedidim Melford Spiro (1958) found no cases of marriage among peer group members. Joseph Shepher, who analyzed census data on some 3000 kibbutz marriages in three generations, specifically notes that there was not a single case in which the partners had been socialized together between the ages of three and six (Tiger and Shepher 1975). Spiro's informants told him that people did not marry peer group members because they knew each other too well, much as brothers and sisters do.

Parker's paper brings together a rich body of data and theory, and his analysis is quite persuasive. Yet the issue has not been fully resolved. Livingstone (1978) has questioned the animal evidence, which he finds inadequate. He also questions the cultural data. For example, a more recent paper by M. Kaffman (1977) reports changes in the sexual attitudes and behavior of kibbutz adolescents that have resulted from the international "sexual revolution." With a change from the puritanical attitudes typical of the kibbutz in the past, he finds that heterosexual relationships among kibbutz adolescents are not rare. Marriages, however, still are rare. At least one of the reasons for this fact, says this author, is that peer groups are small, usually no more than sixteen individuals of the same age. Together with the fact that girls mature earlier than boys, this size means that finding a partner within the group is difficult. Kaffman, however, like Parker and Wolf, also points to the importance of habituation and familiarity in reducing romantic interest.

In contrast to those who argue that genetic factors are at the basis of incest avoidance, Livingstone (1978) suggests that variations in mating behavior, both animal and human, are due to differences in ecological pressures. Cultural changes, such as those that have led to increasing sexual involvement among kibbutz peers and to the disappearance of adoption marriage in Taiwan, might best be understood in this context.

Parker makes an important distinction between the *incest taboo,* a cultural phenomenon, and *incest avoidance,* an earlier biopsychological tendency on which it is built. It is likely that incest avoidance, if not the incest taboo, was part of the protocultural stage of human development. The transformation of biologically based avoidance practice into a culturally formulated prohibition, with its attendant sanctions, is of course dependent, among other things, on language usage to conceptualize it and to communicate the concepts and the rules.

From Protoculture to Culture: The Missing Elements

Having considered the characteristics of protoculture, the necessary but insufficient conditions for the development of culture, we may now ask: what are the missing elements? We have already hinted at the importance of the distinctive characteristics of language. Underlying these characteristics is, in Hallowell's phrase, "the capacity for the symbolic transformation of experience."

In contrast to other animals, human beings are able to share with their fellows private, internal, or "intrinsic" processes, such as subjective versions of experiences, mental imagery, and dreams. We are able to share them because we have "extrinsic" symbolism, means of giving experiences a form that is unrelated to or "outside" those experiences. Language is the primary example of such a symbolic system. The graphic and plastic arts, dance, and ritual are examples of nonlinguistic systems of extrinsic symbols.

As a result of such sharing, the experiences themselves are influenced and modified by group processes. In other animals, such processes—for example, memory or dreams—undoubtedly exist. However, because the animals lack extrinsic symbolism, those processes remain private and are not subject to the modeling influences of sharing, group pressures, and tradition. By contrast, in many human societies, dreams are given serious attention. Because they are told and discussed and evaluated and interpreted, it appears that they are, to a remarkable degree, culturally patterned. Often enough, dreams and the imagery of altered states of consciousness, such as trance states, are sources of cultural innovation. They may have a significant impact on the construction of a culturally constituted behavioral environment. It is in dreams and trances that much mystical and religious inspiration occurs. We shall examine these matters at some length in Chapter 7.

For Hallowell, the key differences between protoculture and culture, made possible by complex, shared symbolic systems, are the universal existence in humans of *self-awareness* and of a *normative orientation.* He notes that, in contrast to the social life of animals, every human social order is also a moral order. Every society has its standards of right and wrong, and each has its system of social control. Social rules of behavior range from those prohibiting in-group murder and incest to those controlling food taboos, property rights, behavior among kin, and even etiquette. Crime and sin are characteristically human phenomena.

This normative system is not merely external to the individual, enforced through law, punishment, and other actions of the group. Rather, the moral order is within the individual, mediated by the development of an individual conscience, the capacity for self-judgment. Therefore, a prerequisite to morality is the capacity for self-awareness and self-objectification, for becoming an object to one's self, to be regarded and evaluated as other objects. Self-awareness implies self-esteem, self-respect, and pride, but also guilt, shame, and anxiety. Self-awareness is always socially patterned and involves the internalization of the society's demands in the process of socialization, during the characteristically long period of dependency of the human young. Language, through the universal use of pronouns and kinship terms, naming systems, and other identifiers, is crucial to the development of this capacity, as we can see in the development of modern children.

Thus, as individuals we learn to appraise ourselves in relation to a socially sanctioned and internalized moral code. The existence of such an appraisal, Hallowell (1960:357) notes, suggests the adaptive value for the society and for the individual of such unconscious psychological processes as the ego defense mechanisms, including rationalization, and repression. These defense mechanisms make it possible to deal with the inadequacies in one's performance and with the conflicts between the demands of one's conscience and those of one's needs.

In summary, the concept of a protocultural stage suggests that culture, human society, the human personality, language, and the underlying capacity for complex symbolic transformations all are products of evolution that developed in interaction. In this light, it would be absurd to expect any abrupt discontinuity in capacity and behavior in the course of hominid evolution, as it would be to expect sudden and startling changes in organic forms. On the other hand, Hallowell (1961:253) rightly stresses, in this connection, the human potential "for transcending what is learned—a capacity for innovation, creativity, reorganization, and change in sociocultural systems themselves."

Hallowell derived this fruitful perspective on human behavioral evolution *from the comparative study of personality structure in contemporary societies.* Each of these societies shares in a "human perceptual world," in Jerison's terms, for all human groups have the same basic organic equipment. Yet each has evolved its own culturally constituted behavioral environment, peopled its world with beings and forces, provided coherent explanatory systems for its experiences and observations, and structured experiences and observations by means of these explanatory systems. (We return to these matters in Chapter 6.) These activities all required a transformation of experience by manipulating shared and conventionalized symbols, substituted for direct experience. The capacity for symbolization does more than facilitate the development of characteristically human social groups living in characteristically human perceptual worlds. The resulting development of self-awareness and of a normative orientation is evidence of a particular, uniquely human articulation between the individual and the society. In a sense, the society may be said to be built into the individual during the socialization process. In addition, characteristically human unconscious psychological processes as well as conscious processes developed. We begin to see that there is a good deal more involved than merely the transmission of social habits or the existence of an open call system.

Hallowell's contribution to the study of behavioral evolution is important not only for the fact that he was the first to sound a call to action or for the pioneering

Human groups use many kinds of symbolic systems. This mask from Northern New Ireland, Melanesia, represents an ancestor spirit. (Collection Paul H. and Erika Bourguignon).

character of his work. Its greatest significance lies perhaps in this fact: he showed us that it is possible for an anthropologist to stress the continuity between humanity and its primate kin without losing sight of that radical innovation, the development of culture, and the role of culture in human life and adaptation. He avoided the twofold trap that awaits the unwary who venture into this terrain: either to see human beings as apes with a little more (or a little less)—the naked ape, the talking ape—or else to see apes as incomplete humans, similar to human children or slightly retarded adults.

Biological Bases of Human Behavior

Hallowell's approach to human evolution was "conjunctive": he sought to take into account the organic psychological, social, and cultural dimensions of the evolutionary process. His work was notably devoid of speculation; he made no attempt, in any of his writings, to invent a scenario to show how human behavioral and sociocultural characteristics emerged at certain stages of development in the remote past. Such scientific restraint has not been typical of many of the popular writers who have taken up the theme of behavioral evolution since the 1960s. Indeed, a whole literature has grown up in which various of the less pleasant aspects of modern Western society have been blamed either on our primate origins or on our distant ancestors.

Two particular aspects of modern culture have received the greatest attention, either separately or in combination: aggression and male dominance. For example, Robert Ardrey, a dramatist turned popular science writer, has us descend from a "killer ape," who modified the course of evolution by turning from the peaceful pursuit of gathering to hunting. The resulting bloodlust in time has given rise to such diverse horrors as modern warfare and juvenile delinquency. "Civilization," says Ardrey (1961:348) "is a compensatory consequence of our killing imperative."

Konrad Lorenz, in *On Aggression* (1966), sees warfare and cruelty as part of the innate human heritage that cannot be changed. He makes these claims in spite of the fact that in his detailed observations of animal behavior he found that aggression occurs in very specific and limited circumstances. His only solution to the problem is to suggest alternative occasions for the expression of the "aggressive instinct," such as substituting sports for warfare.

R. G. Sipes (1973) has investigated the hypothesis that combative sports represent an alternative to warfare, as well as the contrary view according to which they are more likely to appear in warlike societies. On the basis of both cross-cultural and historical analyses, he finds that societies where war is relatively rare are also those where combative sports are absent. He concludes that "rather than being functional alternatives, war and combative sports activities in a society appear to be components of a broader cultural pattern" (Sipes 1973:80). His study also shows that warfare is not a universal social institution.

In discussions such as those of Ardrey and Lorenz we find a confusion between warfare, an institutionalized pattern of complex social organizations, and aggression, which involves subjective feelings on the part of an individual. A separate issue is whether the presumably innate aggression is due to the development of hunting in some early hominid or prehominid species. This second question usually is combined with the first, so that warfare is said to result from hunting. Two observations make this contention unlikely. First, contemporary hunter-gatherer societies are among the most peaceful we know! Second, hunters kill animals of *other* species, just as lions or eagles do. Warfare, murder, and for that matter, combative sports involve aggressive behavior *within* the human species. Arguments like Ardrey's tend to confuse interspecific and intraspecific aggressive behavior. It is, of course, quite possible for a tendency toward aggressive behavior to be innate in *Homo sapiens* without either being due to hunting, or leading inevitably to warfare.

The theory that human culture has its roots in the practice of hunting has been developed more fully by a number of anthropologists. S. Washburn and C. Lancaster have gone so far as to claim: "The biology, psychology, and customs that separate us from the apes—all these we owe to the hunters of time past" (Washburn and Lancaster 1968:303). Hunting, it is said, among other things, led to language, close cooperation among men ("male bonding"), and the dominance of men over women. L. Tiger and R. Fox, who have developed some of this picture, also make the claim that *"agriculture and industrial civilization have put nothing into the basic wiring of the human animal"* (1971:22; italics in original). That is, in the last 10,000 years a genetically determined human nature has not changed. Why the change to hunting and male cooperation required a genetic base, whereas the shift to sedentary life, the great increase in population density, and other drastic modifications of human existence did not require such biological grounding is not made clear. Tiger and Fox also argue that much of modern culture is not adaptive, and that we should therefore attempt to live in ways that are consistent with our "human nature," as they perceive it to be. This is a curious argument. Certainly the nonhunting societies of the past 10,000 years have expanded and grown at the expense of those who have maintained the ways that, presumably, are consistent with our nature as hunters!

These views have not gone unchallenged. Sally Slocum (1975) has proposed that the role of Woman the Gatherer was much more critical to the early development of culture than that of Man the Hunter. Rather than seeing culture as emerging in response to hunting and the interactions among males, Slocum seeks to derive the roots of culture from the mother-child bond. This argument presents a needed balance to the partisans of Man the Hunter. Yet all of these speculative reconstructions remain "just so stories" until data can be found that will help us to test these various sets of hypotheses. Or perhaps we should consider these tales as modern myths, which embody values and beliefs that our society cherishes. Seen in this light, these reconstructions may tell us more about our present than about our past.

A somewhat different approach is to be found in the writings of the sociobiologists. Many of their ideas have long had currency among biologists, but with E. O. Wilson's book *Sociobiology: The New Synthesis* (1975) a lively public debate was launched. Wilson, who is an entomologist, wishes to understand the biological bases of social behavior throughout the animal kingdom, including humankind. The physical anthropologist Frank Livingstone has made the point, in this connection, that

> those who emphasize the biological or genetic determinants of human behavior also emphasize the emotional causes of behavior . . . However, the most striking trend in human evolution has been the elaboration and increasing dominance of the cerebral cortex. This dominance is undoubtedly associated with the evolution of language and symbolic thought (Livingstone 1978:9).

Livingstone goes on to show how the development of symbolic thought has dramatically modified human motivations, so talk of simple genetic programming of behavior appears to be a gross oversimplification.

Such oversimplifications (or overcomplications) are seen in many of the writings of the sociobiologists when they attempt to account for human behavior. The zoologist D. P. Barash uses as one of his examples the Eskimo tradition whereby old people commit suicide by going out on the ice to freeze to death. Barash sets out the following explanation for how such behavior might have become established:

> Assume that geriatric self-sacrifice is initially a phenomenon of cultural tradition and nothing else. Selection could then operate upon the *susceptibility* to such teaching, assuming here that susceptibility genes of this sort exist. Eventually the behavior could be genetically incorporated and thereafter maintained by kin selection (Barash 1977:282, italics in original).

That is to say, individuals who commit suicide favor the successful reproduction of their offspring by not becoming a burden to them when they are unable to contribute to their own support.

Notice the number of assumptions in this statement. Is the susceptibility gene really necessary to account for the maintenance of such a tradition of self-sacrifice? If suicide of the old can develop as a cultural tradition under ecological pressures, and incidentally be rationalized by religious belief and mythological themes, why, as long as the pressures continue, do we need the additional explanatory device of genes? The explanation becomes more cumbersome and complex, rather than simpler and more elegant, by the introduction of this element. Moreover, the fact that such suicides disappeared rapidly under the impact of culture contact and the resulting reduction in the threats of starvation suggests that genes were not involved. If they had been, the cultural pattern would not have disappeared so quickly!

Hallowell's discussion of the important role played in human life by a *normative orientation* may shed significant light on this situation. Rules of right and wrong are set up by social groups, internalized by individuals, and also, in a variety of ways, enforced by communities. These rules, in many instances, may be related easily to problems of group survival. J. H. Barkow has sought to show the importance of Hallowell's work as a corrective to the reductionism of sociobiology. He sees the ideas of "self and social norms" as a "challenge to sociobiology" that it can ill afford to ignore (Barkow 1978:102).

It is certainly true that the behavior of human beings, like that of other animals, has a biological basis, if by that we mean that we cannot develop or acquire behaviors that are biologically impossible for us. Human beings have never learned to live under water or to fly simply by their own force. Some, however, have invented means of supplementing their bodily capacities with artifacts—from snorkels to airplanes. Moreover, this biological basis involves a considerable flexibility to acquire new behavior, to learn, and to unlearn a broad variety of activities.

How broad the cross-cultural range of variations in behavior and in behavioral dispositions may be will be one of our concerns throughout this book. The question of variability is linked to another, that of a shared human nature. This idea, too, in a number of guises, will be our continuing theme.

UNILINEAL CULTURAL EVOLUTION

The paleologician [the schizophrenic patient] has regressed to the egocentric speech of the child ... We know that the child's speech has some elements of the speech of primitive people ... Therefore ... the specific paleological thought and speech processes of the schizophrenics are in essence those of primitive people ... The specific laws of language in schizophrenia show that they are the same as those of primitive people or even those of higher animals (Domarus 1944:122, cited in Goldstein 1960:100).

This passage is taken from the writings of a psychiatrist, a well-known expert on schizophrenia. His notions concerning the relationship among mental illness, childhood, and primitives embody some of the essential ideas of an approach to evolution that had wide currency in the nineteenth century, and which lingered on into recent times in areas outside of anthropology.

The psychohistorian Lloyd de Mause (1974:1) illustrates another aspect of this tradition. Writing on "the evolution of childhood," he states: "the further back in history one goes, the lower the level of child care, and the more likely children are to be killed, abandoned, beaten, terrorized, and sexually abused." Of antiquity, he says: "parents routinely resolved their anxieties about taking care of children by killing them."

Anthropology is a child of the second half of the nineteenth century; it came into being as a named, field of study only a little more than one hundred years ago. Those who became the first anthropologists—in England, Germany, France, the United States, and elsewhere—brought to their studies a variety of backgrounds. They were lawyers and physicians, clergymen, classicists, and philosophers, and their concerns and experiences varied greatly. Yet, in the practice of the time, they shared a common background: they had a knowledge of Greek, Latin, and classical antiquity. Some had traveled widely. Those from the United States, such as the New York lawyer and businessman Lewis Henry Morgan, had the advantage and stimulation of extensive first-hand contact with Indians.

The basic problem these men confronted was to order vast quantities of new information pouring in from all parts of an increasingly complex world. Part of this information came from the colonial expansion of the European empires, as it is now fashionable to point out. However, it must be remembered that colonial expansion began in the Age of Discovery of the fifteenth century, with Portuguese and Spanish explorations in Africa, in the Far East, and in the Americas. At the end of the nineteenth century, only parts of Africa remained to be divided up. On the other hand, systematic archaeology was just beginning in Europe, with the first discoveries of Paleolithic cave paintings and the first recognition of remains of fossil man. The date of the discovery of Neanderthal man (1856) almost coincides with that of the publication of Darwin's *Origin of Species* (1859).

The intellectual climate of the times was dominated by the concept of evolution and by the idea of progress. It was these concepts and ideas predominantly that served the early anthropologists as ordering principles for their collection of information. These principles had to accommodate not only the diverse cultures of exotic peoples—American Indians, Hawaiians, Australian aborigines, Africans, Siberian tribes, and ancient civilizations such as those of India, China, and Japan—but also what was known of the development and traditions of classical antiquity, of the archaeological discoveries in Egypt and Mesopotamia, of European folklore and peasant traditions (research into which was promoted by Romanticism), of prehistoric archaeology, and a good deal more. The dominant method employed was comparison, the linking of elements, often taken out of context, to establish parallels, and building on these, evolutionary stages. Behavior at an "advanced level" that resembled, on some formal basis, behavior at some "lower" level could be dubbed a "survival." In this manner, it was possible to explain a good many oddities. The maypole of English peasants was clearly a survival of the fertility rites of Neolithic peoples, and carrying a bride over a threshold a survival of marriage by capture. Sir James Frazer, in attempting to explain a ritual of classical Rome, in his twelve-volume work, *The Golden Bough* (3rd ed. 1911), plucked information on divine kingship, magic, and fertility rites from among peoples at the ends of the world, removed in time and space, without regard to possible historic connections.

In spite of these strictures, it must be remembered that the nineteenth century pioneers developed a great many of the basic ideas of twentieth century anthropology. They brought together vast quantities of information, and they formulated most of our basic approaches. Science, as Elizabeth Colson (1976) has pointed out, works not by solving one group of problems and then moving on to the next, but rather in a spiral fashion: preliminary, often largely erroneous answers lead to new questions. We ask many old questions today, distinguished above all by a change in language (or jargon), and we often are unaware that our predecessors already have cleared part of the ground.

The basic approach of the nineteenth century anthropologists was psychological. As we have already seen, Tylor's definition of culture contained important psychological elements: learned behavior and cognitive orientations. Tylor (1958 [orig. 1871] vol. 1: 1) tells us that he is interested in the "laws of human thought and action," and that in his work he gives "special consideration to the civilization of the lower tribes as related to the civilization of the higher nations." He refers to "laws of human nature." Although he makes frequent references not only to "lower tribes" but also to "lower races," he also makes the following statement:

> The details of the enquiry will, I think, prove that stages of culture may be compared without taking into account how far tribes who use the same implement, follow the same custom, or believe the same myth, may differ in their bodily configuration and the colour of their skin and hair (Tylor 1958 vol. 1:7).

Thus, human thought and behavior are subject to laws that can be discovered. Human culture has evolved through time. The stages of this evolution can be discerned through the study of living groups. *And though groups of humans may differ as to race, race is irrelevant to the study of human thought and behavior.*

Tylor's definition of culture is a general one that applies to "man as a member of society." He does not limit or specify kinds of societies. However, Tylor and his contemporaries were concerned with "primitive" culture, for they wished to trace the evolution of culture from its earliest stages. The word "primitive" has two meanings: "simple" and "early." It was used in both these senses. Looking at the "simple" cultures to be found in the second half of the nineteenth century, anthropologists identified them with "early" cultures. "Savage life," says Tylor (1958 vol. 2:444) "carrying on into our own day the life of the Stone Age, may be legitimately claimed as representing remotely ancient conditions of mankind, intellectual and moral as well as material."

The "higher cultures" of the day were thought to have evolved from early beginnings, remnants of which could still be observed. But what were the origins, the earliest stages? How, for example, did religion begin? A belief in spirits—Tylor's minimum definition of religion—arose, Tylor held, from a primitive need for explanations of life and death and of dreams and trances. (Notice the reference here to a very "modern" problem, altered states of consciousness.) Tylor speaks of "ancient savage philosophers," "thinking men, as yet at a low level of culture," who sought answers to what are essentially intellectual questions. Thus, he argues, they developed a doctrine of the soul and of spirits. "Evidence" for these claims is produced in the form of examples from many peoples in all parts of the world, ancient and contemporary, who indeed hold a belief in souls, departed ancestors, spirits, and so on. But how can we be sure that, even though a belief in spirits may be universal in all contemporary traditional societies, it was indeed the earliest form of religion, or that it arose in response to questions of the sort Tylor suggests? The fact is, we cannot. Others, such as Durkheim and Freud, proposed that totemism was the earliest form of religion, for they considered the Australian aborigines to represent the oldest type of humankind. None of this speculation, of course, can be proven.

From the point of view of psychological anthropology, one important point is at issue here: the classical evolutionists believed in the evoltuion of the human mind. They sought to show, through the study of contemporary primitives and of the remains of ancient cultures, not only the development and progress through time of technologies and institutions but, first and foremost, of the human mind. They were concerned with the human capacity to perceive, formulate, and resolve problems, both of an intellectual and a practical nature. They believed that there were laws of human thought that would be revealed by their research. Theirs was essentially a psychological enterprise.

The Influence of Evolutionary Theories of Culture

Much of what these early anthropologists wrote was widely read by the educated people of the day. Indeed many popular notions about "primitive" cultures that are still current derive from that period. We need only to look at reports on television or in newsmagazines every time a new "isolated Stone Age" group is discovered, or to read of how rapidly some group in the Philippines or in New Guinea has moved "from the Stone Age to the Space Age," in order to hear echoes of nineteenth century views that somehow equated modern peoples with our prehistoric forebears, making them, by a sleight of hand, our contemporary ancestors. Such reports ignore the fact that all present-day peoples have equally long histories; they have all had time for special elaborations of some aspects of their cultures, even if some have not developed complex technologies.

The early anthropologists stimulated the curiosity of their readers by their reports of exotic materials, and they caused them to think about their own societies as well. There were a great many amateur anthropologists, travelers and observers as well as folklorists, who collected customs, tales, songs, and sayings in their own countries. How widespread this amateurism was is shown by the fact that Charles Dickens satirized it in *The Pickwick Papers,*

Among the educated readers of anthropological works were a number who have deeply influenced the world of our own day. Karl Marx and Friedrich Engels were evolutionists and believers in progress. Lewis Henry Morgan's *Ancient Society* (1877) stimulated Engels' work, *Origin of the Family, Private Property and the State* (1884). Another was Sigmund Freud, the founder of psychoanalysis, whose book *Totem and Taboo* (1912–1913) reveals a wide reading of anthropological theories and ethnographic descriptions.

Recapitulation Theory and Child Animism

From the beginnings of anthropology, some scholars were interested in primitive cultures because they thought that their study could help to solve some basic intellectual questions. We have already referred to the matter of origins. As we have seen in the earlier portion of this chapter, this subject has returned in a different form. We now do not believe that we can reconstitute the specific origins of behaviors or institutions; instead, we seek to identify the roots of human behavior in our primate nature.

Another, related concern of classical evolutionists, as we have seen, was the evolution of the human mind. Now, if that evolution were reflected, as they thought, in the various stages of the evolution of culture, then it would appear to follow that primitive societies are characterized not only by early stages of culture but also by early stages of mental development. It was, and regrettably still is, popular to say that mentally as well as socially and technologically, primitive societies reveal "the childhood of humanity." This analogy with childhood had important intellectual implications, as well as political ones.

At the time this argument was formulated, the converse also was asserted: the child in civilized society relives the development of the species, so a parallel may be seen between stages of childhood and stages of cultural evolution. This assertion is a psychological application of the principle known as Haeckel's Law, which states that individual embryonic development recapitulates the development of the species. It is encapsulated in the phrase "ontogeny recapitulates phylogeny."[8]

Recapitualtion theory played an important role in the growth of developmental psychology, and it was incorporated into some of the tenets of psychoanalysis. Reviewing its impact, Hallowell notes that at the end of the nineteenth century educators in the United States attempted "to correlate the succession of subjects in the curriculum with the 'cultural epoch' theory of ontogenetic development" (Hallowell 1974 [orig. 1939]:15). This attempt is all the more remarkable in that little, if anything, was known of the thought processes of "primitive peoples" except as they were reflected—or supposed to be reflected—in cultural practices, myths, and rituals of living primitives, and even they were known imperfectly. The presumed similarity between living primitives and their, or our, prehistoric ancestors was not seriously questioned. Much of this kind of theorizing was certainly due to a lack of actual contact with "primitives" or even with good fieldwork reports.

Traces of this approach lingered for a long time. Some are to be found in the earlier writings of the influential Swiss psychologist, Jean Piaget. For example, in *Judgement and Reasoning in the Child* (1928), Piaget observes a discontinuity between childish and adult thought in European, "civilized" children. He proceeds to identify childish patterns of thinking as "savage," that is, as characteristic of an earlier stage in the development of humankind. His findings, as Margaret Mead has put it:

were strongly suggestive that there were important parallels between the phenomena which anthropologists had described as animism and the observed spontaneous thought of young children. At the same time this parallelism was essentially inconclusive. The investigator merely compares a series of experiments or recorded observations upon civilized children with a type of thought which could be *inferred* from the myths and institutions of primitive man. Such a comparison was suggestive only (Mead 1967 [orig. 1932]:214; italics added).

Formulating the problem as one of child development, Mead undertook to study it among the Manus of the Admiralty Islands, in Melanesia. She stated the aim of the research in the following terms:

Was the thought of primitive children characterized by the type of animistic premise, anthropomorphic interpretation and faulty logic, which had been recorded for civilized children, or was this type of thought a product of a special social environment? If such thinking were characteristic of the primitive children investigated, what was the result of attaining intellectual maturity in an atmosphere congenial to such thought, rather than under the influence of an education informed by the spirit of western science? (Mead 1967:215).

On the basis of her observations of Manus children under the age of twelve, as well as some ingenious experiments with them, Mead concludes:

Manus children not only show no tendency towards spontaneous animistic thought but . . . also . . . a negativism towards explanations couched in animistic rather than practical cause and effect terms. The Manus child is less spontaneously animistic than the Manus adult (Mead 1967:233).

Furthermore, since the animism of Manus adults is learned as part of adult culture, "animistic thought cannot be explained in terms of intellectual immaturity" (Mead 1967:237).

Commenting on Mead's study, on his own research among the Saulteaux Indians, and several other related investigations, Hallowell remarks somewhat wryly:

We are thus faced with a paradox. The children of savages are often less childlike in some respects than children in occidental society. Yet when these same children mature, their adult mentality has often been equated with the mentality of occidental children at the earliest levels of development. Perhaps we, too, need to make sure that we are not confusing fantasy with reality! (Hallowell 1974 [orig. 1939]:31).

The story of child animism did not end there. In 1958, Gustav Jahoda, who was at that time working in West Africa, conducted what he called "a critical survey of cross-cultural research" on this subject. He found a body of studies using variable methods and showing some inconsistencies in findings. Yet he was able to conclude that, with the exception of Mead's work, all the studies supported the minimum requirements of Piaget's theory. Piaget had defined animism very broadly as "the tendency to regard objects as living and endowed with will," whereas Mead's definition went much beyond that (Jahoda 1958a). Jahoda went on to carry on his own research on animism among school children in Ghana, and his findings also supported Piaget's expectations. What percentage of his group of children responded "animistically" depended greatly on the specific test materials used (Jahoda 1958b).

Mead's full discussion of this issue had to wait for another twenty years. Then, however, she vigorously reaffirmed her position by showing substantial *patterned* evidence of the absence of animistic thought in Manus children (Mead 1978). Her article shows the difference between the work of psychologists and anthropologists. This discrepancy will be discussed fully in Chapter 6 .

Psychoanalysis

Freud recognized universal stages of child development of a different kind. These *psychosexual stages,* which form a keystone of psychoanalytic theory, were originally constructed on the basis of work with adult patients, and only secondarily based on the observation of children. Freud incorporated into his theory the concept of recapitulation together with the hypothesis of the inheritance of acquired characteristics and the general tenets of cultural evolution. Like his one-time associate, C. G. Jung, he read widely in the contemporary anthropological literature. However, whereas Jung believed that the study of the myths and rituals of primitive peoples could shed light on the problems of his patients, Freud, to the contrary, held that the bizarre thoughts and actions of neurotic patients could help to explain the rituals of "savage" societies.

To the equation of child and primitive, Freud added one more item, the neurotic. He considered neuroses to be failures in maturation, that is, fixations at one of the stages of childhood development. Thus, there was an identity—albeit partial—between child and neurotic. However, since childhood was regarded, in the general pattern of the recapitulation theory, as repeating the stages of the development of the human race, it seemed to follow that neurotics were fixated, or arrested, not only at a given stage of individual, or child, development, but also at a given stage of human development, to be identified with that of "savage" society.

Freud was struck with what appeared to him to be important similarities between certain neurotic symptoms of individuals and ritual behavior, particularly, although not exclusively, the ritual behavior of primitives. In his book, *Totem and Taboo,* he sought to explain certain phenomena described by various anthropologists and missionaries in their studies of primitive societies. Specifically, he was interested in totemism and the extension of the incest taboo among Australian aborigines. He thought that these beliefs and practices could be understood by treating them as analogous to symptoms observed among his neurotic patients. At the same time, in the characteristic fashion of his day, he attempted also to reconstruct the origins of these practices and to imagine how totemism and the incest taboo might have come into being.

It should be emphasized that, although Freud, together with most of the anthropologists whom he read, held contemporary primitive societies to represent an earlier stage of humanity than "civilized" Western society, he did not believe it to be the *earliest* stage, at which the incest taboo was instituted or the practices of totemism and exogamy were begun. In his words: "We shall have to admit that even under the animistic system advances and developments took place which are unjustly despised on account of their superstitious basis" (Freud 1950:97). Even more important is his observation that to call primitive beliefs "superstitions" and to hold, as many of his contemporaries did, that the behavior of primitives is due to these "superstitions" is to explain nothing. Rather, Freud argued, it is important to discover the motivations that underlie these "superstitions." He claimed that the methods of psychoanalysis could be of particular value in unearthing these hidden motivations, of which the people themselves are unaware. However, rather than seeking access to primitives, he asserted that they could be analyzed by applying to them the findings derived from the analysis of the symptoms and complexes of neurotic patients. Nonetheless, Freud himself did not believe that there was an identity between neurotics and primitives, but only an analogy. His cautionary remark on this subject has a curious ring to our ears:

> nor must we let ourselves be influenced too far in our judgement of primitive men by the analogy of neurotics. There are distinctions, too, which must be borne in mind. It is no doubt true that the sharp contrast we make between thinking and doing is absent in both of them. But neurotics are above all *inhibited* in their actions: with them thought is a complete substitute for the deed. Primitive men, on the other hand, are *uninhibited:* thought passes directly into action. With them it is rather the deed that is a substitute for the thought (Freud 1950:161; italics in original).

Here, in the conclusion to *Totem and Taboo,* Freud seems to suggest that the apparent similarities between neurotics and primitives actually disguise important differences. What is one to make of this passage? Paul (1976) believes Freud was not referring here to contemporary primitive peoples, but rather to "primordial man." Yet the differences between the reconstructed past and contemporary groups remain uncertain, at best, in Freud's writings.

Anthropological Criticisms of Psycholanalysis

U.S. anthropologists who had fully rejected cultural evolution by the turn of the century and who were strongly steeped in fieldwork and first-hand contact with so-called "primitives"—primarily American Indians—criticized Freud's forays into anthropology severely (for example, Kroeber 1972a, 1972b [orig. 1920, 1939], Du Bois 1937, Hallowell 1974 [orig. 1939]). Among the important strictures they levelled against Freud was the observation that Freud had accepted, perhaps uncritically, a number of indefensible notions of the evolutionists. He had, in other words, read the wrong anthropologists.

First and foremost, there was the idea that contemporary primitives were to be identified with early humans, or that they were in some way childlike. Critics pointed out that Freud did not base his discussion on any first-hand work with "primitives" and that, indeed, remarkably little was known about the psychological life of individual primitives even in the late 1930s. Also, it was argued vigorously that the institutions and customs of human societies, whether primitive or modern, must not be identified with individually developed or "invented" symptoms of neurotic patients. "Primitives" acquire the customs of their society in the process of socialization, whereas neurotics develop their symptoms as part of their own personal psychological distortion. How can we impute unconscious motivations inferred from certain ritual behaviors or social institutions to people who did not invent the particular practices or institutions, but merely accept them as part of a tradition handed down from earlier generations? Although this objection seems well taken, the matter is a bit more complex. As Spiro (1967) has pointed out in his discussion of Burmese supernaturalism, if institutions do not correspond to individual motivations, they soon lose their hold and become obsolete, or are modified in ways that make them personally as well as socially meaningful.

In the 1930s and 1940s psychoanalysis became a major influence on intellectual life in the United States; it affected cultural anthropology deeply, as it affected other fields of intellectual endeavor (for example, Brosin 1952). However, for it to become fully relevant to anthropology, it was necessary for anthropologists to weed out of psychoanalytic theory a series of unacceptable elements, which were not original with Freud, and his associates, but had been taken over from an earlier and outdated anthropology. Both for the anthropologist and the psychoanalyst it became important to study individual life histories and individual development in diverse societies, and to review, among other things, the idea of an invariant series of developmental psychosexual stages through the direct evidence of primitive peoples. As a result, both anthropology and psychoanalysis have been enriched. Not only did culture and personality emerge as a subdiscipline of cultural anthropology from this interaction, but cross-cultural study in turn has had repercussions on psychoanalysis. This mutual benefit can perhaps be seen most clearly in the work of Erik H. Erikson. Discussing his study of the Yurok and Sioux Indians, he notes:

Even "primitive" societies must avoid doing just what our analogistic thinking would have them do. They cannot afford to create a community of wild eccentrics, of infantile characters, or of neurotics. In order to create people who will function effectively as the bulk of the people, as energetic leaders, or as useful deviants, even the most "savage" culture must strive for what we vaguely call "a strong ego" in the majority or at least in its dominant minority—i.e., an individual core firm and flexible enough to reconcile the necessary contradictions in any human organization, to integrate individual differences, and above all to emerge from a long and fearful infancy with a sense of identity and an idea of integrity (Erikson 1963:186).

We have come a long way from that set of imaginary triplets, the child, the savage, and the neurotic!

CONTEMPORARY THEORIES OF CULTURAL EVOLUTION

As we noted in the preceding section, by the early years of the twentieth century classical evolutionism had been rejected by U.S. anthropologists and many scholars elsewhere. In part, this rejection was due to fieldwork which provided a view of "primitives" that did not correspond to the superstition-ridden savages of the armchair scholars. The American Indians, South Sea Islanders, and Africans whom anthropologists encountered were people who concerned themselves with making a living, rearing their children, managing conflicts within their societies and with their neighbors, coping with illness and misfortune, and solving numerous other practical problems of daily living.

The concept of culture revealed its usefulness in this research. Increasingly, anthropologists came to stress the uniqueness of each culture, and the relativity of the ways in which the many cultures under investigation solved what was, essentially, a constant set of problems. Grand theoretical systems were pushed into the background by this effort to collect data and to see each culture as a unique whole. In the resulting books and monographs the "savages" appeared no more irrational than the anthropologists or their readers.

At the same time, the intellectual climate was changing. The First World War, the worldwide economic depression of the 1930s, the coming of fascism, and the shadow the Second World War cast before it all contributed to the destruction of the comfortable Victorian image of progress and of the glory of Western civilization that had formed the cultural and social background of classical evolutionism. Perhaps, some began to wonder, primitive societies, in their simplicity, were at least in some respects superior to modern industrial society with its social and economic ills. The social context of the classical evolutionary theories had collapsed, just as much of the comparative anthropological evidence had destroyed some of the simple assumptions and fragmentary evidence on which these theories had been built in great measure.

The Return of Evolutionism

Prehistoric Archaeology.　During this period, a number of basic facts about human cultural development were being firmly established. Prehistorians had shown that humankind everywhere had lived for a long time in small groups, subsisting on hunting and gathering.

In some respects, such a mode of life could still be observed in a few relatively isolated societies. These societies were surviving in refuges that were then of little economic interest to others: in semideserts, in jungles, and in the Arctic, either where crops could not be grown or where modern technology appeared to be of little use. (By the 1970s, these areas were no longer unusable, and the pressure exerted on the few remaining hunting and gathering societies is now much greater.)

Such foraging had been the only possible pattern of subsistence for human groups until the development of plant and animal domestication in postglacial times. The best known center of this new mode of existence was the Near East. Other centers, particularly in the New World, came to be known later. In the Near East, in time, towns grew up and, eventually, larger political organizations.

This general outline of development began to take shape as prehistoric archaeology of a systematic type enlarged its scope. The Australian-born British archaeologist V. Gordon Childe summarized and popularized it in two widely read and highly influential books: *Man Makes Himself* (1936) and *What Happened in History* (1942). Childe, who has been called a "neo-evolutionist," took the developmental stages of classical evolutionism, as named and identified by Morgan, and gave them new meanings and new life. He redefined the stages in economic terms: *savagery* now referred to an economy of food gathering (including also hunting and fishing), *barbarism* to village life dependent on the domestication of plants and animals, and *civilization* to urban life. Furthermore, Child spoke of the changes from one stage to another as "revolutions": the Neolithic Revolution brought about the domestication of plants and animals, village life, and the development of a large series of crafts and skills; and the Urban Revolution brought about the establishment of town life.

Writing in the less optimistic period of the 1930s, Childe also redefined the word "progress." He sought to give it an objective meaning, to remove its naive, value-laden, even mystic overtones. To do so he turned to an essentially biological sense of the word. Like the Industrial Revolution, he argued, the Neolithic Revolution and the Urban Revolution could each be thought to have been steps of progress, to have been "successful," because each had resulted in an increase of the human population. That is, in biological terms, it could be claimed that each of the "revolutions" had improved the adaptation of the species.

The position Childe outlined was, essentially, an historical one. He was concerned with a series of unique, specific developments in the growth of civilization in the Near East. Even the title *What Happened in History* suggests a historical orientation. His evolutionism consisted primarily of his concept of "progress" and his delineation of developmental stages, the names of which he had taken over from Morgan; also, there was his emphasis, essentially Marxist, on the material and technological basis of cultural evolution.

In spite of his evolutionism, his approach met with little opposition among the generally antievolutionist cultural anthropologists of the period. For example, M.

J. Herskovits, in an influential and widely used textbook, praised Childe's work and his orientation, although he disliked the specific names of the stages, with their pejorative overtones (Herskovits 1948:477). Clearly, variations in cultural complexity were most readily acceptable to the anthropological community when these variations referred to technology. Evolutionism was also more acceptable when stages of development were applied to the archaeological record, where sequences could be observed.

Problems still arose when concepts of complexity and criteria of evolution were introduced in the nontechnological realm, and when attempts were made to apply them to contemporary populations. In this situation, evolutionism ran head-on into the position of cultural relativism, vigorously espoused by Herskovits and others of his contemporaries. To say that certain cultural patterns were more or less complex, or more or less evolved, appeared to be assigning positive or negative values to them, to be saying that they were either superior or inferior. Relativism held that anthropology, like all science, was nonjudgmental, and that each culture provided a meaningful and satisfying life for the people who lived by it.

A second and related difficulty in reintroducing evolutionism was that under the influence of functionalism, cultures were being studied holistically, as total unique entities. Today, we would say that each culture is a system of interrelated parts. However, these very ideas of functional interpretation and of interrelation suggest that at a given level of technological and economic "evolution," we must expect a degree of coherence between the subsistence base and other aspects of the culture. As we shall see, this idea of interrelatedness has had profound consequences for cultural anthropology in general, and specifically for psychological anthropology.

Leslie White's "Culturology".   At about the same time, an evolutionist position also was being advocated in the United States by a cultural anthropologist, Leslie A. White. Virtually alone among his colleagues, he had rediscovered L. H. Morgan, and he saw himself as Morgan's heir. He argued that Morgan and Tylor had been on the right track in their studies of culture in an evolutionist framework, and he strongly contrasted an evolutionist approach of the kind he advocated with the historical emphasis on unique cultures that was dominant at the time.

Like Childe, White sought an objective criterion of progress, and he formulated one in his "basic law of cultural evolution": "culture evolves as the amount of energy harnessed per capita per year is increased, or as the efficiency or the instrumental means of putting the energy to work is increased" (White 1949:368–369). Clearly, there is a great advance in energy available when animal energy replaces human energy, and when the power of wind and water or steam and electricity replaces human and animal energy.

White combined his evolutionist views with an energetic antipsychological stance. Writing in the 1940s, in the heyday of the culture-and-personality movement in this country, he argued that culture must be understood in its own terms, not in psychological terms. He advocated what he called "culturology" or a "culturological approach":

> Of late there has been a falling away from the culturological point of view and objectives. Instead of interpretation of culture as such, many American anthropologists in recent years have turned to the overt reactions of human organisms and to the deep subconscious forces that underlie these reactions. Thus, many men and women anthropologists, who are by training and tradition best qualified to study culture have abandoned it for adventures in psychology or psychiatry for which they have little or no technical training and with but little equipment save a ready intuition. They have sold their culturological birthright for a mess of psychiatric pottage (White 1949:xix).

Elsewhere he writes:

> The culturologist explains the behavior of a people by pointing out that it is merely the response of a particular type of primate organism to a particular series of stimuli ... Culture may be treated *as if* it had a life of its own, quite apart from human organisms ... The behavior of peoples is explained as their response to their respective cultures. It is not mystical at all to treat culture as if it were independent of human beings ... (White 1949:144; italics in original).

Reading these lines, it seems ironic that it was apparently White who first juxtaposed the words "culture" and "personality." He did so in the title of an article published in 1925, while he was a student in psychology at Columbia University, before going on to pursue graduate work in sociology and anthropology at the University of Chicago (Service 1976:612). As Aberle has summarized it, White had then suggested that "the variations in cultural systems promise us a greater opportunity to measure the impact of various factors in the development and functioning of personality than any laboratory setting imaginable" (Aberle 1960:27). Seeking to study the possible impact of culture on adolescence, this assessment had of course been the aim, in a somewhat narrower framework, of Margaret Mead's fieldwork in Samoa.

White, a one-time student of psychology, did not, of course, deny the legitimacy of that discipline. He wished, however, to define the boundaries between anthropology and psychology, and to limit cultural anthropology to "culturology."

George Spindler, in his introduction to *The Making of Psychological Anthropology* (1978), points out that there has been a

> persisting conflict between those who want to deal with culture as a thing in itself, with its own dynamic—culture *sui generis*—abstracted from social and psychological processes (and yet dependent upon these processes) and those who find it necessary to incorporate these dimensions in their theoretical constructs and interpretations (Spindler 1978:13–14).

In reviewing the history of this conflict, Spindler suggests that, particularly in the earlier years of the century, the position of White and other "culturologists" "reflects the struggle of anthropologists to disengage from the bio-racist determinism that ignored the observations about cross-cultural diversity that anthropologists were beginning to assemble" (Spindler 1978:14). Is it possible to recognize the reality of cultural diversity and at the same time recognize the significance of psychological processes for an understanding of human behavior? This is the challenge of psychological anthropology.

M. K. Opler, in an article originally written to honor White, suggested that even in an evolutionary anthropology, psychology could play an important role. Contrary to what he saw as the prevailing mode in anthropology in the United States, he thought psychology should not be used to explain cultural differences, but should be viewed as resulting from them. Thus, Opler argues,

> a generalized psychology of people . . . depends upon the evolution of the culture and is illumined by the material conditions of existence of the culture. Psychology is, then, a result of the environmental influences in which culture and the conditions of cultural existence always operate. There is no doubt *an evolution of behavior* . . . as an ingredient and as a consequence of those developments (Opler 1967 [orig. 1960]: 222–223; italics in original).

Opler criticizes students of culture and personality, as Aberle (1960) did, for giving primacy to psychology, and specifically to personality, rather than to culture. Both Opler and Aberle advocate, as we have seen, that instead of using an approach in which psychology serves to explain culture, anthropologists should develop a research strategy in which personality and behavior are studied as they are affected by culture. Culture, in this perspective, would be seen as the causative agent, and psychology, in Opler's words, as the "dependent variable."

It is interesting to note that, at about the same time, another anthropologist expressed an almost diametrically opposite view. M. E. Spiro (1961) criticized much of the work of the students of culture and personality for doing precisely what Aberle and Opler were urging them to do and what they claimed was lacking in the researches being published. Spiro argued that the initial claim of the culture-and-personality approach had been amply proven: it was by now evident to all, anthropologists and psychologists alike, that culture exerts a significant and powerful influence on personality formation. By persisting in research to demonstrate this connection, anthropology merely becomes a "handmaiden" to psychology, providing it assistance in the solution of one of its central problems. To the contrary, argued Spiro, what was now needed was a reorientation of the culture-and-personality approach: the use of personality concepts to help us to understand the operation of social structures, which, after all, is the central concern of anthropology.

These two positions, summarized here briefly, reflect not only different formulations of the goals of psychological anthropology, but also widely divergent assessments of the work already accomplished in this field. Moreover, they prescribe very different strategies for the achievement of what they perceive to be the goals peculiar to anthropology as a discipline, as opposed to the goals peculiar to psychology. The only point of agreement between these two positions appears to be that cultural anthropology is indeed distinct from psychology, and that it must seek to preserve its own identity and not do the work that properly belongs to psychology.

Julian Steward's Influence.   By the 1940s, cultural anthropology saw itself confronted with the need to bring order into an accumulation of vast quantities of information. Hundreds of descriptions of individual societies now existed, and there was an urgent need for ordering principles and methods of analysis that could be applied to these data. One primary approach that had developed was based on historical and geographic distributions of traits and trait complexes. For example, Julian H. Steward, who edited the monumental *Handbook of South American Indians* (1944–1950), initially proceeded along essentially geographic lines in organizing materials spanning two continents and many centuries.

At least in part as a result of this work, he became dissatisfied with the geographic classification. Instead, he formulated what he termed a "functional developmental" classification, dealing specifically with cultural developments in two regions of the New World, Mesoamerica and Peru (Steward 1948). This limited statement was followed by a more general one, noting regularities and ordering information drawn from six major areas of the world: Mesopotamia, Egypt, India, China, Mesoamerica, and Peru (Steward 1949). Steward later came to speak of "cultural types" and "levels of socio-cultural integration." These levels correspond basically to what others have termed evolutionary "stages." Steward eventually called his theoretical apporach "multilinear evolution" (Steward 1955). One might say, Steward had arrived at an evolutionary position inductively, by looking at cultural data, rather than by reconsidering the work of the classical evolutionists. The emphasis on cross-cultural comparisons in Steward's work is of particular importance.

Steward himself did not contribute directly to psychological anthropology. However, his own work and that of his students and others influenced by him, like that of White and his "school," has had profound consequences for all of cultural anthropology, including psychological anthropology. As Robert Carneiro (1973) has pointed out, in the century that elapsed between the 1860s and the 1960s, the position of evolutionary theory in anthropology has come full circle: whereas it was the dominant theoretical position in anthropology in its earliest phase in the nineteenth century, it came under severe attack at the end of the century and then was virtually eclipsed for almost fifty years. At present, in at least some respects, it has regained a dominant position in cultural anthropology in the United States.

Other Factors Favoring Evolutionism.   The terms "culture and personality" and "psychological anthropology" will both be used in this book. The first of these will refer to the somewhat narrower range of concerns that were the principal subject of the original field of study bearing that label. The second will cover a much larger area that includes, among other topics, such current interests of anthropologists as studies in perception and cognition. This is a subject that has been the concern of social psychologists for a long time. We shall see, however, that there are important differences in the ways in which the two disciplines approach topics in which they appear to have common interests.

In this book, we shall attempt to cast a wide net, to provide the reader with a broad view of our field. Our perspective will be cross-temporal as well as cross-cultural. That is, we shall deal with the study of behavioral evolution, of cultural evolution, and of the psychological relevance of culture change as well as with comparative, cross-cultural investigations. We shall be primarily concerned with work that has been carried out by anthropologists, but at times we shall need to make reference to the research and writing of colleagues in neighboring fields. Our emphasis will be on research among peoples of diverse traditions, yet occasionally we shall find examples closer to home. Since the aim of examples is to reveal principles, readers may well find other examples, from their own experiences, to enlarge on the issues raised in these pages.

In addition to the work of White, Steward, and their students, several other factors have contributed significantly to the present importance of evolutionary theory. One such factor was the Darwin Centennial celebration at the University of Chicago in 1959 (Tax 1960). This event brought together anthropologists of various persuasions as well as representatives of other disciplines. One of Hallowell's important papers on behavioral evolution was presented and discussed on that occasion (Hallowell 1960). A renewed interest in Marxism among social scientists has also contributed to the general revival of evolutionary theory.

The Cross-cultural or Holocultural Method

The introduction of statistical methods for the analysis of large masses of data, made possible by the introduction of computer technology, has had a major effect on anthropological research. They have led to types of studies that previously could hardly have been envisaged. These approaches have been of particular importance for psychological anthropology within an evolutionary framework. We will therefore take a brief look at the development of this area of comparative studies, now generally referred to as "holocultural" research.

The modern cross-cultural statistical (or holocultural) method had its origin in an attempt to bring order into the vast storehouse of cultural data.[7] Beginning in the 1930s G. P. Murdock, at Yale, organized a project that led to the development of the Human Relations Area Files.[8] This project involved bringing together materials on hundreds of cultures and organizing them under topical headings and subheadings. These large quantities of information were coded for analysis by electronic data processing methods. Finally the worldwide distribution of various institutions and cultural practices could be counted, and for the first time a great range of hypotheses could be tested by statistical means. The Files have made it increasingly possible to make meaningful generalizations that are based on more than a handful of societies. Anthropologists, after all, have always engaged in generalizations; yet they have never had ready access to large quantities of comparable materials. In fact, some generalizations in textbooks are rather impressionistic.

A sizable number of the holocultural studies to date have involved ordering data along evolutionary lines. For instance, several scales of subsistence economy and of cultural complexity have been devised. Generally, these scales distinguish hunting and gathering economies from those dependent on animal husbandry and various types of agriculture. Scales of societal complexity have dealt with such variables as class stratification, political organization, urbanization, and so on. Note that, on the whole, such scales do not depend on qualitative judgments, but on quantifiable aspects of culture and social organization. Robert E. Carneiro, who has developed a measure of cultural complexity (The Index of Cultural Accumulation), suggests how to apply it: "In comparative studies of, say, cross-cousins marriage, ancestor worship, or any cultural phenomenon, one might wish to see how the occurrence of the phenomenon correlated with cultural level" (Carneiro 1970:853).

When the term "evolution" is used in the context of cross-cultural studies, we are not dealing with attempted reconstructions of hypothetical past societies that are known to us only fragmentarily, as classical evolutionists often did. Nor are we making any inferences about necessary relationships between societal level and other cultural phenomena, for the statements of association only deal with *probabilities*. Furthermore, we are making no projections about the future of the societies we deal with, as we might if we were thinking of evolution as an inevitable historical escalator, as it were. Many of the traditional societies we deal with in our studies are at present undergoing drastic transformations induced not through the evolutionary processes endogenous to the society but through contact with other, more complex groups. The findings of the studies we are about to report are to be viewed within this limited framework.

Subsistence Levels and Psychological Variables.   In 1959, Barry, Child, and Bacon published a landmark study. They hypothesized that training in later childhood involves, among other things, preparing children to fulfill adult economic roles. In other words, the characteristic child-training practices of a society represent a suitable adaptation to its subsistence enonomy. Therefore, they expected societies with high accumulation of subsistence goods, such as those practicing pastoralism or agriculture or some combination of the two, to pressure their children toward obedience, responsibility, and nurturance, which together are termed "compliance." On the other hand, societies with low accumulation economies, such as hunters and gatherers, who live essentially a hand-to-mouth existence, were expected to pressure their children toward achievement, self-reliance, and independence, that is, toward "assertion." The findings of this study, based on ratings of child-training procedures in 104 societies throughout the world, support the hypothesis: high accumulation societies pressure children toward compliance, low accumulation societies toward assertion.

In a later study, Barry, Josephson, and Marshall (1976) confirmed these results, while introducing some refinements and new categories into the research procedure. They note: "Increasing importance of animal husbandry is associated with increasing inculcation of Competitiveness and Responsibility, but with decreasing inculcation of Trust and Honesty" (Barry et al. 1976:101). They also found that "increasing levels of political hierarchy are associated with decreasing degrees of inculcation in Self-Reliance, but with increasing inculcation in Obedience and Sexual Restraint" (Barry et al. 1976:101). However, these differences do not apply equally to boys and girls: for self-reliance the difference among groups is greater for boys; for sexual restraint it is greater for girls.

When adults inculcate behavior and attitudes in their children, they do so presumably because they are concerned that their children, as they grow up, show the appropriate ways of responding to the economic needs of the society, and to their own economic needs; in this case, that they become successful hunters or good farmers. However, by the same token, they are encouraging the development of certain personality traits: competitiveness and responsibility, self-reliance and independence, and so on. Some traits may not be intended but appear as by-products of the general system of education and of social life in a given society: trust and distrust, honesty and dishonesty, for example. Some traits may indeed be antithetical. Thus, the pressures toward obedience and responsibility may be at odds with the development of trust and honesty.

The findings of Barry, Child, and Bacon have been subjected to several field

In the Peruvian highlands, men and boys herd llamas and carry loads.

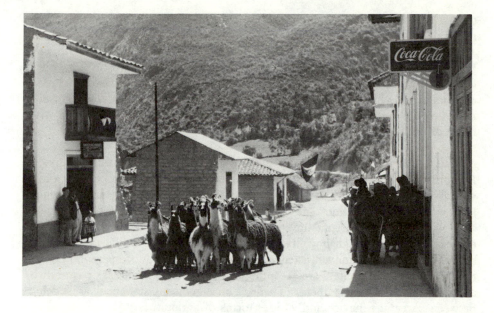

Llamas play an important role in the subsistence economy of the Peruvian highlands. (Note Coca-Cola sign on building!)

tests. In a series of long-term studies called the Culture and Ecology in East Africa Project (Edgerton 1971), comparisons were made among four societies, all of which included both herding groups and agricultural groups. Using direct measures of personality, Edgerton found pastoralists to be higher than farmers on such characteristics as independence, open expression of aggression, cooperation, and quickness of decision making. Farmers, on the other hand, were lower on independent decision making and more likely to resort to indirect means of aggression, such as witchcraft. The result of these studies is a personality picture of herders as "open" and "independent."

Because of the difference between these results and those obtained by Barry, Child, and Bacon (1959), Charlene and Ralph Bolton and their associates (Bolton et al. 1976) attempted to replicate the work of the Culture and Ecology project in their own research in the Peruvian highlands. Choosing two communities, in one of which herding was the dominant subsistence occupation and in the other of which farming was of primary significance, they tested children for a series of characteristics. Here again the herders were found to be self-reliant and nonresponsible, confirming the results obtained by Edgerton and his group in East Africa. The Boltons also interviewed mothers and found that, where some choice existed about which child to assign to herding tasks, the child's personality appeared to play a significant role. Children chosen to be herders are largely those who are less willing or adept in carrying out household chores or the agricultural chores present in the herding community. In other words, there tends to be a reinforcement of preexisting traits, rather than a development of traits in response to the tasks assigned. This finding raises a series of issues that require further research.

Because of the divergence of their results from those of the Barry, Child, and Bacon study, the Boltons reanalyzed the sample used in that investigation. They found that the high accumulation societies were on the whole based on mixed economies, in which herding was rarely of primary significance. These results must be kept in mind when "high accumulation" economies are compared with those of hunter-gatherers.

Subsistence Economy and Parental Behavior.   In a major cross-cultural study, R. P. Rohner (1975) investigated parental acceptance and rejection of children in a worldwide sample of 101 societies. By "acceptance" Rohner means "parental love, warmth, and affection" and by "rejection" he means the "absence or significant withdrawal of parental love" (Rohner 1975:44). Such rejection may be expressed either through hostility or through neglect and indifference. In this study Rohner, too, found subsistence economy to be relevant to parental behavior: he reports that hunters are accepting of their children, whereas pastoralists are more likely to reject them. (There is no significant statistical association between parental behavior and various forms of agriculture.)

Rohner adds the following comment about his expectation of a relationship between subsistence economy and parental behavior:

> We predict that parents in hunting societies cannot reject their children if that kind of social system is going to persist . . . Certain personality characteristics are more adaptive than others for the successful maintenance of a hunting way of life. Young men who are self-confident, self-reliant, and independent and who can cope with stress without undue emotional upset are, in the face of a sometimes hazardous, demanding or uncertain food quest more likely to be successful hunters than youths who do not have these characteristics. Successful hunters therefore have a selective advantage in the Darwinian sense . . . (Rohner 1975:115–116).

Rohner here is saying that in order to survive, societies develop child-training patterns that are adaptive for their particular conditions, specifically for the kind of subsistence economy they depend on. Rohner is concerned with parental behavior—acceptance or rejection of children—because it leads to certain personality traits, both in childhood and later. Accepted children acquire self-confidence and independence; rejected children are more likely to become dependent and to have a low self-evaluation as adults. It is these resulting traits that are either adaptive or maladaptive in the food quest, as well as in social relations. This argument concerning hunting societies is also supported by the findings of Barry, Child, and Bacon (1959), which we have just cited. However, in contrast to hunting, "economic systems such as pastoralism provide neither a necessary nor a sufficient basis for parents to either accept or reject their children; acceptance or rejection does not form a significant natural selective pressure in these subsistence economies" (Rohner 1975:116).

Rohner also finds a relationship between parental behavior and three indicators of cultural complexity: the number of levels of political integration, degree of social stratification, and settlement pattern. In Rohner's words, "the more complicated the political structure, the more likely the children are to be rejected; the greater the degree of social stratification, the greater the likelihood that the children will be rejected" (Rohner 1975:117). Finally, parents in sedentary neighborhoods and compact towns are more likely to reject their children than parents in migratory bands and nomadic communities. The latter groups are, of course, also more likely to be hunters. Again, it should be noted that hunters are also characterized by simpler political organizations, and there is less likelihood for class stratification to exist among them than among people with high accumulation economies. The various pieces of the puzzle, then, all seem to fall together.

Barry and his associates (1957, 1976) explicitly or implicitly deal with child-training variables that are intended to produce certain results in the behavior and the personality of children. Rohner, on the other hand, speaks of the "Darwinian" aspect of the process whereby child-training variables and personality patterns developed:

> Our argument should not be construed to mean that hunters consciously recognize the dangers of rejection or that pastoralists are aware that the effects of rejection are not "lethal" in their type of economy. Rather, our "Darwinian" analysis pertains to the unintended and unrecognized interaction between economy and parental behavior (Rohner 1975:269 n.24).

The implication here is that certain types of parental behavior originally occurred as a result of trial and error, and that the kind of behavior that produced successful hunters became established in time, because it was "adaptive". Presumably, hunters with ill-adapted personalities failed and those with adapted personalities not only had children but tended to treat them as they themselves had been treated, so the adaptive parental behaviors were selected for. Rohner's view, then, must be contrasted with that of Barry, Child, and Bacon (1959), who hold that certain traits are intentionally inculcated in children.

LeVine's Model.   R. A. LeVine (1973), whom Rohner does not cite, presents an "evolutionary model" of "population psychology" that takes this distinction into account. LeVine differentiates four types of adaptation.

The first involves the "adaptation of early child-care customs to ecological pressures" (LeVine 1973:132). He notes that certain aspects of infant and child care may not be the result of parental intent. For instance, it is known that family size varies with subsistence economy: families in hunting and gathering societies are smaller than those in agricultural societies. Not only is there high infant mortality in hunting and gathering groups, but there is likely to be an effort to space children, because a woman cannot carry more than one child. This child-spacing is aided by prolonged nursing and also by occasional infanticide. At the same time, hunting and gathering societies tend on the whole to be monogamous. On the other hand, among agriculturalists, where polygyny is frequent, even where techniques exist for spacing the children of an individual woman, the total number of children per family will be greater. Now, LeVine notes evidence, albeit from the United States, that children from smaller families are higher on achievement than those from larger families, and he raises the question whether unintended early experiences in small families might not provide children with basic personality dispositions "making them easier to train in self-reliance and achievement" (LeVine 1973:132). Conversely, he asks whether "the greater potential for obedience and responsibility of children raised in large families contributed to the selective advantage of large domestic groups once the food producing revolution had occurred" (LeVine 1973:133).

Next, LeVine considers a second kind of adaptation: deliberate socialization. He assumes that basic personality dispositions of children vary randomly in a population, with parents' intentional child-training practices constituting the selective pressure. Through reward and punishment children are pressured to conform to various societal norms. The child is shaped to adapt to society, although adult adaptation cannot be anticipated fully.

This adaptation of the adult is the third part of LeVine's model. He refers to it as "the secondary adaptations of individual personality to normative environments through selective social behavior" (LeVine 1973:133). The adult responds to particular life situations, including required social roles, by modifying attitudes and behaviors. Individuals vary, of course, in the degree to which they are successful in modifying the expression of their underlying personality dispositions, their wishes and strivings, in conformity with the demand of their life situations.

The fourth level in LeVine's model is "the adaptation of aggregate personality characteristics of populations to normative environments through the selective pressures of social sanctions." "Aggregate personality characteristics" means the distribution of observable regularities of behavior in a population or society as a whole, not only in specific individuals. The distribution of behavior patterns is modified by social sanctions to conform to ideals of role performance, social competence, and so on. The social sanctions are rewards and punishment, including the according of social prestige and the possibility of social mobility in some societies. In this case, parents discover what personality characteristics are rewarded by social mobility and attempt to inculcate them in their children. In other words, there is a feedback from the "selective pressures" that act on adults to the child-training behavior of parents. On the other hand, in societies that are stable, where mobility is rare, the norms parents internalized during their own childhood are adequate guides for raising competent offspring.

Ever since the beginnings of investigations into the relationship between a group's personality and its culture, the "fit" between the two has been a subject of considerable debate, and when observers have discovered such a "fit," its origin has been a mystery. LeVine's model neatly explains it by bringing together evolutionary concepts of random variation, selective pressures, and adaptation, and by identifying four levels, on which these evolutionary mechanisms operate, rather than the one level, usually child-training, that other observers have suggested.

Subsistence Economy and Expressive Culture.   In considering the relationship between culture and personality in an evolutionary framework, a number of investigators have studied the association between subsistence economy and those aspects of culture that are often termed "expressive": aspects that are thought to tell us something about the emotional pressures typical of given societies. Examples are studies of games, of the religious use of dreams, and of altered states of consciousness.

Roberts, Arth, and Bush (1959) distinguished three types of games: games of physical skill, of strategy, and of chance. They and Textor (1967) have shown that games of strategy are more likely to be present in agricultural societies, while games of skill and of chance predominate in hunting and gathering societies. Using the child-training variables identified by Barry, Bacon, and Child, Roberts and Sutton-Smith (1962) found games of strategy associated with obedience training, whereas games of skill were linked to achievement training. Games of chance were associated with responsibility training

Roy G. D'Andrade (1961) used the findings of Barry, Bacon, and Child for research into dreams. D'Andrade identified a group of cultural traits that, together, make up a pattern that he terms the "use of dreams to seek and control supernatural powers." He finds strong correlations between this pattern and subsistence economy: the overwhelming majority of the hunting and gathering societies in his sample use dreams in this manner, whereas only one-fifth of the societies that have both animal husbandry and agriculture do so. The societies intermediary in economic form fall between the two extremes in their use of dreams, although a majority employs them in this manner. D'Andrade also finds a relationship between assertiveness training and the use of dreams to seek and control supernatural powers. However, when economy was statistically controlled for, the correlation was drastically reduced. That is, assertiveness training, in the absence of a hunting economy, turned out not to be significantly related to the dream use pattern. On the other hand, societies in which a married son moves some distance away from his parents are also more likely to have this use of dreams. D'Andrade suggests that the pattern should be understood as related to "what happens to adults, rather than to children, and what happens to men rather than to women" (D'Andrade 1961:327).

Not only dreams but also altered states of consciousness (ASC) are culturally patterned. Bourguignon (1973b) distinguished three types of societies by the form that altered states take in their religious practices: 1) societies that use trance (T), a state that includes such experiences as visions and contacts with supernatural beings; 2) societies that use possession trance (PT) linking altered states to a belief in spirit possession; and 3) societies that use both forms of altered states (T/PT).

In a study that carefully controlled for possible diffusion of these patterns among cultures, Bourguignon and Evascu (1977) confirmed the hypothesis that trance (T) was associated with hunting and gathering, with little stratification and low political complexity, whereas possession trance (PT) was associated with agriculture, class stratification, and a higher degree of political complexity. Societies with both types of altered states (T/PT) were intermediate in subsistence base and societal complexity as measured by stratification and political organization.

Both the studies of dreams and of altered states assume that the use to which such states are put by societies reflects their characteristic stresses on individuals as well as the typical personality characteristics of the population.

Culturally Constituted Behavioral Environments

What is the importance of these scattered findings in the context of cultural evolution? It may be helpful here to think back to our earlier review of behavioral evolution, in which we considered the continuities between humankind and our primate relatives. In our discussion of the evolution of language (pp. 35–36), we referred to Jerison's concept of "perceptual world." The perceptual world, he tells us, varies from species to species. That is, the "world" that an animal perceives and to which its actions are adapted is constructed by the animal's sense organs and by its capacity to process the information it takes in from the environment. Humans, as one species, should be living in a single, common "perceptual world." However, as Hallowell has pointed out, in the case of *Homo sapiens* the "world" is always culturally constituted. Information processing is complicated among human beings by the fact that culture, as expressed through language, art, and other symbolic systems, including games, dreams, and altered states, interprets experiences and sensations for us. Not only that: because individuals are born into ongoing cultural systems, they are supplied with a ready set of interpretive categories, so they encounter experiences full of expectations. Therefore members of the same species but of different cultures experience the "same" environment quite differently. Although we may be said to live in the same "objective" environment, we actually live in different "culturally constituted behavioral environments." A vivid comparison of the culturally constituted behavioral environment of two groups with different subsistence economies and at different levels of societal complexity, who are, however, affected by a common physical environment, is provided by Colin M. Turnbull (1965). He contrasts the world of the forest-dwelling Mbuti pygmies of Zaire who live by hunting and gathering with that of the village-dwelling horticulturalists with whom the Mbuti have a special relationship. Turnbull notes that the vast Ituri forest "is considered as generous and friendly from the point of view of the Mbuti hunters and gatherers, and as niggardly and hostile from the point of view of the village cultivators" (Turnbull 1965:17). Whereas the Mbuti live in or by the forest, the villagers live only in spite of it, for they carry on a constant struggle to clear the land for their plantations.

The Mbuti recognize their dependence on the forest and refer to it as "Father" or "Mother" because, as they say, it gives them food, warmth, shelter, and clothing, just like their parents ... Also, like their parents, it gives them affection ... The forest is more than a mere environment to the Mbuti. It is a living, conscious thing, both natural and supernatural, something that has to be depended on, respected, trusted, obeyed and loved (Turnbull 1965:19).

By contrast, the world the forest constitutes for the villagers is quite a different one:

As for the Mbuti, so for the villagers is the forest an entity to be reckoned with, upon which life and death depends; it is also an entity which is natural and supernatural. But instead of acceding to the natural, the villagers with their superior technology combat it; and instead of respecting the supernatural in the sense that the Mbuti respect it, the villagers oppose it with fear, mistrust and occasional hate. They people the forest with evil spirits, and they fill their lives with magic, witchcraft and a belief in sorcery (Turnbull 1965:21).

This example shows more clearly than any abstract discussion could how each group constructs its own "reality," its own culturally constituted behavioral environment. This process involves what is seen, heard, and sensed; in other words, it is perceptual. It is also cognitive, involving practical knowledge by means of which the natural environment can be utilized or modified. Finally, the process of constructing reality is also affective; many types of emotions are to be found in the relationship between a group and its environment, ranging from love and attachment to fear, awe, and even hatred. Some of this feeling is expressed directly, in practical terms, and some of it in the symbolic language of religion and art.

Is it possible to construct a generalized picture from cross-cultural studies? We shall try to construct a model of the world in which hunter-gatherers live. Before we do so, it must be stressed, however, that because these people live at present in marginal environments, any extrapolation of our model to prehistoric hunter-gatherer populations, however tempting, requires considerable caution. Because of their close dependence on their natural habitat, the conditions of life of hunter-gatherers vary considerably among the several ecological settings in which they are found nowadays.

Generally speaking we expect to find in hunter-gatherer societies a simple technology, with only a small total inventory of material culture. The population will be small, local groups numbering 200 or less. There will be no fixed settlements, and the people will move frequently in pursuit of game or opportunities for gathering. We expect to find a sex division of labor, but no occupational specialization. Large animals always will be hunted by men, although women and children may participate in animal drives. However, in many cases more than half of a group's subsistence will be provided by the women's gathering activities. The political unit will be the small band or community, or sometimes the individual family. Under the economic conditions of band life, we do not expect to find class stratification or great differentials in wealth. The only part-time specialist is likely to be a shaman, who enters into direct contact with spirits by means of trance states. Spirits are likely to be concerned in some ways with the animals that are hunted, and hunting will be central to the morality of the group. Spirits also will be concerned with illness, so the shaman may act as diagnostician and healer, and illness is likely to be a punishment for offenses, whether against members of the community or against the rules of hunting. In the socialization of children, overall indulgence of infants is likely to be high, and children are likely to be accepted by their parents; that is, they are treated with warmth and affection. Children, particularly boys, are socialized for assertiveness, self-relieance, and independence. Games of skill and of chance may be expected to exist, but not games of strategy.

As already noted, hunter-gatherer groups are likely to be small. In addition, they are most probably isolated and must therefore be self-sufficient, for the most part. This isolation and self-sufficiency is reflected in their values (such as independence and assertiveness), in their skills, and in their image of the world. They are likely to have detailed and intimate knowledge of their physical environment: the habits of the animals they hunt, the best places to find water, the location of edible plants, the variations in weather conditions, and so on. The spirit world is intimately related to this natural world of work and experience, and good relations, on a one-to-one basis, must be maintained with the spirits. Contacts with spirits occur in dreams, visions, in shamanistic trances, and, as in North America, in the guardian spirit complex.

With the coming of plant and animal domestication much of this behavioral environment must have changed. The relationship between cultivators and the environment is more complex, reflecting both their negative, hostile relations to it and the positive ones. Rather than utilizing to the best of their ability what is available to them for the taking, people now seek to foster and cultivate certain plants and animals and to fight against others. The Bantu cultivators on the margins of the Ituri forest whom we have contrasted with the Mbuti pygmies represent an example of this duality. Consequently, it is not surprising to find that for these people a variety of hostile forces and beings are present in the universe, as well as benevolent ones. The relationship between supernaturals and humans becomes a collective relationship. Religion, in content, organization, and personnel reflects the complexity of the group and the relationship it entertains with the natural and the supernatural. Human groups among cultivators are larger and more complex than those of hunter-gatherers. Their economy can support a larger population and this population is increasingly differentiated, not only on lines of sex and age; there are now craft specialists of various kinds, and we may expect to find social stratification and increasing political complexity as well. The socialization of children now is also likely to be different, as we have seen, as are norms of role performance. Different kinds of personalities are now prized; foresight, management, self-restraint, and obedience are now valued over generosity, self-reliance, and independence.

Among sedentary peoples, ancestors are a major force in the culturally constituted behavioral environment. A Haitian cemetery: tombs have spaces for candles and offerings of food.

All of these changes suggest the possibility that we may be able to speak of an *evolution of types of culturally constituted behavioral environments* of human groups, much as we can speak of the evolution of subsistence type technology, and social organization. Furthermore, we may be able to discern together with it an evolution of adaptive and preferred personality characteristics.

The interrelationship between personality and culture, then, must include a culturally constituted behavioral environment. This culturally variable "reality" is developed and modified in a variety of ways. First, it develops through trial-and-error acquisition of empirical knowledge. This knowledge is accumulated, on the one hand, by individuals in the course of a lifetime, but it is also the property of the group, for it is passed on to its younger members through the teachings of their elders or of more experienced members of the group. Knowledge and skills in humans, in contrast to other animals, is cumulative and grows rapidly when new adaptations are required, slowly when groups have developed a stable adaptation to their ecological niche.

In this regard it is important to remember that a group's "natural resources" are directly related both to need and to the technological capacity to utilize the habitat. The behavioral environment, however, is not limited to this definition and utilization of subsistence resources. As we have noted in the case of the Mbuti and their neighbors, the habitat is conceptualized in both intellectual (cognitive) and affective ways. A variety of elements enter into the construction of a behavioral environment in addition to empirical knowledge. Among these elements are psychological projections. Experiences of dreams and altered states of consciousness may provide guidelines for behavior and a framework of beliefs within which empirical experiences are interpreted. They constitute both a confirmation of beliefs and a source of cultural innovations. Yet, as we have already seen, dreams and altered states of consciousness themselves are culturally structured, and these structures have been shown to be associated statistically with a society's subsistence base, its social and political complexity, its child-rearing patterns, and so forth.

Rather than consider this series of associations as a chain of causal determinants, we are more likely to improve our understanding of the relationship among these various elements if we think of them as constituting a complex network of feedbacks. For example, subsistence patterns favor certain personality characteristics; given, for example, an economy based on hunting and gathering, independence, self-reliance, and so forth, are desirable characteristics. These characteristics result, at least in part, from certain parental attitudes and behaviors. A pattern of using dreams to acquire and control supernatural power also correlates with a hunting and gathering economy. It appears to be related to the stresses experienced by individuals who are, in fact, forced to be self-reliant and independent of human assistance. They express, it would seem, a desire for a magical helper. We shall have occasion to return to these complex interrelationships over and over again in several contexts.

SUMMARY

In this chapter we have seen that an idea of *evolution* is used in anthropology as a basic concept in three different ways, each of which is relevant to psychological anthropology. One of these ways is the *classical theory of cultural evolution* that held sway in the nineteenth century. Although it is now outdated in its original form, it contributed importantly to the development of several approaches in modern psychology. In time it also helped in bringing about the rise of present-day evolutionary theories in cultural anthropology. In addition, we discussed two approaches to evolution that are of great contemporary significance: behavioral evolution, and contemporary theories of cultural evolution.

Behavioral evolution deals with the relationship between the behavior of modern humans and their primate cousins. It seeks to identify both continuities and differences between them, and to reconstruct the behavior of earlier forms of the genus *Homo.* We discussed the theoretical views of Hallowell, who developed the concept of *protoculture.* This term refers to a developmental stage in which a series of preconditions for the emergence of culture were present, yet were not sufficient to bring it about. For the appearance of a characteristically human mode of existence, the growth of shared extrinsic symbolism was required. This symbolism, expressed in language, art, and ritual, brings about, for each cultural group, the development of its own particular *culturally constituted behavioral environ-*

ment. Hallowell stressed the development of *self-awareness* and of a *normative orientation,* which are characteristics of human beings only. Finally, we examined *cultural evolution, modern style.* Among the contemporary approaches are statistical, comparative (holocultural) studies, some of which concern how differences in child rearing and personality types relate to differences in subsistence economy and societal complexity. Based on these studies, and using the concept of a culturally constituted behavioral environment, we attempted to sketch the differences between the world of hunter-gatherers and of more complex societies depending for their subsistence on some forms of plant and animal domestication. Differences between child-rearing patterns and personality were among the variables included. In Chapter 4 we shall return in greater detail to studies of child rearing, and we shall then find it useful to keep these generalized pictures in mind.

The contemporary cross-cultural studies we reviewed contrast present-day societies that have different types of subsistence economies. Although we placed these comparisions within an evolutionary framework, we have actually presented a static picture. That is, we can see what the differences are, but not *how* societies evolve and are transformed. We have not asked in this chapter how, at some point in the past, hunterer-gatherers became agriculturalists and herders, or how modernizaiton occurs today among tribal and peasant peoples. We shall deal with the dynamics of culture change and its psychological aspects in Chapter 9.

What our comparative approach to modern cultures has shown us is that cultural evolution cannot be reduced to an evolution of population size, subsistence economy, technology, and societal complexity. As culture changes and evolves over time, so does the world that is experienced by human groups. Its complexity is related to an increase in empirical knowledge and in practical skills, or a shift in the types of knowledge and skills that are required under new circumstances. At the same time, in ideological or metaphysical terms, it also reflects the image of a more complex social organization. To function effectively personalities must be adapted to this changing behavioral environment, which yet, to some extent, is itself a reflection of the personality type fostered by the group's life style. LeVine's model helps us to understand, in very general terms, the processes whereby personality types evolve. We have attempted to relate this evolution of personality types to an evolution of both culture and of the culturally constituted behavioral environment. In the next chapter we shall turn to the specific evidence of the existence of personality differences among cultural groups.

NOTES

1. See the Reference section for Hallowell's publications on this subject (1956, 1960, 1961, 1963a). The 1963 paper, which contains the fullest statement, has been reprinted in Hallowell (1976a).

2. Students wishing to pursue this subject further may wish to consult Rowell (1972), Jolly (1972), van Lawick-Goodall (1971). The last presents an interesting first-person account of the author's studies of chimpanzees in the Gombe Stream Reserve.

3. K. R. L. Hall, (1963) makes an extensive review of these materials.

4. There is some indication of displacement in the dance of the bees, but it involves an entirely different evolutionary sequence from that found in the development of communication stystems among primates.

5. *Oh's Profit,* a novel by John Goulet (1975) tells the story of Oh, a gorilla with a complex personality, who has been taught sign language, and of the quarrels this successful experiment produces among linguists and psychologists with competing theories. For a nontechnical review of a large number of studies, see Emily Hahn's book, *Look Who's Talking* (1978).

6. In a brilliant book, the paleontologist S. J. Gould has reviewed the long history of the idea of a relationship between the development of the individual organism and that of life forms. He demonstrates the significance for modern evolutionary biology of the *"changes in developmental timing* that produce *parallels* between the stages of ontogeny and phylogeny" (Gould 1977:2). These changes allow him to reconcile continuity and this continuity in evolution and would account, for example, for both the similarities and the differences between human beings and chimpanzees.

7. Sets of the Files are located at member universities, and microcard versions of the Files are available at subscribing institutions. The topical headings were set out in *An Outline of Cultural Materials* (Murdock et al. 1965) and cultures are listed in *Outline of World Cultures* (Murdock 1963). Coding of data on 863 societies is to be found in the *Ethnographic Atlas* (Murdock 1967), and these data have been analyzed by Bourguignon and Greenbaum (1973). Discussions of the cross-cultural statistical method are to be found in the *Handbook of Methods in Cultural Anthropology,* edited by R. Naroll and R. Cohen (1970). In 1978, HRAF published a *Guide to Social Theory: World-Wide Cross-Cultural Tests.* This massive work presents a cross-indexed methodological analysis of some 1375 propositions tested in 300 holocultural studies.

8. G. P. Murdock was greatly influenced by his teacher, the sociologist Albert Keller, and through him, by W. G. Sumner. Tylor, at a time when statistics was in its infancy, had attempted the first correlational study. (See F. W. Moore 1961 for some of the precursors of holocultural research).

CHAPTER 3

Do Group Differences Exist?

I think about my education sometimes. I went to the University of Chicago for a while after the Second World War. I was a student in the Department of Anthropology. At that time, they were teaching that there was absolutely no difference between anybody. They may be teaching that still.

Another thing they taught was that nobody was ridiculous or bad or disgusting. Shortly before my father died, he said to me, "You know—you never wrote a story with a villain in it."

I told him that was one of the things I learned in college after the war (Kurt Vonnegut, Jr., in *Slaughterhouse-Five*).

INTRODUCTION: WHEN SOUTH MEETS MIDWEST

After spending two years in Georgia, my colleague Professor Donald has recently returned to the Midwest. He was glad to be back, he said, because life in the South had made him uncomfortable. People there deal with business contracts as if they were carrying on personal relationships. Even a trip to the bank involves exchanges of pleasantries and personal inquiries instead of being limited to straightforward business transactions. "They are very insincere," he concluded.

A few days after my conversation with Professor Donald I was listening to Mary Ellen, a student from Alabama, who complained bitterly of her experience in the Midwest. She said she could not get used to living among people who are so cold and unfriendly. Here, she thought, people were not concerned with each other, and personal relationships simply could not be established. At home, she said, everyone was warm and friendly and people really cared about each other.

The disagreement between Professor Donald and Mary Ellen could not have been more striking. What one approved and cherished, the other abhorred. They agreed on one thing only: that there are indeed differences in interpersonal behavior between South and Midwest. They disagreed, however, energetically on their interpretations and evaluations of the behaviors, and they did not use the same criteria in making their judgments. Whereas she looked for "warmth" and "friendliness" in human interactions, he spoke of "sincerity" and "businesslikeness." What she expected seemed inappropriate to him, and he therefore saw it as "insincere." What he perceived as "businesslike" she felt to be "cold."

The experiences of Professor Donald and Mary Ellen did not fulfill their expectations. As a result, each was frustrated and disoriented. For us to play our own roles effectively, others must live up to the expectations we have of them. When they do not, the pattern is broken. We are apt to interpret and evaluate others in terms of our own local traditions; we may then respond inappropriately and risk applying criteria that are foreign to the situation.

Behavior, expectations, attitudes, and values are not merely situational and temporary but form part of the image we have of ourselves and that we present to others. Therefore they belong in a discussion of personality. To the extent that they are not unique to an individual but are part of the norms of a given population, we can speak of shared personality features. Our examples suggest that Midwestern and Southern personalities differ in significant respects. According to one set of norms, as we have seen, behavior should be "warm" and "friendly," and according to the other it should be "sincere" and "businesslike."

To what extent do individuals actually live up to these norms? We find that there are variations in the degree to which persons comply. Midwesterners might then say that "Mr. Smith is unusually businesslike, for a Southerner," or Southerners might consider Mrs. James is "an unusually friendly person, for a Midwesterner."

Before we examine scientific approaches to culture and personality, we must consider a basic issue: the contrasting views of those who are primarily interested in cultural diversity and those who seek to demonstrate the existence of a universal human nature. These two perspectives have often been in fundamental opposition, yet both are basic to anthropology.

THE RELATIVITY OF CULTURE AND THE UNIVERSALITY OF HUMAN NATURE

Is it possible to reconcile a recognition of the existence of major cultural differences with a view that there is yet an underlying, single, universal human nature? We have already touched on this point in our earlier discussion of cultural evolution. There Leslie White, a foremost evolutionist, was also vehemently opposed to culture-and-personality studies. Even among those who have con-

In rural Haiti, a little girl stands beside her grandmother and her great aunt. Her mother is at the far right.

A little girl and her mother in a Peruvian highland town. In the background, a Catholic church dating from the Spanish colony.

tributed greatly to the development of psychological anthropology, opposition between a relativist and a universalist view exists.

It is, of course, an easily observed fact that cultures differ widely with regard to a great many matters: they differ concerning standards of behavior in all aspects of life, and they differ, as we have seen, in their interpretations, and apparently in their experience, of the behavioral environment. From this observation, relativists draw important practical implications for child training, mental health, sex roles, and various other matters. On the other hand, universalists stress certain universal constants in "human nature" shared by all members of the species. The various positions we shall examine stress one of these two aspects of the problem, often at the apparent expense of the other.

The classical evolutionists, and the psychologists who were influenced by them, such as Freud and Piaget, were universalists. They dealt with cultural differences by ordering their data within an evolutionary framework, seeing cultural features most at variance with nineteenth century life as "earliest" and most "primitive." Anthropologists of the twentieth century who rejected evolutionary theories attempted to understand cultures as unique, or as specific, historically derived ways of solving common problems faced by all societies. The position formulated by students of Franz Boas, such as Ruth Benedict, Margaret Mead, and Melville J. Herskovits, transformed the observation of variety and relativity into a philosophy of cultural relativism. Relativism denies the possibility of evaluating the practices of other cultures, and makes comparison difficult on any but strictly formal grounds. In psychological anthropology, relativism has had its most important impact on the development of criteria of mental health.

The discovery of the relativity of cultural practices, beliefs, and attitudes has had a profound influence not only on anthropology but on all the social sciences. It is one of the major intellectual developments of the twentieth century. One of its results has been to call into question the concept of a universal human nature. For example, we have already mentioned Margaret Mead's study of the adolescence of Samoan girls, which cast doubt on the universal existence of a period of stress and conflict as a concomitant of the biological transformations of puberty. If the stresses were due to cultural factors, and these factors were variable, what other aspects of the human nature we believed in were, in fact, merely aspects of our own culture? What did it mean when people said, to explain someone's behavior, that "it's only human nature" to take advantage of others, to wish to better oneself, or to be competitive, or, when they said that wars could not be abolished because "it's human nature" to fight?

Introductory college courses in the social sciences began to teach that "human nature" is a meaningless term, because behavior, attitudes, and values are culturally variable. But is this conclusion valid? Is human personality infinitely malleable? Are there no limits to cultural variation? Are there not perhaps certain "built-in" requirements, basic needs and drives that must be satisfied at the peril of psychological as well as physical disaster? If so, can we not attempt to evaluate human cultures with regard to the degree to which they achieve the satisfaction of human wants, and conversely, and perhaps more easily, with regard to the degree of stress to which they submit human psychological and biological functioning? We have become increasingly aware of the impossibility of separating the biological and the psychological aspects of human existence; psychological stresses are reflected in physical ailments. The basic questions about human nature to be answered, open a perspective that must be confronted in a world that gave rise to German concentration camps and the Russian prison camps of the Gulag Archipelago.

Knowledge of cultures outside Western civilization has long been used to question the certainties of that civilization. In the eighteenth century, travel literature reporting true or imaginary adventures among foreign peoples was used to challenge familiar institutions and values. Swift did so with *Gulliver's Travels,* Montesquieu with his *Persian Letters,* and Diderot with his spurious *Supplement to the Voyages of Bougainville to the South Seas.* These reports raised doubts about the institutionalized constants of individual and social life.

To question the immutability of society is a revolutionary act; it implies that observations of alien ways of life may shed some light on our own. The differences between human groups are not so radical that we cannot recognize ourselves as we are, or as we might be, in others. Unless we draw this conclusion, we will find ourselves arguing that others are less than human, like the proponents of slavery who argued that Africans had no souls.

The development of psychology raised further questions. Psychology proceeded from the assumption that human psychological functioning was amenable to scientific study, as was all else in nature. Scientific study meant the search for regularities, for laws of nature that were valid universally. We find this assumption of the existence and discoverability of universal regularities in behavior equally in the laboratory work of Wundt and in the clinical work of Freud.

It is psychoanalysis, the personality theory of Freud, that gave a major impetus to culture-and-personality research in anthropology and, in a number of modified forms, gave it its major theoretical orientation. Even those who have taken other theoretical positions have often done so in order to disprove some aspect of psychoanalytic theory. The history of culture and personality may thus be seen as a dialogue of sorts between cultural anthropology and psychoanalytic personality theory.[1]

As we saw in Chapter 2, Freud was interested in anthropology in the early years of the century, and anthropologists have criticized him in large measure for the anthropological theories he incorporated into his work. A psychology of "primitive" societies remained to be constructed on the basis of better comparative data and of what, at each period, has been perceived to be a more adequate anthropology. It could then also utilize Freud's theoretical constructs, without much concern about his specific views on primitive society.

Psychoanalysis grew out of Freud's work with neurotic patients. It is both a therapeutic method and a theory of personality, which changed and evolved in the course of his lifetime and which has been further developed by his successors.

It is primarily as a dynamic theory of personality that it has been of relevance to culture and personality. As such, it is first of all rooted in human biology. Therefore, insofar as human biology is constant without reference to culture, the laws of human psychology may be assumed to be constant also. In other words, psychoanalysis denies the dichotomy of mind and body that has so profoundly affected Western thought for such a long time. Secondly, a personality is held to be the result of the individual's life history.

Freud delineated a series of maturational stages of psychosexual development. These stages correspond both to the physical and emotional development of the child and to the disciplines imposed on it. An individual who encounters distortions and trauma at one stage of development will develop corresponding personality distortions. It is part of the therapeutic process to uncover the infantile sources of adult disturbances, be they character disorders, neuroses, or psychoses.

It is largely under the influence of Freud's formulation of the stages of infantile development and their significance for personality development that anthropologists have paid considerable attention to child-care practices in their studies of culture and personality. There has been interest in discovering whether the stages are universal; specifically, it has been asked whether the Oedipus complex occurs in all societies or whether it is a function of a particular social organization. The universality of a latency period, prior to puberty, also has been questioned. Another aspect of psychoanalysis taken up by anthropologists deals with the consequences of child care for adult personality. This issue has involved both direct studies of individuals and the study of cultural products, such as myths, religion, and other institutions. In part, this approach was already initiated by Freud and some of his students, when they saw an analogy between dreams and myths (for example, Abraham 1913), and when Freud likened the institutions of primitive societies, the rituals and taboos of the Australian aborigines, to the expressions of neurosis in European patients. With regard to field research, psychoanalytic practice has suggested the significance of acquiring psychological data by collecting dreams together with the dreamer's associations, life history, open-ended interviews, and so forth. As we shall see, some problems have been encountered in operationalizing psychoanalytic theory, that is, in setting up clear-cut tests of the theoretical propositions.

Whereas anthropology has been heavily influenced by psychoanalysis, anthropology in its turn has influenced psychoanalysis in this country, particularly in the 1930s and 1940s. Certain Neo-Freudians, such as Karen Horney, Erik H. Erikson, and Erich Fromm, have been interested in reducing the emphasis Freud placed on the physiological basis of psychological development and in allowing room for social and cultural factors.

A number of anthropologists have attempted to construct a perspective that brings together both an awareness of cultural diversity and a conception of a universal human nature. Hallowell, as we have seen, viewed a human psychological level of adaptation as an emergent of human evolution. He stressed the universal existence of extrinsic symbolic processes, of cumulative learning, and of the ability to transcend learning. He pointed to the fact that every human social order is a moral order with a normative orientation (although specific norms are culturally variable), with reflexivity (the individual's self-awareness and self-judgment) and with the ego defense mechanisms posited by Freud, which permit compromise between individual drives and social demands. He posited the construction of a culturally constituted behavioral environment, so that the "reality" to which individuals and societies adapt is, in fact, a variable reality.

Melford Spiro (1954, 1978) also has sought to define a universal human nature while recognizing cultural variability. In his second analysis of the problem, he concludes that there is much greater constancy than he had envisaged earlier, and he describes how he arrived at his conclusion on the basis of fieldwork in four drastically different societies: among Chippewa Indians, on Ifaluk atoll in Micronesia, in a kibbutz in Israel, and in Burma. Spiro defines personality as "a system of cognititive, perceptual, motivational and affective dispositions 'underlying' behavior" (Spiro 1978:351). This definition leads him to question the simple identification of cultural and behavioral variability with personality variability. Instead he points out:

> however much societies may differ, they all must cope with man's common biological features, especially his prolonged infantile dependency; the adaptively viable means for coping with the latter condition exhibit common social and cultural features across a *narrow range of social and cultural variability;* these common biological, social, and cultural features are a set of constants which, in their interaction, produce a universal human nature (Spiro 1978:355; italics added).

This position does not mean that culture and cultural diversity may be neglected in our investigation of human nature. Rather, Spiro's approach requires that personality, as a system, be investigated separately from culture and behavior. Group differences in behavior tell us about cultural differences, but not about differences in personality, as he defines it, nor about the relativity of human nature.

We shall see how this dialogue between the constant and the variable, the universal and the relative, appears again and again in the context of specific investigations of numerous cultural groups. Note that Spiro's 1978 statement comes much later than his own earlier, more relativistic views, and that our review of the work of culture-and-personality anthropologists will now turn back to an earlier era.

THREE APPROACHES TO THE INTERACTION BETWEEN CULTURE AND PERSONALITY

The existence of differences among cultural groups seems to be self-evident to all who have ever come into contact with individuals outside their native community. It is precisely the "otherness" of outsiders that makes them "aliens." Yet, although at a commonsense level such differences appear beyond dispute, at a scientific level they are not. Those who have attempted to develop evidence have found their work beset by a variety of serious difficulties. In order to obtain valid data we need agreement on three issues: 1) How is the relationship between culture and personality to be conceptualized? 2) What categories are to be used in describing personality? 3) What methods are to be used in assessing personalities cross-culturally to produce comparable data?

Each of these questions has received different answers in the course of the past half century. The studies that have been carried out and that we shall be considering in a roughly chronological order fall into three groups. They represent three approaches: the *configurational* approach, the *psychoanalytic reductionist* approach, and the *personality mediation* approach.

The Configurational Approach

Ruth Benedict's epoch-making book, *Patterns of Culture,* was first published in 1934 and has been reprinted many times since. Benedict selected three culture areas for her analysis: the Pueblos of New Mexico, as illustrated principally by the Zuni; the Dobuans of Melanesia; and the Northwest Coast of North America, centering on the Kwakiutl. In addition, the culture of the Pueblos is contrasted with that of the Plains Indians. The analysis of Zuni culture is based primarily on Benedict's own fieldwork among these people, the Dobuan data were furnished by Reo Fortune, and those on the Kwakiutl by the work of Franz Boas. Each culture is identified by a dominant configuration, and for this purpose two key terms—Dionysian and Apollonian—are taken from Nietzche's analysis of Greek tragedy. The third term, Paranoid, is taken from psychiatry. The Dionysian seeks ecstasy, and the "illuminations of frenzy." The Apollonian, to the contrary, distrusts all extremes and "does not meddle with disruptive psychological states" (Benedict 1961 [orig. 1934]:79). The Pueblos are Apollonian; the Kwakiutl and their neighbors are Dionysian, as are the Plains Indians. The Dobuans are Paranoid, fearing and hating each other. The Kwakiutl, in addition to their Dionysian propensities, show traits of megalomania, an aspect of paranoia.

Benedict has been much criticized for these labels. Mead, in her preface to later editions of the book, notes:

> She was building not typology; she held no belief that Nietzschian or psychiatric labels were suitable for all societies. Nor did she believe that any closed system could be constructed into which all human societies, past, present, and future, would fit. Rather, she was committed to a picture of developing human cultures for which no limit could be set because the possible combinations were so many and so varied as to be inexhaustible (Mead, in Benedict 1961:viii).

Patterns of Culture was Benedict's attempt to bring order into the vast "diversity of custom." Something more than a catalog of that diversity was required:

The significance of cultural behavior is not exhausted when we have clearly understood that it is local and man-made and hugely variable. It tends to be integrated.
A culture, *like an individual,* is a more or less consistent pattern of thought and
action. Within each culture there come into being characteristic purposes not necessarily shared by other types of society. In obedience to these purposes, each people
further and further consolidates its experience and in proportion to the urgency of
these drives the heterogeneous items of behaviour take more and more congruous
shape ... We can understand this only by understanding first the emotional and
intellectual mainsprings of that society (Benedict 1961 [orig. 1934]:46; italics added).

Notice, here, the likening of culture to "an individual." Like individuals,
cultures are said to have "purposes"; the question of how these characteristic and
distinctive purposes come into being is not investigated. The need for congruity
and order is seen as a "drive," and the purposes a society has are said to be its
"emotional and intellectual mainsprings." They are characterized in the terms we
have already cited: Apollonian, Dionysian, and Paranoid or following Spengler
for Western Civilization, "Faustian."

Culture then, is isomorphic with individual personality, and it can be discussed
by means of studying the personality of its bearers. Conversely, the personality
pattern that typifies individuals is also the one that typifies a culture. The analysis
therefore can shift back and forth between these two concepts with ease, particularly because culture is said to "mold" personality:

If we are interested in human behavior we need first of all to understand the institutions that are provided in any society. For human behavior will take the forms those
institutions suggest, even to extremes of which the observer, deep-dyed in the culture
of which he is a part, can have no intimation (Benedict 1961 [orig. 1934]:236).

In a sense, then, culture is *built into* human individuals, and it is discovered,
or some parts of it are, by studying individual behavior. Yet individuals do not
appear in this book at all. Cultural forms are illustrated through reports of
individual acts, but there is no assessment or presentation of individual personalities. The end product is necessarily a picture of fairly homogeneous communities,
although the existence of deviants is recognized. Deviation and adaptation are
related to the concept of "temperament," which, however, is never made clear.
Because culture and personality are in fact one and the same thing in this
presentation, separate methods of studying each are not necessary, nor is the
evaluation of a "fit" between them.

Benedict holds that the particular patterns that characterize a given culture are
the result of "selection": each culture actualizes only some part of the human
potential. However, she presents no theory of why some aspects of this human
potential are selected for actualization by a given culture, rather than others.
Although there is emphasis, as we have seen in Benedict's statement, on the
integration of culture, she also recognizes that some cultures are better integrated,
such as the Zuni, or less well integrated, such as the Kwakiutl. The possibility

that selection might in some way be related to ecological and technological factors, or that the degree of integration might be related to culture change, are not considered. Such ideas have received greater emphasis only more recently.

Essentially, Benedict's approach, as represented here in its first major expression and as later developed both in her own work and in that of Margaret Mead, stresses cultural—and therefore psychological—variability. Cultures are "understood" by revealing their patterning—the way various parts of the total picture fit together. "Understanding" does not involve a search for causes or a discovery of correlations, a testing of hypotheses or even an unravelling of historical sequences. The principal problem to be solved in this approach, in addition to a discovery of the pattern, is the way in which culture (and thus typical personality) is transmitted from one generation to the next. The pattern is seen in all aspects of culture, and in the culture of childhood as well as in that of adults. Cross-cultural comparisons are used primarily to show incomparability.

Benedict's approach has been criticized on the one hand by those who reject a psychological approach altogether, such as Leslie White and Marvin Harris. It has also been criticized by those who search for a fit between personality on the individual level and the cultural demands resulting, for example, from the adaptation of a society to its particular ecological niche, and by those who search for causes or test hypotheses concerning cross-cultural regularities. As Robert LeVine remarks with regard to the work of both Benedict and Mead: "We are asked to forfeit the aim of explaining cross-cultural differences in personality in favor of simply appreciating them" (LeVine 1973:55).

On another level, Benedict's choice of labels also has been questioned. In the remarks quoted earlier, Mead argues that this criticism is based on a misunderstanding, and that Benedict was not seeking to establish a finite typology. Two other points deserve attention in this connection.

First, both the Plains Indians and the Kwakiutl are identified as Dionysian. Here is some of the evidence Benedict offers to show that in both areas there was a seeking after ecstasy and transcendence. In the Plains, men sought visions with "hideous tortures":

> They cut strips from the skin of their arms, they struck off fingers, they swung themselves from tall poles by straps inserted under the muscles of their shoulders. They went without food and water for extreme periods. They sought in every way to achieve an order of experience set apart from daily living (Benedict 1961:81).

The purpose of the Plains Indian vision quest was to receive power from the spirits in a private, personal encounter. It was a "cultural mechanism which gives a theoretically unlimited freedom to the individual . . . It gave individual initiative a scope which is not easily equalled" (Benedict 1961:83).

The context in which the Kwakiutl on the Northwest Coast sought ecstasy was different. Here the altered states of consciousness were part of the rituals and ceremonies of secret societies, into which persons were initiated, presumably, by the spirit patrons of the societies. In the Cannibal Society, the period of initiation involved several months of seclusion and "a demonstration of frenzy" during the ritual of the initiate's return:

> The whole Winter Ceremonial, the great Kwakiutl series of religious rites, was given to "tame" the initiate who returned full of "the power that destroys man's reason" and whom it was necessary to bring back to the level of secular existence (Benedict 1961:177).

There was, then, a striving for ecstasy, but the context of the Kwakiutl experience and its personal and social significance were quite different. Among the Plains Indians it was individual power that was sought and a supernatural support for personal initiative and independence. Among the Kwakiutl, the initiate was received into membership in a secret society, the Cannibal Society having highest prestige and rank. Indeed, whereas the Plains Indians lived in equalitarian societies of buffalo hunters and raiders, the Kwakiutl lived in a hierarchically organized society of settled villages. The people were divided into nobles, commoners, and slaves, and there were great differences in wealth, prestige, and power. The Plains Indians, to use the terms employed by Barry and his associates (1959), lived primarily by hunting and had a low accumulation subsistence economy. The Kwakiutl, who were sedentary salmon fishermen, by contrast, had a high accumulation economy.

Both types of societies may be considered to be Dionysian, in Benedict's classification, yet with regard to just about any other aspect one might wish to choose, these two cultural areas represent drastic contrasts. As a result, we see that even the Dionysian aspects play different roles in the total cultural fabric and have different personal meanings.

A second problem in labeling is that by using the terms Apollonian and Dionysian as a contrasting pair of labels for different cultural types, Benedict appears to suggest that a single cultural emphasis or personality type could be used to characterize a total culture. She implies a high degree of cultural and psychological homogeneity in a society. Nietzsche, who coined the terms, had actually used both of them in his analysis of Greek tragedy; he found *both* patterns to be present in the single culture of classical Greece.

Whether a single configuration, or pattern, can be said to characterize all the elements that make up a given culture, or whether at least some cultures might not be more complex, is ultimately an empirical question. Benedict herself presented a more complex picture of a culture a dozen years later in *The Chrysanthemum and the Sword* (1946), her wartime study of Japanese culture. The problem, here, is not primarily the matter of labels, but rather the basis on which a typology is established, what is assumed to begin with, and what is discovered in the process of investigation.

With regard to labels, a third, more serious problem was raised by the use of terms, such as "paranoid" and "megalomania," taken from the language of psychiatry. Benedict's concern was to show that behavior that might resemble that of pathological individuals in Western society might be institutionalized in other cultures, and therefore be "normal." Thus, like everything else about human behavior, the "normal" and the "abnormal" were to be understood as culturally relative.[2] Unfortunately, the language of psychopathology came to "taint" the culture-and-personality enterprise. In fact, it was, in part, used in the psychological warfare of World War II. In the contemporary period, when the people studied by anthropologists read the books written about them, when anthropologists have been tarred with the brush of "colonialism," and when much scientific work has been politicized, the overtones carried by the psychiatric terminology have, at times, been taken to be insults and political exploitation.

All of this criticism was far in the future when Benedict published *Patterns of Culture* in 1934. Indeed, by stressing relativism, she intended to strike a blow for tolerance and to express a hope for harmony among human societies. Curiously, the extent of criticism to which this book has been subjected is itself one measure of its great impact within the anthropological profession, as well as among a wider readership.

Criticism of quite a different sort has turned on the issue of Benedict's data and of her interpretation of them. John W. Bennett reviewed a large body of writings on the Pueblo Indian cultures of the Southwestern United States. He documents two points of view concerning them in the anthropological literature: On the one hand, he finds, writers like Benedict, see Pueblo culture as highly integrated, with a consistent and harmonious set of values and with an ideal personality "which features the values of gentleness, nonaggression, cooperation, modesty, tranquility, and so on" (Bennett 1956:204). On the other hand, some writers claim that "Pueblo society and culture are marked by considerable *covert* tension, suspicion, anxiety, hostility, fear and ambition . . . the individual is suppressed and repressed. Witchcraft is covert, but highly developed" (Bennett 1956:204; italics in original). Bennett suggests that these two views reflect differences in the writers' values. The first group appears to approve of Pueblo ways of life, not merely to describe them. This group stresses the positive character of some features of Pueblo culture that one might consider to be clearly at variance with modern Western civilization. The second group stresses aspects the first seems to give little attention to: the cost to the individual at which the "harmony" is achieved. The two views appear to be complementary rather than contradictory as far as the information itself is concerned. They do, however, lead to a rather different picture of the Pueblo way of life and of the Pueblo individual. The second group of writers, in particular, looks to ecology as a framework within which the development of Pueblo social organization and child training have taken place.

This disagreement raises several matters of considerable importance. Regarding cultures where several anthropologists have carried out fieldwork, there may be a high degree of agreement on certain aspects of the materials and less on others; there may also be a great deal of difference in the interpretations the data are given. The interpretations, although perhaps not the data themselves, may reflect unstated, and even unconscious, premises and value orientations of the fieldworker. It follows that where we have the report of only one fieldworker, no such check is available to us, and questions concerning the validity and reliability of the picture we are offered must be kept in mind.

In the Pueblo case, not only do we have reports by a series of fieldworkers, but these reports extend over a decade or more—even longer if we include those prior to Benedict's formulation and the psychologically oriented studies of the thirties. The changes in the field reports therefore reflect not only individual views and values, but also changes in theoretical perspectives within anthropology. For example, researchers like Esther Goldfrank (1945), who see Pueblo culture as repressive of individual development and expression, distinguish conceptually between culture and personality in a way that the configurationists do not, and it is the latter who emphasize the picture of harmony and integration. The concern with ecology, mentioned earlier, also appears to be an example of such a shift in theoretical interest, and this shift is clearer now than at the time of Bennett's writing. Incidentally, most of the studies cited by Bennett appeared after *Patterns of Culture,* which gave a strong impetus both to the configurationist view and to contrasting views.

In summing up the configurationist approach initiated by Benedict and further developed by Mead and her coworkers, LeVine argues that it focuses on the concept of culture and reduces "personality to a mere individual reflection of culture, and personality development to the intergenerational transmission of culture" (LeVine 1973:55). Margaret Mead has written extensively on a broad variety of subjects, yet throughout one of her principal concerns has indeed been the subject of cultural transmission.

In summary, several difficulties were encountered in the process of trying to demonstrate and delineate group differences in personality. These difficulties have to do with the conceptualization of the problem on the one hand and with the acquisition and analysis of the data on the other. The debate between the protagonists of the configurationist approach to Pueblo culture and their opponents suggests another difficulty, if we are to believe Bennett: anthropologists have often argued that studying alien, "primitive" societies made it possible to be a good deal more "objective" than studying one's own society. Nonetheless, this debate suggests that unadmitted and often unanalyzed biases may creep into the study of a foreign society as well as into the analysis of one's own way of life. The debate also shows the importance of restudy, or of the study of a single society by more than one anthropologist. Likewise the selection of conceptual tools, of hypotheses to be tested, or of concepts to be applied tends to structure our findings. Observers who use different concepts and different methods of analysis and of data acquisition will necessarily produce results that are hardly comparable.

We now turn to students of personality and culture who have treated the field as involving the interaction of two systems, or portions of two systems, rather than as a single system.

Psychoanalytic Reductionism

At about the time Benedict was formulating the configurational approach, another view of the interrelationship between culture and personality was being developed by Géza Róheim, a Hungarian anthropologist trained as a psychoanalyst. In 1928, Róheim was given the opportunity to carry out psychoanalytically oriented fieldwork by Marie Bonaparte, Princess George of Greece, herself a student of Freud. He chose to go to Australia, among other societies, because he regarded the Central Australians as the most primitive human group living, and because information on the Australian aborigines had been basic to Freud's argument in *Totem and Taboo*. Róheim sought to check, in the field, Freud's hypotheses concerning the relation between primitives and neurotics, cultural evolution, and the universality of the developmental stages and psychic mechanisms identified by Freud. He attempted to close the gap that "had made itself felt in psycho-analytic ethnology, since psychoanalysts have never been in a position to gather ethnological observations in the field" (Róheim 1932:2). Among the Aranda, he collected and analyzed folklore and mythology, as well as dreams and the dreamers' associations to their dreams, which he compared to the mythological materials. He studied ceremonies, interviewed individuals, and observed children at play. He also utilized a form of play analysis. His book, *Children of the Desert* (Róheim 1976) was published only long after his death. In it, he described a way of life that has now, for the most part, disappeared.

On the basis of his anthropological and psychoanalytic fieldwork, Róheim developed his "ontogenetic theory of culture." This theory views culture as the result of the human "delayed infancy." It considers the "group character" of a given society as the outcome or response to the infantile trauma typical of that particular society. That is, he holds that in each society there is one particular aspect of the interaction of infants and adults that is especially painful. Róheim recognizes the existence of individual variations in this situation in every society. However, he suggests that variations are smaller in primitive societies than in modern ones.

By "delayed infancy" Róheim means the great length of time during which the human infant, compared to the young of other primate species, is dependent on adult caretakers.[3] During this extended period, the infant develops strong attachments, particularly to the mother or mother substitute. Freud had drawn attention to the existence of infantile sexuality, which had been denied by nineteenth century ideology. Róheim points out that the child's sexual development is premature in relation to both its physical and its emotional development. He argues that the disproportionate rates of development are responsible for the constellation of feelings Freud had discovered and had named the Oedipus complex. Róheim points out that, since the biological facts that he holds responsible for that complex are a human universal, the complex itself must be generically human. He therefore rejects Freud's explanation of the Oedipus complex on the basis of a collective unconscious and on the inheritance of acquired characteristics, for in *Totem and Taboo* Freud had traced the origins of the Oedipus complex to events in the earliest stages of humanity.

Moreover, Róheim notes, Freud had claimed that neuroses were due to various kinds of trauma experienced in early childhood. Since parents in different cultures vary in the ways in which they treat their children—a finding he confirmed through his fieldwork—it follows that each culture is characterized by its own typical "ontogenetic trauma." That is, each culture is based on a particular, specific, childhood trauma, which also accounts for the specific character type to be found in each society. According to Róheim, then, the origin of culture in the evolution of humanity is to be found in infantile trauma, and each specific culture results from a particular trauma. He goes so far as to say that such infantile experiences are more important than the "real conditions" of life:

> The Australian native has never undergone the trauma of being weaned. The children will go on sucking as long as they like and will easily get another woman to let them do it if their own mother has no milk . . . The Australian native lives in an environment that can hardly be called favorable . . . And yet nobody has ever heard that an Australian native feels anxious about tomorrow's meal. Facts might well justify such an attitude, but there is no basis for it in the libidinal development. With such yielding mothers, we are all heroes (Róheim 1932:78).

Róheim is saying, in effect, that because there is no trauma of weaning for the Australians, even harsh economic conditions are not able to break their faith in being always provided for. In more general terms, then, since the pattern of life is established by infantile experiences, all adult activities are seen as derivative, involving sublimation or acting out on the level of reality (as in economic activities) or on the level of fantasy (as in rituals).

Róheim has been criticized for, in effect, denying adulthood—the existence of rational adaptive strategies—in favor of seeing adult behavior and institutions as based on childhood experience. However, the opposite position, which would deny the irrational component in adult personal and institutional behavior, is certainly also quite off the mark. As we saw in our discussion of the culturally constituted behavioral environment (Chapter 2), "realistic" behavior must be seen in relativistic terms.

Since Róheim wished to test Freud's theories in the field, he was open to the possibility that cultural variability might affect Freud's stages of psychosexual development. In fact, he claims that among the Aranda, the latency period does not exist (Róheim 1932), an observation which had been made earlier by Malinowski with regard to the Trobriand Islanders. However, while Malinowski had claimed that the Oedipus complex as described by Freud did not exist among the matrilineal Trobriand Islanders (Malinowski 1927), Róheim reported the existence of this complex among the Normanby Islanders, who are also a matrilineal group, in many respects culturally similar to the Trobriand Islanders. (We shall return to the Oedipus complex in Chapter 4).

Róheim collected a substantial amount of observational material, in part by innovations in field research. He collected dreams and the dreamers' associations to them; he observed children at spontaneous play and also set up play situations for them. Although he emphasized the biological basis of psychological development and of personality structure, stressing the universal aspects of human nature, he was willing to admit the possibility of cultural variations. In fact, the whole basis of his ontogenetic theory of culture traces differences in culture to differences in child care.

Róheim's theory has found little acceptance among anthropologists. For example, F. L. K. Hsu states emphatically that "psychological anthropology is not simply the psychology of the individual, and it must shun psychoanalysis of whole cultures in the manner of some of Freud's disciples" (Hsu 1972a:10). Róheim has also been criticized for not allowing room in his theory for cultural change, although he argues for cultural evolution. Because adults are, in effect, condemned to act on the basis of their own childhood trauma when dealing with their children, there appears to be a vicious circle: personality results from childhood trauma, and the same trauma is perpetuated in the next generation by the parents as a result of their own personalities.

This brief discussion has emphasized some of the difficulties Róheim's contribution has encountered. However, in spite of these strictures, it contains many valuable insights and observations, and represents a significant element in the development of psychological anthropology.

The Personality Mediation Approach

The next important step in the development of theories about the relationship between culture and personality came from the collaboration between a psychoanalyst, Abram Kardiner, and several anthropologists, in particular Ralph Linton and Cora Du Bois. LeVine (1973) called it the "personality mediation view."

In their first book, *The Individual and His Society* (Kardiner 1939), the culture of the Marquesas and that of the Tanala of Madagascar are described by Linton and analyzed by Kardiner. A second volume, *The Psychological Frontiers of Society* (Kardiner 1963), includes three cultural descriptions: Linton describes the Comanche; "James West" (Carl Withers) describes a midwestern American community dubbed Plainville; and Cora Du Bois describes the Alorese. The cultural descriptions in these two volumes were based on research carried on under a variety of circumstances and for diverse purposes. Only Du Bois' work was specifically designed to provide the cultural and psychological data required for Kardiner's analysis as it had been developed in his earlier trial formulations. She also presented her materials at much greater length in her book, *The People of Alor* (Du Bois 1960). This book should be read together with a shorter description and Kardiner's analysis, both of which are included in the *Psychological Frontiers of Society*. In addition to obtaining a good deal of general ethnographic materials on which her description of the culture is based, Du Bois also collected eight rather full life histories from both men and women and obtained personality test protocols and children's drawings. The life history materials and the tests could then be used as a basis for personality analysis, which could be related to the cultural materials, including information on child training and parental attitudes.

Kardiner uses specific information on individuals to derive what he calls a society's *basic personality structure.* (Du Bois prefers the term *modal personality*). This term refers to those characteristics shared by the majority of a group's members as a result of their common formative experiences. These formative experiences are the result of the childhood disciplines of a society, family organization, and so on, referred to as *primary institutions.* Certain other aspects of culture are termed *secondary institutions:* religion, folklore, mythology, art, and so on. Secondary institutions are products of the "projective systems" or "projective screens". According to this model, a society's primary institutions create its basic personality structure, which in turn projects or expresses certain psychological content—conflicts, fantasies, and so on—in the form of the society's secondary institutions. Thus, personality "mediates" between the two types of institutions.

To understand this model, it is necessary to know what Kardiner and Linton mean by "institutions." As Kardiner puts it (1963:25), "Institutions should be defined to mean what people do, think, believe, or feel. Their locus is within the

A youngster in a Haitian slum. Child training practices constitute the "primary institutions" in Kardiner's system. Clothing infants wear is one indicator of parental attitudes towards elimination and modesty.

human personality; and they have an accommodative or adaptive function." The primary institutions are taken as givens. Their origin or source is not investigated, nor is a hypothesis advanced to account for their existence: "The origin of an institution has nothing to do with the effect it creates on the growing individual" (Kardiner 1963 [orig. 1945a]:25). Furthermore, the model does not claim to account for the entire culture or social system. Kardiner thinks that practices of "purely rational origin" are likely not to be involved with the basic personality structure, either as cause or effect.

This approach has been criticized on a variety of grounds. Let us consider the matter of the data, first of all. As already mentioned, of all the cultural descriptions included in the two Kardiner volumes, only that of the Alorese by Cora Du Bois draws on fieldwork conducted specifically to provide data for the purpose of this analysis. Sometimes sketchy information is used to construct formidable theoretical edifices. For example, after Linton's description of the Tanala of Madagascar Kardiner summarizes as follows:

> The old Tanala society had as its basis the cultivation of dry rice. This technique permitted a certain type of social organization, based on communal ownership of land . . . under the extreme authoritarian rule of the father. The basic needs of the individual . . . were completely satisfied notwithstanding . . . submission to despotic rule . . . When the wet method of rice cultivation was introduced, communal ownership of land had to be abandoned. The individual suddenly became important, and his rights were threatened by the competitive needs of other individuals for the same means of subsistence. This led to the disruption of the whole family organization. This resulted in a great increase in crime, homosexuality, magic, and hysterical illnesses. These social phenomena indicate quite clearly that when the personality, as shaped by the customs suited to the old method of economy, encountered, in the new economy, psychological tasks it was in no way prepared to meet, the result was an enormous outbreak of anxiety (Kardiner 1945b:113).

This analysis is an oversimplification of Linton's description. In fact, Linton speaks of two neighboring societies, Tanala and Betsileo, of whom he says: "basically we can regard Betsileo as Tanala culture, after all the changes consequent upon wet rice have become consolidated, organized and institutionalized" (Linton, in Kardiner 1939:283).

Linton's work has been widely quoted as evidence for a relationship among economy, family structure, and personality structure. It is also a hypothesis about the relationship among ecology, economy, and social and political organization. As such it has recently been the subject of a restudy by Aidan Southall, who states that, having worked among both the Betsileo and the Tanala, he undertook this exploration "in a spirit of piety to the ancestors" but that he has "become increasingly uncomfortable as the sense of piety dissipated" (Southall 1975:604). He summarizes Linton's hypothesis as follows: "He [Linton] assumed, perhaps plausibly but without evidence, that the Betsileo had once been a stateless people occupying a forested plateau, but that by clearing the forest and developing terraced, irrigated rice cultivation, they had also developed kingship and a caste structured society. He argued that the Tanala were developing in exactly the same direction in the late 19th century until the process was altered by the French occupation of 1895" (Southall 1975:604).

Because Linton published his ethnography of the Tanala in 1933, evolved the hypothesis in question in 1937, and developed it further in the Kardiner volume in 1939, Southall is able to compare three versions of the materials.[4] He finds that "Linton himself contradicts *all* the crucial elements of his celebrated hypothesis" (Southall 1975:606; italics in original). He goes on to say: "It almost seems as if, in these later writings, he became so enamoured with an exciting idea that he proceeded to elaborate it without any regard for the facts which he himself had previously recorded" (Southall 1975:607). Finally he concludes:

> The moral of the story would seem to be that ecological interpretations of social change should not be applied mechanically without due regard for the facts of history as well as social structure ... Linton's worst theoretical mistake was to pose two similar sequences of socioeconomic development and political change for two quite dissimilar ecological niches (Southall 1975:608). As far as the psychological implications of the supposed developments are concerned, Southall makes no reference to them at all.

What, then, is left of the Linton-Kardiner analysis of the Tanala-Betsileo? It appears that we can no longer say with Kardiner that Linton has offered us "a remarkable text for the study of the dynamics of social change" (Kardiner 1939:329). We can no longer consider that the Betsileo show us what the Tanala are in the process of becoming. Could we argue, on the other hand, that the Tanala show us what the Betsileo once were? Southall says this idea is "plausible," but "without evidence." Perhaps, then, we can use the separate descriptions of the two societies for purposes of comparison, seeking to identify patterns of concomitant variations in both culture and personality. However, Linton provides only cultural data for the two, and it is Kardiner who infers differences in basic personality structure from these descriptions. Kardiner tells us that among the Betsileo, a society with irrigation, permanent villages, and despotic rulership, there is greater anxiety than among the Tanala, where there is dry rice farming, shifting cultivation, and the joint family. He infers this anxiety from Linton's claim that among the Betsileo there are more forms of spirit possession trance and there is more sorcery than among the Tanala. This last is a curious claim, because we have learned to expect from numerous studies (Hallowell 1940, Kluckhohn 1944, B. B. Whiting 1959, Swanson 1960) that sorcery is more likely in societies where there is no superordinate authority. The Betsileo-Tanala comparison appears to suggest the opposite. As to spirit possession, one would need a good deal more information to be able to draw Kardiner's and Linton's rather audacious conclusions.

In sum, Kardiner concludes that the changes or differences in basic personality structure that he infers from the cultural data must be the result of changes or differences in the subsistence economy, because, he says, there are no differences in the family organization. Yet Linton tells us that while there is a joint family organization among the dry rice Tanala, this organization does not exist or "has broken down" among the wet rice Betsileo! Kardiner also says that the "basic disciplines" (the child-training practices) are the same in the two societies, but the information on which this statement is based is not provided. Given then, that the difference in the subsistence economy is the only one among the primary institutions that he can locate, he suggests that the greater anxiety he finds among the Betsileo, as compared to the Tanala, is due to scarcity. But would one not be justified in expecting the opposite—that irrigation agriculture produces more of a surplus than shifting cultivation?

Although comparison between cultures is a useful technique to shed light on concomitant variations, the approach does not work here because the information we are given is too slight to support such a major edifice of inferences. The description of a basic personality structure for the two societies is drawn from cultural materials; primary and secondary institutions are outlined and a basic personality structure mediating the two is inferred from them. No independent personality data or measures of personality are available.

The People of Alor.   Cora Du Bois' work on the Alorese represents a great step forward. Her fieldwork was specifically designed to provide, for Kardiner's analysis, a body of detailed psychological materials, together with cultural data providing information on both the "primary" and the "secondary" institutions. *The People of Alor* (Du Bois 1944) offers a rather full ethnography of childhood, as well as an overall picture of the culture. The book also presents the full text of autobiographies of eight individuals, four men and four women, together with Kardiner's analyses. Kardiner also provides an overall analytic chapter. In addition, there are summaries of findings based on several psychological tests: the Proteus Maze Test, word associations, children's free drawings, and the Rorschach test. This last was submitted to a "blind" analysis by the Swiss psychiatrist and Rorschach expert, Emil Oberholzer; he was given none of the cultural information. The children's drawings were interpreted by Trude Schmidl-Waehner in the same "blind" manner. Both of these experts utilized the formal properties of the materials rather than the content for their analysis. The resulting agreements between Kardiner's interpretations and those of the other two specialists are remarkable, although, of course, imperfect.

The detailed information Du Bois was able to provide made it possible for Kardiner to formulate models of Alorese basic personality structure at several developmental levels, through adolescence and early adulthood. Kardiner draws psychological conclusions from cultural data, but he also uses the autobiographies to confirm his picture of the basic personality structure.

To understand the great significance and impact of this study, it is important to place it in its historical context. Cora Du Bois herself has done so in her introduction to the paperback edition of *The People of Alor* (1960). She notes that "In the 1930s anthropology was preoccupied with functionalism, patterns and configurations. Cultural relativism was rampant, to the detriment of careful

comparative studies" (Du Bois 1960:xvii). This relativism had a number of implications. One of these was that each society was studied, and presented, as a unique
whole, and no parallels were drawn with other cultures. This limitation was
serious for theory building, but in their training anthropologists had been exposed
to information on many different cultures, so at least implicitly a comparative
framework existed for them. However, when they published for a broad public,
as Mead and Benedict did with such books as *Coming of Age in Samoa* and
Patterns of Culture, such a framework was not made explicit. The situation was
even worse when anthropologists began to collaborate with professionals trained
in other disciplines.

This lack of comparative references is evident in Kardiner, in spite of his
exposure to anthropology. One need only consider a few passages to become
aware of this lack, as well as of a number of inconsistencies. For example, Du
Bois tells us: "The Alorese mother has economic responsibilities that make her
welcome the birth of a child less cheerfully and care for it less solicitously than
she might in another culture" (Du Bois 1960:38). A great deal of emphasis is
placed by both Du Bois and Kardiner on the mother's work and the neglect of
the infant, although Du Bois herself notes the lack of quantitative data and urges
caution in drawing conclusions. She also notes differences between the care of
infants born in the early dry season, when mothers are freer, and infants born at
busier times (Du Bois 1960:34). Here, on the other hand, is one of Kardiner's
summaries of this situation:

> The influences to which the child was subjected in this society were of a unique
> character. Owing to the peculiar division of function between males and females, the
> woman bore the brunt of the vegetable food economy. She worked in the fields all
> day and could take care of her children only before she went out to the fields and
> after she returned. Maternal neglect was therefore the rule, and by this is meant that
> the supportive influences of the mother in establishing the structure of the ego were
> in default (Kardiner 1945b:115).

What makes Kardiner think that this situation is unique? There are a great
many societies in which women carry the principal burden of the subsistence
economy, whether horticultural societies (where farming does not involve the
plow) or hunting and gathering societies. Besides, Margaret Mead had already
published her work on the Mundugumor of New Guinea, among whom women
provided most of the food, and who disliked having children, while the men spent
most of their time on head-hunting and other "nonproductive" activities (Mead
1935). Furthermore, is there a necessary relationship between the women's agricultural work and child neglect? Kardiner seems to think so, for here is another
version of this situation, as it appears in *The Psychological Frontiers of Society:*

> Poor maternal care in Alor was an accident resulting from the mother's having to
> work all day in her fields. The basic institution is that the mother works in the fields
> all day; the neglect of the children is not institutionalized, although almost universal
> (Kardiner 1963 [orig. 1945a]:24).

By "not institutionalized" Kardiner appears to mean that there are no sanctions against the good care of children, nor is there a social ideology that requires child neglect. One of the sources of criticism against the Alorese study was based precisely on this point, since a number of anthropologists were able to point to societies where the mothers took their children along to the fields. Du Bois herself says explicitly: "It is not customary for the mother to work with the child on her back, or even near her, *as it is in some societies.*" (Du Bois 1960:34; italics added)

Kardiner also makes references to the women's unconscious hatred of the mother and of the maternal role. The male's frustrations are expressed in an unconscious denial of their dependence on women, and this denial is at least a partial explanation of their elaborate prestige economy, which involves complex financial transactions and other "important" but unproductive activities. It would appear, then, that it is inaccurate to say that women's economic responsibility causes child neglect; rather, its primary source is the women's attitudes toward their children. Rohner (1975), incidentally, uses the Alorese as his type case of a society in which parents reject their children.

Kardiner draws a number of conclusions from the Alorese study. For instance, he comments:

> A culture which sacrifices adequate maternal care for infants to other interests starts a cycle which never ends. Adequate maternal care, as judged by Alor, means assisting the ego in the early years to the formation of adequate executive capacities to deal both with the outer world and with other members of the community (Kardiner 1963 [orig. 1945a]:253).

He finds the Alorese case distressing and full of implications for Western society:

> The whole situation appears all the more absurd in view of the fact that the women do not need to take over the subsistence economy and tend to the fields instead of aiding the child in the formative years. The men do not contribute, save very sporadically, to the subsistence economy and do nothing with their time except dun for debts in what seems to us a meaningless although complicated financial system (Kardiner 1963 [orig. 1945a]:254).

This comment is rather disconcerting, for it shows that the anthropologists with whom he had worked over a period of several years had not succeeded in indoctrinating their psychoanalytic collaborator with the then "rampant" relativism of which Du Bois speaks. The fact that the financial system of the Alorese appears "unproductive" and "meaningless" to us, does not, of course, mean that it is not of the highest significance to the Alorese themselves, nor that it does not require analysis in terms of its relation with, and impact on, Alorese social structure, political organization, and ecology. Kardiner perceives it only in a psychological framework, which is interesting, to be sure, but from the point of view of the 1970s, this approach offers us an incomplete understanding of the situation.

Alorese men actually do raise chickens and goats for food; the pigs they raise play an important role in their financial transactions, and although they are ostensibly not raised for food, they are eaten at feasts. The men also hunt for wild pigs and wild rats. Moreover, until the recent past they were involved in warfare and head-hunting.

With reference to a system in which women work in the fields and neglect their children as a result, while men do nothing "useful," Kardiner adds the following interesting comment:

> It can be safely said of the Alorese that they are totally devoid of social insight and have no idea of the effect of the institutions by which they live. However, in that regard, *neither are we concerning our culture* (Kardiner 1963 [orig. 1945a]:254; italics added).

Moreover, Kardiner is quite aware of his occasionally ethnocentric position, and he notes explicitly that:

> all value judgments used in the appraisal of Alor were drawn from our culture . . . There is no need . . . to maintain the pretense of disinterestedness, since there are no absolute values which we can use as a yardstick. However, the value judgments . . . were not based on *moral* issues but on purely psychological grounds. We can call an adaptation effective or ineffective without lapsing into moralization (Kardiner 1963 [orig. 1945a]:252–253; italics in original).

In the Alorese case, for the first time, actual personal data on individuals were available. It was therefore possible to compare the character of individuals as it appears in the life histories and the psychological tests with the basic personality structure derived from the cultural materials provided by the anthropologist.

On this very score, Kardiner has been criticized heavily. Wallace (1970:124–125) for example, is scathing in his juxtaposition of Kardiner's occasionally inconsistent comments on specific individuals and on the "typical" Alorese personality. However, Kardiner himself appears to be not unaware of some of these discrepancies. Furthermore, he himself raises the question of "whether the concept of basic personality structure is validated by these studies," that is, by the autobiographies and their analysis. He answers his own question by remarking:

> The concept is essentially a check on *institutions* and not on character. What we see in each of the four men is a highly individual character. Each has some features of the basic personality structure, but each is molded in turn by the specific factors in his individual fate (Kardiner in Du Bois 1960 [orig. 1944]:548; italics in original).

On the whole, there was considerable agreement among the analysis of the Rorschach test data, the children's drawings, the picture of the Alorese that emerged from the cultural data, and that which Kardiner drew from the auto-biographies. There were, however, also some discrepancies. With regard to the

Rorschach, Kardiner makes a most illuminating remark: "The psychologist who operates only within the knowledge of the psychopathological entities found in our society," he says, "has an insurmountable handicap—he is capable of identifying only those entities found in our society." That is to say, as a practicing psychoanalyst, Kardiner was limited in his understanding of the personality structure of people in other societies, such as the Alorese, by his training and experience. The Rorschach test, by contrast, "demonstrates emotional combinations which are not identifiable in the psychopathological entities common in our society.... [It] is an instrument not only for checking conclusions already reached but for discovering new entities inaccessible to other techniques" (Kardiner 1945b:117).

As we have seen in several of these comments, it is evident that Kardiner has in mind, for the most part, a standard of "normal" personality development based on "adequate" care in infancy and childhood. Deviations from this pattern are viewed in terms of pathology. Benedict's use of clinical terminology, as we saw, was coupled with a relativistic view of psychopathology; this is not true of Kardiner, who maintains a constant, although not fully articulated, standard of "normal" and "healthy."

In spite of the interesting developments in theory and the collection of important new data, the collaboration between Kardiner and the anthropologists has been criticized further on various grounds. Some critics have attacked the research methods. One important element in the research design used by Du Bois was the collection of autobiographies. As Du Bois herself points out, the individuals who were willing to collaborate with her in this time-consuming task were not necessarily the most typical or representative of the society. After all, the anthropologist has only limited control over available sources of information. The method whereby the material was collected has also been questioned. The anthropologist inquired about dreams and tried to get free associations to them; the interviews were not structured, and on the whole an attempt was made to make these autobiographical accounts as comparable as possible to the kinds of materials a psychoanalyst might obtain from patients. As several commentators have pointed out (for example, Powdermaker 1945, Ortigues and Ortigues 1966) an unwarranted assumption is involved here: the patient, who seeks a cure, is motivated to cooperate with the therapist, to tell the truth, and not to withhold anything. The informant interviewed by the anthropologist has no such motivations, even if he or she understands the instructions concerning "free associations." We cannot tell, therefore, how much is withheld or presented with the intent of giving a particular kind of picture.

Kardiner's approach has been criticized as "too psychoanalytic" by some social scientists, and as "culturalist" by some psychoanalysts. He himself was critical of the orthodox Freudian views of psychosexual development, and although he makes casual references to the Oedipus complex in the analysis of the Alorese and other data, nowhere does he treat the subject systematically. He uses the language of psychoanalysis without defining his own theoretical position vis à vis the concepts involved in his terminology. On the other hand, he himself has expressed criticism of both Freudians such as Géza Róheim and NeoFreudians such as Karen Horney and Erich Fromm.

Most of the criticism of Kardiner's work appeared at the time of the publication of the several studies that we have reviewed, when they stimulated a good deal of discussion and debate. However, specialists working in the same general area have continued to find it necessary to define their own position on both theory and research method by taking Kardiner's work as a significant point of departure.

The comments of Ortigues and Ortigues (1966) are an example. (M. C. Ortigues is a psychoanalyst who works in Dakar, Senegal, with disturbed children from several African ethnic groups.) These authors characterize Kardiner's view as "a very optimistic conception of the effects of education." Commenting on Kardiner's distinction between primary and secondary institutions, they note that in traditional societies the primary institutions (child care) belong to the domain of women and the secondary institutions (religion, mythology) to the domain of men. They suggest that by seeking to explain the public life of a society (the man's world) through the private life of that society (the women's world) one loses the means of understanding the difference between the position of men and of women in the society as a whole. For Ortigues and Ortigues, the essential problem the child must face is to grow up. This task of growing up they hold to be the essence of the Oedipus complex as conceptualized by Freud. We shall return to a discussion of the Oedipus complex and its curious history in Chapters 4, when we deal more systematically with the subject of socialization.

Ortigues and Ortigues bring up two additional points: First, they, like numerous other critics, find Kardiner's model circular. Second, they critize his concept of the "secondary" institutions as involving "projection." The fact is that Kardiner has transformed Freud's concept of projection, without making that transformation explicit. To Freud, projection is a defense mechanism of the ego in which an individual assigns to others ("projects" onto them) some unconsciously held emotions. A well organized system of projections might be found in patients suffering from paranoia. Kardiner instead implicitly uses the term to describe a social ideology. That is, not unlike Benedict, he treats the society as a whole as having a personality; the secondary institutions may then be considered to be its fantasies. While aspects of the religious system may find support to some extent in the private fantasies of given individuals, they are not over and over created and reinvented by individuals, whose characters actually show a considerable amount of variation. In fact, Oberholzer, in his analysis of Alorese Rorschachs remarked on the great range of variations presented by the test protocols, an observation which tends to weaken somewhat Kardiner's stress on a common basic personality structure.

The View from Psychohistory.   The criticism that Kardiner's model is circular has been made repeatedly. Lloyd de Mause (1974) raises this objection not only against Kardiner, but also against Róheim and against Freud himself. As a psychoanalytically oriented historian, he comments: "That child-rearing practices are the basis for adult personality was proven again and again. Where they originated stumped every psychoanalyst who ever raised the question" (de Mause 1974:2).

De Mause himself presents a "psychogenic theory of history," which argues that "the central force for change in history is neither technology nor economics, but the 'psychogenic' changes in personality occuring because of successive generations of parent-child interactions." Thus, rather than viewing the parents' treatment of their children as a repetition of how they themselves had been treated, as other psychoanalytically inclined writers had done, de Mause hypothesizes "the ability of successive generations of parents to regress to the psychic age of their children and work through the anxieties of that age in a better manner the second time they encounter them than they did during their own childhood" (de Mause 1974:3). The source of the child-training practices of each age, he suggests, is the reduction of the adult anxiety that results from the closing of the psychic distance between adult and child, for "the history of childhood is a series of closer approaches between adult and child, with each closing of psychic distance producing new anxiety." Furthermore, "a society's child-rearing practices . . . are the very condition for the transmission and development of all other cultural elements" (de Mause 1974:3). Based on these hypotheses, de Mause proposes an "evolution of childhood," from antiquity (infanticide mode) to the present (helping mode).

Kardiner was not unmindful of the charge of circularity in his view of society. Speculating on the matter, he comments: "our researches up to now indicate that institutions change first and that personality changes follow. While not inaccurate, this formulation does not establish the continuity and interrelatedness of institutions and personality; both change each other in a continuous cyclic process" (Kardiner 1963:256). Although this statement suggests a way out it does not fully resolve the problem, particularly since by "institutions" he appears to be referring to child-training practices. In brief, Kardiner appears to be aware of a larger number of problems than he can handle, and his approach, although highly provocative, is not sufficiently systematic.

The Alorese in Comparative Perspective.   In spite of its limitations and handicaps, the study of Alorese culture and personality was a landmark event. Its analytic framework produced much fruitful discussion and debate and represented a necessary step forward. Cora Du Bois' rich data remain valuable today for comparative purposes. We have already referred to their use by Rohner (1975) in his important work on the acceptance and rejection of children.

To Kardiner, the Alorese appeared to be "unique" and "peculiar" in both their institutions and their basic personality structure. In the intervening thirty years, a good deal of additional research has been carried out on child training, personality, and social institutions. Attempts have been made at ordering materials for cross-cultural comparison, so that we need no longer look at each society as totally novel. How do the Alorese look to us when we place them in a comparative perspective?

First, let us consider the division of labor. In Alor, women provide the major portion of the subsistence economy, which is based on crops that they plant and harvest. Kardiner says that the women do not need to work, because, after all, the men do not do anything useful. How widespread is subsistence dependence on women's work?

Murdock's *Ethnographic Atlas* (1967) gives us information on the division of labor by sex for 639 societies in all parts of the world where some form of agriculture is practiced. In 36 percent of these societies, women do the agricultural work alone or do appreciably more than men, and in another 32 percent there is equal participation in agricultural work by both men and women (Bourguignon and Greenbaum 1973, Table 14). That is, women are heavily involved in agricultural work in two-thirds of the societies, and in only one-third do they not participate in it to any significant extent. (Where there is substantial dependence on gathering, women predominate in this work in 78 percent of the societies). On the other hand, women are much less involved in working with animals in animal husbandry, hunting, or even fishing. Consequently, with regard to women's work, the Alorese no longer seem quite so strange.

Second, let us consider the treatment of Alorese children. Kardiner claims that because mothers work in the fields of Alor, the children are neglected. This neglect does not necessarily follow. As we have noted earlier, in many societies women take their children along, whether working in the fields or gathering. Indeed, among gatherers, Rohner tells us specifically that children are accepted, not neglected. Nor does it follow that children are neglected when their mothers do not take them along. In fact, Rohner (1975:114) cites some evidence to suggest that in societies where there is more than one adult caretaker, children are accepted rather than rejected. Among the Alorese the neglect, particularly the inconsistency and unreliability of caretakers, applies not only to mothers but to substitute caretakers as well, be they grandmothers, fathers, or older siblings. On the other hand, neglect, and rejection of children as the typical pattern of a society is not rare. Rohner (1975:187) shows for a sample of forty-two societies that sixteen (or 38 percent) reject their children. For this sample, he finds a high correlation between rejection and emotional instability, a finding that applies well to the Alorese.

Third, let us take a cross-cultural look at adult behavior. Alorese child rearing quite predictably produces adults who are hostile and aggressive and who believe in hostile spirits. Their emotions are shallow and unstable. The men engage in litigations and continuous quarreling. Could it be that that kind of personality is adaptive to both the natural environment and the behavioral environment in which they find themselves? To answer this question, it would be desirable to have a modern ecological study of the area. A number of points might be explored. The area appears to have been under some population pressure at the time of

Du Bois' fieldwork, although the evidence is not clear. The group she studied had been relocated some twenty years before by the Dutch colonial government from a mountain site to one on the valley floor. The social and economic consequences of this relocation, as well as of the cessation of warfare and head-hunting, were not explored. The population of the island is divided into a number of linguistic groups, a situation that tends to reflect social distance between them and may have also been related to earlier intergroup warfare. The hostile character of the Alorese, together with their belief in hostile spirits might suit such a situation quite well!

As we have seen, Kardiner takes the division of labor and the child-rearing practices as given. He sees the secondary institutions as resulting from the basic personality structure, which, in turn, results from the primary institutions, the child-training practices of the society. When we seek to understand the relationship between culture and personality we may, however, formulate our question in somewhat different terms, and ask instead: Given the fact that the Alorese child is born into an ongoing social system, what does it take to be a well adapted, successful individual by Alorese standards? We have seen that, from the point of view of subsistence, the women carry a heavy burden. However, they also have relatively high status, since all agricultural produce is owned by women, and women as well as men inherit fields. Also, at ceremonial feasts food is distributed to the women who take it home for redistribution within their families. From the point of view of the needs of the society, as the Alorese perceive them, the work of the men is even more important: they control the political structure of the society, which involves access to power and prestige. This is a society of self-made men, in which status is not inherited but must be achieved. The financial system of credit, debts, and litigation is directly related to male status-seeking. Thus power, money, marriage alliances, and dealings with supernaturals, as well as head-hunting and warfare in former times, all fall into the male domain. It may well be that in order to be successful in such a system, it is necessary to be aggressive, hostile, deceitful, and without strong emotional attachments.

It is interesting to note that the emphasis on pigs, finances, debts, and achievement—as well as the presence of intergroup conflict and warfare—is widespread in Melanesia and New Guinea.[5] Alor is on the margin of this area, and presents the complex only partially. However, a more thorough comparison between Alor and similar societies in the region might well provide us with a basis for understanding how such a system could have grown up.

The adjectives used to describe Alorese personality tend to be consistently negative: hostile, aggressive, deceitful, shallow, unstable, uncreative, and so on. At least some of them could be phrased more positively: aggressive, enterprising, clever, free of emotional entanglements, and so on. One wonders whether the hostile reaction the Alorese stimulated in analysts and readers in the United States might not be due to the fact that in many respects they appear to represent a caricature of our own prestige structure.

The People of Alor in Retrospect.   It is, of course, easy to be critical of Kardiner's contribution from the hindsight provided by more than thirty years of work in the field of culture and personality, much of which would have been difficult without his contribution and that of the anthropologists with whom he collaborated. A different perspective is provided by the psychohistorian R. J. Lifton, who comments: "Kardiner's analyses of anthropological data taught a generation of psychiatrists important empirical lessons" (Lifton, 1971:7).

When her book was republished in paperback in 1960, Cora Du Bois looked back on the whole venture. Her comments are of importance, for they help us put this study into proper perspective. In contrast to the comments by Kardiner, who was impressed by the high degree of agreement between his own analysis and the findings that resulted from several other psychological approaches, she writes:

> It is not surprising that the undertaking failed to reveal any very high degree of consistency between the aspects investigated. It is doubtful that any culture is fully integrated in this sense . . . nevertheless, given the theoretical climate of the times, the subsequent analysis of the data stressed, and may have oversimplified, the congruities that did emerge, and largely ignored the incongruities and discrepancies (Du Bois 1960:xviii).

She concludes:

> *The People of Alor* was a partial, preliminary and provocative sally into a broad, significant and inchoate field. Today, the common sense observation that groups of people in different socio-cultural environments differ in the configuration and distribution of personality traits and processes has been given some degree of scientific confirmation. The explanatory dynamics still offer a rich field of research. It is quite probable that man's intrapsychic constitution is less complex and diverse than his sociocultural constructs in terms of institutions, roles, values, and beliefs . . . Human personality variables are in all probability less numerous than the sociocultural variables in which they are expressed (Du Bois 1960:xxvii).

By the time Du Bois was writing these lines, a number of other issues were being raised and some different approaches were coming to the fore. We shall turn to one of these important issues next.

TWO VIEWS OF CULTURE: THE "REPLICATION OF UNIFORMITY" VERSUS THE "ORGANIZATION OF DIVERSITY"

We mentioned earlier A. F. C. Wallace's criticism of Kardiner's attempt to establish a fit between the characters of Alorese individuals, as revealed by their autobiographies, and the basic personality structure of the Alorese deduced from analysis of their primary and secondary institutions. This criticism is placed in the context of a more general argument. To Wallace, Kardiner's approach is only one of many taken by those who have sought to identify a single personality type for each society. In these studies, which constitute the bulk of the culture-and-personality literature, the investigator's interest is focused on "the extent to which members of a social group, by virtue of their common group identification, behave in the same way, under the same circumstances," notes Wallace. He goes on to say: "Under such circumstances, the society may be regarded as culturally homo-geneous and the individuals will be expected to share a uniform nuclear charac-ter" (Wallace 1970:22).

The primary interest of these researchers concerns the "mechanisms of social-ization by which each generation becomes, culturally and characterologically, a replica of its predecessors" (Wallace 1970:23). Using such an approach, one assumes that the individual's personality will reflect faithfully the culture of the society in which it develops. One also assumes an essentially static situation; the mental model used does not allow for culture change, for it is basically circular. All of the approaches we have discussed so far belong to this category, which Wallace calls the "replication-of-uniformity" approach.

By contrast, Wallace presents another view, which focuses not on the shared aspects of culture and of personality but rather on their diversity. Instead of stressing stability, this view enphasizes the modifications and variations in culture and social organization over time. "Culture," Wallace comments, "shifts in policy from generation to generation with kaleidoscopic variety and is characterized internally not by uniformity, but by diversity of both individuals and groups, many of whom are in continuous and overt conflict in one subsystem and in active cooperation in another" (Wallace 1970:24).

These two contrasting conceptions of culture imply differences in research goals and research strategies. They also involve different concerns with personal-ity. The first group looks at socialization, to find out how personality is molded by culture, how child training creates both personality and certain other aspects of culture, or even how personality causes patterns of child training and all other aspects of culture. Certain assumptions are made, usually more or less Freudian, about what the structure of personality is and how it develops over time. It is assumed that human motives can be known, and behavior is explained in terms of these motives. The second group, on the other hand, which stresses diversity, also emphasizes the predictability of behavior. It is possible, argues Wallace, that the same behavior may flow from different motives, and from different percep-tions of a given situation. Personality, in this view, is essentially a "black box" —we do not know what is in it, nor need we know. The only thing that concerns us is to know what it does, how it behaves.

In support of his view, Wallace points to the fact that total homogeneity would render the operation of society impossible. On the contrary, every society consists of individuals occupying a number of different status positions. These statuses, for example, may involve differences of age and sex: children and adults, young adults and elders, men and women, and so on. The positions in a kinship system furnish another instance: father and son, mother and daughter, older brother and younger brother, brother and sister, husband and wife, uncle and nephew, and so on. These statuses involve complementary roles, and by virtue of their positions, people have not only different rights and obligations, but also different perceptions of a given situation. Relationships among individuals, in this view, are based not on *shared* expectations, but rather on *complementary* expectations. To the extent that these expectations are realistic, they constitute in effect a social contract. It is this social contract, which we may call culture, that is shared. The motivation of the individuals involved in these transactions is basically irrelevant to the operation of the contract, that is, to the social system.

Wallace is drawn to this position as a result of several research experiences. The first involves his 1952 study, *The Modal Personality Structure of the Tuscarora Indians.* Here Wallace utilized the Rorschach test on a sample of seventy adult Indians, both men and women, ranging in age from sixteen to seventy-one. At that time, early in his career, Wallace was looking for shared personality characteristics within the population under investigation. However, his work was innovative in two respects: First, he used the Rorschach *to discover* personality characteristics of the Tuscarora, *not to confirm* a picture derived from a cultural description and analysis. Second, instead of assuming the existence of shared features, he sought to discover how widespread features actually were.

In previous studies using the Rorschach test, it had been the practice to construct a single test profile for the population sample by averaging the Rorschach scores in each of the several categories into which the test is broken down for purposes of analysis. Instead, Wallace proceeded differently: he counted the frequency distributions of responses in each of the scoring categories and used these distributions to identify a modal type. Just over one-third (or 37.2 percent) of the total number of cases fell within that modal group. Wallace tells us of this group that it consists of

> Rorschach records . . . [whose] quantitative aspects cannot be distinguished from one another, at conventional levels of statistical significance, insofar as their relationship to the modal value of the total is concerned (Wallace 1952:78).

It is well known to social psychologists analyzing test results that the larger the number of items one deals with, the smaller the number of responses will be in which there is coincidence of all the items. Also, as G. Spindler (1978b) has noted, the Tuscarora sample is likely to have been made up of individuals at different levels of acculturation.[6] Yet in reacting to the expectations derived from the writings of Kardiner, Wallace notes:

> The variability of personality data in general, within the confines of any given society, and of the Rorschach data in particular presented here, cannot be easily discussed as long as one assumes every individual to have been "subjected to exactly the same cultural influences." One can, indeed, describe Tuscarora culture. But, simply because a culture can be described, one need not assume that every individual's forma-

tive experiences will be identical. This is because it is not "culture" which feeds and cleans and rocks a child to sleep, administers punishment and praise, offers advice and acts as a model. It is the parents . . . The situation is analogous to that of the physicist, who recognizes that his "laws" are really statements of probability (Wallace 1952:63).

Thus, the question Wallace must deal with is this: if only a limited percentage of a population shares a modal personality, how then can we account for the operation of a social system, the sharing of some values, a certain cultural heritage, and so on?

The second important element in Wallace's thinking relates to another aspect of his work with the Iroquois, of whom the Tuscarora are one group. It has to do with his research into culture change, and more particularly, into a type of radical cultural transformation for which he has coined the term "revitalization movement." It will be remembered that the replication of uniformity model is also an essentially static model. A concept of diversity makes it somewhat easier to deal not only with gradual change over time, but also with dramatic and sudden cultural innovations. We shall return to this question at greater length in Chapter 9.

It should be noted that Wallace's position appears to be sharpened for polemical purposes. No one has really argued for total cultural and psychological homogeneity. The differences between Wallace and the other authors we have discussed are, at least to some extent, differences in emphasis. Likewise, Wallace argues strongly against the reification of culture. This danger, too, is recognized by other investigators. Its appearance may be attributed in large measure to a casual use of language, or if one prefers, to a certain lack of methodological rigor, more than to any real confusion on the issues.

Another point of difference between Wallace and those he criticizes lies in the perceived aims of culture-and-personality research. Wallace has expressed his own views in the following terms:

> Culture-and-personality is . . . significant in the field of cultural anthropology because it is concerned with certain aspects of the theory of cultural processes . . . culture-and-personality is least significant in the monitoring of specific cultures, since a good ethnography permits far more accurate prediction of specific behavior than any national character study. Its *raison d'être* resides in the fact that it systematically takes account of noncultural data in explaining and predicting cultural phenomena (Wallace 1970:4).

For Wallace, then, culture and personality is a field of anthropology, not of psychology or psychiatry. Personality is not to be explained through an understanding of culture, nor does he wish to study the operation of cultural processes on personality. Rather, it is cultural processes and phenomena that are to be explained and predicted through the use of personality data. The same point is phrased in somewhat different terms in the following lines:

the true function of the culture-and-personality approach in anthropology lies not in its ability to provide . . . descriptions of the psychological correlates of culture . . . Culture-and-Personality takes the documented facts of cultural evolution, cultural change and cultural diversity as the phenomena to be explained (Wallace 1970:243).

Here Wallace is in clear agreement with Spiro (1961), who also argued in favor of using personality concepts in seeking to understand social structures.

The concept of the "organization of diversity" comes into its own in the study of complex societies, to which we next turn our attention.

STUDIES OF "NATIONAL CHARACTER"

Although the term *national character* is sometimes treated as synonymous with basic or modal personality, it is customarily used in a particular kind of research. National character studies typically deal with the psychological patterns observed in the populations of complex, large-scale, diversified, modern nation states. Such research has not been limited to anthropologists, but usually has been carried out by interdisciplinary teams, including sociologists, social psychologists, historians, political scientists, and others.[6] The term *culture and personality,* on the other hand, is specifically identified with the work of anthropologists studying small-scale, traditional societies. These societies may be tribes, so-called "primitive" people, or a single traditional peasant village.

This difference in the *scale* of the societies studied is important because it implies differences both in research methods and in the theoretical approaches of the investigators. For example, whatever psychological tests, techniques, and concepts may be utilized by students of culture and personality, the basic research involved is rather standard, primary ethnographic fieldwork. It is generally carried out by one or two individuals living in a community for several months or longer, interacting with people face to face. Often these communities have not been studied previously, and as a rule the people are nonliterate, or have been nonliterate until recently. Usually, few written records are available, and those that are may be of an ethnohistorical kind, provided by outsiders like explorers, missionaries, or colonial administrators. Because the group is small, it will be relatively homogeneous, and because little, if any, historical information is available, changes in culture and society over time are not easily discovered. The anthropologist's fieldwork is carried out within a limited time, so the result may well be a study that has the static appearance of a snapshot. And because individuals cannot be observed throughout their lives, it will be assumed that the child-rearing practices observed today are the same as those that gave rise to the adult personalities manifested by the population at the present time. The picture of homogeneity that Wallace complains of, and the circularity in the theoretical models that we have discussed, relate in part to such conditions of research.

Typically, then, culture-and-personality studies are investigations of small-scale, traditional groups, based on a form of ethnographic field research and limited in time depth by the scarcity of written documents.

On the other hand, national character studies deal with large-scale, modern societies that include millions of people. These societies are known to have considerable time depth, and much written documentation of changes over time is available. The people are literate and have written about themselves for a long period of time. For the recent past, there will be elaborate statistical data concerning demography, economics, and other aspects of social life. Ethnographic methods of investigation—a single researcher or a small team studying a single community for several months—under such circumstances could produce only a fragmentary, local picture, which could be generalized to the total society only with difficulty. In particular, such a small community is likely to include only a limited range of status positions and occupations, and it is therefore not fully representative of the society as a whole. James West's Plainville as analyzed by Kardiner (1963) is an example of such an attempt. For a total study, the methods of history, sociology, demography, political science, social psychology, and even literary analysis are required. Hence the emphasis on interdisciplinary teams. Because such societies are heterogeneous far beyond any single band or village community, field research should involve sampling procedures. Diversity of responses will necessarily be found when interviews are conducted or tests are administered.

One of the major problems to be confronted by researchers into the national character of a large-scale complex society involves the problem of generalizations, which can be easily distorted beyond their justifiable limits into stereotypes. This likelihood increases when researchers see culture as consisting of traits that are shared by all its "carriers," or of an all-pervading, all-integrating pattern revealed in diverse institutions as well as in the behavior of specific individuals.

National character studies were popular in the United States in the years centering about World War II and the cold war that followed it. It must be remembered that these studies grew up, developed, and were supported in a particular historical, political, and international context. Most of the studies dealt with societies with which the United States was in conflict. Here, then, the methodological problems referred to earlier were compounded by at least two additional difficulties: First, the studies were carried out, implicitly or explicitly, with political motives. The war, and later the cold war, necessarily colored the view that the United States and its allies were able to have of enemy countries and their societies. The very formulation of the problems to be researched was structured by political facts. Part of the problem, from the point of view of the Western democracies, was to explain the psychology of totalitarian societies: How can we understand the mentality that accepts and fosters the development of totalitarianism? During the six-year period before the war, most Germans, by all appearance, were enthusiastic supporters of Hitler. How could that be?

Haiti and Peru are both complex societies, that include urban centers as well as rural areas. A view of the city of Port-au-Prince, Haiti

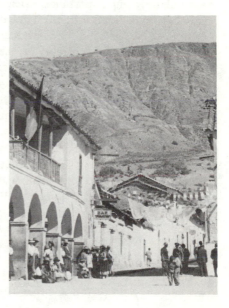

A view of the city of Ayacucho, Peru

A second difficulty lay in gaining access to information—first about Germany and Japan, later about the Soviet Union and other East European countries. This problem included finding not only written sources but also potential informants for anthropological research. The only informants in the West accessible to the researchers were former members of these societies. This difficulty applied to the World War II studies of Japan, for example, of which the most brilliant and successful was undoubtedly Ruth Benedict's *The Chrysanthemum and the Sword* (1946). For this large-scale, collective research it was necessary to interview Japanese and Japanese Americans living in the United States. It will be remembered that these people were then in a hostile environment; in many cases they had been removed from their homes and placed in relocation camps. Also, many had been away from Japan for a number of years and were incompletely informed about changes that had taken place in that country.

One interesting additional difference between national character studies and traditional anthropological studies lies in the fact that members of modern societies want to read what has been written about them. Benedict's book was soon translated and published in Japan in 1948. In 1953, J. W. Bennett and M. Nagai reviewed the Japanese reaction to the book. By 1952, they reported, it had gone through eight editions and had been reviewed and commented on widely. Bennett and Nagai summarized several scholarly symposia and professional articles devoted to it. They note that "much that Benedict had said was well known in Japanese social science and scholarship, but the organization of the material was unique, the insights unusual, and the fact that the book had been written by an *American,* a *woman,* and one *who had never visited Japan* made it an object of vast and intriguing importance" (Bennett and Nagai 1953:404; italics in original). Although many critics in the United States attacked the patternist approach exemplified by Benedict for inadequate quantity and interpretation of data, the Japanese commented favorably on this aspect of the study. Also, they liked the use of an intuitive approach in the construction of patterns or configurations. Specifically, the Japanese critics approved of the attempt to draw together data from many different sources to construct a single total configuration.

On the other hand, a series of negative criticisms leveled at this work are of considerable importance. Questions were raised about just who "the Japanese" are that Benedict speaks of: whether many of her statements do not apply only to some specific segment of the society and are unjustifiably generalized to cover the society as a whole. The Japanese critics focus on the heterogeneity of Japan, whereas Benedict sees it as essentially homogeneous. Furthermore, the critics noted that, since many of Benedict's informants had been reared in Japan at the beginning of the century, the picture refers more accurately to an earlier period than to the 1940s. The Japanese scholars were also critical of Benedict's "reliance on data concerning child rearing for making pattern generalizations at the cultural level," and they argued that "the purely logical or plausible matching of the two cannot yield anything other than imaginative hypotheses" (Bennett and

Nagai 1953:409). In other words, they argued for empirical substantiation, rather than imaginative or intuitive interpretations, to confirm the claims concerning the relationship between child rearing and the overall pattern of Japanese culture that Benedict constructs. In conclusion, Bennett and Nagai quote one of the Japanese scholars who offers the following harsh assessment of Benedict's effort:

> This book is instructive in the sense that it tells us that the social anthropologist is unable to analyze, single-handedly, the social behavior of a modern society (Miniami, cited in Bennett and Nagai 1953:410).

Since World War II, a great many studies of a variety of aspects of Japanese culture and character have been carried out by scholars from the United States and Japan, and a much more complex and diverse picture has emerged. With regard to child rearing, notably the rigid toilet training emphasized by U.S. wartime investigators, there has been only limited confirmation of the picture constructed by Benedict and other anthropologists such as Geoffrey Gorer (1943) and Weston LaBarre (1945). With regard to the investigation of psychocultural factors Japan is now probably the best-studied country in the world, for intensive research work has been carried out there over a period of more than thirty years by both Japanese and foreign scholars. Many of the wartime conclusions have had to be modified as oversimplifications. At the same time, it has been possible to observe the considerable changes that Japanese society and culture have under-gone during that period. Moreover, research during this period has been more highly focused, and attempts at constructing an overall configurational synthesis have not been pursued.[8]

With regard to the Soviet Union and other East European countries analyzed in the immediate postwar period it has on the whole not been possible to carry out on-the-spot verification of the various hypotheses. This research was con-ducted by a team at Columbia University, and much of its information is pub-lished in a volume edited by Margaret Mead and Rhoda Métraux and aptly entitled *Studies of Culture at a Distance* (1953). The emphasis on selected specific childhood disciplines, such as Geoffrey Gorer's "swaddling hypothesis," created a vigorous debate (Gorer and Rickman 1949). Margaret Mead, who strongly supported Gorer, argued that his position had been grossly misrepresented and caricatured by his critics. In a spirited defense of the national character approach she restated Gorer's hypothesis in the following terms:

> *The prolonged and very tight swaddling to which infants are subjected in Russian child-rearing practice is one of the means by which Russians communicate to their infants a feeling that strong authority is necessary* (Mead 1953:644; italics in original).

She goes on to note that, by taking culture into account as a "mediating variable," this statement insists that when it is Russians (who themselves embody their whole culture) handle their own children (who are in the process of becoming Russians) in a particular way that this way of handling becomes a form of communication between parents and children in which the child learns something the adult has already learned . . . (Mead 1953:644–645).

In spite of Mead's vigorous defense of the national character studies of this type, by 1953, when this article was published, they were already on the wane. Both psychological anthropology and the anthropological study of complex societies were moving in other directions. One direction involved cooperative research with scholars in the countries under investigation. As we saw in the case of Japan, research became generally more narrow in scope, and specific subjects were investigated in greater detail.

An important and highly innovative approach in the study of complex civilizations is that of F. L. K. Hsu. Chinese in origin, trained in Great Britain under Malinowski, and working in the United States, Hsu has been impressed with the importance of a comparative perspective. In contrast to most anthropologists, he believes it important that one study not only alien cultures, but also, systematically, one's home culture. The results of this orientation have been a series of important studies by Hsu on the Chinese (1948, rev. 1972), on Americans in comparison with the Chinese (1953, rev. 1970), on Chinese, Indians, and Americans (1963,) and on the Japanese (1975).

Holding that "man's most important environment is the social environment," Hsu (1978b:156–157) divides social relations into two aspects: role (or usefulness) and affect (or feeling). While role differentiation increases as society grows more complex, affects are limited in number, including "love, hate, rage, despair, hope, anxiety, forbearance, loyalty, betrayal" (Hsu 1978b:157). Hsu suggests that *patterns* of affects vary among cultures, and that the basic pattern of affect of each society is likely to persist over thousands of years. Hsu sees differences between various European societies and the United States and between the modern West and ancient Greece as local variations, when contrasted with the great differences between the West and China. Anthropologists should give greater attention to these differences in the ways in which people express feelings and in the factors that produce the various feeling states.

A second point of importance in Hsu's thinking is the hypothesis of the "dominant kinship dyad." He suggests that in China the principal relationship is between father and son, and all other social patterns derive from this relationship, whereas in the West the prime relationship is that between husband and wife. The traditional U.S. emphasis on independence and self-reliance is associated with this kinship pattern, whereas the Chinese emphasis on the group and on continuity through time has its root in the father-son relationship.[9]

Hsu speaks of "affective needs" that are developed in the context of the kinship system, and as the individual grows up, in contact with the wider institutions of the society. Human beings, says Hsu, must maintain a Psychosocial Homeostasis

(Hsu 1971a); that is, they must maintain the pattern of affective needs acquired in the course of socialization. As a result, major changes in the patterns of social roles, in technology, economy, and political systems, even when these changes are brought about by culture contact or by revolutions, may take place without modifying the basic pattern of affects.

The study of complex societies will increasingly attract the attention of anthropologists, including psychological anthropologists. In this connection it is important to remember that many of the peoples of small societies and village communities who have been the targets of anthropological research in the past are now becoming members of nation states. Many are moving to the cities, while others find that the cities are reaching out to them. The line between simple and complex, traditional and modern, nonliterate and literate societies is less and less evident as the peoples of the world undergo massive transformations in all aspects of their lives. Not only must we study the ongoing changes and their psychocultural implications, but also in our conceptualizations of the problems we must take these new realities into account. Concepts such as Hsu's "psychosocial homeostasis" and Wallace's "organization of diversity" may help us to deal with some aspects of our contemporary situation.

SUMMARY

We started this chapter by asking: do group differences exist? We found the answer to be a complex matter. One underlying issue we examined concerns the shifting emphasis on cultural relativity and its relationship to a universal human nature. Another debate we reviewed deals with ways in which culture, personalities, and their interactions have been conceptualized by different students of the subject. In our survey we distinguished three major approaches.

First we examined the configurationist approach of Ruth Benedict and Margaret Mead. Here primary stress is placed on the *transmission* of culture, which is said to "mold" personality. Applied to complex societies, this approach was utilized in the early national character studies.

Second, we looked at the approach of some psychoanalysts. This approach is most clearly illustrated in the work of Géza Róheim. It sees childhood experience as responsible for the development both of adult personality and of culture. Because psychological factors are interpreted as primary, the approach has been called reductionist.

Third, we discussed the personality mediation approach. Here certain aspects of culture (the childhood disciplines) are said to be "primary" and to give rise to personality, which in turn gives rise to "secondary" aspects of culture such as religion. Personality, in other words, "mediates" between two segments of culture. This model was originally formulated by Abram Kardiner. Although it has been exposed to various criticisms, in modified form it is still influential, affecting both studies of childhood and holocultural studies of various expressive systems.

In much of the research based on these approaches stress was placed on the shared elements of culture and psychology. This uniformity was obviously an oversimplification and distortion. To correct it, an analytic model was required that could take individual variation into account. Wallace's concept of the *organization of diversity* does just that.

In the early studies much stress was placed also on the cultural influences on personality formation. In reaction, Wallace and Spiro, among others, began to urge a reorientation of the field. They emphasized the role of psychological factors in maintaining social systems, an understanding of which was seen as the primary goal of cultural anthropology. Hsu's concern with patterns of affects also emphasizes the psychological dimension, starting, however, with a typical kinship structure derived from the cultural tradition.

For the most part then, we have learned that, over a period of years, there has been much discussion of methods and concepts among cultural anthropologists; that research has consisted of a series of more or less successful attempts and approximations, which have led to transformations of many of the original questions, but not to truly definitive answers. Anthropology, like other social sciences, is continuously exposed to the impact of social and political currents, and some of the theoretical formulations and some of the choices of problems to be studied can only be understood in such a context. Furthermore, in an interdisciplinary field such as psychological anthropology, the growth of related disciplines, in this case the various specialized fields of psychology, has made itself felt significantly. This interdisciplinary effect is, as we shall see, a two-way street.

As for the tangible results of research on group differences in psychological features, we may echo Robert LeVine's assessment of the situation:

> Humans exhibit more behavioral variation from one population to another than any other species, and it seems likely that some of it is stabilized in individual dispositions that are more than immediate situational responses. A growing body of cross-cultural evidence supports this view . . . But problems of measurement in the psychology of personality . . . have so far prevented the generation of conclusive evidence (LeVine 1973:11).

NOTES

1. Beginning in the early 1960s, there appeared to be a decline in interest in the possible applications of psychoanalytic theory to anthropological data. More recently, there is evidence of a lively revival of a psychoanalytic orientation.

2. This important subject will be discussed in Chapter 8.

3. Spiro also refers to the lengthy period of infant dependency. This concept is related to S. J. Gould's discussion of the evolutionary significance of "changes in developmental timing" (Gould 1977). See note 6, Chapter 2.

4. Although neither Linton nor Southall mentions it, there is an intriguing similarity between Linton's hypothesis, as it took shape over time, and the Marx-Wittfogel model

of "oriental despotism," positing a relationship between irrigation agriculture and the development of the centralized state dominated by an autocratic ruler (Wittfogel 1938, 1955, 1957).

5. A number of anthropologists have attempted to explain the widespread pattern of warfare in New Guinea as due to population pressures resulting in a shortage of land. Divale and Harris (1976) go further and argue that in band and village societies in general warfare is best understood as an attempt to keep population stationary. However, these arguments are not universally accepted among anthropologists, or even among New Guinea specialists. Paul Sillitoe (1977), for example, points out that the essential demographic data on New Guinea are lacking, and he concludes on the basis of a review of available data from that area that only a small number of wars can be accounted for in ecological terms.

6. The concern of this section is with the development of Wallace's views. Others at about the same time also discovered diversity on American Indian reservations, particularly in acculturation. An important demonstration of this diversity was made by G. D. Spindler (1955) in his study of the Menominee of Wisconsin. The Menominee studies will be taken up in some detail in Chapter 9.

7. There is also an extensive literature of national character studies authored primarily by sociologists and political scientists. For reviews of this literature, see Inkeles (1972) and Inkeles and Levinson (1968). The sociologist Daniel Bell has suggested a number of ways in which national character studies, having fallen on hard times, might be revived and "rehabilitated." See Bell's article in Norbeck, Price-Williams, and McCord (1968).

8. Books such as G. DeVos, *Socialization for Achievement: Essays on the Cultural Psychology of the Japanese* (1973) and T. S. Lebra and W. P. Lebra, eds., *Japanese Culture and Behavior* (1974) are excellent sources for a review of these newer studies. DeVos has reviewed the twenty-five–year history of his own, generally cooperative, research on Japanese cultural psychology (DeVos 1978).

9. In a paper entitled "Passage to Understanding" (1978b), Hsu has traced the evolution of his thinking in autobiographical terms. *Kinship and Culture,* edited by Hsu (1971b), brings together articles by a number of authors, describing a series of diverse cultures within the framework of Hsu's dominant kinship dyad hypothesis. We shall return to the hypothesis of the dominant kinship dyad in Chapter 4.

CHAPTER 4
Growing Up Human

INTRODUCTION: TWO SCENES OF CHILDHOOD

In the summer of 1978 a California court heard a case against the National Broadcasting Company. An eight-year-old girl had been sexually assaulted by a group of girls who had seen such an attack four days earlier in the TV movie *Born Innocent*. The leader of the group was said to have told police that she had "got the idea" from the movie. The victim's mother was therefore suing the network that had shown the film.

Eight years earlier, the psychologist Urie Bronfenbrenner had written:

> Given the salience of violence in commerical television, including cartoons especially intended for children, there is every reason to believe that this mass medium is playing a significant role in generating and maintaining a high level of violence in American society, including the nation's children and youth (Bronfenbrenner 1970:114).

Still, childhood in the United States is not all TV, violence, and sex. At Easter, for example, the familiar ritual of the egg hunt is widely practiced. At about the same time as the story of violence appeared, a Columbus, Ohio neighborhood newspaper announced that "thousands of candy eggs are ready for the Easter Bunny to deliver" to the park where the hunt is to take place on the day before Easter. The article continued, "areas will be designated according to age groups as follows: Red—ages four and under; Orange—ages five and six; Blue—ages seven, eight, and nine". Prizes were being donated by an amusement park, a fast-food chain, and a civic organization.

The Easter egg hunt is a traditional event in many parts of the country, with one variant even taking place on the grounds of the White House. Like the gift-giving rituals of Christmas and the "trick or treat" of Halloween, this practice is associated with the transformation of religious celebrations into lay festivals centered about childhood. Three other aspects of the news announcement also bear mentioning: 1) The egg hunt is a competitive activity, in which prizes are awarded. There will be a minority of winners and a majority of nonwinners or losers. 2) To make the competition "fair," the children are divided into age groups. 3) The organizations that offer prizes combine in this manner advertising directed at children with the creation of "good will" by community participation. (To the commercial establishments the cost is tax deductible.)

Competition is seen by the organizers as a "natural" ingredient of the event, which is required to make things "interesting" to the participants. It expresses the attitudes of the adults and transmits them to the children. Establishing age groups causes children to be involved with their "peers" rather than primarily with their kin, and children of the same family may compete in different groups. Note that although there is age segregation, a pattern widespread in the United States, no other type of segregation is announced, whether by sex, race, or ethnic group, nor is it specified that the event is limited to people living in a particular neighborhood.

Bronfenbrenner has suggested that TV and peer groups represent the major socializing influences on U.S. youngsters. Yet TV is created and directed by adults, just as the community ritual of the Easter egg hunt is. The segregated peer groups act within the field of influence created by adults, who transmit their attitudes, values, and even their fantasies to the children: age stratification, competition, violence, and the Easter Bunny all play their role in this picture.

The influence of the adults is, however, often unplanned and indirect, and perhaps the adults are, at times, unaware of the impact they have on children. Bronfenbrenner comments in the context of a comparison of systems of education and socialization:

> The Soviet peer group is given explicit training for exerting desired influence on its members, whereas the American peer group is not . . . The Soviet peer group is heavily—perhaps too heavily—influenced by the adult society. In contrast, the American peer group is relatively autonomous, cut off from the adult world—a particularly salient example of segregation by age (Bronfenbrenner 1970:115).

Bronfenbrenner attributes much of the violence, delinquency, and alienation of U.S. youth to the lack of adult involvement with the lives of youngsters, and the resulting major role played by self-directed peer groups; yet one might argue that age segregation in childhood prepares individuals for the segmentations of later life. Also, aggression and violence are given major significance in this country, in daily life, fiction, and sports.

What do we have to know about our society and culture to put the two events cited here into context and to make sense out of them? The first example appears to be a unique case, and the second one an event that is repeated over and over again, with variations from place to place. What else do we need to know? The reader's own experience may serve as a guide. Imagine explaining these events to a foreigner, not the proverbial Martian or "primitive." Think instead of someone from a complex society, where both TV and seasonal rituals are known, perhaps from East Europe or from the Middle East. What do these events tell us about our childhood, society, and culture?

How a society and its culture affect the development of its children, and how, in turn, childhood experiences influence society and culture are major subjects in psychological anthropology. Research in this area will be our concern in this chapter.

SOCIALIZATION AND ENCULTURATION

The interest in the relationship between culture and personality has had as one of its most significant and lasting results the stimulation of research into various aspects of childhood in different cultural settings. This development in anthropology has coincided in recent years with the growth of similar interests in a number of disciplines in the social and behavioral sciences. Such a trend is clearly recognized by LeVine, who goes so far as to write:

> The socialization of the human individual, his transformation from an infant organism into an adult participant in society, has emerged as the foremost topic of interdisciplinary concern in the behavioral sciences (LeVine 1973:61).

LeVine lists a series of specialists, ranging from primatologists to legal scholars, who have conducted overlapping and mutually relevant research in this broad area. The work of anthropologists, specifically, has had an important impact beyond the confines of their own speciality. For example, a review of emotional behavior and personality development in young children, by a team of developmental psychologists, contains the following passage:

> Cultural anthropology has changed popular thought as few sciences have done in the past. We know, as did no earlier age, that the typicality shown by various nations and tribes is due largely to a lifetime of learning and social interaction within given milieus. One can see on film the Balinese boy, Karba, growing from a universal infancy into a withholding, muted, graceful, suspicious child, typical of the Balinese (Freedman, Loring, and Martin 1967:476, referring to Bateson and Mead 1942).

Although the authors of this passage do not question the claims Bateson and Mead make in their film concerning the typical Balinese character, they do go on to question the notion of a "universal infancy" and wonder about the possible genetic effects of inbreeding in Bali on personality development such as that illustrated in the film.

On the whole, the relations between anthropological studies of child rearing and those carried out by other specialists have been reciprocal. Anthropologists have learned some methods of observation from colleagues in other fields, and they have, at times, attempted to test in a cross-cultural setting theories developed in Western culture. The research by anthropologists in this broad area has gone under a number of names: socialization, enculturation, cultural transmission, child care, child rearing, childhood disciplines, and so on. These terms are not strictly synonymous and deserve a closer look.

The term *socialization* was first introduced by psychologists and gained currency in the 1930s. It is certainly the one used most widely today, in the several disciplines that deal with the broad subject area it covers. However, its specific meaning and definition appear to vary somewhat with individual writers. Sociologists, primatologists, and some anthropologists have emphasized the *learning of social roles.* Therefore, anthropologists who have taken a somewhat broader view of the total process have tended to find the term too confining and misleading. To remedy this situation, other terms have been proposed.

M. J. Herskovits coined the term *enculturation,* which he favored. Defining socialization as "the process by means of which an individual is integrated into his society" (1948:38), he remarked that social animals, such as other primates, deer, wild dogs, or any other group-living species are socialized.

In a distinction, he noted:

> The aspect of the learning experience which marks man off from other creatures, and by means of which, initially, and in later life, he achieves competence in his culture, may be called *enculturation.* This is in essence a process of conscious or unconscious conditioning, exercised within the limits of a given body of custom (Herskovits 1948:39; italics in original).

Elsewhere he elaborates on this definition:

> The enculturative process includes the whole of that aspect of adjustment of the newly-born individual to the group of which he is to become a member, and more. . . . The enculturative experience, however, also includes those reactions to aspects of life that, as expressions of the creative drive, are only secondarily reactions to the social structures which make of society an organized unit (Herskovits 1948:640).

Among the patterns to which the individual is enculturated Herskovits lists music, art, dance, and philosophical speculation. The concept implies that although specific cultural coloring is given to original innovative arts, innovation is possible. *Enculturation and socialization do not limit the individual to becoming a replica of a preexisting model.*

Margaret Mead has taken over the term "enculturation" but has redefined it for her own purposes. She uses "socialization" to mean "abstract statements about learning as a social process," limiting "enculturation" to refer to "the actual process of learning as it takes place in a specific culture" (Mead 1963:185). Mead also has favored the term *culture transmission*. This term includes not only what children learn from their elders or from peers, but also how culture is transmitted from one society to another.

The Developmental Processes

Considering the changes that occur in the individual from birth through infancy and childhood, we may distinguish, for analytic purposes, a series of developmental processes that occur more or less simultaneously and are of primary interest to somewhat different groups of researchers. In fact, however, in the experience of children and of parents, they are part of a single development of growing up. Although many of these processes are studied separately in a Western context, in the cross-cultural field they all may become subject matter for the anthropologist.

We may distinguish among them the physiological processes of maturation and seek to understand how they relate to genetics, nutrition, maternal and child health, the physical environment, and the cultural environment. In the last, specific methods of handling and caring for the child are of interest. In recent years such studies in traditional societies have increasingly been carried out by psychologists, often with the cooperation of anthropologists. Such carefully detailed investigation is possible and meaningful only within the context of a larger ethnographic study, or when the relevant background information is already available. The general subject becomes of broad interest to anthropologists when comparisons are made among human groups, or when generalizations are made about humanity at large.

In an evolutionary context, the immaturity of the human infant at birth, its total dependence on caretakers, and its slow rate of maturation as compared to the young of other species, all have been linked to the great amount of learning that occurs during this period and that, given the infant's initial helplessness and its relative lack of innate responses, are required to insure survival. Because this very early learning takes place in a particular social and cultural setting, cultural variability has its roots in the formative stages of personal and social development of the individual.

Among the learning processes that begin virtually at birth is the learning of a particular language. This process, with few exceptions (for example, Kimball 1970, 1972), has been studied almost exclusively among children in Western society, in groups speaking an Indo-European language. The development of the perceptual and cognitive capacities of the child constitutes another area of research, on which there is now a growing comparative, cross-cultural body of publications.[1] Personality development and the development of social and cultural competence intertwine with all of these other processes, and the distinctions have not always been spelled out clearly in the anthropological literature. Indeed, anthropoligists have tended to focus on some, but not all, of these processes, in part because of their lack of detailed specific training in these areas of developmental psychology. As already noted, however, more recently, some psychologists have become involved in this comparative, cross-cultural research. We shall consider some of this work now, and some of its impact on contemporary anthropological research.

Two Major Problems

During the past fifty years, anthropologists have laid emphasis on different aspects of infant and child development and the acquisition of culture. As we saw in Chapter 3, interest in the past has centered basically around two problems.

First, how do children acquire culturally appropriate behavior and attitudes? How are they "molded" by culture? How is culture transmitted to them? This issue has interested Benedict, Mead, and their associates. Mead has stated emphatically:

> Everything that has been patiently accumulated on the subject of child-rearing in different cultures has demonstrated the most minute correspondence between the over-all pattern of a culture and the patterns of child-rearing in that culture (Mead 1963:134).

Elsewhere she has suggested (Mead 1964) that each culture involves a particular continuum of three different types of learning: empathy, imitation, and identification with the source of learning. These types appear not only in intergenerational learning, but also in learning from peers, by adults as well as by children. Moreover, Mead stresses inhibitions to learning—messages that certain behavior is socially inappropriate and must *not* be learned. Mead's work focuses on cultural differences and stresses the considerable malleability of human beings.

A more limited but significant interest of students of cultural transmission concerns formal education; specific educational institutions, such as schools, are examined in cross-cultural perspective (for example, Spindler 1974).

The second major problem is how child care affects the formation of the basic personality structure of adults in a given society, and how various aspects of culture result from that personality structure. In Chapter 3 we discussed this subject at some length; it is essentially the model put forth by Kardiner, who conceived of personality as mediating between two facets of culture. This formulation has been elaborated further in the work of J. W. M. Whiting and his associates, to which we shall turn shortly. Strong emphasis is placed by these investigators on factors that influence child-care practices. They note the ecological setting and subsistence patterns. Also, they study specific aspects of social structure, such as household composition, sleeping arrangements, work load of mothers, and so on. Although adult personality and adult culture are still part of the overall picture, the primary interest of this research approach is children and childhood.

The study of child care, socialization, enculturation, and transmission of culture, then, has acquired some degree of independence from the earlier area of culture and personality. It may be said to have become an end in itself, with its own methods, theories, specialties and subdivisions. The broad intuitive generalizations of the classical period of culture and personality research have largely been relegated to history.

However, before we turn to a review of some of this more recent research, we need to take another look backwards, into the history of the comparative study of personality development as related to cultural variations.

The Oedipus Complex: A Classic Debate

We remarked earlier that much of the cross-cultural research in psychological anthropology has revolved around the issue of a universal human nature. This focus is particularly strong in studies of stages in child development. One of the best known arguments in this area of research concerns the universality of the Oedipus complex.

Freud described a stage in the life of small boys in which the youngster has a strong sexual attachment to his mother and considers his father as a hated rival against whom he harbors death wishes. He found a model for this constellation of feelings in the Greek myth of King Oedipus, as represented in the tragedy by Sophocles. Freud and other educated men of his time had received a strong classical education, and the label clearly encapsulated the major elements of the complex: it was the fate of Oedipus to kill his father and to marry his mother, although he attempted to avoid that fate and actually committed his crimes unknowingly. Nonetheless, he had to suffer punishment for his deeds. In Freud's view, the child's wishes are inescapable, and they are fearfully associated with the threat of punishment. In the normal child, the complex is eventually resolved and the memory of the emotions is repressed; the boy becomes a man, using his father as a model. His sexual interests are turned to women outside his family. Only in neurotic patients, in dreams, and in legends do traces of this complex remain in disguised form.

The anthropological debate on this subject began with Bronislaw Malinowski, who spent two years in the Trobriand Islands during World War I. His friend and mentor, C. G. Seligman, sent him some of Freud's writings and drew his attention to psychoanalysis. Malinowski proceeded to compare the matrilineal family of the Trobriand Islanders with the patriarchal European family of Freud's acquaintance. When he returned to England after the war, he presented his view on a Trobriand "family complex" radically different from the Oedipus complex. A debate ensued between him and the psychoanalyst Ernest Jones.

Malinowski published his exposition, together with his responses to Jones, in 1927 in *Sex and Repression in Savage Society.* He claimed that among the Trobriand Islanders no friction exists between father and son, "and all the infantile craving of the child for its mother is allowed gradually to spend itself in a natural, spontaneous manner" (Malinowski 1955 [orig. 1927]:74). At this point the maternal uncle, the boy's mother's brother, begins to exert his authority. It is he from whom the boy will inherit and to whose village the boy will move when he marries. This relationship, Malinowski tells us, is an ambivalent one, tinged with resentment and veneration. In many respects, the uncle in this society is said to play a role similar to that of the father in the European family of the period. At the same time, a severe avoidance rule is established between brothers and sisters. It is largely this rule, Malinowski suggests, that helps to make the sister the target of strong but repressed incestuous wishes. He finds evidence for both elements of this complex in the dreams of Trobriand Islanders as well as in their myths.

The argument between Jones and Malinowski revolved largely about concepts derived from the classical evolutionary anthropology, which Malinowski considered outworn. (Yet more than a little of the old terminology and the old concepts still lingers on in Malinowski's own part of this discussion.) Most important is the fact that Malinowski appears to think that up to the age of about six or seven when the Trobriand "family complex" begins, that is, when socialization with regard to the role of the mother's brother and the brother-sister taboo starts to have its impact on the child, the Trobriand youngster's development is "natural," and that it is only at that time that his "nature" is beginning to be molded.

There is no evidence that Malinowski carried out a detailed study of infancy and childhood among the Trobriand Islanders. Róheim, in an attempt to check Malinowski's findings, carried out research on Normanby Island, among another matrilineal Melanesian group, and reported finding an Oedipus complex of the classical type there. In criticizing Malinowski, he writes with some disdain:

> Fancy! Somebody who admits that he has never analysed a dream himself—for the obvious reason that he does not know how to do it—is *testing* Freud's theory! (Róheim 1932:7; italics in original).

Victor Barnouw (1973) offers a detailed analysis of all of Malinowski's writings on the Trobriand Islanders and dealing with sexuality and social organization. He concludes that there is evidence that they do, after all, have the classic type of Oedipus complex. He also notes Róheim's claim to have found it in Trobriand mythology. However, regardless of what one concludes about the Oedipus complex among the Trobriand Islanders, it does not invalidate Malinowski's claim to have discovered a different sort of family complex, one that has its roots in later socialization and in which unconscious hostility is directed toward the maternal uncle, whereas incestuous desires are directed toward the sister.

The debate between Malinowski and the psychoanalysts has had an impact on psychoanalysts and anthropologists alike. In part because of it, for example, Erich Fromm (1948) has argued that the true basis of the hostility of the son to the father is conflict over authority. In the European family, the roles of authoritarian and of sexual rival are both combined in the role of father, whereas in the matrilineal situation the two functions are separated. The same point is made by

Campbell and Naroll (1972). Freud dealt with a family triangle consisting of three individuals (child, mother, father) and three relationships (child-mother, child-father, mother-father). Malinowski also deals with three individuals (boy, sister, mother's brother), but there are only two relationships (boy-sister, uncle-nephew).

Following Malinowski, anthropologists have sought to identify the particular critical family relationships that typify a given society, with some students finding both the sexual and the rivalry aspects of the family triangle discovered by Freud, and others focusing on only one or the other of this pair of attitudes. A third attitude, affection and support offered by the father to the son, has too often been neglected. In an important article that seeks to reassess the significance of psycho-analysis for anthropology, R. A. Paul (1976) argues that the male intergenerational problem is universal. The Trobriand Islanders, he says, have solved it by using two cultural roles, that of the affectionate father and that of the authoritarian mother's brother. Together they represent the image of the primal father:

> What makes cultures different is not whether all these emotions are present, for they are; but rather how they are symbolically distributed, and what devices are employed to express them, and to try to resolve the inherent conflicts among them (Paul 1976:348).

From quite a different perspective, Margaret Mead writes:

> the oedipal situation, in the widest meaning, is a way of describing what any given society does with the fact that children *and* adults are involved in the growing child's sexual attitudes, especially toward the parent of the opposite sex (Mead 1952:411; italics in original).

She notes that "crises of relationships between parents and children" may occur at a variety of developmental stages; the parents' behavior should be seen as resulting from their situation as adults, and not merely as delayed responses to their own childhood experiences. As an example she mentions "the current crises in the American middle-class male" at a daughter's marriage or at the birth of her first child. Mead suggests that such crises may be traced to the youth cult in our society. Although she speaks in connection with the "oedipal situation," about "the nature of human growth and human parenthood," she denies any fixity, or universality, in the process of the child's growth. Instead, she looks at the variety of family forms and household groupings, as well at the background of cultural factors, in order to explain the developmental crises that are characteristic of specific societies.

Mead draws our attention to the reaction of adults to the Oedipal situation, not only to that of children. The observation that the attitudes of children, and of adolescents as well, have a reciprocal term in the behavior of their parents or other significant adults is of major importance. Herskovits and Herskovits (1958), in their analysis of Dahomean folklore, find much evidence on the one hand of the fathers' fear of being replaced by their sons and of rivalry among brothers. On the other hand, they find little evidence of hostility of sons toward their fathers. Whereas Mead stresses the sexual aspects of the Oedipal situation—the attitude of the father toward his daughter, in her example—Herskovits and Herskovits consider the other significant dimension of the paradigm, the hostility among males. This emphasis on the relationship among brothers is also brought out in a study by Ortigues and Ortigues (1966), which is based on psychotherapy of children in three West African ethnic groups (Wolof, Lebu, and Serer) in Dakar, Senegal. Although they hold that an unconscious rivalry between boys and their fathers exists, Ortigues and Ortigues see in the clinical data that this rivalry is displaced onto brothers and members of the child's peer group. However, since this rivalry is culturally inadmissible, it is overcompensated emphatically by expressions of group solidarity. It is the rejection by members of the group of brothers and peers that causes the greatest anxiety for the African child, and not rejection by parents. However, this pattern is modified by varying degrees of Westernization among the Senegalese.

F. L. K. Hsu (1971b, 1972b) in a series of studies, has distinguished four types of *kinship content,* each dominated by a particular *dyad*—a relationship between two individuals occupying particular positions within a kinship structure. Of the four types, one is dominated by the father-son relationship. This type is illustrated by the traditional Chinese family. A second one, characteristic of Western society, is dominated by the husband-wife relationship. A third one is dominated by the mother-son dyad and is exemplified by the traditional society of India. Finally, the fourth one, which Hsu finds in Africa, is identified in the following terms: "Mutual dependency seriously undercut by rivalry which coexists with the emphasis on brother-brother dyad and practically no worship of ancestors" (Hsu 1972b:515). It is interesting that Hsu arrives at this characterization from a general reading of African ethnography, in contrast to the use of clinical data by Ortigues and Ortigues and of mythological materials by Herskovits and Herskovits. The three approaches appear to confirm each other in their findings, although their formulations are quite different.

Hsu sees the key dyad as the determinant of a particular kinship content, and with it of a total culture. The Oedipus complex in this context is merely a feature of Western society, characteristic of the particular kinship content in which the child must compete with the father for the mother's attention.

Still another family configuration, termed a "nuclear complex," is identified by Anne Parsons (1964) on the basis of her study of South Italians. Here, she tells us, the strongest family tie is found in the relationship between son and mother, much as in Hsu's analysis of Indian society. It is seen, in highly sublimated form, in the Madonna complex of which virginity is the central symbol. The relationship between father and son is a frankly hostile one, a hostility which is neither repressed nor outgrown as one would expect from the Freudian model. This pattern is reflected in a triangle of relationships that Parsons calls the "South Italian nuclear complex": the relationship between a man and his daughter on the one hand, and his son-in-law on the other.

Parsons, who began her presentation of the South Italian data with a review of the Malinowski-Jones debate, concludes:

> For the original question of whether the Oedipus Complex is universal or not, we would sum up by saying that it is no longer very meaningful in that particular form. The more important contemporary question would rather be: what is the possible range within which culture can utilize and elaborate the instinctually given human potentialities, and what are the psychologically given limits of this range? (Parsons 1964:328).

As we have seen, anthropologists have been intrigued by the hypothesis of the Oedipus complex. In their investigations over the last fifty years they have, however, redefined this hypothesis over and over. In part, this redefinition has been a response to the great variety of family situations they have had occasion to observe. The redefinitions have also been a response to what was felt, at any given moment, to be a more meaningful and significant problem, testable by the means at the disposal of the anthropologist. Instead of dealing with clinical data and unconscious repressed materials from early childhood, anthropologists have looked at evidence of intergenerational hostility among males, sources of conflict to be discovered within the social structure and the value system, and so on. Therefore rather than finding that the original hypothesis has been either confirmed or disconfirmed, we cannot claim that it actually has been tested, or assert whether or not the Oedipus complex is universal. Instead, we have a series of different formulations and noncomparable answers. The story of the Oedipus complex is a good example of how science proceeds in a spiral fashion, finding unsuspected complications when attempts are made at answering questions, and rather than answering them, moves on to redefine them.

COMPARATIVE STUDIES OF INFANCY AND EARLY CHILDHOOD

In 1976, M. J. Konner, who conducted a comprehensive study of infancy among the !Kung Bushmen of Botswana, listed reasons for carrying on such research: it broadens the range of variation of our information concerning infant behavior and development as well as maternal care, it adds another set of leads to what may be universal features of human infancy, and it provides data that can be used for comparisons between humans and other species. That is, the data collected in a study of !Kung infancy can help us in resolving the following questions: in what respects are human beings similar to other primates, particularly the great apes, and in what respects are they unique? We may be interested in a particular study of infancy and maternal behavior to discover 1) what is culturally unique, 2) what is universally human, 3) what is unique to the human species, and 4) what it shares with other related life forms. Konner adds another point, which he finds of particular relevance in a study of the !Kung. Such research, he says,

> adds a temporal or evolutionary and (potentially) causal dimension to the extent that we can guess, by extrapolation from modern hunter-gatherers, what adaptation in infant care and development must have characterized *ancestral* populations of hunter-gatherers (Konner 1976:220; italics in original).

The reasons Konner offers for his work illustrate clearly a series of interests that are currently in the forefront of comparative research into human infancy. They also show us a great difference between present-day orientations and those on which most of the studies of the "classical" period of culture and personality were based. Information on infancy is increasingly sought as an end in itself. Studies of specific cultural groups are considered desirable for comparative purposes in an evolutionary framework, not merely to add documentation to the thesis of cultural relativity. Moreover, in contrast to earlier work such as that of Du Bois, or even that of Mead and her associates, no questions concerning personality are asked. No attempt is made to extrapolate from infant or child experience to adult personality. Conversely, no attempt is made to explain adult behavior as resulting from infantile experiences. Instead, the work on infancy focuses specifically on aspects of physiological maturation, interpersonal contacts, group composition, and so on. Also, in contrast to earlier studies, instead of offering a generalized picture of !Kung infancy, Konner explains his methodology in detail and presents his data in statistical form, so that information on variation among individuals is available.

The possibility that Konner suggests of drawing inferences concerning ancestral hunter-gatherer populations on the basis of research among the modern !Kung must be approached with considerable caution, however. The !Kung live in the particularly harsh environment of the Kalahari Desert. Certain other contemporary hunter-gatherer groups, such as the Pygmies of the Ituri Forest, to the contrary, live in a relatively positive environment to which they have worked out an optimal adaptation. Still others, like the Eskimo, who also live in a harsh environment, must face problems of adaptation of quite a different character than those confronting the !Kung. Furthermore, ancient hunter-gatherer groups, before the development of agriculture during the Neolithic period, must be assumed to have lived in much more hospitable enviorments, which must have presented different types of problems.

The ecological, demographic, and social context of infant care is given considerable attention in modern studies. In the case of the !Kung, such data were available to Konner, for his work was part of a large project, continuing over a decade and involving many different specialists who have focused on a variety of aspects of !Kung life. Team research of this type differs from earlier studies where the researcher—Du Bois, for example—was alone in the field. Also, the extensive modern technology available to the fieldworker, such as the tape recorder for obtaining data and the computer for analyzing it, have transformed anthropoligical fieldwork in many important respects.

Neuromotor Development

One of the subjects Konner deals with concerns the neuromotor development of !Kung infants. He studied the age at which infants attain independent sitting, rising, and walking and compared his findings with those of investigators who have tested infants in the U.S. and in Great Britain. Although Konner observes no differences between !Kung babies and the other groups at birth, the !Kung are substantially ahead of the other test populations soon thereafter. For example, some of the !Kung infants were able to sit up at less than two months of age (50 days), and all of them were able to do so at less then seven months (just over 200 days). At the same age, only 50 percent of the sample in the United States had reached that level of performance. Similarly, 50 percent of the !Kung infants were able to stand up at the age of 250 days, while none of the infants in the U.S. at that age were able to do so. Although !Kung infants were found to reach the first phase of independent walking at about the same time as infants here, they reached the full, mature state of walking sooner.

These findings are of particular interest when they are placed in the context of a debate that was begun in 1956, with the publication of a series of remarkable findings by the French investigator Marcelle Géber. She reported that infants she studied in Uganda (mostly Ganda but also some others) showed greater skeletal maturity at birth and were also precocious with regard to motor abilities, compared to European infants (Géber 1956, Géber and Dean 1967). For example, 107 Ugandan infants, most of whom were born in the hospital rather than at home, were examined within the first week after birth, the majority of them within two days. Of these infants it is reported that their motor behavior resembled in many ways that of the four- to six-week-old European infants, and even older ones. Moreover, precocity of African infants in neuromotor development is found to continue into the third year of life. Using the Gesell tests, it was found that all the babies of six months or less were ahead of the European averages, as were most of those tested during the second six months. The percentage of those exceeding the European averages decreased at later age levels. African infants were also found to be precocious in language development and personal-social behavior.

Although all of these findings require explanation, the matter of precocity at birth has been seriously questioned, because it suggests a possible genetic factor, race differences in prenatal development. Konner (1976:231) reports, on the basis of unpublished research, that Géber was not able to replicate her original findings concerning differences at birth in an investigation of infants in Zambia, nor was N. Warren, of Sussex University, who worked in Uganda. Warren (1972) has offered major criticisms of Géber's methodology. However, the findings concerning the developmental advance of African infants after birth are generally accepted by specialists in this field. Freedman and his associates (who do not question Géber's findings concerning African development at birth) cite similar findings on black-white developmental differences in the United States and conclude: "There is little choice but to acknowledge the genetic aspects of the racial differences found in the first years" (Freedman et al. 1967:477). In spite of this comment, it is clear that not all students of the subject are quite so ready to admit a racial factor in this precocity. Freedman and his associates refer to studies in the United States, specifically the work of Nancy Bayley (1965), who found black infants to exhibit precocity in motor behavior for the first six months, when compared with white and Puerto Rican infants. These findings were not affected when the groups were divided by socioeconomic characteristics or child-training practices. However, another study by Williams and Scott (1953) found black infants from homes the authors rated "permissive-accepting" to be precocious, while those from "rigid-rejecting" homes were not. Thus, the information we have on black-white differences in the United States is not consistent.

While there is no *a priori* reason to reject the possibility that racial differences may exist in developmental rates in highly inbred populations, the linking of East African and U.S. Black populations does present some difficulties. Because most blacks here are descendants of West Africans, it entails the tacit assumption that the findings of Géber (1956), Ainsworth (1967), and others for East Africa hold for West Africa as well, and that African populations may be regarded as consistently precocious compared to white populations. Moreover, the substantial admixture of European and American Indian genes into the gene pool of blacks in the United States would have to be considered irrelevant to the issue. Konner's findings on the !Kung add yet another important complication to this discussion because the !Kung are unrelated to other African populations.

Although some of the African data have been questioned by such authors as Warren (1972), the general findings concerning differential rates of motor development appear to be well established. For example, Kilbride, Robbins, and Kilbride (1970) in a carefully designed study, found Ganda infants to be more highly advanced in motor development than Bayley's sample (1965) of both white and black infants in the United States. E. E. Werner (1972) brought together material from some fifty studies, which shows that in almost all non-Western societies children exceed youngsters in Europe and the United States in psychomotor development. Some of these data come from Latin America as well as from Africa. To speak of the "precocity" of the Non-Western child seems rather ethnocentric; we might as well speak of the "retardedness" of the Western white child!

To sustain the racial or genetic argument it would be necessary to conduct a series of carefully controlled studies, and to eliminate all possible environmental influences with regard to infant precocity.

In addition to genetic or racial causes, two other types of factors ought to be considered. First, we should consider effects on the mother during pregnancy: the mother's general health, her nutritional status, her activity level, and her attitude toward the pregnancy. The preliminary information we have appears to go in opposite directions: Western mothers are likely to have better nutrition and general health, but also to be less active physically, and, it has been argued by some, more likely to have a negative attitude. There is little systematic research available here.

For example, Géber and Dean (1967) mention the positive attitude toward pregnancy of African mothers. However, as Munroe, Munroe, and LeVine (1972:78) point out, there have been no studies to show how widespread such positive prenatal attitudes are among the Ganda. They note that it is not legitimate to use general positive cultural attitudes toward human fertility as a basis for assuming that individual mothers, in such societies, typically have anxiety-free pregnancies. Moreover, because of the relatively high rates of mortality for both infants and mothers in Third World countries, the general prevalence of such untroubled positive attitudes would be surprising. A second, related factor is stimulation of infants in the course of child care. Kilbride, Robbins, and Kilbride (1970) mention that Ganda mothers carry their children on their backs, which affects the child's ability to support his head and to adjust to the mother's movements. Kimball (1975) mentions that Malay children are carried on the hip. Through participant observation she became aware that children learn to grasp the hip with their thighs, and that this action is a prerequisite for this mode of transport. Children who have not learned it simply slip off the hip. Konner (1976) has paid particular attention to the carrying sling used by the !Kung and the specific *vestibular stimulation*[2] he believes results from it for the child.

In Peru, as in many other societies, women carry young children on their backs.

A number of experimental studies have been carried out in this country on the relationship between vestibular stimulation and neuromotor functioning and development in both humans and animals. D. L. Clark (1977) at the Ohio State University, has specifically tested the influence of vestibular stimulation on the motor development of normal infants between three and thirteen months who have not yet learned to walk. In another study, by Kanters, Clark, Allen, and Chase (1976), the effect of such stimulation on developmentally impaired infants was investigated. Both groups showed significant improvement in motor performance as a result of vestibular stimulation. In these researches a specially designed rotary chair was used to spin the child, who was held on the lap of an adult.

Konner (1976:234) reports discussing child motor development with !Kung parents. He tells us that:

> They insist that a child not taught to sit, crawl, stand, and walk will never perform these behaviors (even as late as age three) because the bones of the back will be "soft" and "not tightened together." So they go through training routines for each of these behaviors. Infants too young to sit are propped up in front of their mothers in the sand with a wall of sand around their buttocks to support them. When they fall they are propped up again. Incipient walkers are lured with bits of food to push to the limits of their ability. And so on (Konner 1976:234).

Furthermore, Konner notes that among the !Kung "infants are rarely permitted to lie down while awake. Mothers consider that this is bad for infants and that it retards motor development" (Konner 1976:222). He parenthetically contrasts this belief and the behavior that flows from what he terms:

> folk belief in the northeastern United States where grandparents, at any rate, say that vertical posture is bad, at least for very young infants. Hence, presumably, the American parental pattern of laying babies down most of the time (Konner 1976:222).

During this first year of life !Kung babies are in constant physical contact with their mothers or other caretakers while awake. Only when sleeping may they lie on the ground, near their mothers. Otherwise, they are held on laps or carried in a sling on the mother's hip. In this latter position the infant sees what and whom the mother sees and participates in her social world. The child also can nurse whenever it wants to because it is close to the mother's breasts. Since neither mother nor child wears clothing, there is constant skin contact between them. When placed on her lap or in the sling, the child can play with the mother's ornaments. There is thus continuous physical and social contact and sensorimotor stimulation.

Although the situation and the sociocultural context is quite different for the black children in the United States Young reports on, here, too, there is a considerable amount of contact and stimulation, compared to the general picture we have of the middle-class white child: "The baby finds," writes Young (1970:275) "that its environment is almost wholly human. Cribs, baby carriages, and high chairs are almost never seen. The baby is held and carried most of the time and when it is laid down it is seldom without company." She goes on to note that there is an intense relationship and constant interaction between the holder and the child. Moreover, there is a high density of social context; households are crowded, and older children and other adults, men as well as women, take an active interest in infants. Konner makes a similar observation concerning the !Kung.

This great amount of social contact is important for mothers as well as for children. We may contrast the atmosphere of the !Kung camp provided for child rearing as well as that of Young's Southern black community with the picture offered by an urban middle-class white mother in the following passage:

> My daughter was born in New York City in 1965. She was lonely and cranky and bored stuffed up in an apartment and I was too. Whitney's father worked in an office all day. And there wasn't a grandmother in five hundred miles. There were all these other mothers and babies living within blocks of us, but we didn't know each other ... This was the way it was supposed to be, one woman and her children alone (Harlow 1975:1).

She goes on to tell us about the baby's need for continual care and attention: "She was mine. *All* mine. I hated the every-minute-of-every-day responsibility I was saddled with and the loneliness."

!Kung children in Africa and black children in the United States appear to be advanced in neuromotor development compared to white children in the United States and Europe during the first two to three years of life. There is no material offered on later development of !Kung infants, but for other African populations it appears that the early advances may be lost. Géber found that among non-nursery school children in Uganda at about three years the African children fall behind their European counterparts on test results. She has suggested that these reversals are the result of the traumatic experience of abrupt weaning. Munroe, Munroe, and LeVine (1972) point out that evidence suggests that the weaning experience may be only temporarily traumatic, but that the changed attitude toward the child, of whom new independent behavior is now expected, may be equally traumatic. Moreover, there is some evidence that weaning in the tropics leads to more or less prolonged protein deficiency. The nature of the tests themselves may also be an important factor in yielding these results. As Géber (1961) herself has pointed out, by the age of twenty months to twenty-six months, the infants in her sample had mastered all the elements of the neuromotor tests, and they could therefore make no further gains. The verbal tests appropriate for older children are standardized on Western populations and contain a considerably greater cultural component than the neuromotor tests. However, the latter, too, are by no means "culture-free"; they include such items as "walks up and down stairs" and "jumps over rope."

Certainly many questions remain to be answered about the varying rates of neuromotor development among different populations, as well as about individual differences within given populations. For some aspects of this process it is important to develop more appropriate tests. Also, as Konner's work, in particular, has shown, it is important to pursue research aimed at obtaining as complete a picture as possible of the cultural context in which child development takes place. This picture should include not only a maximum of information on the behavior of caretakers, but also their views of child development.

Our present, admittedly incomplete, picture suggests that cultural factors intervene from the very beginning of an individual's life; their influence is obvious from the moment of birth onward, but they probably have an important impact on intrauterine development as well. Maternal nutrition during pregnancy may be modified by various food taboos. Her physical regimen may affect the development of the fetus. Her attitudes toward pregnancy and toward the unborn child are likely to be influenced by cultural factors, and they, in turn, will have implications for her attitudes toward the infant after it is born. For example, Sears, Maccoby, and Levin (1957) show a correlation among mothers in the United States between a positive attitude toward pregnancy and warmth toward the infant.

One implication of the studies of neuromotor development that we have been discussing is that there exists an interrelationship between such aspects of biological maturation as neuromotor development and cultural factors. *Biology and culture must be seen as intertwined at every stage of human development, not as separate and independent causal factors.* Another implication is that what we, in the Western world, take to be scientifically established knowledge, in this case concerning neuromotor maturation, may contain a number of unanalyzed and unsuspected folk assumptions.

Bonding and Interactions

Another aspect of infant development that has attracted a good deal of attention centers about the development of a mutual attachment between mother and infant, sometimes referred to as mother-infant "bonding." Because of the total early dependence of the human infant on its caretakers, this process of attachment formation is crucial to its survival. It has been the subject of considerable research by psychologists and psychiatrists with human infants as well as in a cross-species perspective. However, only a limited amount of work has been done cross-culturally. Much of the research has had its starting point in various types of pathological phenomena in infant and child development, and it has therefore centered about what has come to be called "maternal deprivation." The work of Spitz (1945) and Bowlby (1952) in particular has had important implications for the improvement of child care, especially in institutional settings.

M. S. Ainsworth (1977), who carried on comparative research in this area for many years, has summed up the importance of the concept of attachment by pointing out that it implies genetic determinants of early social behavior [of infants] that for all societies place certain limits beyond which a society cannot push its efforts to mold the child to conform to social demands—at least not without risking gross and maladaptive anomalies of development inimical to the survival of that society (Ainsworth 1977:65).

Cross-cultural research should help us to discover what these limits are.

As is shown clearly in this citation, we are again confronted with the possibility, indeed, the great likelihood of the existence of a general human nature that imposes limits on cultural variability. More correctly, it may be argued that different cultures represent experiments in adaptation, and those that push beyond "certain limits" pay a price in evolutionary terms.

Rohner (1975), who investigated rejection and neglect of children cross-cultur-ally, claims that few societies reject infants, for if they did the survival of the society might be jeopardized. Even among the Alorese, where the maternal role seems to be accepted with some reservation, as we have seen, women stay with their newborn infants for two weeks at least before returning to work in the fields during the heavy agricultural season. It is evident, however, that societies differ substantially in the ways in which infants are handled and treated from the beginning. There are few detailed studies available on this subject. Mary Ains-worth (1967) investigated the psychosocial development of infants in Uganda. The twenty-seven babies she studied ranged in age from four to fourteen weeks, and their families varied in degree of acculturation or westernization. The infants fell into three groups, classified as *secure-attached, insecure-attached,* and *non-attached.* Ainsworth found the type of attachment of the infant to be a response to three aspects of the mother's attitude and behavior, as shown in interviews with the mothers: the amount of care she reported giving the child, her enjoyment of breast-feeding, and her excellence as an informant. Ainsworth considers that these factors reflect the mother's interest in the child and her concern for it.

Much of the research dealing with infant attachment has focused on two matters: disorders of childhood traceable to maternal deprivation and their reme-dies on the one hand, and on the other, the process whereby mother-infant attachment develops. For example, in this country it has long been the practice to isolate newborns from their mothers and others during the immediate postpar-tum stay in the hospital. This isolation was originally instituted in order to reduce dangers of infection and infant mortality. Since the 1950s there has been a gradual growth of interest in keeping infants with their mothers, the "rooming-in" prac-tice. Several investigators have studied the effect on "mothering" of routine hospital separation, and found that it has negative effects on the mother's capacity to deal effectively with the infant. M. H. Klaus and J. H. Kennel write:

Observations in human mothers suggest that affectional bonds are forming before delivery, but that they are fragile and may be easily altered in the first days of life. A preliminary inspection of fragments of available data suggests that maternal behavior may be altered in some women by a period of separation, just as infant behavior is affected by isolation from the mother (1970:1035).

They go on to suggest a "thorough review and evaluation of our present perinatal care practices." Among the questions they wish to see investigated, two are directly related to cultural factors:

Has the hospital culture, which has taken over both birth and death, produced disorders of mothering which last a lifetime?
Are the diseases of failure-to-thrive, the battered child syndrome, and the vulnerable child syndrome in part related to hospital care practices? (Klaus and Kennel 1970:1035).

As a first step in observation of mother-child interaction, Konner (1976) noted what percentage of the time !Kung infants were in physical contact with their mothers. He compared his findings with some reports on home-reared and institution-reared infants in the United States. He reports that !Kung infants spend as much as 70 percent of the time in passive physical contact with their mothers during the first several weeks of their lives. This figure declines to 30 percent by the middle of the second year. There are some differences between males and females, the female infants being in contact with their mothers somewhat more from the beginning, and this difference increases throughout the period of observation. At fifteen weeks of age, when the !Kung infant is in contact with the mother about 70 percent of the time, the home-reared infant in this country is in contact about 20 percent of the time, and the institution-reared infant less that 10 percent. Moreover, the contacts of the !Kung infants are not limited to their mothers; they interact with and are held by a sizable number of other individuals, including older children. Although they gradually move about and venture away from their mothers, they still like to be carried even after they are weaned, and it is the "weaning from the back," the cessation of being carried, that the !Kung child experiences as a particularly difficult transition.

In some societies, infants and young children may be in primary contact with persons other than their mothers. For example, Margaret Read (1960) reports that among the Ngoni of Malawi in Southern Africa, the mother was secluded in her hut with the new baby until the falling of the umbilical cord. Shortly thereafter a nurse girl was assigned to its care by the child's grandmother. These girls were teenagers who took care of the child and carried it about from morning to nightfall, bringing it back to its mother periodically for nursing. The child continued to spend much of its time with the nurse girl even after weaning. Often infants were more strongly attached to their nurses than to their mothers.

Cross-cultural differences have been found both in the amount and in the kind of interaction that takes place between infants and their mothers or mother surrogates. William Caudill (1972) reports observations of mother-child interactions in two samples of thirty families, one in Japan, the other in the United States. He finds a number of statistically significant differences between them. For example, when the child is awake, the Japanese mother is likely to be present even when not engaged in child-care activities. In the United States, on the other hand, when the mother is with the child, she tends to be specifically occupied with it. When the child is asleep, the Japanese mother is by far more likely to be present, whether or not she is engaged in child-care activities, whereas here the mother is more likely to be absent.

In another study, comparing child care in the United States and Japan, Caudill and Schooler (1973) show that for children both at two and one-half and at six years of age, there is a much higher activity level in both the child and the caretaker in the United States than in Japan. Also, there is a much greater amount of physical contact and encouragement of dependency behavior among the Japanese. Caudill notes that there is much greater emphasis on vocal contact and deemphasis on physical contact by U.S. mothers; the reverse is the case among the Japanese. He seeks to understand these differences by placing them in the context of differences in the concept that mothers have, both of their babies and of themselves. For instance, he suggests that for the mother here, "the baby is from birth a distinct personality with his own needs and desires which she must learn to recognize and to care for." By contrast, the Japanese mother "views the baby much more as an extension of herself, and psychologically the boundaries between the two are blurred . . . She knows what is best for the baby, and there is no particular need for him to tell her what he wants, because, after all, they are virtually one." Because the U.S. mother views her child as a separate person, she stresses "vocal communication, so that he can "tell" her what he wants and she can respond appropriately. She deemphasizes physical contact . . . and encourages the infant through her voice to explore and to deal with his environment by himself" (Caudill 1972:43). The Japanese mother, who knows what the child wants, does precisely the opposite: she stresses physical contact between herself and the child, and deemphasizes vocal communication. Furthermore, because of the concept of separateness, the U.S. mother also values time for herself, which she may have when the child is asleep. The Japanese mother has no such concerns. Instead of the independence that is emphasized in the United States, the Japanese stress interdependence in adulthood as well as in childhood. The differences in basic maternal caretaking behavior thus are expressive of basic cultural values, as Caudill shows, and expressive of the mothers' personalities as well. The differences need not be articulated consciously in order to communicate to the child basic attitudes toward the self and toward others. Caudill strikingly summarized the findings of several years of comparative research into child care and child development in the two cultures in the following terms:

> It seems the American mother wants a happily vocal, active, and exploring baby, and the Japanese mother wants a quiet, inactive, and contented baby. Our data indicates that by three to four months of age infants in the two cultures have already learned to behave in culturally patterned ways, well before any development of the ability to use language. Thus, culture would appear to be "built into" the person, at least in nascent form, even by three months of age (Caudill 1976:40).

Therefore, for behavior as for neuromotor development, culture has an early and profound impact on the human individual.

A New Focus

As we see in these few examples of studies conducted in the 1970s, it is evident that they differ from work carried out in the 1930s and 1940s in a number of important respects. The classic studies sought to describe the "typical" childhood of a given society, and to relate it, in causal sequence, to adult personality and to aspects of culture viewed as expressive of that personality. Many of the contemporary studies are more limited in scope, and more highly systematic and empirical in their methods, not only in the collection of data, but even more importantly, in the reporting of data. For example, Caudill's observations are highly focused; they involve time sampling, and comparisons are reported in statistical terms. Although much of the earlier work undoubtedly involved equally careful observations, the observations tended to be more diffuse and all-encompassing, and in the reporting little emphasis was placed on noting either the range of variations in behavior or the specification of intracultural variations that might be related to particular variables. In other words, just as cultural anthropologists in general have become more interested in problem-oriented research and in the testing of specific hypotheses, so have students of child development and socialization.

Moreover, there has also been a general change in the view of culture held implicitly or explicitly by anthropologists. We have seen that the earlier emphasis stressed cultural relativity and cultural uniqueness, which tended to discourage comparisons and generalizations. In part, this approach probably was due to the earlier, excessive, and unwarranted grand generalizations, against which the relativists reacted. We have come full circle, and dominant interests are again turned toward the search for answers to broader questions, which are thought to be obtainable through *systematic cross-cultural research.*

CROSS-CULTURAL AND COMPARATIVE STUDIES

We mentioned earlier that the vast accumulation of descriptive information on hundreds of societies led anthropologists by the 1950s to recognize a need to take stock and to create order. David French wrote a bit caustically, that anthropologists "do not know what they know, they do not know the questions for which they have accumulated the answers" (French 1963:417).

Although French's comment still holds a good deal of truth, some progress has been made in sorting out the questions as well as the answers. Essentially, two strategies have been used in this situation. One has been to carry out large-scale, cross-cultural statistical, or holocultural studies to test specific hypotheses, culling the data from the available ethnographic literature. The other has been to set up a series of highly focused field studies, to be conducted either simultaneously or successively in a number of different societies, so that the results might be compared. Both of these approaches have been used over the past twenty-five years by John W. M. Whiting, Beatrice B. Whiting, and their numerous associates, first at Yale and later at Harvard.

As John W. M. Whiting (1966) himself has stressed, this research grew out of the work carried out at the Institute of Human Relations at Yale during the 1930s and 1940s. There, anthropologists collaborated with psychologists and sociologists and developed an "integrated behavioral science approach" that combined elements from a number of sources: psychoanalytic theory of personality development, learning theory, and cultural anthropology. In this setting, anthropology was a rich source of data on which hypotheses derived from a combination of psychoanalytic theory and learning theory could be tested.

A Milestone Study and Its Limitations

A major contribution to the process of formulating and testing hypotheses of this type was made in 1953, with the publication of *Child Training and Personality,* by John W. M. Whiting and I. L. Child. In this innovative work the then new cross-cultural statistical method was used for the first time to test hypotheses concerning the interrelationship of certain child-training variables with cultural practices, used as indicators of personality.

Child training was divided into five "behavior systems." Such a system was defined as "a set of habits or customs motivated by a common drive and leading to common satisfaction." It was assumed that the five systems chosen would be found in all societies (Whiting and Child 1953:45). Three behavior systems were selected on the basis of the Freudian theory of psychosexual development. They concerned nursing and weaning (oral); toilet training (anal); and masturbation, sex play, and modesty training (sexual). To them were added two other systems, derived from the work of Dollard and his associates on aggression (Dollard et al. 1939): dependence, expressed in parental reactions to crying and asking for help, and aggression, expressed both physically and verbally. A more strict Freudian view would have held that these latter behavior systems were in fact already subsumed in the other three. Each of the five behavior systems was divided into two phases, initial indulgence and socialization. For example, in the oral system, nursing constituted the phase of initial indulgence, weaning, the phase of socialization.

These behavior systems constituted the independent variable. The dependent variable selected concerned native theories of disease and native therapeutic practices; it, too, was two-pronged. There was, then, no direct measure of personality; rather, aspects of culture considered to be expressive of personality were correlated with child-training variables. In a theory of "personality integration of culture" it was held that the personality typical of a society constituted a link between the child training and the cultural beliefs and practices under study.

A sample of seventy-five societies from all parts of the world was selected, and information on the degree of indulgence and the severity of socialization in the five behavior systems was rated by three assistants who were not aware of the hypotheses being tested. The information on the dependent variables was similarly analyzed by another group of "naive" raters.

A number of hypotheses, derived from psychoanalytic theory and reformulated in terms of learning theory, were tested in this manner. One of them concerned the psychoanalytic concept of "fixation." Whiting and Child note that in the psychoanalytic literature this term is applied to consequences of experiencing either "extreme frustration" or "extreme satisfaction" in early childhood in any one of the behavior systems. Because they infer from learning theory that quite different consequences should flow from such opposite types of experience, they propose to differentiate between "positive fixation" and "negative fixation." Negative fixation in the oral behavior system, for example, would be evidenced by a relationship between "high socialization anxiety" (harsh weaning) and an explanation of illness as due to oral causes (eating, drinking, or verbal spells). On the other hand, positive fixation would involve a relationship between initial satisfaction in a given behavior system and the use of that same system for purposes of therapy, such as the taking of oral remedies.

High socialization anxiety in three of the five behavior systems was found to be statistically related to native explanations of illness. The three were the oral, dependence, and aggression behavior systems. Significant results were not obtained with regard to the anal and the sexual systems. On the other hand, as far as therapeutic practices are concerned, only the sexual system showed significant results. However, here the numbers involved were very small, for there were only two societies with adequate child-training data, where sexual intercourse was reportedly used for curing purposes. Therefore we may conclude that "fixation" is a meaningful term when applied to "extreme frustration" in the socialization of behavior systems. The study gives no support for the concept of "positive fixation."

Like most new departures in research, this study is of much greater importance for the work to which it gave rise than for its immediate findings. Because of its newness, it necessarily suffered from a number of weaknesses. Writing in 1966, Whiting himself lists some of its principal difficulties.

The basic and most evident handicap of this study is to be found in its data. The materials that were available had been collected by anthropologists who varied widely with regard to their interest in child training, and consequently the quality and quantity of the data on which raters based their judgments were not adequate. The sources were not strictly comparable, and vital information was frequently lacking.

Whiting notes, furthermore, that a number of questionable assumptions were built into the research. First, it was assumed that there was little intracultural variation, so a single judgment, say on age of weaning, could be made for each society. Whether or not there is such homogeneity ought to be investigated, not assumed. Second, it was assumed that there was intergenerational stability in child training. That is, Whiting assumed that child-training practices reported by the anthropologists had been in force for some time, so as to give rise to the cultural practices with which they were being correlated. Although this assumption was probably true for a majority of the traditional societies that made up the sample, it was not necessarily true of all. Third, in Whiting's words:

> the use of a cultural belief system (theories of disease) as a projective index of personality assumes a "modal" personality that was not directly measured. Such cultural indices would be more convincing if they could be buttressed by some estimate of the characteristic behavior of individual members of the society being studied (Whiting 1966:viii).

Some other criticisms and comments also should be mentioned. For example, from a strictly technical, statistical point of view, the sampling of societies was faulty, with no attention given to how the societies in the sample related to a larger universe of human societies. This problem is a subject to which much attention has been paid since 1953, and more recent cross-cultural studies are more carefully designed in this respect. Another problem concerns the model used in this research. We actually learn little about societies or cultures; instead, we learn about the statistical interrelation of variables. We do not glimpse the modal personality that is assumed to be integrating the elements of a given cultural system. Moreover, the model assumes, by implication, that each culture is characterized by a *single* fixation and has *one* typical explanation of illness. In fact, in any given culture we may find more than one behavior system in which socialization is traumatic, and we may find more than one characteristic type of explanation of illness. In other words, the procedure used in this study takes cultures apart, but it does not put them together again.

This criticism may become clearer if we apply it to a concrete example. Among Haitian peasants, a variety of explanations of illness are used. An individual who is ill may believe the illness is a result of an enemy's oral aggression in the form of verbal spells or magically poisoned food. On the other hand, a *vodoun* specialist may say that an enemy has sent spirits of dead persons to possess the one who is ill. This cause falls into the category of dependency explanations of illness. In yet a different manner, illness may be diagnosed as being due to supernatural punishment. Whiting and Child found this last type of explanation to be significantly linked to severity of punishment for aggression in childhood. This experience certainly fits the Haitian case, where children are expected to be submissive to elders, including elder siblings. We might expect the oral explanations of illness also, for although children are nursed on demand, the nursing is somewhat unreliable. Moreover, the child will be put to the breast to calm it, even though the discomfort may be due to some other cause. Weaning generally takes place at one and one-half years, which is below the median age of weaning (over two years) found in the Whiting and Child sample of societies. With regard to dependence, children are pushed early to accept responsibilities, whether for the care of younger siblings, or for a variety of chores. It is, of course, difficult to guess how the project analysts would have rated a society not in their sample, but on the whole the type of explanations of illness we see in Haiti might indeed have been expected on the basis of Haitian child-training customs. It is interesting that much of the aggression is oral in nature, and much of the therapy similarly is oral.

The Haitian materials also highlight another problem of such research: what is illness? For example, Haitian peasants believe in the phenomenon of the *zombi,* who, according to their view, is an individual who has died and then has been partially revived by a sorcerer. In that condition, Zombis remain under the control of the sorcerer and do not have an independent existence. They do not know their name or identity. Feeding *zombis* salt, however, will cause them to remember who they are and to die, or perhaps to go home. Some *zombis*, it is believed, are transformed into animals. Is a *zombi* a sick person, and if so, how is this sort of explanation to be categorized?

The Haitian psychiatrist Louis Mars (1947:76–82) has published the results of his examination of a woman who was purported to be a *zombi,* a dead person returned from the grave. He diagnosed her as syphilitic and schizophrenic, unable to identify herself or to give an account of herself. By Western medical criteria, this *"zombi"* was mentally deranged, a sick person; by Haitian peasant criteria, she was a creature of quite a different sort.

For purposes of comparative research, then, there exists a problem of definition. Some people who are sick by Western standards may be seen as something else in another cultural interpretation, and conversely, some who are adjudged sick in another culture may not be sick according to Western medical views. Thus, matters that seem to be straightforward and to involve "commonsense" concepts may turn out to be complicated by problems of cultural relativity. Whiting and Child (1953) were interested in the variability of explanations of illness and of therapeutic practices, but they did not consider variability in the very concept of illness. Illness was coded whenever the authors of the original field reports used that term, and no further questions were raised. The problem of cultural variability in one way or another, lurks in the background of cross-cultural research.

A More Complex Research Strategy

As a result of what they had learned from their 1953 study, Whiting and Child proceeded to develop a more complex research strategy that involved a combination of cross-cultural statistical research with a series of field studies. These studies would take into account intracultural variation and would provide an opportunity for the intercultural replication of research (the Six Cultures Project, to which we shall turn presently). In order to carry out research along these various lines, they turned toward directly observable, behavioral child-training variables that could be expected to exist in all cultures. They also wished to avoid a research strategy that called for inferences about internal states, such as anxiety.

This ambitious enterprise involved the development of a more complex model than that used in the original 1953 study. Its most recent version was published

Environment and History are shown in these contrasting landscapes: Haiti: The deforested mountains show heavy erosion. The peasant hut is built on an African pattern.

Peru: The climate and altitude limit the plants that can be grown in the highlands. Stones are available for housebuilding. The tile roofs show Spanish influence.

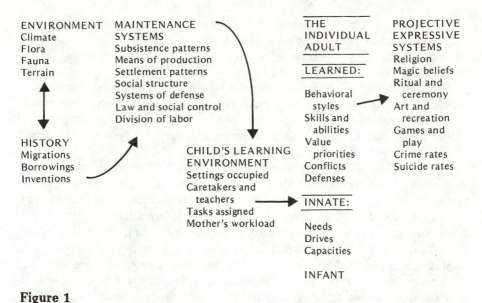

ENVIRONMENT   MAINTENANCE
Climate   SYSTEMS
Flora   Subsistence patterns
Fauna   Means of production
Terrain   Settlement patterns
                Social structure
                Systems of defense
                Law and social control
                Division of labor

HISTORY
Migrations
Borrowings   CHILD'S LEARNING
Inventions   ENVIRONMENT
                        Settings occupied
                        Caretakers and
                            teachers
                        Tasks assigned
                        Mother's workload

THE   PROJECTIVE
INDIVIDUAL   EXPRESSIVE
ADULT   SYSTEMS
                    Religion
LEARNED: Magic beliefs
                    Ritual and
Behavioral   ceremony
    styles   Art and
Skills and   recreation
    abilities   Games and
Value   play
    priorities   Crime rates
Conflicts   Suicide rates
Defenses

INNATE:

Needs
Drives
Capacities

INFANT

Figure 1

A MODEL FOR PSYCHOCULTURAL RESEARCH FROM WHITING AND WHITING, CHILDREN OF SIX CULTURES (1975).

in 1975, in *Children of Six Cultures,* by Beatrice and John Whiting. Termed "a model for psychocultural research," it includes six major components. Remember that the original model dealt with child training but not with the antecedents or causes of that training. The new model, by contrast, goes back several steps. It begins with environment and history. Environment includes such aspects as climate, flora, fauna, and terrain, and history includes migrations, borrowings, and inventions. Together these two components are thought of as giving rise to the *maintenance systems,* which include such segments of culture as subsistence patterns, means of production, settlement patterns, social structure, systems of defense, law and social control, and division of labor. The maintenance system, so conceived, gives rise to the *child's learning environment.* Under this heading are considered the settings occupied, caretakers and teachers, tasks assigned, and the mother's work load. These factors act on the infant with its innate needs, drives, and capacities to produce the individual adult, who has acquired a series of learned characteristics: behavior styles, skills and abilities, value priorities, conflicts, and defenses. The psychological dispositions of individuals, combining innate and learned elements, give rise to the *projective expressive systems.* Here are listed not only religion, magic beliefs, and ritual and ceremony, but also art and recreation, games and play, crime rates, and suicide rates.

The resultant research, whether library-based cross-cultural studies or field studies, deals with interrelationships among several of these elements. Antecedents are considered as independent variables and consequences as dependent variables, the causal chain being assumed to run from environment and history to the projective expressive systems. It is recognized that feedback exists among various of these elements, and that in some instances causality may run the other way, but the primary emphasis is placed on the causal chain presented in the model.

The resulting cross-cultural and comparative studies have focused, for the most part, on the relationship between various aspects of the maintenance system and the child's learning environment or the specifics of child training, and between child training and various aspects of the projective expressive systems. Only a few studies have dealt with ecological variables.

Whiting (1966, 1974) has summarized these research efforts in historical terms. In doing so, he points to two imporant difficulties with the original work (Whiting and Child 1953), which were fundamental to the new formulations employed in the subsequent studies. In reviewing the type of information available in the ethnographic literature on the training of infants and young children, Whiting notes that "parents in most cultures were more concerned with interpersonal relations than with body functions," which had been stressed by using the oral, anal, and sexual behavior systems. The approach therefore was defective in that it stressed the wrong features and in that "it left out of account the personal relationship between mother and child, and the role of the father in the socialization process. Oedipal rivalry, identification and super-ego development had been bypassed" (Whiting 1974:4). That is to say, one aspect of psychoanalytic theory, the concept of psychosexual development, had been incorporated into the study, albeit stripped of the idea of a sequence of stages. At the same time, in translating Freudian theory into the language of learning theory, another, equally important aspect of psychoanalytic theory had been omitted, namely the interpersonal relationships that form the social and cultural context of infant and child development. It is on this aspect of psychoanalytic theory that much of the cross-cultural and comparative work under discussion here has been constructed. Now, however, the biological dimensions of infant development have been, on the whole, deemphasized.

Biological and Ecological Cross-Cultural Studies

There have been a few studies dealing with biological and ecological variables. For example, Whiting and Landauer (1968), in one of several related studies, considered physical stress as part of the child's learning environment, and investigated its relationship to adult stature. The hypothesis was derived from experimental research with animals that showed that physical stress and repeated separation of infant and mother lead to increased growth rates, greater adult stature, and a greater tendency on the part of the mature animal to explore its environment. Although the findings confirmed the hypothesis, this study has been received with a good deal of criticism.

In another study, J. W. M. Whiting (1964) worked out a long chain of statistical associations, starting with climatic factors and including relationships of pairs of variables that had been established in several previous studies, to account for the observation that harsh male initiation rites appear to be limited to sub-Saharan Africa and Oceania. The chain begins with a hot, rainy, tropical climate. It is known that under such conditions there is a great risk of protein deficiency disease (kwashiorkor) in infancy and early childhood. Such climatic conditions are statistically linked to a long postpartum sex taboo, which is in turn associated with polygyny, a prolonged period of nursing, and mother-child households. Polygyny makes the sex taboo on the mother tolerable for the male and results in the spacing of children. In such a setting, there is a strong and lasting tie between mother and child. Such mother-child households are found in societies with patrilocal residence. At puberty, boys undergo vigorous collective initiation rites. The argument here is that because of the long association between child and mother, and child training practiced virtually exclusively by women, it is important for the establishment of male sex identity to separate boys impressively from women and to impose on them a new group and sex identity.

This ecologically based study is a follow-up on earlier work by Whiting, Kluckhohn, and Anthony (1958), in which they found a link between such initiation rites, a prolonged postpartum sex taboo, and exclusive mother-child sleeping arrangements. In both of these studies an aspect of infancy is linked to an aspect of later socialization, initiation rites. Furthermore, the infancy sleeping arrangements are themselves linked to household organization and the rules governing the relations among husbands and wives.

Slater and Slater (1965) have given a psychodynamic dimension to this complex of relationships among elements. They developed a score for narcissism and discovered high narcissism to be related to a weak marital relationship, which is shown by the presence of the prolonged sex taboo and polygyny. They suggest that strong male narcissism leads to a weak marital relationship, which in turn affects the relationship between the mother and the male child. The mother, who in such a situation is herself sexually deprived, reacts to this situation by being both demanding and depriving toward the child. This treatment leads to narcissism in the child and in turn, to a weak marital relationship. Slater and Slater thus suggest a circular scheme with two types of feedback, rather than a linear causal chain.

This scheme does not deny the possibility that, given certain environmental constraints, specifically the dangers of high infant mortality due to kwashiorkor in the humid tropics, a long infant nursing period, favored by a lengthy postpartum sex taboo, is indeed adaptive in biological terms. It makes sense to think that societies that have invented these practices have been selected for. It also makes sense to think that given the prolonged, exclusive mother-son association, the invention and institution of harsh male initiation practices was also adaptive in resolving the identity problems that developed for boys in such a situation. Slater and Slater note the psychological consequences for mother and son of their association, and the way in which the narcissism developed in this manner in men helps to perpetuate the weak marital relationship that is a necessary social institution in this series of interconnected elements. This psychological dimension provides the motive force, as it were, of the whole complex.

While the Slaters as well as Whiting have related male initiation ceremonies to aspects of infancy, other students of the subject have sought and discovered other statistically significant relationships. For example, Young (1962) found such rites to be linked to the existence of exclusively male organizations, and Cohen (1964) has found them to be associated with the presence of unilineal descent groups and with the existence in a society of the legal concept of joint liability.

It is important to understand that one given feature of culture, in this case male initiation rites, may be significantly related to a number of other cultural and ecological features. As Wallace (1966) has stressed, the various explanations offered for initiation rites are better understood as complementary than as contradictory.

Other Approaches to Puberty and Initiation: A Digression

It should be pointed out that the initiation ceremonies these authors are concerned with, which involve the inflicting of pain and the segregation, for a time, of boys from women and girls, are associated with male puberty and constitute a *rite of passage* into adulthood. They are tribal initiations that groups of boys undergo jointly. They are *not* initiations into secret societies, such as the hazing of pledges who wish to join college fraternities in the United States. They are also different from the type of tribal initiation that exists, for example, among the Hopi, in which both boys and girls learn certain tribal secrets; these rites are not limited to boys and do not involve the element of segregation. The specific types of male initiation treated in holocultural studies we have just reviewed are characteristic of only a particular kind of society: they are located in the tropics of Africa and in the Pacific, they have unilineal descent and polygyny, men and women live very different lives, and until initiation boys are closely associated with their mothers and with women in general. This particular type of initiation and its social context represent an intriguing problem, and therefore they have attracted much attention. However, the subject of the transition from childhood to adulthood, and its ritualization, is a much broader one, and these holocultural studies, important though they are, do not exhaust it.

More broadly interpreted, rites that separate adulthood from childhood are widespread. They serve to mark the attainment of a new position, while at the same time they induct the individual into a new set of roles. C. W. M. Hart (1963) suggests that childhood learning experiences in primitive societies in general are unstructured and informal, whereas the puberty rites are formal learning situations, in which the novices are taught about the sacred world as well as the society at large. The initiation is conducted by strangers rather than by family members, and where no strangers are available, masks disguise the identity of familiar persons. This point is interesting, for masks are widely used in puberty initiations.

Hart suggests that the informality of childhood learning makes it highly unstandardized and diversified, and he argues that this fact accounts for the great variations in individual personalities the fieldworker in any primitive society is likely to discover. The standardization of later, postpuberty learning results in the acquisition of knowledge and skills, not of personality characteristics. Although Hart refers to reports on a number of different societies, his starting point is his own extensive observations among the Tiwi of Northern Australia.

W. E. Precourt (1975) has considered both initiation ceremonies and secret societies as educational institutions. He suggests that in addition to the explicit content of these institutions, a *hidden curriculum* is conveyed to the participants. His hypothesis is that in egalitarian tribal societies there will be initiation rites for all young men, whereas in societies that have some social stratification, such as chiefdoms, only some will be initiated into secret societies. In the first case the hidden curriculum speaks of equality; in the second the message is that there are differences. Precourt confirms his hypothesis by means of a holocultural study.

When Precourt speaks of "egalitarian" societies he, like others who use the term, is speaking of societies where there are few status distinctions between men, especially men of the same age group or generation. Nothing is implied concerning the status of women. Because the male rites we have been discussing are spectacular, they have been much studied. Female initiation rites tend to be less widespread and less spectacular, and perhaps for this reason they have been given less attention. There are important differences in the growing up processes of boys and girls. For boys, there is always a move from the women's side of society to that of the men. In matrilocal societies, a shift from the mother's home to wife's home is added. As a rule, boys' initiations occur on a group basis. For girls, on the other hand, there is a marking of first menstruation, and so the initiation rite is a personal, individualized event. In numerous societies where girls marry early, the marriage ritual may be seen as a type of initiation, or a substitute for it, because marriage produces a drastic change in status. This change is particularly great in patrilocal societies, such as traditional India or China. Here the girl goes off to live among strangers, and there is now a physical as well as social separation between her and the household in which she grew up.

Where male initiation rites concern such matters as social structure and religious concepts, female rites, whether on an individual or group basis, strikingly often concern sex and fertility, as well as the ritual demonstration of domestic and economic skills. Where there are sexual operations, a pattern widespread in East Africa and in the Arab world, the emphasis is on the effect of such operations either on sexual behavior, or on risk in childbirth, or both.

A particularly interesting example of a girls' initiation rite comes from the Tsonga, who live in the border area of Mozambique and South Africa. We are told that " 'Khomba,' the Tsonga girls' initiation school, teaches the women's role as husband-pleaser, infant-bearer, home-keeper, and tiller of the soil, in that order" (Johnston 1977:219–220). The ritual, which emphasizes fertility, makes the girls eligible for marriage. If the young married woman is infertile, she will not have fulfilled her social obligation and will bring disgrace on her father and male relatives, who will have to return the marriage gift of cattle to the husband's kin. Because infertility is such a grave matter, it is often attributed to witchcraft. In the khomba ritual, fertility is assured by the use of drugs, recitation of secret formulae, vigorous dances, and various symbolic acts and gestures. The drugs and the rituals with which they are linked produce visions of supernatural snakes, which support the traditional beliefs concerning fertility.

Rites of Passage and Adult Roles.   Ceremonials that transform an individual's position in society, in this case changing a child into an adult, are called *rites of passage.* How these rites are carried out and what their overt and symbolic contents are appears, as we have seen, to depend on a variety of cultural and social factors. In our own society, there seem to be numerous such rites, yet there is a characteristic hesitancy or incompleteness about the sequence. When might we say that a youngster in the United States becomes an adult? What are the clearest markers? School graduation? We have graduations every few years, from nursery school to doctorate! After each graduation, one starts again at the bottom of the next sequence, whether first year in senior high school, freshman in college or in medical school, or beginning graduate school. Acquiring a driver's license, permission to drink alcoholic beverages, or voting age? They do not necessarily come at the same time, nor are they connected with full adult status. Marriage, or being self-supporting? Again, these two circumstances need not be connected, and numerous are the individuals who are married and have children but still are not either self-supporting or out of school. The implication seems to be that there are many rituals and markers of status change, but the pattern is inconsistent, and to the one going through the sequence, often confusing. Moreover, since the system requires both competition and conformity, it is important to keep up with

Among the Dogon of Mali, West Africa, carved masks representing animals that are important in the myths of the lives of the founding ancestors, are worn by men during the boys' initiation rites. (Collection Paul H. and Erika Bourguignon).

one's age cohort, or better, to be slightly ahead of it. "I'll have my M.A. before I'll be able to drink full strength beer," complained an Ohio State student who was a bit ahead of her age cohort.

There is a great contrast between the complex modern industrial societies and those of traditional American Indian tribal groups, who were, in the majority, hunter-gatherers. Guy Swanson (1973) deals with a characteristic feature of many of these societies, the search for a guardian spirit. Swanson's thesis is that this search by the individual youth for a vision and for the power bestowed on him by a spirit is a rite of empowerment "for the office of manhood." Whereas the male initiation rites that we discussed earlier are corporate rites initiating the individual into a group, in the guardian spirit quest no groups are involved. The individual acquires power on his own; he initiates himself into a new status by his own effort. Swanson finds the guardian spirit complex to be present in societies depending largely but not exclusively on hunting and fishing. He also finds it associated with a type of political organization with room for both common and special interests, rather than those that are completely individualistic or those that are dominated by common interests and allow for little individual autonomy. That is, both economy and political organization are relevant to the existence of this practice. Two other variables are also related to the existence of the guardian spirit quest: the residence rule of virilocality, whereby married brothers reside in the same community; and linguistic stock, suggesting that cultural diffusion, a historical factor, also helps us to account for the distribution of the guardian spirit complex in North America.

Note that in Swanson's explanation of the guardian spirit complex there is no reference to infancy or child training. Instead, economic and sociological factors are given principal importance. Swanson took as his starting point an important earlier study by Barry, Child, and Bacon (1959) to which we referred in another context (p. 61). These authors, it will be remembered, sought to understand the relationship between child training and one aspect of the maintenance system, subsistence economy. They dealt with childhood, a period later in life than that emphasized in the original work of Whiting and Child (1953). They hypothesized that different types of economies require different sorts of personality attributes and that children would be pressured to acquire those traits useful for the fulfillment of adult economic roles. They selected the dependence behavior system of the original study and broke it down into six separate aspects of training: obedience, responsibility, nurturance, achievement, self-reliance, and general independence. A sample of 110 societies was chosen, and the training of boys and girls was rated separately for each of the six aspects. It was hypothesized that societies with high accumulation economies (agriculture and animal husbandry) would favor conscientious, conservative, and compliant individuals and would therefore pressure children toward obedience, responsibility, and nurturance. On the other hand, societies with low accumulation economies (hunting and fishing) would favor independent, venturesome individuals and would therfore pressure children toward achievement, self-reliance, and general independence. The findings confirmed the hypothesis. However, this study, as well as an earlier one (Barry,

Bacon, and Child 1957) showed important sex differences: girls were consistently pressured more toward compliance (obedience, responsibility, and nurturance) and boys more toward assertion (achievement, self-reliance, and general independence).

This statistical research is partly confirmed by an intensive field study by Patricia Draper (1972, 1976) among two groups of !Kung Bushmen with different types of subsistence economies. Among one group, which had recently become sedentary and agricultural, she found pressures on children toward compliance (obedience, responsibility, and nurturance), while among the hunter-gatherer !Kung she found no such pressures. This finding is as expected. The first observation is, however, of particular interest, because it indicates a shift in child-training practices and parental attitudes as soon as a change in subsistence economy takes place: there is no time lag between economic change and change in child training. This fact suggests a virtually immediate change in adult attitudes, unrelated to their own experiences and to the value system in which they themselves had been reared.

Among the nomadic hunter-gatherer !Kung, Draper notes that children, contrary to expectation, are not pushed to accept an early orientation toward achievement, self-reliance, and independence. However, Shostak (1976), in reviewing the autobiographical statement of a !Kung woman among the hunter-gatherers, remarks on the considerable amount of independence that children are permitted. There is, then a distinction to be made, it would seem, between *positive pressures* toward independence and *permissiveness* with regard to the independent behavior exhibited by children.

The Six Cultures Project

More ambitious than the series of statistical studies testing the Whiting model, which we have been discussing, was the important Six Cultures Project conducted by John and Beatrice Whiting and their associates. This project involved the simultaneous, coordinated study of child training in six communities. The people of five of these communities were subsistence farmers, the exception being the people of Orchard Town, a New England community. Three of these communities were rated as more complex, three as less complex by such criteria as degree of occupational specialization, differentiation of settlement pattern, political centralization, social stratification, and religious specialization. J. W. M. Whiting (1974) notes that the findings of this project appear to contradict those of Barry, Child, and Bacon (1959): in the simpler societies of this group, children are pressured toward compliance, as one would expect; however, in the more complex ones they are pressured toward achievement. Since all six of the societies have, in the terms used by Barry, Child, and Bacon, "high accumulation economies," this variable does not distinguish among them.

Whiting proposes that the differences can be understood in terms of the mother's work load. In societies where women carry a heavy load of economic respon-

In a Peruvian mountain village, a child nurse carries a younger child on her back, just as adult women do.

sibilities, children will be pressured into helping by being assigned chores in domestic work and child care. In more complex societies, where the mother's work load is less and where schooling exists, children will be pressured to succeed and to achieve in the context of the schools. Whiting (1974:8) concludes that the findings of the Six Cultures Project do indeed support those of Barry, Child, and Bacon in that the tasks assigned to children vary with the maintenance system of the culture in which the child is being brought up. The observation that complex societies, like hunter-gatherer societies, stress achievement, whereas agriculturalists (tribal and peasant societies) stress compliance fits well into a picture of curvilinear relationships, which have been suggested for other elements of culture. For example, matrilineal descent and matrilocal residence are more likely to appear in middle range societies than among the simplest or the most complex.

Nevertheless, these findings raise a number of questions. Given the importance that is placed on the mother's work load in the Six Cultures Project, it would now be interesting to recode the sample of societies used by Barry, Child, and Bacon (1959) for this variable, and to note whether it also produces a significant correlation with socialization pressures on children. An inspection of this sample, however, reveals the lack of representation of the type of complex society in which the comparative ethnographic studies discovered stress on achievement. The mother's work load makes sense as a differentiating variable among societies, for we can easily see how it might act to draw children, particularly girls, into the mother's sphere of responsibilities. For example, Draper (1975), comparing sedentary agricultural and migratory hunter-gatherer !Kung, finds that the differences in women's economic responsibilities affect the assistance they require of their daughters, and as a result, the kind of socialization pressures for compliance that they bring to bear on them. The boys, who are off with the animals they help tend, are not affected in the same way by the mother's activities.

In complex societies, Whiting considers that it is the presence of both schooling and "a social class structure with achievable statuses" (Whiting 1974:8) that causes pressure on children to achieve. Thus he implies that in two of the five societies in which schooling is present (Juxtlahuaca in Mexico, and Tarong in the Philippines) schooling is not perceived as an avenue to social mobility.

It is interesting to compare these communities with high accumulation economies to another community a different sort: the type of communal-collective village in Israel called a *kibbutz*. [3] Here children are reared in groups and interact with parents primarily, if not exclusively, in leisure time. From the age of six, when they begin formal schooling, they also begin regular work assignments in the dormitory, the schoolroom, and the children's community's own farm. In the school program there are no grades, and students are not failed. In this setting, children develop a strong sense of social responsibility and learn to strive for the success of the group, rather than for personal achievement, which would imply competition among group members. There is no striving for individual success or for the acquisition of property. The things that give prestige, which individual children seek to achieve, involve contributions to group welfare. The mother's work load is irrelevant, for children do not interact with their mothers in situations involving work. Task assignment is largely organized through the children's own community: children plan the school curriculum, and they allocate work assignments. Nor is there a class structure and social mobility within it.

In this case, we have a society that was consciously planned to achieve certain social and educational goals, and it has been highly successful. The social organization of the kibbutz, however, as well as the specific information available on child behavior, are so different from the other societies under discussion here that a true comparison is not possible. Nonetheless, the kibbutz appears in many respects to cut across our several types of societies.

Contrasts between Holocultural Research and the Six Cultures Project.   Both the cross-cultural statistical studies we have reviewed so far and the Six Cultures Project investigated the effects of various antecedents, primarily elements of the maintenance system, on child training and child behavior. Before taking a closer look at the Six Cultures Project it may be useful to stop for a moment to consider the differences between these two approaches, their advantages and disadvantages, their strengths, and their limitations. As we have already seen, there is important feedback between them, and our knowledge of the possible effects of various antecedents is advanced in this way.

The statistical studies are designed to test hypotheses on a large sample of societies. The answers we obtain from them are formulated in terms of probabilities. On the other hand, when we do fieldwork and discover a pattern in a given society, we cannot generalize beyond that society. For example, among the !Kung, we find low pressure on children for compliance. We cannot know from that case alone whether the !Kung are, in this respect, typical of hunter-gatherer societies. Nor can we infer that their economy is relevant to their child-training practices, although we may be able to trace multiple relations between them as we study the full context of child training. For example, we note not only that children are not assigned child-care chores, but also that infants are spaced far apart, perhaps as much as four years, and are also nursed for a long time. Moreover, we know that the !Kung spend a relatively small amount of time on subsistence activities: Draper (1976) estimates approximately three days a week. Some of the relationships among type of economy, total amount of work, mother's work load, and child involvement in work responsibilities become clearer when we compare the hunter-gatherer !Kung with others of their kin who have taken up agricultural activities. Unlike the statistical studies, this limited, controlled comparison shows us changes in the whole pattern of interrelated elements.

Statistical studies provide us with correlations among the variables we suspect to begin with as having important bearing on each other. The method of research limits us to the testing of preformulated hypotheses. We cannot generate new, unhypothecated information. Also, we are limited by the information available in the literature: most of the ethnographic studies we must draw on were not originally designed for the purposes for which we utilize them. In this instance we must use reports on certain specific aspects of child training, of the subsistence economy, and of other elements in the maintenance system.

The Six Cultures Project allows us systematic comparison not only between cultures but also with regard to variation within cultures. Yet it must be remembered that this ambitious project—which required about two years of data collection by six teams of investigators and has now involved more than two decades of analysis, the work of some two dozen people, and the utilization of electronic data processing, and which has not yet been fully completed—has dealt with only six communities. In realistic terms, it is clear that such intensive, coordinated studies must be limited to only a few communities and can be significantly complemented by the broad statistical test of hypotheses they generate. Both research strategies, then, have important contributions to make, despite their characteristic limitations.

The Six Cultures Project: A Closer Look.   The fieldwork for the Six Cultures Project was carried out by six teams in 1954 and 1955 on the basis of a common research plan, jointly developed by them and the principal investigators, John W. M. Whiting, Irving L. Child, and William W. Lambert. The communities selected for research were "Orchard Town" in New England; Nyasongo, a community of the Bantu-speaking Gusii tribe in Kenya; Taira, a village on the island of Okinawa; the Rajputs, a caste in the village of Khalapur in Northern India, some ninety miles from Delhi; Tarong, a barrio, or community of scattered hamlets, on the island of Luzon in the Philippines; and finally, Mixtecan-speaking Indians in the town of Juxtlahuaca, in Oaxaca, Mexico.

Three major books have resulted from this research, as well as a large number of articles and other publications, including an important research guide (J. W. M. Whiting 1966). The first of these books was edited by Beatrice Whiting, who acted as research coordinator. It was published in 1963 under the title *Six Cultures: Studies in Child Rearing.* It consists of a general discussion of the research plan and of the conceptual model as then conceived, and it contains six parts, each by one of the research teams. These individual monographs,[4] which have also been published separately, present a general ethnography of the specific culture as background for a detailed description of the child-rearing practices of the society. In spite of the fact that fieldwork was structured by a common research plan, there are some differences in emphasis in the resulting reports, largely because each culture presents its own particular challenges and its special elaborations.

In addition to the collection of the background materials presented in the 1963 volume, the research also involved the selection, on the basis of census information, of a sample of children, both boys and girls, between the ages of three and eleven. These children were observed systematically, and a standardized interview was administrated to their mothers. The protocols of the observations and the interviews were sent back to the United States for coding and analysis. A study based on the interviews was published in 1964 by L. Minturn and W. W. Lambert under the title *Mothers of Six Cultures: Antecedents of Child Rearing.* The results of the study of child behavior have been presented by Beatrice and John Whiting, in collaboration with Richard Longabough, in *Children of Six Cultures: A Psychocultural Analysis,* which was brought out in 1975. There is enough repetition and summary of the related work, so that each of these volumes can be studied separately.

The specific aim of the Six Cultures Project was to investigate child personality in relation to a series of independent variables. The children's social behavior, observed in a natural setting, was used as a measure of personality, rather than responses to tests or behavior in experimental situations. The researchers observed the behavior of each sample child in interaction with others—infants, peers, or adults—during a five-minute period. A total of 9581 such samples were collected. The social behavior of children, then, constituted the dependent variable. The independent variables were five in number: culture, that is, the child's specific learning environment; sex; age; target(s) with whom the child is observed in interaction; and differences within a culture that distinguish some children from others. Analysis of the behavior samples in terms of these five variables makes it possible to identify the effect of both cultural and noncultural factors on child behavior and on child personality. In coding the observational protocols, the behaviors were broken down into twelve types of "acts" that occur in all cultures. With the exception of "acts sociably," which ranks first in all six cultures, the remaining acts vary in frequency cross-culturally.

The analysis of this rich body of information has yielded a number of important results. On the one hand, it is evident that culture "makes a difference." Certain aspects of the child's learning environment have an important impact on the child's behavior. Furthermore, behavior is not merely situational, but does involve consistency across targets; for example, children who were above the median in sociability in relating to peers were also above the median in relating to infants. In other words, it is, indeed, appropriate to speak of social behavior as a measure of child personality, and this personality is shown to affect behavior in specific situations.

At the same time, there are a number of remarkable consistencies that cut across cultures. We shall consider them first, particularly because such cross-cultural regularities often are not appreciated fully by anthropologists. For example, Whiting and Whiting (1975) distinguish between "childish" and "adult" styles in the behavior of children between the ages of three and five. They note sex differences and changes in behavior with age. They summarize some of their findings for the total sample as follows:

> At the 3–5 age period both boys and girls have different "childish" styles of social behavior. Boys engage in more horseplay . . . girls seek help and touch each other more frequently. These behaviors decrease sharply with age. Acting sociably . . . is another form of "childish" behavior on which both young boys and girls score high, but which also decreases with age. Boys remain more aggressive in the older age group, insulting and continuing horseplay, and they increase in seeking attention and dominance.

Sex distinctions are not limited to "childish" behavior styles, but appear also in "adult" styles:

> Boys and girls are equally nurturant during the 3–5 age period, but the proportion of nurturant behavior exhibited by girls increases rapidly as they grow older, while the nurturant scores for boys remain relatively constant. Suggesting responsibly and reprimanding are not sex typed; they start low and increase rapidly with age for both boys and girls (Whiting and Whiting 1975:182).

It is interesting that these effects of sex and age on behavior generally hold true for each of the six cultures separately as well as for the total sample. The authors are particularly impressed by the cross-cultural "consistency of sex differences." They draw specific attention to the fact that horseplay and intimate dependency (seeking help and physical contact), are differentiated by sex everywhere between the ages of three and five but not later, and they suggest that such age-specific sex differences may be due to innate factors. By contrast, sex differences that increase with age, they suggest, "are more likely to be culturally determined, and their similarity can be attributed to the similarities in the roles of men and women in the six cultures" (Whiting and Whiting 1975:182).

Another interesting finding that is consistent cross-culturally is that children in the total sample acted differently toward infants, peers, and parents. Children everywhere were more likely to be nurturant toward infants, sociable with peers, and intimate dependent with parents although the rank order of behaviors varied somewhat among cultures. At the same time, certain dominant personality traits, that is, behaviors generalized across targets, have been identified. "Thus, our findings suggest," say Whiting and Whiting (1975:184), "that, throughout the world, two of the dominant personality traits of children between the ages of seven and eleven are self-righteousness and bossiness."

Other cross-cultural consistencies emerged from the analysis of the interviews with the mothers in the six cultures, carried out by Minturn and Lambert (1964), who also attempted to test some of the research hypotheses on a sample of societies drawn from the Human Relations Area Files (HRAF). The basic conclusion of this study is that, regardless of cultural differences, the number, age, and status of the people who make up a household have important effects on the ways in which mothers treat their children. In the words of the authors, "mothers in widely different cultures react in the same fashion to comparable pressures from their families" (Minturn and Lambert 1964:279).

Specifically, the analysis of the data shows that where there are several adult women in a household, mothers spend less total time with their children. Where other women relieve the mother of some of the burdens of child care, mothers are warmer and more emotionally stable than where they do not. Conversely, mothers with larger numbers of children who have little assistance available to them are less warm and less emotionally stable. Where other children and other adults are present in the household, peer aggression is more severely inhibited than where neither additional children nor additional adults are present. That is, where households are crowded and friendly relations must be maintained, children are more severely punished for fighting than where nuclear families live alone. Aggression directed against the mother, on the other hand, is inhibited when additional adults are present, for example grandparents, but the presence of additional children does not affect the results.

Birth order also was found to have an effect on the treatment of children in all of the societies. Older children in a family receive less warmth and more work assignments than their younger siblings. The last born, everywhere, is more greatly indulged, and only children are treated like the youngest in larger families.

The twelve types of behavioral acts of the children in the six cultures, as reported in the observational protocols, were analyzed by means of multidimensional scaling. This method produced two dimensions. Dimension A contrasts *offers help, offers support,* and *suggests responsibly*, on the positive side, with *seeks help, seeks dominance,* and *seeks attention* on the negative side. The first group is termed "nurturance" and "responsibility," and the second "dependence" and "dominance." On the other hand, Dimension B contrasts, on the positive side, "sociable-intimate" behavior *(acts sociably, assaults sociably, touches)* with "authoritarian-aggressive" behavior *(reprimands, assaults)*, on the negative side. When the six cultures were compared on each of these dimensions, groupings were found above and beyond the uniqueness of each culture.

For Dimension A, cultures that ranked high as nurturant-responsible turned out to be the simplest three of the six: Nyasongo, Juxtlahuaca, and Tarong. The three most complex cultures, Orchard Town, Khalapur, and Taira, ranked high on the dependence-dominance end of the dimension. In attempting to understand these differences, the authors considered the mothers' work load and the resulting assignment of tasks to children. The nurturant-responsible behavior of the children is seen as a direct consequence of the assignment of infant care and household chores to them. Because these tasks are given more often to girls than to boys, girls are everywhere socialized to be nurturant and responsible to a higher degree than boys.

Although women in all the six cultures are responsible for childcare, food preparation, and housework, how much work each of these responsibilities entails varies considerably among the societies and depends on the number and kinds of specialized agencies available in the societies. Also, in the simpler of the six societies women have specific responsibilities for gardening. The societies vary a good deal in their assignment of tasks to young children. For example, three-and-four-year-olds among the Gusii of Nyasango had as many as five tasks to perform, and among the Mixtecans of Juxtlahuaca and the Ilocos of Tarong two and three tasks, respectively. In the three most complex societies, they were responsible for only one task. A larger number of tasks are assigned as children get older, and Whiting and Whiting suggest that performance of many different kinds of tasks is one of the mechanisms by which children, particularly in the simpler societies, learn to be nurturant and responsible. Moreover, they suggest that in the simpler societies, the tasks assigned seem reasonable, and it is self-evident how these tasks contribute to the welfare of the family and to the economy. On the other hand, in urban societies tasks that children are assigned may seem to be arbitrary and less related to the overall welfare of the family. In these more complex societies, children score high on dominance-dependence. "Competition for good grades," the authors remark, "is training in egoism and does not encourage a child to consider the needs of others" (Whiting and Whiting 1975:107). (In this connection, it is interesting to note that it is the Rajputs of Khalapur, and not the people of the most complex culture, Orchard Town, who have the most extreme score on dominance-dependence.)

Task assignment, moreover, is related to obedience training. In the simpler cultures mothers claim that they insist more strictly on obedience than in the more complex cultures. Also, they have less tolerance of aggression against themselves and more overall control of the child.

Whereas Dimension A differentiates societies by complexity, Dimension B is related to another variable, household composition. The three cultures that have nuclear households (Orchard Town, Juxtlahuaca, and Tarong) score high on the sociable-intimate end of the dimension. The children in the cultures with non-nuclear households (Nyasongo, Khalapur, and Taira) are more typically authoritarian-aggressive. This dimension, as can be seen, cuts across the differentiation between simpler and more complex cultures: two out of three of the simpler cultures have nuclear households, but so does Orchard Town; and on the other hand, two out of the three of the more complex cultures have non-nuclear households, but so have the Gusii of Nyasongo, the simplest of the six cultures. In Orchard Town, for example, the children in this culture with nuclear households are sociable-intimate rather than authoritarian-aggressive, but at the same time, they are also dependent-dominant. Of the six cultures, Orchard Town is the only one that presents this constellation of behaviors. In this society, where there are few tasks assigned to children and mothers have a low work load, mothers also claim less overall control of the child than do mothers in the simpler societies.

In their conclusions, Whiting and Whiting observe that the social behavior of children is generally consistent with the way in which they will be expected to behave as adults. The complexity of the socioeconomic structure and the organization of the household, in effect, dictate the appropriate behavior of adults. This demand is expressed in the values of a culture:

> Nurturance and responsibility, success, authority, and casual intimacy are types of behavior that are differentially preferred by different cultures. These values are apparently transmitted to the child before the age of six (Whiting and Whiting 1975:179).

The types of chores assigned to children seem to be of crucial importance here. Giving children responsibility for the care of infants encourages the development of nurturance and discourages dependent-dominant behavior. This observation helps to explain differences both among cultures and among individuals within cultures. The contrast between authoritarian-aggressive and sociable-intimate children appears to be related to the children's identification with adults and to their imitation of adult role behavior. Presumably, there is considerable tension and conflict in extended family households, and children observe it. Like their elders, they become authoritarian-aggressive, which, in the simpler societies, is combined with being nurturant and responsible. It is particularly interesting that the mothers of aggressive children claimed to punish aggressive behavior more than the mothers of sociable-intimate children.

The results of the Six Culture Project appear to have amply justified the original plan with its limited goals. Its conclusions could not have been arrived at on the basis of research in a single society: comparison makes it possible to distinguish significant variables and to identify features that cut across cultural differences.

Reviewing twenty-five years of their own work, John and Beatrice Whiting conclude:

> We remain dedicated to developing and testing hypotheses designed to be true for all people at all times. We are also interested in explaining the individual, culture, and the interaction between them. And we remain convinced that child rearing involves more than the simple and intentional transmission of culture (Whiting and Whiting 1978:58).

In the Six Cultures research, the Whitings have brought us a long way toward identifying the basis of personality differences among cultures as well as the mechanisms by which these differences are passed on from generation to generation.

SUMMARY

As we have seen, there are diverse approaches to the subject of socialization. In the preceeding pages we have sampled them and pointed to a number of significant problems, research strategies, and findings. We referred to this broad subject earlier, and we do so elsewhere in this book, for early experiences and formative stages seem to be at the heart of the processes, insofar as we are able to identify them, that underlie human behavioral regularities—regularities within cultures, which lead to cross-cultural differences, as well as regularities across cultures. We have seen evidence of both in data from the societies studied in the Six Cultures Project.

In general, studies that emphasize comparison (sedentary versus hunter-gatherer !Kung, or child training in Japan versus the United States) tend to show how the groups under discussion differ. Studies that focus on a single culture can show differences within a single group—by sex, age, birth order, class differences in stratified societies, and so on. In addition, even within homogeneous groups and within a single category we can see a *range* of variations. Nonetheless, anthropologists tend to emphasize averages or typicality rather than diversity and variation.

Variation is important for a number of different reasons, in spite of our stress on regularities. It helps us to discover why some individuals in a group are better at what they do than others, more likely to choose certain roles, happier and better adjusted, more eager to learn new ways, more exposed to emotional (and perhaps physical) ills, innovative or conservative, and so on. These questions should be kept in mind as we look at ways of assessing adult personalities in our next chapter.

NOTES

1. See Chapter 6 for a discussion of cross-cultural studies of perception and cognition.

2. Stimulation of a portion of the inner ear, which makes an important contribution to the regulation of balance.

3. For details on kibbutz education, see Bettelheim (1969), Rabin (1965), Rabin and Hazan (1973), and Spiro (1954, 1958).

4. The studies of the individual communities were published separately in 1966 as the *Six Culture Series.* Volume 1 of this series is the *Field Guide for the Study of Socialization,* by J. W. M. Whiting, I. L. Child, W. W. Lambert, et al. (1966), on which the research was based. The other monographs in the series are: 2) R. A. LeVine, (1966) 3) L. Minturn and J. T. Hitchcock (1966) 4) K. Romney and R. Romney (1966) 5) J. Fischer and A. Fischer (1966) 6) W. F. Nydegger and C. Nydegger (1966) 7) T. W. Maretzki and H. Maretzki (1966).

CHAPTER 5

Assessing Adult Personality

INTRODUCTION

In Chapter 3 we discussed how some anthropologists have attempted to show differences among the characteristic modal personality structures of cultural groups. These differences are frequently said to result from the varying types of enculturation to which children are exposed, and enculturation in turn has been linked by some to maintenance systems (Chapter 4). How can we discover differences in the typical personalities of adults except by inferring them from cultural data?

As we consider the *methods of personality assessment,* we must keep some basic questions in mind. How can we speak of personality differences among groups without constructing stereotypes or basing our descriptions on ethnocentric judgments and evaluations? Such problems are not unique to anthropology. They have also troubled psychologists in their efforts to construct personality concepts and tests based on them (for example, Holtzman 1964). Anthropologists, it must be remembered, have established neither their own theories of personality nor, for the most part, their own tests. One part of the answer to the problem of stereotyping must lie in the language used in setting up our questions and in describing our results. Another lies in the methods of research we choose. As we saw in Chapter 1, much of the terminology in the first culture-and-personality writings was derived from clinical psychology and psychoanalysis; it therefore contained many overtones of pathology. Is it possible to use a "neutral," nonevaluative, or nonclinical language? Should the anthropologist maintain a relativistic, value-free stance? What research methods allow for unbiased cross-cultural comparisons?

A related question deals with the problem of generalization. Can a single modal personality structure be identified for each society, or would it be more correct to speak of a number of personality structures, each typical of a particular cultural subgroup within a society? This may depend on the type of society being studied. The least successful of the investigations that have been conducted appear to have been the national character studies. They have suffered from a number of handicaps and have been criticized severely, as we have seen. Among these difficulties have been the political motivations underlying much of this work and the limited access to first-hand data that characterized many of the situations in which the research was conducted. On the other hand, a difficulty also resulted from the level of complexity of the societies with which the national character studies dealt. Certainly the research problems associated with the investigation of personality types characteristic of societies that include millions of people, and that are stratified in social and economic terms, are quite different from those that confront the anthropologist who studies the inhabitants of a village of several hundred individuals, or fewer.

Yet another problem we must keep in mind in the following discussion concerns the definition of personality, or the aspects of personality researchers wish to invesitgate and the aspects of personality functioning their research instruments are capable of identifying. Because students look for different features and employ methods that reveal different aspects of psychological functioning, their studies are not comparable. We cannot ask, on the basis of the studies that have been carried out, how the societies in a sample of, say, fifty compare with regard to some specific psychological parameters. As Margaret Mead has remarked:

> Cultural anthropologists suffer from an occupational disease which demands that the results from studying each culture yield a new vocabulary and some insight that can be claimed as a major theoretical contribution (Mead 1975:639).

Anthropologists have attempted to assess personality primarily in two ways, which we may call the *inferential* and the *direct*. In the first case, certain cultural behaviors, usually termed "projective" or "expressive," are taken to be indicators of a group personality, which is inferred or deduced from them. In the second case, some attempt is made to describe or measure the personality of individuals in a given population, and a general picture is derived from these specific cases.

INFERENTIAL ASSESSMENT

We have already noted the roots of the inferential approach in the work of Abram Kardiner in his collaboration with such anthropologists as Ralph Linton and Cora Du Bois (Chapter 4). It will be remembered that Kardiner spoke of a basic personality structure (bps), which, according to him, results from child training (primary institutions) and gives rise to the projective system (secondary institutions). When no direct evidence of personality was available to Kardiner, as in the data reported by Linton and several other anthropologists, he inferred the basic personality structure from these two types of institutions. When direct evidence was available, as in the work of Du Bois on the Alorese, the inferential approach was relegated to the background, and Kardiner's analysis focused on the direct evidence—the life history materials and the results of two projective tests (the Rorschach test and the children's drawings).

Comanche and Cheyenne: A Comparison

Since the early work of Kardiner, the inferential approach he developed has had a number of applications. For example, among the societies he discussed were the Comanche Indians, buffalo hunters of the Great Plains, whose way of life Linton described (in Kardiner 1945a:81–100). Thomas Gladwin (1957) observed that the tribes of the plains shared a common way of life at the end of the nineteenth century—a recent development, since they had all come to the Plains from other areas. The specific way of life of the buffalo hunters had become possible only as a result of the acquisition of horses. This observation led Gladwin to ask: "Did they shed their old personalities at the same time as they abandoned their old ways of life?" (Gladwin 1957:113).

The Comanche are relatives of the Shoshoni and Paiute of the Great Basin. Before becoming buffalo hunters, they lived, like them, by simple hunting and gathering. They had the same simple band structure, and brought with them an informal style of life. Gladwin contrasts them with the Cheyenne, who came to the Plains from quite a different ecological and sociocultural background. The Cheyenne moved into the Plains from the eastern edge of the region and were related to the peoples of the Woodlands. They had been sedentary agriculturalists, with more complex social, political, and religious structures than those of the Comanche.

As a result of a new, common cultural emphasis on warfare as well as on the buffalo hunt, the Comanche and the Cheyenne shared, as Gladwin points out, a stress on "masculine vitality and courage." Although there were many similarities in child training, there were some major differences that centered about the expression of emotions, especially with regard to sexuality and aggression. Among the Comanche, there was great freedom in these respects, particularly for boys and men, whereas among the Cheyenne there was a great emphasis on moderation and even repression. Furthermore, a great social distance and a stress on respect between children and parents, and adults in general, existed among them. The emphasis on moderation went so far that the ideal couple would wait as long as ten years before having a second child, continence being considered a high virtue. Moreover, a young man could not marry until he had proven himself in battle, so that sex and warfare became necessarily linked. Among the Comanche, on the other hand, both boys and girls enjoyed great sexual freedom, there was no emphasis on virginity or continence, and there was no linkage between sexuality and warfare. Among the repressed Cheyenne, it may be added, unfaithfulness in a wife was punished by gang rape by the offended husband's soldier society.

All these differences with regard to sex, aggression, and self-expression are evident on the overt level. Gladwin argues that they appear on the covert level as well. For example, sorcery, which is clearly an expression of aggression and of the anxiety surrounding it, was treated differently in these two societies. The Comanche, who freely expressed their aggressive impulses, had little fear of sorcerers; occasionally, an individual suspected of sorcery might be killed. Among the Cheyenne, on the other hand, there were a few powerful sorcerers, greatly feared, against whom no defense was believed to exist. Such blocked aggression, Gladwin suggests, may be turned inward against the individual. For example, in the vision quest the Cheyenne tortured themselves and received little support from their spirits, while the Comanche, whose quest was far less painful, acquired reliable power in their contacts with guardian spirits. It is also not surprising, then, that self-mutilation in the Sun Dance reached its peak among the Cheyenne. In other words, the psychological pressures created by the buffalo-hunting, war-centered cultures of the Plains were largely directed *outward* by the Comanche and *inward* by the Cheyenne.

Both cultures represent the cultural patterns developed in their previous areas of adaptation. For example, the differences in handling aggression are consistent with a more recent finding by Edgerton (1971) and his collaborators, working in East Africa, who confirmed that witchcraft or sorcery is more likely to occur in sedentary agricultural communities than among nomadic (in this case, herding) peoples who are more openly aggressive.

Although societies share subsistence techniques, some other aspects of the maintenance system, such as social organization and certain specifics of child-training patterns may vary, as may some aspects of the projective system, for historical reasons. Consequently, these two societies, adapted to the same ecological niche, differ significantly in basic or modal personality structure, in the ways in which they handle and control impulses, and develop and respond to stresses. Gladwin infers a basic personality structure involving anxiety surrounding sex and aggression among the Cheyenne from cultural data. No reference is made to specific individuals or to differences among individuals.

Some Holocultural Studies

More recently the inferential approach to personality assessment has been used primarily in holocultural studies. The first of these studies, using an elaboration of the Kardiner model, was Whiting and Child's 1953 study of child training and personality, which we discussed at some length in Chapter 4. It must be remembered that in studies of this type, in contrast to the work of Kardiner and of Gladwin, the basic personality structures characteristic of individual societies are not assessed or discussed. Rather, we have here the *testing of hypotheses* concerning the relationship between certain aspects of child training and certain aspects of the projective system. In the case of Whiting and Child, the hypotheses being tested dealt with five behavior systems, their socialization in childhood, and their relationship to curative practices and theories of illness. Such questions are quite different from those that deal with personality constellations that might typify some particular group, Haitian peasants, say, or Saulteaux Indians.

A number of such studies have been conducted over the past twenty-five years, many of them growing directly out of the collaboration of Whiting and Child and their associates. In Chapter 4 we considered several such studies dealing with the maintenance system and its effects on child training. We shall now consider briefly several that test hypotheses concerning relationships between child training and the projective system. Here child training is seen as the antecedent of a modal personality that is not present directly but is expressed in the projective system. It is interesting that, for the most part, these studies historically precede those dealing with the effects of the maintenance system.

For example, a number of studies have tested the hypothesis that parental treatment in infancy or early childhood is related to a perception of spirits and the dealings of adults with them. Spiro and D'Andrade (1958) confirmed the hypothesis that in societies where infants are highly indulged, adults are likely to believe that the behavior of gods can be controlled by compulsive rituals. That is, there exists an analogy between the behavior of the infant who fantasizes having control over the behavior of caretakers, and the behavior of the adult who fantasizes having control over the behavior of spirits conceived in the image of the indulgent parents.

A number of other studies also have dealt with a possible relationship between the treatment of children and the view of the supernatural. For example, Lambert, Triandis, and Wolf (1959) found a relationship between the harsh treatment of infants and a belief in aggressive gods. They also discovered a correlation between strong pressure placed on boys for self-reliance and independence, and a belief in aggressive gods. In contrast to most of the authors of cross-cultural studies dealing with the relationship between childhood and adult institutions, who treat religious beliefs as projections resulting from stresses set up by childhood experiences, Lambert, Triandis, and Wolf argue that beliefs in aggressive gods lead people to train their children for self-reliance and independence, for such traits are necessary in a world that is viewed as hostile. It must be remembered that *correlational analyses do not allow us to identify causes, but only to confirm hypotheses about associations among variables.*

At an earlier point (p. 64), we discussed Rohner's complex study of parental acceptance and rejection. In a test of his own, Rohner (1975:107–108) finds a relationship between parental rejection and a belief in malevolent gods, and parental acceptance and a belief in benevolent gods. Rohner (1975:109) is, futhermore, able to show that in societies where gods are viewed as hostile, adults are more likely to be hostile, whereas in societies where gods are viewed as benevolent, adults are more likely to be cheerful and nonhostile.

Other types of cultural products also have been studied by means of cross-cultural, statistical investigations seeking to relate them to childhood experiences. For instance, G. O. Wright (1954) found confirmation for his hypothesis linking severe socialization of aggression to the typical handling of themes of aggression in folklore. J. M. Roberts and B. Sutton-Smith (1962) found that the presence of games of strategy in a society is related to the society's complexity and to an emphasis on obedience training. In a follow-up study Sutton-Smith, Roberts, and Kendon (1963) showed that folktales the outcome of which involved strategy were found also in societies that had games of strategy. In contrast to theorists, who consider folktales, as well as religious beliefs, as representing projections and displacement of emotions derived from childhood experiences, these authors speak of a "conflict enculturation hypothesis." This hypothesis holds that obedience training leads to emotional conflict in childhood. This conflict is expressed in games and tales which constitute a type of learning or enculturation adaptive both for societies and for their individual members. In other words, games and tales are said to represent an imaginary reflection of the real social world.

Herbert Barry III (1957) has approached the subject of the graphic arts through holocultural research. He established a correlation between severity of socialization for independence and complexity of art styles. Barbara Ayers (1968) related stress in infancy to polyphony in musical styles and absence of stress to monotonic styles of singing.

Although, as we have seen most of the holocultural studies that take child training as the antecedent variable have concerned themselves with the expressive projective system, that is, with indirect indicators of personality, at least one has attempted to use descriptions of behavior to assess personality. To do so, M. G. Allen (1967) established a seven-point scale of ego strength, ranging from a minimum of passivity and ineffectiveness to a maximum of activity and effectiveness in meeting problems of everyday living. Allen rated cultural behavior reported in the ethnographic literature along this scale and then investigated its relationship to the societies' physical environments and to the child-training variables rated by Whiting and Child (1953). He found that variations of ego strength were unrelated to the harshness of the environment, but were indeed related to childhood training. Specifically, high average socialization satisfaction was related to it positively.

There are a number of difficulties with this study. As is the case in many such investigations, we have here a single rating for a whole society. Groups within the society, such as men and women, specialists in certain activities, and so on, are not differentiated, so that ego strength is not an individual but a collective characteristic. Also, we may ask how adequate ethnographic reports are for that kind of judgment. Finally, although harshness of environment is rated, other possibly relevant factors are not treated: specifically, one would like to know what bearings the level of technological complexity and of subsistence economy might have on ego strength.

Personality Seen Through the Arts

The folklore of individual societies frequently has been utilized in intensive culture-and-personality studies as a source of information on psychological themes of importance. The graphic arts have been used more rarely in this context by anthropologists, and musical styles least of all. A number of assumptions are generally made when cultural products are employed in this manner about the relationship of the products, their authors, and their audience. It is assumed that a narrative or a graphic style expresses basic psychological themes shared by its creator and the community, and that the appeal of the product lies precisely in the symbolic expression of themes or feelings that generally are not acknowledged explicitly. Such analyses work best when basic ethnographic and psychological information about the cultural group is available to provide independent confirmation for the interpretations based on the cultural products. Only a small number of such studies can be mentioned here.

In Chapter 4 we discussed Malinowski's writings on the absence of the Oedipus complex in the Trobriand Islands. In his book on the subject, *Sex and Repression in Savage Society* (1927), he uses myths, along with other kinds of information, to buttress his argument for the existence of what he termed the "matrilineal complex," which involves incestuous attraction between brothers and sisters and the hostility of the nephew toward the maternal uncle.

Still on the subject of the Oedipus complex, we referred earlier to the work of M. J. and F. S. Herskovits. In their book, *Dahomean Narrative* (1958), they show how the myths and tales of this West African people contain many references to hostility and rivalry among brothers. Also, they note frequent reference in the tales to the fearfulness of fathers and their hostility toward their sons, rather than the hostility of sons towards fathers one might expect from Freudian theory. They suggest that these themes reflect conscious as well as unconscious conflicts in Dahomean society.

In what he himself calls "the first anthropological monograph written from a psychoanalytic point of view" (1964:xvii), Jules Henry tells us that the Kaingáng Indians of Brazil, among whom he lived in the 1930s, express "their psychic structure constantly and clearly" in stories of feuds and murders. The stories deal with "murder committed in every imaginable way and on all relatives except sons. Stories begin with murders committed for no reason and rehearse over and over again the whole wearisome theme of treachery and retaliation . . . The one elaborate art form that the Kaingáng have, their folklore, is overwhelmingly concerned with their own destruction" (Henry 1964:62). The stories represent realistically the events of their social world and their own feelings. "Kaingáng feud stories," says Henry (1964:126), "are direct expressions of the fear-wish-to-kill-guilt obsession that drives them constantly to acts of violence and panic."

As our final example of folklore analysis we shall take a brief look at the case of the Haitian peasants. These people have a rich body of oral narratives, which are told by skilled storytellers in a special setting. In addition, however, there are a great many anecdotes of supposedly real and recent events. Among the most popular of these are accounts involving *zombis,* cannibalism, werewolves, and other evil beings. *Zombis* are believed to be people who have died and have been incompletely revived by sorcerers. To keep them from knowing that they are dead and indeed who they are, the sorcerers do not allow them to eat salt and supposedly keep them away from the area where they lived and where they might be recognized. Some sorcerers, it is held, turn *zombis* into animals and sell them for meat. That is how a link is established between *zombis* and the thought of eating human flesh.

In an analysis of such anecdotes and the beliefs expressed in them, I have shown (Bourguignon 1959) how they are interrelated with the Haitian peasants' general world view and also with their patterns of interpersonal relations. Specifically, these beliefs reflect a strong fear of others, particularly of strangers. After all, some strangers may be sorcerers, *zombis,* demons, werewolves, and so on. Much of this fear, however, is expressed in terms of oral concerns: eating, feeding, ingestion of magical substances, oral spells, and so on. Oral concerns are also a major theme of the *vodou* cult, where gods must be fed and cared for, if one is to have their protection rather than be the object of their wrath. At the same time, the oral concerns involve expressions of aggression: whether through gossip or through magic, attack is likely to be expressed in oral terms. This emphasis on the oral, it is suggested, is related to childhood experiences such as irregular and unreliable feeding and harsh weaning. It is also related to realistic fears of hunger, if not outright starvation. Moreover, much of the fear and hostility that is felt against strangers and frightening figures, such as sorcerers, werewolves, demons, and the like, may best be understood as having its roots in a strictly hierarchical social structure; it is displaced from authority figures onto such more or less imaginary beings. The *vodou* cult, which in part codifies some of these fears, may also be seen as a bulwark against them by providing rituals of protection.

Compared to the psychocultural study of folklore, the use of music or graphic works of art in this manner is far less systematized, and it has been much more rarely utilized by anthropologists. An interesting exception is a study of Mayan art by A. F. C. Wallace (1950). Wallace used the methods and concepts of drawing analysis developed by such experts as Schmidl-Waehner, and also the categories employed in the analysis of the Rorschach test. The method is ingenious, and the resulting psychological picture fits well with what we know of the Maya, both from historical sources and from modern ethnographic studies.

DIRECT ASSESSMENT

For the most part, two approaches have been used for the direct assessment of personality cross-culturally: the "life history" or "personal document," and personality tests. The most widely used of the tests, the Rorschach test, and the Murray Thematic Apperception Test (TAT), are referred to as "projective tests," because they do not seek specific answers but allow the subjects to interpret relatively unstructured stimulus materials, "projecting" personal thoughts and feelings in their responses. Historically, the growth of the field of cultures and personality coincided with the development of personality tests in clinical psychology, which had an important impact on the work of anthropologists. In fact, in numerous studies involving the use of such tests anthropologists collaborated closely with psychologists, either receiving training from them or obtaining interpretations from them, as we saw in the case of *The People of Alor*. There, it will be recalled, Cora Du Bois brought back Rorschach records to be interpreted by the Swiss Rorschach specialist Emil Oberholzer, while Alorese children's drawings were interpreted by another specialist, Trude Schmidl-Waehner.

Life History

Of these approaches, the use of the life history is, in some respects, the oldest. The first such documents were collected not from an interest in assessing either the impact of culture on personality, or of personality on culture, or even in delineating the personality of non-Western individuals. Often they were published for their intrinsic interest and as such obtained a sizable popular appeal. In recent years, for example, the life story of Ishi, the last survivor of a California Indian tribe, was written by Theodora Kroeber (1961) and drew much attention among readers of all kinds of backgrounds. As L. L. Langness (1965b) has pointed out, numerous such accounts have been published, and even more have been collected from individuals in all parts of the world, but only a modest beginning has been made in the cultural and psychological utilization of these documents.

Perhaps the first full-length American Indian biography published by an anthropologist was Paul Radin's *Crashing Thunder* (1925), the autobiography of a partially acculturated Winnebago Indian. This influential work stimulated other anthropologists in the United States to collect lengthy personal narratives from other Native Americans. Many years later, Nancy O. Lurie (1961) met Crashing Thunder's sister, Mountain Wolf Woman, obtained her autobiography, and published it.

Radin's primary interest was cultural; in using informants to reconstruct a waning culture, he wanted to get as full a picture as possible of this old way of life through the remembrances of a typical, middle-aged individual. Certainly this resource is important, particularly in the case of so-called "memory cultures," where the anthropologist does not have the opportunity to observe the details of the life of an on going culture. Individuals who are willing to talk frankly about their lives may offer important insights into how the rules actually operated. For example, Crashing Thunder told Radin that when he went out, as a boy, to fast for a vision, and the vision did not come, he made one up. This anecdote perhaps shows the breakdown of the old values. But how general were such practices? We cannot know on the basis of a single report. And if this was a rare occurrence, what made Crashing Thunder different?

Part of the difficulty, then, with understanding and utilizing life histories has to do with placing the individuals in their society, as typical or deviant. Often enough, our information is too limited to allow us to do so. When we have more than a single life history, they are likely to be shorter and more fragmentary.

Moreover, by virtue of the circumstances under which they are collected, the majority of detailed life histories, including those of Ishi, Crashing Thunder, and Mountain Wolf Woman, deal largely with the impact of social and cultural change on the lives of the individuals and their communities.[1] It is much more difficult and rare to obtain insights into the relationship between individual and society in a stable traditional group.

Life histories collected by anthropologists, and sometimes psychologists and psychiatrists, from non-Western informants partake of a number of literary genres; they are part biography, part oral history, part autobiography, and part case history. They are not true biographies in the sense in which that form is understood in Western tradition, for only rarely does the anthropologist have access to, or even interest in, documents and sources other than the narrator. There is rarely any attempt or opportunity to confirm or disconfirm the informant's accounts.

In some respects, the enterprise is similar to that of the oral historian, but it precedes the age of the tape recorder. In reading such reports, we often do not know how much of the narrative results from the questions and the promptings of the investigator, or even how much of the final document has been edited. Nor are these oral accounts true autobiographies. This fact is partly due to the role played by the collector, and partly to the fact that a tradition of autobiography may not exist in the culture under study. Also, particularly when the aim is a psychological analysis of some kind, the account may resemble a clinical case history, in that the questioner seeks certain kinds of information and is less interested in other types of reminiscences. In short, the anthropological life history presents itself in many forms and does not neatly fit into any one category.

It may help us to understand one aspect of this problem when we remember that the "autobiography" is a relatively modern phenomenon even in the West, and that it has evolved over time. Thomas Cooley, in a study of its development in the United States, points out that

> well over one-third of all autobiographies written in this country before 1850 were religious narratives, including spiritual autobiographies, reminiscences of missionary work, and the life stories of clergymen. . . . In autobiographies and journals, the pious could record lives of soul-searching for the enlightenment of others and, at the same time, take inventory of their spiritual stock (1976:4).

Some popular autobiographies of the period were "confessions," accounts of the sins, suffering, and redemption of the narrator. Others were stories of adventures, often of captivity among American Indians. These stories were full of thrills and excitement, offering rich entertainment for their readers. Only in the second half of the nineteenth century did writers of autobiographies in this country center their attention on a search for personal identity.

The writing of autobiographies and biographies implies, as Cooley notes, a theory of human nature; it also contains a conception of the world in which human beings move and live, although this conception is often taken for granted, as a series of shared tacit assumptions. Indeed, writers or speakers may not be conscious of the views and motives that underlie the picture of the self that they present or wish to present. There is also, of course, the intentional distortion, based on the wish to offer a particular view or on the speaker's interpretation of the anthropologist's questions.

All of these difficulties bring us back to a subject we broached earlier: the culturally constituted behavioral environment, which varies from society to society, from period to period. Hallowell (1974 [orig. 1954]) has pointed out that the conception of the self is culturally defined and culturally variable. Here we need to add that, as a consequence, there will be differences in what individuals of different cultural backgrounds include or exclude from autobiographical statements. Furthermore, there will be differences in how they view the course of life. For example, we saw that some presentations deal with life as a spiritual progress, as a striving for redemption, or, as an adventure. The purposes of telling the tale —which influence the manner in which it is told—may be just as diverse: to instruct, to convert, or to entertain. Quite another purpose in autobiography may be to carry on an exploration of one's life and to seek a clue to one's identity. In some psychoanalytically oriented accounts, the search may be for therapy by facing one's past and coming to terms with it. In other societies, other perceptions of self and of life may be evident. Although it has not always been done explicitly in the anthropological analysis of personal narratives, it is clear that the delineation of a culturally defined concept of "life" and of "self" are important first steps in an attempt to understand what the narrator is telling us. That is, placing the individual in a social and cultural context requires not only a definition of the social structure and religious beliefs, for example, but also an attempt to understand how the narrator's own conception of self and of life structure what we were told. Some examples may help to clarify this discussion.

Khady Fall and Her World.   Andras Zempleni (1977) reports the life history of a woman named Khady Fall, a priestess among the Wolof people of Senegal. The story consists of a series of episodes, told without concern for chronological sequence. Her "entire story is organized," as Zempleni remarks (1977:120), "like a destiny tenaciously held to myth, and not like a psychological or family novel." This destiny or fate is the result of the behavior of family spirits, who indicate that they want her to renew their relationship by sending illnesses and disasters. However, to discover the will of the spirits, and which spirit is responsible for a particular event, is often complicated, and alternative interpretations are available. The entire account, with its many episodes, falls into three periods: at first Khady Fall refuses her fate, then she is subjected to a series of trials, and finally she submits and accepts.

In this life, a great many "persons" other than the self play a role. There are a number of living individuals, who belong to the several ethnic groups of the region around Dakar. They are matched by spirits of these same groups, ancestors and others, who play an important part in her life: some appear in dreams, some are said by healers and diviners whom she consults to have an influence over her, and some possess her during trance states. In other words, the *dramatis personae* of her story extend beyond the living people she encounters. Her self is structured, as is her behavioral world, to include the significance of dream experiences, possession trance, omens, the mystical explanation of illness, and so on. Illness and disaster are perceived and interpreted in special spiritual terms. They may be seen as due to conflict with spirits, intentional or unintentional disobedience on her part, her willingness to accept her spiritual inheritance, and so on.

When we want to interpret such a life history, our primary concern clearly cannot be to verify the events reported to us, or, in an attempt to make sense out of what we are told, to deal with them as if they had been told to us by a member of our own society. We must attempt to find out what the events mean to the narrator and to others among whom she lives. How much of this story happened in the waking world, and how much of it was dreamed or fantasied or reconstituted in the telling, is perhaps only of secondary importance. More importantly, what is the effect of having such dreams? How do they influence the behavior of the narrator and others? Unless we can place the individual in a culturally constituted behavioral environment, and unless we can delineate the concepts of self and other in such a context, we cannot hope to make sense of a personal narrative.

In the case of Khady Fall, Zempleni suggests that her history is both symbolic and typical of the history of her people. The spirits she deals with represent four ethnic groups whom she can identify among her ancestors, as well as the foreign, European element with which her people must deal. Also, the cult of the spirits was at one time men's business. However, since the men have increasingly turned to Islam, the spiritual inheritance has become women's responsibility, so it is not surprising that this woman has inherited the care and worship of the spirits of her several family lines. In exchange, as it were, she has become a priestess and healer.

What Individual Lives Can Tell Us About a Society.   The autobiography helps us to see the world through the eyes of the narrator, and to see how cultural and social constraints are brought to bear on an individual's experiences. In this benefit lies one of its major advantages as a research instrument. It has been utilized in a number of different ways. Zempleni's approach, which we have just reviewed, is only one.

In a study entitled *The Psychosocial Analysis of a Hopi Life-History,* David F. Aberle (1967 [orig. 1951]) used autobiography differently. For this analysis, he utilized the life history of a Hopi Indian, Don C. Talayesva, which had been published by Leo W. Simmons in 1942 under the title of *Sun Chief.* Rather than attempting to assess the personality of the narrator or to place primary stress on how his development was influenced or determined by society, Aberle wishes to gain information from the life history of this one individual about Hopi society in general. He tells us that

> only by seeing the individual in the social network, only by understanding the range of individual reactions, can we advance to an encompassing view of Hopi society in operation (Aberle (1967:130).

He concludes:

> Although in many respects Don is a unique *person,* the beliefs with which he operates, the social system in which he lives, and the human and nonhuman environment he faces are those which our analysis of Hopi society would lead us to expect . . . it follows that *whenever* Hopi face certain situations, then certain typical problems arise for them . . . From the ethnological materials and from Don's own life a fairly satisfactory picture of the *range* of possible alternative responses to chronic features of Hopi life can be derived (Aberle 1967:129–130, italics in original).

In analyses such as Aberle's we may discover the subjective view of behavior we have observed and about which we are able to make broad sociological statements. The aim of such research is to throw light on the society and its functioning. The life history is the tool by means of which we may achieve this goal.

A similar goal is pursued in the best known life history studies, those of Oscar Lewis. Using the tape recorder, Lewis and his associates conducted extensive and intensive studies of families first in Mexico City and later among Puerto Ricans, both on the island and in New York City. The result is a stunning series of books, which critics have compared to the best of the works of the great Russian novelists. *Five Families* (1959) portrays a day in the life of each of several members of each of five families at several levels of the social structure. A full-scale portrait of one of these families is presented in *The Children of Sánchez* (1961). Here five persons tell their own accounts, which often overlap, so that the same events are illuminated from different perspectives. In *La Vida* (1965) we get the picture of a Puerto Rican family.[2]

These books make excellent reading; they are often dramatic and highly colored, and the narrators emerge with great clarity and individuality. Yet there is virtually no analysis, and to interpret these stories, readers are left to their own devices. It is true that the life history volumes are only part of a series of much larger research projects from which Lewis drew, at least in part, his concept of the "culture of poverty." His introductions to the various volumes allow us to follow some of the development of his thinking. Specifically, Lewis is interested in *families,* rather than in the individuals of which they are made up; to him, "whole family studies bridge the gap between the conceptual extremes of culture at one pole and the individual at the other; we see both culture and personality as they are interrelated in real life" (Lewis 1965:xx).

In an example on a much smaller, more highly focused scale, Marjorie Shostak (1976) reports the childhood memories of a fifty-year-old !Kung woman, which she obtained through taped interviews. The author selected the principal topics. For example, the woman describes in some detail how angry and unhappy she was when her mother had another baby and refused to let her nurse. The childhood resentment of this woman appears not to have been overcome, for she blames what she considers to have been early weaning and inadequate feeding for her physical shortcomings as an adult. Shostak is able to make interesting point-by-point comparisons between her subject's reports of her memories of experiences in early childhood and contemporary observations by Draper (1976) of corresponding situations in the rearing of children. Thus, we know that among the !Kung children are nursed for a long time and weaned only at three or four years of age when the mother is again pregnant. Although the informant's detailed report seems to be more a reconstruction than a memory, it also corresponds to the observed behavior of newly weaned children. It is important here that in the almost fifty years since the informant's childhood, little had changed in the !Kung's way of life and in the way they were rearing their children. This consistency is an exceptional situation; at the time of the study many changes were beginning, and the life of the !Kung is currently undergoing drastic transformations. Such cross-checking between memories and observations is possible only in stable societies, which are now rare.

Problems of Method.   It is important to remember in reading such memories, or other personal narratives, that collecting such documents is an interpersonal transaction that reflects on both the investigator and the subject. When questions structure the interview, the investigator can be sure that certain topics will be covered, as Shostak made sure of getting information on specific stages of childhood and youth. On the other hand, even if the questions are as nondirective as the interviewer is able to make them, the fact that the undertaking is still stimulated by the investigator and does not proceed from a special desire of the subject to recount the events of a meaningful life, tends to structure the situation in important ways. Subjects interpret the situation, the questions, and the interviewer's motives in ways that are not always evident. On the other hand, subjects interpret questions in terms of how they see themselves and the world, what they consider significant and important experiences, and what they censor as not to be revealed to a stranger.

This problem is illustrated by the Alorese life histories collected by Cora Du Bois and analyzed by Kardiner. The guiding principle in collecting these accounts was to obtain information suitable for Kardiner's psychoanalytic interpretations. The life histories, it will be remembered, were intended to provide data for the construction of a model, the basic personality structure of the Alorese, and to show how this model was reflected in specific individuals. This purpose meant a concern with childhood, with dreams, and with an attempt to encourage free association on the part of the informants. As H. Powdermaker (1945) pointed out in her criticism of this approach, the accounts given to Du Bois by the several Alorese individuals and those given to a psychoanalyst by Western patients are *not* comparable, and the materials therefore cannot be treated in the same way.

In the one case, it is the patient, motivated by a wish to get well, who seeks out the analyst and who, to gain release from suffering, is willing to try to obey the rule not to hold anything back. In the other case, it is the anthropologist who initiates the relationship, who is taken up by some, often deviant, individuals who are willing to talk about themselves in exchange for money or other compensation. The informant, moreover, is in no way motivated not to hold anything back but, to the contrary, is likely to present a self-portrait that witholds certain information. The resulting accounts are a mixture of more or less censored or elaborated memories, influenced by various distortions, rather than "true" accounts of events that did occur.

Du Bois is well aware of this distortion. She points out, for example, that Alorese accounts, as well as their institutions, are greatly concerned with food and hunger, quite beyond what one would expect from the realistic conditions of their existence. She relates this concern to their childhood experiences, their unreliable nursing, and later, the fact that preadolescent boys, in particular, are largely on their own in scavenging for food (Du Bois 1941).

It is important to remember that the significant events in an individual's life depend on several factors. As indicated in the Alorese case, they may be events that, for psychocultural reasons, have a particular emotional loading. Also, the cultural definition of what is real may vary importantly. Great significance may be attached to dreams, visions, or the power of certain individuals.

In this painting by the Haitian artist Hector Hyppolite, who was himself a *vodou* priest, we see that in their imagery, as well as in their dreams, Haitians represent the spirits in the form of human beings. (Courtesy Centre d'Art, Port-au-Prince).

The Case of Nelly.   These points may be illustrated from a brief life history I obtained from a young Chippewa woman whom I shall call Nelly.[3] Nelly was about twenty-five years old; she had two children and was at the time living with the father of her younger child, a distant kinsman. The account is dominated by two themes: frequent moves from one locality to another in search of work, and much violence, usually in the context of heavy drinking. Her father, the person she had felt closest to, had been killed a few years earlier. He had died when his house was burnt down by some men who were drunk, and Nelly had been the one to find him. Afterwards she had nightmares, and also, she thought, had contact with her father:

> If I was walking some place alone, I used to hear him whistle . . . call me. He had lots of pet names for me. It got so I could understand his whistle. I used to go out to the woods all the time. Just sit in a tree. Two times my mother lost me. They found me in a swamp some place. It was in the winter time. I never knew what I was doing. (Pause) It seems like I was the only one he was around after he died. He bothered me. I could hardly breathe, my ears were ringing . . . just couldn't move. That's why my mother took me away from there. (Pause. Question: Did it stop when you came here? Shakes head). Mmm . . . I had it for a while. My grandfather used to stay up with me . . . talk to me . . . after a while it didn't bother me any more (Bourguignon 1956).

These contacts with her dead father seemed to have been of several types, if we interpret them for a psychiatric point of view: dreams, hallucinations, and fugue states. To Nelly and to her grandfather, a priest of the Medicine Society, they appeared to be real events: the dead father returned to be with his favorite child. The Western psychiatrist, to the contrary, would interpret these experiences rather as attempts by the bereaved daughter to deny and undo the reality of her father's death.

Nelly's story also contains a number of references to people being "witched." Sometimes this action was a revenge or a continuation of a fight that had occurred between two people while they were drunk. In part, these tales just reflect the general atmosphere of violence on the reservation. On the other hand, they represent a continuation of the tratitional past, when violence was covert. Indeed, the contemporary fighting was rarely carried on when sober. The picture we get of the social and psychological world in which Nelly lives fits well with that given us for the same group by Hallowell (1974 [orig. 1951]) and Victor Barnouw (1950).

Dreams

Freud called dreams "the royal road to the unconscious." Anthropologists have collected dreams as part of life histories and other personal documents, and there has been a considerable amount of discussion concerning the possibility of using psychoanalytic interpretation of dream symbolism in non-Western societies.[4]

In cultures in which dreams are considered real, they may also be used by the anthropologist as the royal road to the understanding of the culturally constituted behavioral environment. Not only can they tell us about the unique narrator of a life history, but by using the manifest content of a large collection of dreams, we may discover or confirm cultural preconceptions, expectations, and perceptions. We may get indications of how culture is built into the individual, and how in turn the individual makes personal use of cultural materials.

Dreams, therefore, may be valuable as part of life histories both for their unconscious, latent content and for their manifest content. Several aspects of this problem have been treated in the anthropological literature. However, since they have been treated for different societies, we cannot generalize effectively from these studies. They do raise some important questions, however, that should be followed up; findings in one society should be tested in others to see how widespread some of the phenomena are.

How are dreams experienced? A Haitian informant on one occasion told me about a dream she had had, in which a female spirit had asked her to return to the city from the rural hamlet where she was staying with me. It occurred to me to ask her what the spirit had looked like. This question was prompted by the fact that many of the spirits are represented as Catholic saints in chromolithographs that are sold in the marketplace. Also, the spirits are believed to possess people during *vodou* rituals, so that for a time, any man or woman present may embody a given spirit entity. In response to my question, I was told that, in fact, my informant had not seen a female being in her dream at all, but rather a man. She esplained that the spirit, Erzili, had sent another, the male spirit St. Jacques, and since this spirit was known to be a warrior, he was dressed in a military uniform. When I asked whether the man in the dream was known to the dreamer, the answer was yes. In short, a woman has a dream of a man she knows, who asks her to return to the city; she tells it as a dream of a female spirit.

What is one to make of such an account? To understand it fully, it is important to know that the woman had a shrine for both the female and the male spirit in her small room in town, and that the dream included the request that she attend to the shrine. Moreover, the woman explained to the spirit that she (or he) would have to wait a while because I was keeping her away in the country. We also have to remember that, through the mechanism of possession, spirits may appear in any human or other form they choose, so that in this context, seeing an individual's bodily form is not sufficient to know what personality one is dealing with.

It seemed to me that in this interview there was a discrepancy between the imagery of the dream and how that imagery was experienced. That is, the experience involved a translation from the visual context of the dream to its meaning for the dreamer. The interpretation, in other words, was not simply the secondary elaboration that occurs in the telling of the dream. I would never have known about it if I had not fortuitously asked about the spirit's appearance.

There is, of course, also a rather thinly disguised unconscious, latent meaning in this dream, the message to the anthropologist that says: "Let's go back to town,

I'm tired of being here." This latent content was made explicit, but discretely, in the discussion that followed the account of the dream. It must be remembered that Haitian society is highly hierarchical in nature, and the young peasant woman would not have dared to tell me directly what the dream made so very clear.

There is one more point that should be made here: the dream has the same truth value as a waking experience. It was not necessary for my friend to make an offering at her shrine now that she had had her conversation with the spirit in her dream.[5]

Dream Imagery. Another question one might ask about dreams deals with their imagery. Dorothy Eggan (1961) collected more than 650 Hopi dreams, 362 of them reported to her by Don Talayesva, whose autobiography we discussed earlier (Simmons 1942, Aberle 1967). This individual, although he is, in many respects, not a typical member of his society, makes much use myths and ritual symbols in his dreams (Eggan 1955).

In another article, Eggan (1966) analyzes a group of dreams from several informants in which there is reference to beliefs and rituals centering about a particular spirit, the Hopi water serpent. The water serpent is a figure concerned with fertility, and as such, says Eggan it is "a *conscious* sexual symbol" for the Hopi. This spirit condemns "sexual misconduct, gossip, quarrels and physical aggression" (Eggan 1966:260–261; italics in original). Therefore when he appears in a dream the Hopi interpret it to mean that either the dreamer or the person in the dream are guilty of some transgressions. Now, it is important to remember that among the Hopi a "bad" dream must be confessed, and "Hopi rules about dream discussion thus start a frequently successful probing of the dreamer's situation" (Eggan 1966:251). Therefore, says Eggan, "when a Hopi *hikwsi* (psyche) researches through *dimoki*—the 'bundle' of his dream thoughts—he finds it richly populated with cultural images that act as a rudder to push a demanding self back into the coercive tide of social process" (Eggan 1966:263).

To understand the "meaning" of dreams, then, we must know a number of things: the cultural sources of dream content, the place dreams have in cultural life, the complex of behavior surrounding dreams, and so on. Eggan's analysis of dreams confirms much that has been written about the Hopi elsewhere, for example, in general cultural analyses and in the life history of the Sun Chief, Don Talayesva. It is this cultural information that is summed up in Eggan's remarks: gossip, quarrels, and physical aggression are bad, as are sexual transgressions. All of these acts must be confessed, when they appear in dreams, for not only are they wicked in waking life, but dreaming about such behavior is wicked. The "coercive tide of social process" allows little room for "a demanding self." Social and cultural controls are exerted not merely on behavior but also on private thoughts and impulses.

Another interesting example of such internalized controls comes from a study of dreams of a group of Australian aborigines. In the 1930s, Lauriston Sharp collected 149 dreams from 51 individuals among the Yir Yoront. More than thirty years later these dreams were published with an analysis by David Schneider (Schneider and Sharp 1969). Schneider analyzed the manifest content of the dreams under a number of headings: sex, aggression, death, and contact with whites. It is interesting that in dreams involving sexual themes, the complex kinship system, which specifies who is and who is not a potential partner, is clearly reflected. In most instances, the partner is of the proper category. More striking is the observation that when he or she is not, intercourse is prevented by a variety of interruptions, and Schneider remarks: "the magnitude of the interruption correlates with the strength of the prohibition on sexual relations" (Schneider 1969:51). There are also striking findings concerning dreams involving aggression. In the majority of these cases (56 percent), the dreamer is the victim of aggression. The dreamer is the aggressor in less than one-fifth of the cases (19 percent). That is, the dream is more frequently an expression of a fear of being attacked than of the wish to attack others. It is particularly revealing of the social reality of these people, and of the feelings associated with it, that the men's mothers' brothers and their own elder brothers are most often seen as the aggressors in the dreams. On the other hand, wishful thinking occurs most clearly in death dreams in which the dreamer dies, for here death is often followed by resurrection; the death is not "permanent." This fantasy occurs in spite of the fact that, we are told, there is no cultural belief in resurrection in this group. The dreams in which whites appear seem to be more realistic, for in them, says Schneider, the Yir Yoront see themselves as "playing subordinate, passive roles" (Schneider and Sharp 1969:53).

In analyzing the manifest content of these dreams, Schneider has shown us how the universal themes of sex, aggression, and death are characteristically handled in the fantasy life of one particular group. With the exception of personal death, the Yir Yoront appear from this analysis to be quite a realistic people, who face the frustrations of their kinship system, in the dominance-submission relations between maternal uncles and nephews, older and younger brothers, and relatives who stand in such classificatory relations to each other. They have internalized the sexual prohibitions, and they recognize their position as a dominated group. The manifest content of their dreams does not offer them much escape from these realities.

If we compare Schneider's use of the manifest content of dreams with that of Eggan, we see that their concerns are quite different. Schneider uses the dreams of one group to discern its typical treatment of universal themes. Eggan, on the other hand, identifies the use individuals made in their dreams of culture-specific myths. These, however, are not the only possible approaches to the subject. For example, R. A. LeVine (1966) in a rather complex study, hypothesized differences in achievement motivation among three Nigerian ethnic groups on the basis of ethnographic evidence. He tested his hypothesis by the use of the manifest content of dreams.

LeVine predicted differential achievement motivation on the basis of the precolonial status system of the Hausa, the Yoruba, and the Ibo. Among the

Hausa there was, traditionally, little personal mobility, with the best chances being open through the role of subservient follower of the powerful. Among the Ibo, on the other hand, groups were small, and the diligent, energetic person was able to achieve a place through independent efforts. The Yoruba fell somewhere in between in their traditional systems.

LeVine assumed that young people in the 1960s would reflect in their personality orientation the social structure of their grandparents' generation, due to the existence of sociocultural lag. Reports of dreams were collected in the form of classroom essays and were scored, by someone not acquainted with the ethnic differences, for the frequency with which achievement imagery appeared in the dreams. LeVine's hypothesis not only was confirmed, but also was supported by the use of another method, the analysis of an essay on a related subject. Significantly enough, group differences were not influenced by westernization as shown by the amount of Western education of the parents. The subsequent history of Nigeria, including the ill-fated attempt at independence by Biafra under the leadership of the Ibo, clearly supported LeVine's findings.

The use both Schneider and LeVine made of dreams in their studies is similar to the employment of projective techniques for personality assessment, in that they treated dreams like other fantasy products of individuals. In fact, LeVine's research was modeled on the work of the psychologist David McClelland, who analyzed stories subjects told when presented with the picture cards of the Murray Thematic Apperception Test (TAT) (McClelland 1961). However, in contrast to test responses, dreams may be considered spontaneous fantasy products. They differ from fantasy products such as folktales and myths, however, as we have seen, which also have been used for psychocultural analysis, in that they are products of specific, identifiable individuals and not, like folklore, the result of contributions by many persons over time; they express *personal* rather than *collective* fantasies. Yet it is apparent that dreams are as characteristically revealing of the central personality dispositions of a group as is the content of folklore or the style of artistic production.

For the optimal utilization of dreams in psychocultural research, then, it is desirable to have, on the one hand, a series of dreams of a single individual, together with life history materials and other relevant data. On the other hand, it is valuable to obtain a large number of dreams from many persons in the community, so that the individual might be placed in the larger context. Dreams then may be analyzed from all three of the perspectives we have discussed.

Projective Techniques

As early as 1938, A. I. Hallowell began to experiment with the cross-cultural utilization of the Rorschach inkblot test, under the influence of the psychologist Bruno Klopfer. At about the same time, a number of Japanese investigators began parallel studies, which were then not known in this country (for example, Fujisawa 1953; for a summary, see Huzioka 1968).

The particular appeal of the Rorschach lay in the nature of the test: it was unstructured and therefore thought to be culture-free. The inkblots were accidental shapes and did not represent anything. The forms were vague and there were no "correct" answers to the test. Moreover, the emphasis in the test analysis—in which lay the true originality of the test's inventor, the Swiss psychiatrist Hermann Rorschach—did not rest primarily on the content of the responses. That is, although subjects are asked to look at the inkblots and to state what they see in them, the analytic procedure focuses on the way in which the unstructured stimulus material is organized perceptually. Personality implications are drawn not principally from *what* is seen but from *how* it is seen. The test protocols are scored to determine how much, and which parts, of the blots are utilized, what elements of the blots determine the response (form, shading, color), and whether forms are perceived as static or in motion. The specific content is grouped into categories (human, animal, inanimate, and so on). Responses, moreover, are grouped into those that are frequent in a given population (populars) and those that are not. The productivity of the subject and the complexity and organization of the responses are also significant elements of the analysis.

All of these features contrast with picture tests, which, first of all, require experience with pictures, perception of perspective, and recognition of the objects represented. The Rorschach, therefore, had an important appeal for anthropologists. When Hallowell and others began to try them out on American Indians, and Du Bois on the Alorese, it became plain that cultural differences did not represent an obstacle to obtaining test protocols.

However, the Rorschach also has one major disadvantage: it requires a considerable amount of training, not only for interpretation, but also for proper administration. The very idea of testing is alien and even threatening in many societies. Also, it may be difficult to find individuals alone to take the test and to obtain answers that are not influenced by the comments of bystanders and observers. The test situation, the way in which the test is presented and administered, and how the subject interprets the situation as well as the test, all, it has been claimed, play a role in the results.

In the early years, projective tests acquired a rapid and extensive popularity among U.S. anthropologists. For one thing, it was felt that here was something tangible that could be brought back from the field and that could be used as an objective validation of the claims of the fieldworker, particularly if these materials were to be analyzed by someone else. Perhaps, too, the peculiar U.S. taste for gadgets played a role in this development. At any rate, projective tests, for a while, became a fad, with every student, whether adequately trained or not, feeling compelled to take test cards along as part of the required research equipment. As is the case with much in U.S. culture, overdoing made the enthusiasm for projective testing burn itself out rapidly; projective testing became somewhat discredited, and only a small percentage of the large number of studies carried out produced a significant legacy. At the same time, clinical psychologists began to raise questions concerning the reliability and validity of the tests. The fads in anthropology now grew elsewhere, and all these factors, taken together, led to a great decline in the use of projective tests in the most recent period.

Anthropological uses of projective tests have been reviewed by several authors (see in particular Hallowell 1956b, Lindzey 1961, Spain 1972). The most extensive of these reviews is Gardner Lindzey's book-length study. His conclusions are worth citing:

> There is enormous variation in personality even within apparently homogeneous, nonliterate societies.
>
> Varying degrees or levels of acculturation are accompanied by varying personality attributes and perhaps by variations in general level of adjustment.
>
> Individuals representative of different socialization practices and different cultural backgrounds respond differently to most projective techniques.
>
> Personality inferences based upon the widely used projective techniques appear consistent with parallel inferences derived from ordinary field work methods. (Lindzey 1961:311–312).

Among the studies that Lindzey praises is one by Thomas Gladwin and Seymour Sarason (1953) dealing with the people of the Micronesian atoll of Truk. This study is a replication, with some improvements, of the researches on the Alorese by Du Bois and Kardiner. In addition to the collection of ethnographic data, Gladwin obtained life histories, Rorschach records, and TAT stories. In doing so, he made a specific attempt to draw a representative sample of the population. Sarason, a clinical psychologist who analyzed the test protocols, was given no access to the ethnographic information and life histories; he knew only the age and sex of each individual. In contrast to the traditional methods of scoring and evaluating the tests, he treated the responses as samples of behavior in novel situations. On the basis of these samples, he formed hypotheses about how a given individual would act in specific life situations. As Gladwin reports in a separate paper on this research, Sarason found, to Gladwin's surprise, "that the men were notably more anxious than the women and would tend to respond less adequately to any situation of conflict or doubt." Moreover, according to Sarason's analysis, the women used food production, food distribution, and sexual activities, in which the men hold dominant positions, "as a means of subtle aggression toward men and as media for expression of their assertiveness" (Gladwin 1953:307). Upon reanalysis of his data, however, Gladwin revised his own views.

His summing up is worth citing:

> Dr. Sarason's conclusions, based exclusively on his analysis of the projective tests, provided a substantially more economical and inclusive explanation for the data I had collected on the roles of men and women, in spite of the fact that, after four years of contact with the Trukese, I continued to assume that the superficial dominance

of men in the society reflected also a corresponding sense of security at the psychological level (Gladwin 1953:308).

The fact that the analysis of the test materials provided an independent basis for the interpretation of Trukese personality made it possible for the psychologist to offer a check on the interpretation the anthropologist had drawn from other types of data. *Truk: Man in Paradise,* the final common statement on the Trukese by Gladwin and Sarason, with its ironic title, however, does not show the evolution of the psychocultural picture on which the two authors came to agree.

Projective Tests and Cultural Differences.   In addition to their use in defining modal personalities of some communities or societies, the Rorschach and TAT have also been employed to test the existence of psychological differences among groups among whom there are known cultural differences. The cultural differences may exist at various levels: people of a common cultural tradition, but living in different communities and at different levels of acculturation; historically unrelated peoples; people within a single community, but differentiated by level of acculturation, sex, class, or other factors.

Hallowell (1974 [orig. 1951]) compared three groups of Ojibwa Indians representing stages in acculturation. The least acculturated were the Berens River Saulteaux in Canada, the Lakeside Saulteaux were intermediate, and the Lac du Flambeau Chippewa, in Wisconsin, were the most acculturated. This last group showed significant signs of poor psychological adjustment. Hallowell also compared these American Indian groups with a sample of white Chicagoans, and here too he found the Wisconsin group more poorly adjusted than the whites. On the other hand, a comparison between the Chicagoans and the two Canadian groups of Ojibwa led him to conclude that "while the Indian pattern is distinctive, it is certainly no less healthy than the American one" (Hallowell 1956b:528). He goes on to point out that the sociocultural data he had gathered concerning these American Indians provided "empirical validation of the inferences drawn from the Rorschach data."

In the study of a single community of Menomini Indians, G. Spindler (1955) identified four levels of acculturation, using religious identification as an important criterion. He found that these groups also differed by a whole series of sociocultural features. When he administered the Rorschach to a sample of male subjects, he found statistically significant differences among the four groups with regard to this test as well. L. Spindler (1962) tested a sample of women, and here too differences among the four groups appeared. Finally, differences between men and women at each of the four levels were also found to exist (L. Spindler and G. Spindler 1958). We shall come back to this important investigation in another context.

Other group comparisons are offered by G. A. De Vos, who developed a system of scoring Rorschach responses for their emotional or affective content; this scoring enabled him to establish indexes for the expressions of feelings such as hostility, anxiety, dependency, bodily preoccupations, and so on. In one interesting study, De Vos (1961) compared a number of cultural groups and subgroups (Americans, Japanese-Americans, urban and rural Japanese, urban and rural Algerian Arabs) along these lines. He found, among other things, that groups exposed to acculturation, such as immigrant Japanese-Americans and urbanized French-influenced Algerian Arabs, showed much greater evidence of psychological stress in their test responses than comparable rural groups. He concludes:

> Fear, hostility, dependency, positive feelings and mental mechanisms described by Freud as the basic mechanisms of the human mind in handling the relationship of feeling and cognition are probably represented in the production of Rorschach percepts in surprisingly similar terms from culture to culture (DeVos 1961:362).

It is the existence of such basic similarities in mechanisms and processes that makes it possible for us to establish comparisons between groups, as well as to see that the differences that exist fall within a limited range. The relation between feelings and thinking, between perception and behavior, are among these basic universal factors in human psychological functioning.

The Rorschach as an Interview.   At times, the Rorschach test situation may function as a specialized interview situation, in which subjects tell us things that are on their minds that we might not have learned about, at least not so characteristically, in another context.[6] Such a situation occurred in my work in Haiti, and it offered me some important insights. I have presented the full case with my analysis elsewhere (Bourguignon 1969), and I shall summarize it here briefly.

A young man of the Haitian upper class—I shall call him R. J.—agreed to take the test at the suggestion of a friend, a psychiatrist, from the United States. This man was present during the test, and it seemed clear that R. J. wished to impress him by his performance. He gave a total of one hundred responses to the ten cards; of these, however, forty-four were not percepts—things that he could recognize in the inkblots—but associations to his percepts. For example, in Card 1 his first response was "a bat." This response, together with "bird" or "butterfly," is frequent among Haitians, as it is in most groups that have been tested. To this response he presented four associations: a house in which he had lived; a story of demons told about this house; a young girl who was unwell, who played a role in this story; and, finally, verses by the French poet Mallarmé. The second thing he saw in the card was a tattoo the psychiatrist was said to have; this image reminded him of a spirit of the *vodou* cult. So it went throughout the ten cards. In this small sequence R. J. drew both on Haitian traditions and on French literature. He continued to do so throughout the protocol, but he also referred to Africa and the United States, both to help him interpret the forms and to fill out his associations. He thought of Africa and of Haitian *vodou* religion as mysterious and frightening, but also as heroic. As soon as he spoke of one or the other of these topics, he was drawn immediately to France or the United States. In fact, Haiti, Africa, France, and the United States represented four poles of attraction and repulsion to him. His fantasy constantly pulled him away from Haiti and back to it. In short, both the general content of the protocol, and the specific sequence in which the materials are presented, revealed a high degree of ambivalence in this young man.

M. J. Herskovits (1937a:295) coined the term *socialized ambivalence* with regard to the Haitian personality, and observation suggests that it is particularly characteristic of the upper class, or élite. Ambivalence is reflected in the simultaneous holding of contradictory attitudes toward and evaluations of the same situations, institutions, persons, or other objects of feeling and opinion. This ambivalence, however, is not the unique characteristic of a particular individual; because it is such a widespread typical emotional disposition, it is referred to as "socialized." In expressing such ambivalence in response to the ambiguous stimulus offered by the Rorschach cards, R. J. shows us a picture of the relationship between the upper-class Haitian and the various cultural sources of contradictory teachings and attitudes to which he is exposed.

I have attempted to understand this pattern of socialized ambivalence as resulting from what Ruth Benedict (1938) has called a "discontinuity of cultural conditioning" or socialization. In the case of the child of the Haitian élite, the early years of training are largely in the hands of servants, who are members of one cultural tradition. Later socialization, particularly in the context of the schools, emphasizes a second cultural tradition. Servants are Creole-speaking members of the peasant class, with a strongly *vodou*-based tradition. The schools teach French, and the French tradition plays an important role there. The Creole language is therefore associated with a private world of intimate relationships, the French language with formal relations and the public domain. This discontinuity is important for the life of individuals and for the development of their picture of themselves and the world. The upper-class world rejects the practices of the peasants as ignorant and superstitious; yet there is a strong nationalistic identification with a black tradition and with African roots. Yet again the élite see themselves as a group of modern, Western people. Each point in this sequence sends the individual back to the opposite pole for a contrasting and contradictory evaluation.

This analysis received strong confirmation from a comprehensive study of Haitians living in France, by Bastide, Morin, and Raveau (1974). These authors show clearly how socialized ambivalence plays an important role in the personality of these transplanted Haitians and in the problems of adjustment they face in a different kind of society.

Although Haiti may represent a special case, as a result of its unique history as the first independent black nation, such conflicts are not rare today in many parts of the developing world, where radical transformations are taking place and where individuals and groups are forced to cope with incompatible orientations and teachings.

This discussion of methods of personality assessment has led us to deal with a matter of much contemporary importance—culture change and acculturation, and its psychological impact. We shall discuss this subject more fully in Chapter 9.

Other Tests.   Let us look briefly at some other projective tests, such as the Thematic Apperception Test (TAT) and the Sentence Completion Test (SCT). Reviews of these and other techniques have been published by psychologists who specialize in this work (for example, Rabin 1968). There is much diversity in this area of psychological testing, and many of the instruments have gone through a large number of modifications and adaptations for specific uses.

The TAT originally consisted of a series of twenty pictures. The subject is asked to tell a story about each. The interpretation of these stories may proceed along a number of different lines, but the basic assumption is usually made that what happens in the stories represents some aspect of the fantasy life of the storyteller. Also, it is generally assumed that the central character of the tale in some ways stands for the narrator. Beyond that, various investigators have concentrated their attention on some particular theme or themes in the stories, often to the neglect of other possible content categories. For example, as we mentioned earlier, McClelland and his associates (1953) used the TAT to study the achievement motive in the stories of their subjects. Others have looked for evidence of aggression, anxiety, or other emotions.

Lindzey (1961:69–70) in his general survey of projective techniques contrasts the TAT and the Rorschach. He notes that investigators generally consider that these two techniques provide somewhat different types of information. The Rorschach is held to offer primarily insights into the *structure* of the personality; the TAT, on the other hand, with its greater potential for tapping the imagination of subjects, is thought to yield information on the *content* of personality. In other words, the TAT is generally used to reveal the specific nature of the individual's conflicts and attitudes, both on a conscious and on an unconscious level. In contrast to the Rorschach, little training is required to administer the TAT. Also, it is a flexible technique. It is generally believed, for example, that the specific pictures of which the test is made up are much less important than their ability to elicit responses from subjects. Because the original pictures, which contain scenes involving white people in the United States, are obviously not culture-free, different sets of pictures have been prepared to facilitate the subject's identification with the characters portrayed. These special pictures often show persons with the appropriate racial and cultural characteristics, and when investigators are interested in particular themes, the pictures might present situations that are expected to produce responses dealing with these themes.

On the other hand, the TAT also presents its particular problems. When shown to people who have little or no experience with the representation of three-dimensional objects in two-dimensional space, perceptual difficulties may intervene. For example, a special set of pictures drawn for use in Micronesia was employed by Gladwin on Truk in the study to which we referred earlier as well as by several other investigators. One of them, M. E. Spiro (1959), used these cards on the atoll of Ifaluk. According to a note by Hallowell (1956b:487) Spiro's subjects saw canoes shown not as being in the background, *behind* figures in the foreground of the drawings, but *above* them. They therefore interpreted what they saw to signify that the men, appearing to be placed beneath the canoes, were carrying them. H. Silverthorne (1951), who used specially drawn TAT pictures among Haitian peasants, had a similar experience. He found that subjects frequently interpreted forms in the foreground of pictures as either standing or sitting on the feet of persons lying in the background; persons in the background appeared to them to be placed higher than those in the foreground and therefore to be lifted or carried by them.

It may also be asked whether the use of different pictures, adapted to varying cultural situations, produces comparable results. However, unlike those using the Rorschach, investigators employing the TAT and its variants often pursue quite different goals; the non-comparability of the results may therefore reside as much in their research aims as in their experimental tools. In any event, few systematic comparisons of results obtained through diverse TAT-type pictures have been attempted.

French-English Bilinguals: A Test of a Hypothesis.   The number of applications of the TAT and its various modifications has been very large. One particularly interesting and well-designed study may be cited here both for its approach and its results. The study in question was conducted by Susan Ervin (1964) with a group of French-English bilinguals living in the Washington, D.C. area. On the basis of the descriptive literature on culture the author hypothesized that subjects from France and the United States would express themes of aggression differently in their TAT stories. Specifically, the former would deal with aggression as expressed in verbal exchanges, whereas the latter would deal with physical expressions of agression.

Ervin further hypothesized that when bilinguals speak English they may be expected to tell U.S.-type TAT stories, whereas when they speak French, their TAT stories would conform to the French model. This hypothesis, indeed, was confirmed. The TAT stories, told by the same subjects in two different languages, appeared to reveal two distinct personality patterns, coherent with the culture that is associated with the language being used. The author interprets this to mean that, for subjects who have learned each language in a different cultural context (they are termed "coordinate bilinguals"), each language acts as a system of cues, conjuring up associations linked to that particular cultural system.

The implications of these findings are of major significance for an understanding of multilingual societies, for our analysis of culture change and its psychological implications, and for anthropological fieldwork. Anthropologists working with bilingual informants or interpreters must be aware of the psychological complexities that are involved in such multiple levels of participation and personal involvement.

This point is also underscored by a further example: Leonard Doob (1957,

1960) reports on research in three African societies. He tested bilingual individuals, asking them to agree or disagree with a series of statements in each language. He found that there were important differences of opinion, depending on the language in which the statement was presented.

Intragroup Differences.   Ervin's study, as we have seen, does not attempt to construct the modal personality of a group, but seeks to test some psychocultural hypotheses. In this respect it resembles the numerous TAT studies in Western societies dealing with achievement motivation, aggression, and other specific themes. In fact, such a tendency toward focused research has become increasingly evident in psychological anthropology.

Another trend has also become evident, based on the greater awareness that even relatively small groups, undifferentiated with regard to sociological variables, include a range of individual personalities. Lindzey, as we saw earlier, drew this conclusion from a study of research utilizing projective techniques. Therefore the practice of testing hypotheses that relate personality differences to some antecedent variables, which is common in studies in complex societies, has been extended to research in traditional societies.

This practice is well illustrated by the research of Ralph Bolton among the Qolla, an Indian group of the highlands of Peru, in the region of Lake Titicaca. Among these people, Bolton found a high degree of aggressive behavior, a characteristic that had been noted in much of the literature on the Qolla and their neighbors, the Aymara of Bolivia. His original research aim was to discover the roots of this behavior in social and cultural factors, but he was unable to do so. He therefore proceeded "to an examination of the possible biological factors which might be responsible for the apparently irrational aspects of Qolla agonistic behavior" (Bolton 1973:228–229). He was particularly struck by the fact that their aggressive behavior is in contradiction to their moral code, which values and demands "charity, compassion, and co-operation with all men" (Bolton 1973:229).

Although the community as a whole is characterized by high homicide rates and other indicators of aggression, not all individuals are equally agressive. It is then possible to ask why some individuals are more aggressive than others, that is, to find correlates of aggression that distinguish some people from others. On the basis of the literature in the field of physiology, Bolton proposed a relationship between mild hypoglycemia (abnormal blood glucose levels) and aggressiveness. His interesting study did in fact confirm that in this population more than half of the men in his sample had hypoglycemia, a condition that appears to exist in only a small fraction of the population in the United States. Moreover, he found a statistically significant relationship between aggression and hypoglycemia (Bolton 1973).

Among the psychological instruments used in this study was the Sentence Completion Test. Here Bolton (1976) discovered differences in the responses of hypoglycemics and individuals with normal blood sugar levels. Not only were hypoglycemics more likely to give aggressive responses to the test, but they did so more frequently when the sentence stems dealt with certain specific subjects, such as money, women, figures of authority, male relatives, and land.

This study is important in the context of our present discussion in a number of respects. First of all, it is an example of a type of investigation in which personality assessment is not an end in itself, but is part of a larger research design. In this instance, an attempt is made to link personality traits and behavior with physiological states. Secondly, this study is also important in that the projective test findings are consistent with other data, such as evidence of aggression in the form of homicide rates, statistics on litigation,[7] and so on. Where projective tests are the only source of information on personality traits there is always the question whether the results are in part a function of the specific test and whether another instrument might have produced different results, or whether the investigator is, in some way, responsible for the results of the study. In this study, there is considerable supportive evidence for the claim that the Qolla are highly aggressive and that some individuals are much more aggressive than others.

Bolton's research is of importance in another respect, also. There is, at the present time, a greatly increased interest in the possible relationship between psychological functioning and physiological states. Two aspects of Bolton's work must be considered in this context: hypoglycemia is found to be frequent among the Qolla (and possibly other Andean populations), and it is associated with high levels of aggressive behavior. A large number of individuals experience this physiological condition and respond to it by certain types of behavior and certain types of feeling states. Also, individuals who are hypoglycemic experience this condition with greater intensity at certain times, which appear to be the periods when their behavior is most likely to be aggressive. We shall return to this matter of a possible relationship between physiology and psychology when we discuss altered states of consciousness (Chapter 7). Here, however, we need to point out that Bolton's research among the Qolla indicates that personality features typical of a given group may be considered not only in relation to such antecedents as child training, which we have discussed at length, but also in terms of physiological states that may result from particular ecological adaptations (or maladaptations). Moreover, these ecologically derived factors appear to act on behavior directly, without the mediation of childhood training variables.

Photography

Let us turn to a different kind of direct approach. Both still photography and films have been used in cultural anthropological fieldwork, specifically in psychological anthropology, primarily to provide illustrations of behavior and to document cultural differences. These documentary still photographs and films are important instructional tools. However, only relatively rarely has photography been used as a true research instrument. There are a few important examples of such use, to which we may now turn briefly.

One of the most important examples is the work of Bateson and Mead in Bali. Their book, *Balinese Character: A Photographic Analysis* (1942) represents a landmark in psychocultural research. In it, they note in the introduction, they wished to show in photographs how the Balinese, as individuals, embody their culture in their characteristic behaviors. Bateson (1976:58) describes the book in these terms: "The plates, each with from five to nine pictures, were built according to what we thought or felt were cultural or characterological themes . . . Every plate is a complex statement, illustrating either different facets of some quite abstract theme or the interlocking of several themes." Mead, referring to a plate in this book, representing a sequence labeled "sibling rivalry in Bali," notes:

> It is during scenes of this sort that the field worker often develops new insights about the culture, and, if these are recorded on the spot, then later one can go back to the exact visual situation which gave rise to the insight. Furthermore, if a large number of sequences of interpersonal relations are shot immediately upon entering the field, it is possible to check the effect of a developed hypothesis in the distortion of the field worker's perception, by going back to the photographs which were taken *before* the insights were articulated (Mead 1956:85; italics in original).

In a study influenced by the work of Bateson and Mead, Walter Goldschmidt (1976) used photographs as data in research among the Sebei of Uganda. What is methodologically interesting about this particular article is that an impressionistic observation about mother-child interaction was confirmed by systematic review of a series of photographs that were not originally taken to document this observation. The pictures of mothers carrying or nursing small children show the mother "disengaged" from the child: in most instances neither her eyes not her hands are on the child. In fact, in no instance are both hands on the child, and in less than one-fourth of the pictures is one hand on the child. "What I see in these photographs is an absent mother—an emotionally absent mother" (Goldschmidt 1976:70). Clearly, an inference is made here that characteristic posture in interpersonal situations reveals an underlying emotional disposition, in this case, lack of emotional involvement of the mother with her child. Goldschmidt goes on to suggest that this behavior on the part of the mother constitutes a form of communication to the child, a socialization for low affect.

Goldschmidt's pictures of the Sebei are strikingly different from pictures of mother-child interactions among the Fore of New Guinea, presented by E. R. Sorenson in *The Edge of the Forest* (1976), a volume based on a series of research films.[8] The book contains almost 150 plates of photographs, most of which present a behavioral sequence. One major focus of this research is child development and interactions of adults with children and of children with peers. The rich data, however, are not analyzed fully.

As part of this research, Sorenson wished to study the expression and recognition of emotions among the Fore. He did so in part by showing them a set of pictures of Western subjects expressing a series of emotions, which had been used

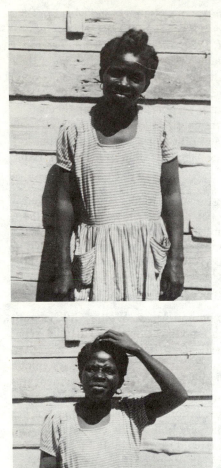

The expression of emotions: Young Haitian woman poses, relaxed, pleased to have her picture taken.

Her facial expression and posture change to show anger at a nasty remark by a neighbor.

previously among college students in the United States. The emotions represented were happiness, sadness, anger, surprise, disgust and contempt. The author remarks: "the most striking result was that the Fore saw anger more often than did Westernized subjects, particularly in the pictures representing sadness or fear" (Sorenson 1976:142). Moreover, when a Fore individual was asked to pose for a picture looking angry, the expression seemed to Sorenson to look more like sadness than anger. Other Fore, however, agreed that the man looked angry.

Sorenson argues that emotions are neurophysiological human universals that, to some extent, are shared with other animals. However, he wonders to what extent culture is relevant to the manner in which emotions are expressed. With regard to what seems to him to be an "atypical" response of the Fore—their contamination of fear and sadness with anger—he suggests the following: Fore traditional social organization is "affiliative," that is, it is informal and based on personal rapport. It is therefore fragile and precarious, and vulnerable to anger. Anger thus represents a danger to the stability of the group. Because they are, presumably, aware of this danger, the Fore have become sensitive to the element of anger in any expression of sadness and fear.

The Study of Affective Reactions

Sorenson's research on the Fore leads to interesting questions concerning the relationship of emotions to their physiological substrate and their bodily expressions. Cultures clearly vary both in the level of affective intensity and in the types of emotional expressions that are sanctioned. They appear also to differ to some extent in the emotions associated with specific facial expressions or bodily symptoms. The first point is clearly illustrated by Goldschmidt's study of Sebei photographs, mentioned earlier. In fact, a large proportion of the culture-and-personality literature argues this difference in affective level, beginning with Mead's (1927) study of Samoan girls. She explained their conflict-free adolescence, it will be remembered, as related to the lack of intense emotional involvement in Samoan interpersonal relationships. Benedict's concept of a Dionysian personality addresses the same subject. In contrast to the low affectivity of the Samoans, we have the high emotional intensity of the Dionysian Plains Indians. Also, groups may be said to differ in the choice of emotions that are repressed while others are given intense development. We have seen in Gladwin's (1957) discussion of the Cheyenne how sexuality and in-group aggression are repressed, and are compensated for by warfare and aggression turned inward against the self in the self-mutilations and tortures of the vision quest and the Sun Dance.

LeVine (1973) has suggested the usefulness of a comparative study of affective experiences for the cross-cultural study of personality dispositions. Following the lead of psychoanalysis with its concern with the emotions, he remarks:

> The expression of fear, rage, sadness, surprise, joy, disgust, shame or sexual arousal, in situations where they are culturally inappropriate; . . . is an indication that a personal motive of some strength and depth is affecting the individual's adaptation in his sociocultural environment (LeVine 1973:226–227).

Specific bodily symptoms of the emotions can be used, he suggests, as "anchor points" for research on affective states, since their investigation may lead from the "social surface of individual behavior" to unconscious strivings. Such comparative research is possible because the symptoms, such as weeping, blushing, and trembling, exist in all human groups, and they are everywhere related to affective states. The specific emotions to which they are linked, however, may vary. In fact, whether or not they vary and how much is in itself a significant research problem. (It must be recalled that Darwin believed in a continuity in the expression of the emotions in animals and man, and many ethologists have taken such a continuity for granted. It would be better to investigate it in the framework of possible cultural differences.)

It is well-known that specific bodily symptoms may be associated with a wide variety of emotions in a single culture. In a small-scale experimental study, a group of my graduate students found that people in the United States report that they weep with grief, rage, joy, disappointment, relief, frustration, fatigue, pity, or self-pity, or when they feel "moved" (as by a film or a musical selection). This list suggests that a limited bodily repertoire of physiological reactions is associated with a much larger repertoire of felt emotions.

There is also reason to believe that an element of learning may intervene between a physiological state of arousal and its subjective interpretation as a particular emotion. The psychologist A. Bandura (1973:106) goes so far as to assert:

> Whether people experience their emotional arousal as fear, anger, euphoria, or some other state depends not on internal somatic cues, but on a number of external defining influences.

Such a social learning position receives strong support from various experimental studies. For example, Stanley Schachter (1964), in a discussion of the "interaction of cognitive and physiological determinants of emotional states," reports on some of his own experiments in this area. In one instance subjects were injected with a drug substance. Some were told they would experience certain side effects, and they did. Others were given no information on the sensations they might experience. Of these subjects, some were exposed to a confederate who behaved in a hostile fashion. These experimental subjects, modeling their interpretations of their aroused state on the confederate, experienced aggressive feelings. Others, exposed to confederates who were cheerful, experienced euphoria. The implication for the anthropologist appears to be that such a patterning of subjective emotional states on models exists not only in individuals in specific, perhaps aberrant, situations, but that socialization may lead to culturally patterned emotional states and behavioral responses to physiological arousal. The evidence for such cultural learning, however, is much less clear than the great quantity of ethnographic materials that illustrates the cultural patterning of the expression of emotions.[9]

LeVine suggests that "public displays of affective reactions with bodily symptoms are usually inconsistent with cultural norms concerning the maintenance of composure in adults" (1973:228). Therefore, the occurrence of such symptoms is a temporary, more or less serious breach of these norms. The investigation of instances of such behavior may lead to the discovery of the norms and of how individuals cope with their infraction. We may also observe that sanctions may be applied to those who violate these norms.

Note, for example, that in the United States we use the expression "to break down" to mean both "to weep" and "to confess." Men, in particular, are expected to show strength of character by exhibiting self-control, and not weeping. It is therefore not surprising that in the 1968 presidential primary campaign Senator Muskie was vigorously criticized for shedding tears in public in responding to the attacks of an opponent. Indeed, this incident was widely believed to have been directly responsible for his losses in that campaign.

Traditionally, norms of emotional expression have differed for men and women. Although weeping was taboo for men and boys in this country, it was acceptable and "to be expected" in women and girls. As the roles of women here are changing, it is not surprising that attitudes toward weeping on the part of women are changing also. This change is illustrated by the story of the female graduate student who, when her work being criticized by a male professor, "broke down." Reportedly, the professor went on to criticize her for her "unprofessional behavior." The implication appears to be, "if you want to have a professional career, like a man, you must live up to male norms of self-control."

The converse of LeVine's assertion is also true, for there are rules that govern when certain bodily symptoms of affective reactions are expected to be displayed. Failure to display them on these occasions may also be considered a breach of norms. Therefore, an investigation of what emotional expressions are considered culturally required in given situations is also psychologically revealing. Examples are readily available: well-bred Victorian young ladies in this country and in Europe were expected to blush at the mention of "delicate" subjects, and an inability to blush might cause the offender to be considered to be lacking in "purity" or "shame." Women of the "better classes" were expected to faint in shock or grief rather than to cope matter-of-factly with certain situations. Fainting in the face of emotional stress represents one way of removing oneself, quite literally if only temporarily, from a difficult situation. Other dissociative reactions may also offer a way out. In societies where a belief in spirit possession exists, a spontaneous possession trance (which is a type of dissociative reaction) represents a possible response to a difficult situation. In Haiti, I heard a number of accounts from *vodou* cult members of situations in which they were frightened and where, they said, a protective spirit took over, as it were, by "possessing" the individual at the critical moment.

A comparison of funeral customs clearly shows different requirements placed on emotional expression. For instance, William Douglass, describing funerals in the Spanish Basque village of Murelaga, observes: "Overt grief is carefully controlled. Immediate female kinsmen (sic) may weep, but men are denied this outlet for their grief, and are expected to remain stoic" (1969:23). This behavior may be contrasted with the description of a funeral maong the Tiwi of Australia by Jane Goodale. Here mourners wail, beat their bodies, and cut their heads with vigorous blows of knives, shovels, and other instruments:

The close relatives directed their grief toward the grave, and they had to be restrained
from doing real bodily harm to themselves . . . The others were given knives and
clubs, which they used on themselves without restraint while facing the immediate
family of the deceased (Goodale 1971:249).

Goodale goes on to suggest that the bloodletting by nonrelatives indicates their
feelings of guilt and that:

all the self-injury in the ritual expression of grief is to show the deceased . . . that they
are sorry if they had anything to do with his death rather than to encourage real
nonritual tears and wails (Goodale 1971:249).

On the one hand, wailing and weeping may be expressions not of grief but of guilt.
On the other hand, ritual requirements of shedding tears may lead to mimed
expressions of emotions. Although we cannot always be sure of the subjective
feelings of actors in ritual situations, we observe that among the Tiwi value is
placed on intense public demonstrations of emotions, which is quite the opposite
of the situation in Spain or the United States. Clearly, societies differ in the degree
to which they value self-control, or, to the contrary, open and intense expressions
of emotions. These values have implications for the ways in which individuals
judge their own feelings and behavior as well as those of others. The Basque may
judge the Tiwi to be "hysterical," excessive, and lacking in restraint or respect-
ability, while those who value demonstrative behavior may consider the others
to be cold, selfish, emotionally unresponsive, and so on.

E. L. Schiefflin, in his small book *The Sorrow of the Lonely and the Burning
of the Dancers* (1976) provides a fascinating example of how emotionally expressive behavior is culturally patterned. The book centers about the Gisaro ceremony
of the Kaluli people of Mt. Bosavi of Papua, New Guinea. Like the Fore, these
people remained isolated from the outside world until quite recently; they were
contacted by Europeans barely forty years ago.

The Gisaro ceremony takes place at night. It is performed by guests, acting as
dancers and singers, for their hosts. The dancers are splendidly decorated with
paints, feathers, and shells. The songs are specifically prepared for the occasion
and deal with the past locations of gardens and houses and with the deaths of the
loved ones of the hosts. It is the specific aim of the dancers and their songs to
provoke the grief of the hosts, who, in anger, burn the dancers with torches. The
burning relieves the hurt feelings of the hosts, who weep and wail, but it does not
compensate them for their pain. At the end of the ceremony, the dancers pay
compensation to their hosts for having made them weep. The author notes that
there is in this ceremony a "painful tension between grief, anger, intimacy and
violence" which "becomes visible when someone from the audience angrily
thrusts the torch out at the dancer's shoulder and then throws his arms around
him, hugging him affectionately and wailing uncontrollably" (Schiefflin
1976:190). The Kaluli feel not only that the creemony provides them with com-

pensation for what they have lost, but also that the ceremony itself is "death-averting." A ceremony, to be good and successful, must cause many people to weep, and they perform it whenever they feel the community is in danger. Schiefflin links this behavior to characteristic processes of their society and the symbolism of their world view. In the present discussion, however, what is of importance is the characteristic patterning and valuing of emotional expressions, which are so alien to us. We find this ritual difficult to understand precisely because the juxtaposition of actions and emotions is foreign.

A comparison between the Tiwi funeral and the Gisaro ceremony of the Kaluli reveals some interesting similarities and differences. In both cases, there is wailing, weeping, violence, and loud public acknowledgement of emotions. Tiwi mourning, however, combines grief with guilt, which is linked to a fear of ghosts and their potential vengeance. The Tiwi express this guilt by turning their aggressive actions against themselves. Both men and women participate in these activities. The sorrow of Kaluli men, on the other hand, combines grief and anger, which is released by turning aggression against other men, who are, however, not blamed for the original loss, but only for having revived the sorrow and caused its expression in weeping and wailing. The anger is pacified through the payment of compensation. Although fear does not appear to be expressed in the Gisaro ritual, it seems to be the motivating force behind its performance. Schiefflin suggests that the ritual, with its joining of sorrow with violence and compensation gives the Kaluli men a sense of self-respect, proving to them that they are not helpless in the face of adversity.

In studying the expression of emotions both in violation of norms and in the fulfillment of norms, we may find the opportunity of exploring the operation of personalities and the definition of sex differences, as well as the operation of the society and the patterning and conceptualization of a particular culturally constituted behavioral environment.

SUMMARY

In this chapter we have reviewed methods used in studying personality in different cultural settings. We have stressed the work of anthropologists, particularly anthropologists from this country, who have been concerned with cultural differences and cultural comparisons.[10] Because we discussed studies of children at some length in Chapter 4, our principal emphasis here has been on the personalities of adults.

We have distinguished two kinds of personality assessments, the *inferential* (or *indirect*) and the *direct*. The inferential methods use cultural products such as belief systems, folklore, art, and games as indicators of central tendencies in the personality type of a cultural group. Many of these studies set out to test specific hypotheses about the relationship between antecedent factors, usually aspects of child training, and cultural products that are interpreted as consequences of these antecedents. A number of the studies of this type that are reviewed in this chapter employ the holocultural method.

The direct methods of personality assessment are techniques of fieldwork. They involve administering specific tests or instruments to a sample of the population under study. Because the tests, for the most part, were developed in Western societies, some modifications in procedures of administration and interpretation may be required. The methods used vary from informal, unstructured interviews to formal, highly structured testing procedures. Among the methods we discussed are the life history, the analysis of dreams, projective techniques (Rorschach, Thematic Apperception Test, Sentence Completion Test), photography, and the study of affective reactions. Although dreams are products of individuals, their content has at times been treated in the same way as folklore.

A number of methods have been used in research with children that are not found or only rarely, in work with adults. In particular, the highly focused time sample observations of behavior, used both by the Whitings and their associates and by Caudill, do not have a major place in work with adults.

It must be stressed that, when any or all of the methods mentioned are used in the field, they are only a portion of a larger enterprise. The basic methods of the anthropologist are always participant observation and the interview. The tests may then constitute only a special type of variant of the basic interview.

A number of conclusions emerge from this rapid review of various methods utilized in cross-cultural research on personality. First, for the most part the several methods yield noncomparable results; that is, they do not yield the same kind of information. Some investigators are primarily interested in certain dimensions of personality, such as the levels of emotional intensity, whereas others wish to discover the typical intrapersonal conflicts encountered in a given culture; still others are concerned with the goals towards which people direct their energies (such as achievement motivation) or the characteristic patterns of interpersonal relationships. Given a sufficiently broad scope of research, it may be necessary to utilize a number of different methods that complement each other. In selecting our methods, then, we must take care to choose those that will yield the information we seek.

Caution is required also in deciding which language we use in our investigation. This fact was shown in the work of Ervin and Doob with bilinguals. As we shall see in our next chapter, language is not only a system of cues that may influence responses. It is also a system for codifying reality, and the realities presented by different languages to their speakers may differ considerably. How these differences influence what people see and hear and how they think about the world is a matter of considerable interest in itself. It may also affect test performance to an important degree.

We shall also mention some of the personality tests discussed here in Chapter 9, in the context of cultural change. As we have already seen, a number of the studies we have reviewed briefly are, in fact, investigations of the effects of acculturation and of the adaptation of individuals and groups to social and cultural changes. The tests reported on in this chapter have been important tools in such research.

NOTES

1. Most of the life histories or autobiographies discussed in this chapter are based on unstructured interviews. Some investigators have obtained life history materials for specific purposes and therefore provided some direction to the reminiscences of their informants. For example, Louise Spindler (1962) used the technique of the "expressive autobiographical interview" in working with a sample of sixteen Menomini women. This study of the adaptation of women to culture change will be referred to again in Chapter 9.

2. To this list we might add *Pedro Martinez* (1964), *A Death in the Sánchez Family* (1966), and with Ruth M. Lewis and Susan M. Ringdon, *Four Women: Living the Revolution: An Oral History of Contemporary Cuba (1977)*.

3. The complete text of Nelly's life history is in Bourguignon (1956).

4. Whether psychoanalytic interpretations of symbols in dreams can be useful in the analysis of non-Western dreams has been discussed by Seligman (1924), Róheim (1947), Kluckhohn and Morgan (1951), and Honigmann (1961), among others. Bruce (1975) discusses dream symbolism among the Lacandon Mayas of Chiapas, Mexico, and shows both the interpretational system of the Lacandon and an application of Freudian principles.

5. This dream and dreaming in Haitian culture are discussed in Bourguignon (1954).

6. A number of anthropologists have noted over the years that the Rorschach Test is a valuable interview device for the fieldworker, yielding a great deal more than merely a set of scores. See G. Spindler (1978c) for an interesting discussion of this point.

7. The Boltons have shown the importance of adultery in much of the violence and litigation among the Qolla (Bolton and Bolton 1975).

8. See E. R. Sorenson's interesting film, *Growing Up as a Fore* (1971).

9. See Weston La Barre's article, "The Cultural Basis of Emotion and Gesture," in *Journal of Personality*, 1947 (16):49–68. This important contribution has also been reprinted in *Personal Character and the Cultural Milieu* (3rd ed.), edited by D. G. Haring, Syracuse University Press, 1956.

10. Psychologists have devised a broad range of testing methods, many of which, however, have not found cross-cultural applications. Much current personality research in this country is carried out in a laboratory setting, under controlled experimental conditions. For a review of the field, see Blass (1977).

6
Perception and Cognition

INTRODUCTION: CONSTRUCTING THE WORLD

A jungle raised Kpelle child is taken at around age ten to the capital city of Monrovia (Liberia), where large tanker ships can be seen far at sea from a tall hotel on a hilltop. The child, who has never seen such a view before and who was not familiar with tankers, commented on the bravery of the men who would go out to sea in such small boats (Cole and Scribner 1974:97).

The Nuer have no expression equivalent to "time" in our language, and they cannot therefore, as we can, speak of time as though it were something actual, which passes, can be wasted, can be saved, and so forth. I do not think they ever experience the same feeling of fighting against time or of having to coordinate activities with an abstract passage of time ... (Evans-Pritchard 1940:103)

Among the Tetum people of Eastern Timor, in Indonesia the wombs of women and buffalo cows, the rear room of the house, and pregnant stones symbolize the sacred world. When a child is born, a buffalo cow is expected to give birth to a calf and a pregnant stone to give birth to a baby stone ... (Hicks 1976:23).

What are we to make of such reports? Are there differences in the way in which members of different cultural groups perceive the world? Are there differences in how they think?

THE BACKGROUND OF THE PROBLEM

Anthropologists have collected much interesting and striking, although mostly anecdotal, information concerning the cultural relativity of perception. Whether there are differences among cultural groups in the processes, as well as the content, of thought has been much debated. Yet there is still too little systematic knowledge available to provide even tentative answers.

Part of the difficulty in obtaining answers lies in the choice of methods of investigation. The research falls somewhere between anthropology and psychology; the problems encountered have reflected some of the conflicts, disputes, and uncertainties both within these two disciplines and between them.

The contact between studies of perception and cognition on the one hand and personality and culture of the other has been even more recent; in fact, most of the reviews of psychological anthropology do not deal with this subject area at all. For one thing, the systematic experimental work in this field has been done by psychologists, who have ventured only rarely into cross-cultural research. In particular, psychologists from the United States rarely have worked among "primitive" peoples. At present, however, the situation has changed drastically from what it was only a few years ago. Gradually, in the years since World War II, an increasing number of psychologists from the United States and Europe have been working in the former colonial areas of Africa and in other parts of the Third World.

S. Biesheuvel, of the University of Witwatersrand, has written of

> the demand for educational and vocational selection tests in the developing countries. Pressure for the rapid advancement of the indigenous populations, coupled with limited scholastic and training resources, compelled the sorting out of those who could make the best use of available opportunities. Measuring devices of proved validity in Western contexts generally required substantial modification, or entirely new approaches had to be devised, for effective prediction in different cultures (1974:xi).

Among the fields of comparative interest, under these circumstances, Biesheuvel further stresses that

> cognition . . . deserves priority because of its major role in the process of adaptation to change and acculturation to Western technological demands with which all developing countries are currently confronted (1974:xii).

These practical problems, together with the growth of school systems and institutions of higher learning in the developing countries, have led to a mushrooming of studies by psychologists on differences between cultural groups in perception and cognition. There is now a *Journal of Cross-Cultural Psychology* and an International Association for Cross-Cultural Psychology, which held its first meeting in 1972 in Hong Kong. However, cross-cultural psychology is taught systematically in few universities here as yet.

Anthropologists usually have dealt with perception and cognition in broader contexts such as world views and belief systems. Sometimes also the relationship between language and culture has been a focal point for discussions of group differences in thought processes and the perception of reality. However, there exist, as we shall see, more specific points of contact between research into perception and cognition on the one hand and into personality on the other. We mentioned some of them in Chapter 5. For example, in our discussion of the Rorschach test we noted that subjects are required to tell what they "see" in the inkblots, and their responses are referred to as "percepts." The blots are "seen" or read, as it were, rather than "interpreted." Then the subjects are asked to state what caused them to see what they saw: the form, the color, the shading, the portion of the blot utilized, and so on. It is held that a subject's perceptual approach to the inkblots reveals personality dispositions. Another, rather different, reference to perception came in our discussion of picture tests, in which mention was made of the observation that inexperienced subjects had difficulty in dealing with perspective in drawings and thus misread the pictures. Also, we saw that the Fore, in looking at photographs of facial expressions, misperceived certain emotions, and this was interpreted by the investigator in that case as indicative of their own affective orientations. Thus, both in interpreting data and in applying certain research techniques, we had to deal with the subject of perception. We also referred to perception in Chapter 2, in our discussion of behavioral evolution. Here we noted, following Jerison, that the brain labels and organizes information acquired by means of the sense organs. In humans, the resulting behavioral environment is culturally constituted, for culturally learned orientations define, specify, evaluate, and interpret the information derived through the senses. This framework is culturally variable, a point we shall pursue in more detail and with greater precision in this chapter.

Defining Our Terms

Let us begin with some definitions. *Perception* and *cognition* are terms derived from laboratory psychology. Cole and Scribner (1974:2) suggest a possible definition of cognition, on which psychologists of different persuasions might agree: "those processes by which man acquires, transforms and uses information about the world." By perception, they say, psychologists usually mean "processes by which people organize and experience information that is primarily sensory in origin" (p. 61).

Anthropologists have generally used the term more broadly. Segall, Campbell, and Herskovits, after reviewing some major anthropological studies dealing with the subject of perception, remark:

> While we would be hard put to specify the boundary between perception and cognition—since both processes can be inferred only from overt behavior—we would argue that the more cognitive the behavior actually studied, the more equivocal the evidence provided for the proposition that culture influences perception (1966:25).

However, it was precisely that proposition they wished to test, because it is of considerable importance to both psychologists and anthropologists. One of the most vigorous and long-lasting debates in psychology has been carried on between "nativists," who hold that perception is governed by universal constant laws, and "empiricists," who argue for the importance of learning and experience as factors in perception.[1] The research undertaken by Segall, Campbell and Herskovits had its beginnings in a running debate between the anthropologist, M. J. Herskovits, who argued that cultural differences are so pervasive that they might well also affect perception, and the psychologist, Donald Campbell, who expected to find confirmation only for the operation of basic constant laws of perception.

Does Culture Influence Perception?

To shed light on whether or not culture influences perception, Segall, Campbell, and Herskovits sought an area of testing in which cognitive processes, such as classification or memory, were not called upon. They decided to investigate cross-culturally the susceptibility to optical illusions. In formulating hypotheses to be tested, they argued that both cultural and ecological factors influence visual perception. Therefore they expected that Westerners, living in a "carpentered world," with right angles that do not exist in nature, would be more susceptible to two optical illusions, the Müller-Lyer illusion and the Sanders parallelogram, than people who are not habituated to such an environment. These illusions involve "figures constructed of lines meeting in nonrectangular junctions." People accustomed to a "carpentered world" should tend to "rectangularize these junctions" (Segall et al. 1966:96). That is, they would be likely to treat the forms as if they were drawings representing three-dimensional objects in perspective in two-dimensional media. On the other hand, they expected people living in open spaces with wide horizons to be susceptible to two forms of horizontal-vertical illusions. This hypothesis is ecological rather than cultural. A horizontal-vertical illusion "results from a tendency to counteract the foreshortening of lines extended into space away from the viewer" (Segall et al. 1966:97). The hypothesis assumes that this tendency would be useful to people living in situations of open terrain and broad vistas. On the other hand, people who have less opportunity to see the horizon, such as forest, canyon, and city dwellers should be less susceptible to the illusion.

These tests were used on some fifteen cultural groups, including twenty-three different samples and close to 2000 individuals. Of the cultures included, thirteen were African, one (the Hanunóo) was located in the Philippines, another was a group of South African Europeans, and two samples were studied in Evanston, Illinois. On the whole, the results of this large-scale study supported the original hypotheses. Segall and his associates conclude cautiously:

> Cross-cultural differences were found that we consider to be reliable, and not artifactual . . . and probably best understood as the results of experience and reasonably in line with the particular empiricist hypotheses (1966:194).

Test materials consisted of fifty different drawings, each illusion being represented by several variants, and performance results were not uniform. That is, in each group some people behaved counter to the hypothesized manner. There were other inconsistencies in the data. One of the deviant cases consisted of a sample of black South African mine workers. These people live in a carpentered environment; yet they were little susceptible to the Müller-Lyer illusion. A possible explanation was that they had lived in this environment only relatively recently.

Another investigator, M. L. Bonté (1960, cited in Segall et al.) attempted to test a group of Bambuti pygmies. The drawings were incomprehensible to the people, so she used a movable wooden model instead. On this instrument Europeans, Bambuti, and an agricultural African group, the Bashi, showed little difference in performance.

It is important to mention these details because the methods employed in the tests may very likely affect the results, and only results obtained with identical procedures may, strictly speaking, be compared. G. Jahoda (1966) sought to replicate the study of Segall and his associates with three different cultural groups in Ghana. Two groups, the Lobi and Dagomba of Northern Ghana live in round huts without carpentered furnishings, in open parkland country. The Ashanti of Central Ghana were the third group. There subjects were selected in villages located in the tropical rain forest. Their houses, which contain carpentered furniture, are rectangular in form. Both the Northern groups and the Ashanti subjects were illiterate. Jahoda stresses this last point, for he argues that literacy is a significant variable that Segall and his associates had neglected to take into account. The Müller-Lyer illusion, he notes, includes two distinct elements: the "carpentered environment" and the interpretation of two-dimensional drawings, and a distinction between the two is important in dealing with illiterates unaccustomed to drawings. For materials, Jahoda employed constructions of white plastic with black lines. Segall had used both black and red lines.

The results of Jahoda's experiments did not support the original hypotheses. On the horizontal-vertical illusion, the Ashanti, in their closed-in rain forest villages, were intermediate to the two Northern groups with their wide open spaces and broad vistas. On the Müller-Lyer illusion, the Ashanti, with their rectangular houses, were not significantly different from the two other groups. For this illusion, Jahoda suggests that illiteracy is the major factor, operative in addition to the carpentered world element. Results on the horizontal-vertical illusion are puzzling to him, although he suggests the possibility that the apparatus used might have been of importance.

Does Biology Influence Culture?

The studies by Segall and his associates, Jahoda, and several other investigators clearly show that group differences in susceptibility to optical illusions do exist. However, there were enough discrepancies in the data to suggest that factors other than those hypothesized might also be operative. Some of those factors are the exact methods and materials used in testing, literacy, and familiarity with the graphic representation of three-dimensional objects. R. H. Pollack (1970) has suggested yet another possible factor, neither ecological nor cultural, but physiological. Pollack, presenting children with the Müller-Lyer illusion on a tachistoscope, found a relationship between density of optical pigmentation and the ability to discern contours. This ability is, in turn, related to performance on the Müller-Lyer illusion: the greater the density of pigmentation, the less the susceptibility to the illusion. Denser eye pigmentation is related to skin pigmentation, and Pollack found that darker-skinned children in this country were less susceptible to the illusion than lighter-skinned children.

Pollack's work encouraged several other investigators to pursue this physiological line of reasoning in their research. Jahoda (1971), for example, found African and Scottish subjects performing differently depending on whether the stimulus material for the Müller-Lyer illusion consisted of blue or red lines; however, contrary to the original expectations, the Africans turned out to be more susceptible to the illusion than the Scottish subjects.

M. C. Bornstein (1973) suggested that susceptibility to the Müller-Lyer illusion is a function of visual acuity, and that acuity varies with intraocular pigmentation. He found support for this thesis by reanalyzing the original test data obtained by Segall, Campbell, and Herskovits (Bornstein 1975). In fact, the pigmentation hypothesis appeared to account better for the data than the "carpentered world" hypothesis. Specifically, it seemed to account for certain deviant cases, such as the South African mine workers, who now fitted in with other dark-pigmented groups, as did the Ashanti of Jahoda's research. Bornstein concludes that environment, culture, and physiology must all be taken into account in attempting to explain perceptual behavior.

Seeking to deal with group differences, on what appear to be, at first blush, simple perceptual tasks, has turned out to be a most complex and difficult undertaking! For the story does not end with Bornstein, either. A number of other investigators have proceeded to test Bornstein's hypothesis. Bolton and his associates (1975) sought to set up a "critical test" to evaluate the relative merits of Bornstein's physiological hypothesis in contrast to that of Segall, Campbell, and Herskovits, who look to learning and environmental cues to account for differences in illusion susceptibility. According to Bornstein, eye pigmentation should increase (and visual acuity decrease) with proximity to the equator. Bolton's group adds a further variable, altitude. They selected two settings for their test: one with high altitude and broad vistas in the Peruvian high plains, and another with lower altitude and limited view in the Peruvian jungle. Both, however, are equally close to the equator, and both had equally carpentered environments. Moreover, there appeared to be no significant differences in pigmentation. They conclude that their results provide no support for the visual acuity hypothesis, but do confirm the hypothesis formulated by Segall, Campbell, and Herskovits.

Bornstein's main interest, however, does not lie in the phenomenon of susceptibility to illusion. This phenomenon is only part of a larger problem, differences in visual acuity and, in particular, color vision. Bornstein (1975) argues that color vision varies with optical pigmentation, which, in turn, is related to distance from the equator. Differences in color vision should be reflected in the geographic distribution of color vocabularies. He therefore studied such vocabularies for a sample of 145 societies. In this sample he found that 50 percent of the languages used only one term for blue and green, others identified blue and black, and still others grouped blue, green, and black together. Pursuing the matter further, Bornstein (1975) goes on to argue that physiological differences cause differences in color perception that are revealed in language. Reversing the title of the book by Segall, Campbell, and Herskovits, he called his 1975 article "The Influence of Visual Perception on Culture," culture being represented by color vocabularies.

The basic structures of the human eye that make color vision possible are three different types of photoreceptor cells, which are sensitive to blue, green, and yellow-red. However, Bornstein argues, density of pigmentation in the eye, which screens the light waves that reach the photoreceptor cells, differs by region. As a result, color vision also differs. As Coon (1965:235) points out, "eye color is correlated in general with skin color, but in some parts of the eye more than in others. Pigment is found in four parts of the eyeball: the sclera, the deep layers of the iris, the outer layers of the iris, and the retina." Although there is some association between skin color and the color of the iris (the colored part of the eye we can see), the greatest correlation appears to exist between skin color and retinal pigmentation, which can be examined only with optical instruments. Bornstein refers primarily to the pigmentation of the retina. He finds evidence that this pigmentation, which is genetically determined, is adaptive in responding to ultraviolet light, which is of greater intensity in the tropics. By protecting the eye under these circumstances, the pigments have positive, adaptive value in these environments, and they also promote visual acuity by screening out harmful rays. On the other hand, they do so at the cost of reducing sensitivity to blue. It is this physiological difference in color vision that, Bornstein suggests, underlies differences in color vocabularies. He concludes, "Color at its most basically organized level is, apparently, subject to absolutist rather than relativistic interpretation" (Bornstein 1975:791). Or, in the terms used by Segall, Campbell, and Herskovits, according to Bornstein it is the nativists rather than the empiricists who, after more than one hundred years of controversy, win this particular argument. Whereas Segall and his associates argue for ecological adaptation through cultural invention and learning, Bornstein argues for biological adaptation of which culture (language) constitutes merely a reflection.

COLOR VOCABULARIES AND COLOR VISION: A BRIEF HISTORY

Several authors, including Segall, Campbell, and Herskovits (1966), Berlin and Kay (1969), and Bornstein (1975), have reviewed the lengthy history of the controversy surrounding the relationship between color vocabularies and visual color discrimination. Depending on the authors' points of view and the conclusions reached, the history is evaluated somewhat differently, although many of the principal protagonists considered are the same.

The argument began in 1858, with the British statesman William Gladstone, who, as Lowie (1937:105) put it "piqued himself on his classical scholarship." He noted the paucity of color distinctions in Homeric Greek, where one word was used for *blue, grey,* and *dark.* Similarly, only one word was used for *white* and *bright.* On the basis of this observation he argued that the ancient Greeks could not have seen colors as modern English-speaking people do.

The argument was taken up by a number of other scholars, and a heated debate ensued. According to Lowie, "the upshot . . . was to rule out deficiencies in vocabulary as indicative of racial inferiority" (Lowie 1937:105). Nevertheless, various of Gladstone's successors in this debate, who explored color vocabularies in ancient writings, including the Bible, and among contemporary primitives as evidenced in the ethnographic literature, came to the conclusion that ancient and primitive peoples had "defective" color vocabularies and "defective" color vision. They argued on the basis of this observation, in the temper of the times, that both color vision (biology) and color vocabulary (culture) had evolved over the ages, contemporary primitives being remnants of an ancient past.

Probably the first attempt to put the idea of a linkage between color vocabulary and color discrimination to the test came when Rudolf Virchow (1878:79), the famous German pathologist, examined several Nubians. He found that although their vocabulary lacked certain color terms, they were able to distinguish hues adequately in several different kinds of tasks. This finding raised the possibility that color vocabulary might, after all, not be an adequate indicator of visual ability. Virchow's findings were supported by the work of a comparative psychologist, Grant Allen (1879), who was interested in human color perception within a larger framework of cross-species comparison. Again collecting data from literary sources, as well as from missionaries and others in remote places, Allen concluded that there is no difference in color perception among human groups, although there are differences in vocabulary. To account for the differences in terminologies, he developed a theory of the evolution of color vocabularies.

The major early field research in this area was carried out by W. H. R. Rivers (1901), initially as part of the 1899 Cambridge Expedition to the Torres Straits (between Northern Australia and New Guinea), where he participated in a major study of several ethnic groups, and later in his work among the Dravidian-speaking Toda of South India. Among other data, Rivers collected color vocabularies, and he also tested natives of various groups for color discriminations, using equipment he had previously employed in England. He, too, found "deficient" color vocabularies that failed to distinguish among several hues; as Bornstein points out, in particular, the distinction between blue and green was lacking. He also found a certain visual insensitivity to differences between certain colors. Rivers concluded that vocabulary reflected sensory perception. Yet shortly thereafter, other experimenters, such as Woodworth (1905–1906), obtained contrary results. Working with members of several Filipino groups whose languages lacked verbal distinctions among blue, green, and violet, he found that they were none-theless able to make discriminations among them on sorting tests.

In attempting to assess the results of the tests conducted by Virchow, Rivers, and Woodworth, which seem to be clearly in contradiction with each other, it appears likely that the specific tools, methods, and settings that were used in the testing of visual discrimination may have been important factors in the results obtained. After the early years of the century, however, psychologists ceased to carry on comparative cross-cultural experiments of this sort, and we have to wait until a much later period before this part of the story continues.

Does Language Make a Difference?

The next phase of this research shifts from psychological tests of visual acuity and theories of biological and cultural evolution to considerations of cultural and linguistic relativity. In the United States, linguists Edward Sapir and Benjamin Lee Whorf, in particular, argued that linguistic categories are highly variable and that people experience the world in terms of the categories of their languages. Whorf (1956), in a series of brilliant papers, showed how dramatically different American Indian languages, such as Hopi, are from what he termed Standard Average European. Observed reality is divided differently: where English has one word for "water," Hopi has two, distinguishing between moving water and water in a container. Moreover, while English has tenses, differentiating actions by periods of time (such as past, present, and future), Hopi has verb forms that distinguish what Whorf calls different kinds of "validity." That is, Hopi distin-guishes statements of fact, whether past or present, from statements based on memory, on expectation, and so on.

If natural objects such as water, or experiential dimensions such as time are labeled and experienced differently, could not the same hold true for categories of color? One might then argue, on the basis of linguistic relativity, that if there is indeed an association between sorting behavior and language categories, such an association shows the priority of language over behavior. Language provides categories for behavior that override sensory input. Roger Brown (1958:211) observes that, considering three dimensions of color—hue, brightness, and satura-tion—7500 million color differences can be identified; yet

> the largest collection of English color names runs to less than 4000 entries. Evidently there is categorization of colors among speakers of English. It seems likely that all human beings with healthy visual apparatus will be able to make much the same set of discriminations. This ability is probably standard equipment for the species . . . This is not to say that people everywhere either see or think of the color world in the same way. Cultural differences probably operate on the level of categorization rather than controlled laboratory discrimination (Brown 1958:238).

Various bits of evidence may be cited in support of this position. For example, the neuropsychiatrist Kurt Goldstein (1948) worked with soldiers who had received head injuries in the First World War. Some of these men were aphasic, and among the words they had lost were the names of colors. In seeking to test the effect of their injuries, Goldstein had them match colored yarns. Those who lacked the appropriate words had difficulty sorting the yarns by hue. Having lost the word, they appeared to have lost the category on which their actions (matching) were to be based. Their visual acuity had not been affected.

Quite a different example comes from Leonard Doob (1960:199), who carried on research among the Zulu. The Zulu language has a single term for red and yellow, and another term for blue and green. In a sorting task, combinations based on the color terms would be expected to occur by chance 33 percent of the time. A sample of rural Zulu women and a sample of urban Zulu women were both asked to sort deflated balloons. Among the rural women, sorting followed the color terms 50 percent of the time, whereas it followed them in only 23 percent of the cases among the urban women. That is, the color terminology influenced sorting to a much higher degree among the rural women than among the urban women.

If color terms reflect visual sensitivity, how can we account for such great differences between rural and urban people of the same pigmentation? The importance of acculturation and possibly the learning of a Western language appear to be significant factors here. In this connection, Doob also mentions that Ganda, which does not distinguish between blue and green, has borrowed the English word "blue" to facilitate such a verbal distinction. This borrowing, too, suggests that the dark-pigmented Ganda can see the difference between blue and green and will make a verbal distinction when the words are available in the vocabulary. It seems to be the contact with English-speaking people, however, that created the need to do·so.

In Haitian Creole a distinction between blue and green is also absent.[2] The problem of the visual discrimination between the two hues arose when I administered the Rorschach test in French to a young schoolteacher. He had grown up speaking Creole, and French, used in formal situations, was a second language to him. Looking at Card 9, he pointed to the green area of the blot and said, "Here, in the blue. . . ." When asked about this color word, he replied rather testily that he knew that such a distinction was made in French, but to make it he had to attend to it; it was not a difference that mattered to him. This reply is reminiscent of comments made by native speakers of French who can distinguish, and also pronounce, the initial *h* sound in English words such as "hear" and "hall," but who find it of no significance because the *h* sound is not phonemic in French, that is, it does not alter the meaning of syllables to which it is attached. Yet it is obvious that we are not dealing here with a defect in hearing!

Do Lexical Differences Imply Cognitive Differences?

A number of studies have sought to test this theory of linguistic relativity as it applies to the relationship between color vocabulary and color recognition.

Brown and Lenneberg (1954), in a study that has been widely referred to and that has led to a number of later explorations, devised experiments to test a proposition inherent in Whorf's thesis: that the existence of lexical differences implies the existence of cognitive differences. In contrast to the earlier studies we have reviewed, this research was no longer directed toward the discovery of group differences in sensory acuity or the capacity to discriminate between colors visually. Rather, the investigation concerned cognitive processes such as classification and memory.

In setting up their experiments, Brown and Lenneberg developed a variable they called "codability." A highly codable category is one that is named by a single, short word; a category with low codability, on the other hand, requires a paraphrase of several words. They expected, and confirmed experimentally, that categories labeled with one short word, that is, having high codability, will be produced readily and with little hesitation, and also will produce a high degree of agreement among subjects. Given the fact that color vocabularies differ among speakers of different languages, a stimulus that has high codability for one group may have low codability for another. This fact does not mean that it cannot be recognized and described by circumlocutions. There would, however, be more hesitation and less agreement.

Such a difference in codability is, of course, not limited to the domain of color. In fact, it represents a constant practical problem to the anthropologist who wishes to describe in English practices and institutions for which there are no simple English words. For example, the person an Ojibwa man calls his *ninəm*, we would have to describe in English as his female cousin who is the daughter of his father's sister or mother's brother or another relative so categorized. Anthropology has invented a shorter technical phrase, which is still cumbersome: "female cross-cousin, man speaking."

Although, as we see, we are able to specify the category *ninəm* in English, what we produce to do so is closer to an explanation than to a label. We have no comparable category in English.[3] We lack the word because we lack the social institution to which it is linked. There is, of course, a major difference between kinship terms, which refer to institutions that vary from society to society, and color terms, which refer to aspects of nature that are presumably constant throughout the world.

In their study of color codability, Brown and Lenneberg worked with students at Harvard and Radcliffe whose native language was English. They began by presenting to a group of judges the series of 240 Munsell chips and asking them to pick out the "best examples" of the eight English color terms most widely in use: red, orange, yellow, green, blue, purple, pink, and brown. There was high agreement among the judges. Using this series as a basis for a grouping of twenty-four chips, they asked another group of subjects, tested individually, to name each color as rapidly as they could. Of this group of subjects, five were retested a month later. They found significant relationships between the length of the color term (number of syllables), reaction time, agreement among subjects, and for those who were recalled, consistency of response. However, the strongest indicator of codability—the item most strongly related to length of term—was agreement among subjects.

Once this study was completed, the authors proceeded to investigate the relationship between codability and the ability to recognize colors. A new set of subjects was used, and they were exposed to four of the original twenty-four color chips. They were then asked to identify these four in a larger set of 120 chips. The results showed a high correlation between codability and recognition. How were subjects able to recognize the colors? On the basis of interviews with several subjects in a pretest, Brown and Lenneberg found that subjects said they had remembered the names of the four colors and had used these names as an aid in recognition. Brown and Lenneberg further tested the relationship between codability and memory, by comparing recognition after various time intervals. The best recognition was found when the time interval was the longest and the subjects were occupied with other tasks during that period. This finding again suggests that it is the storage of the verbal label that facilitates the task of recognition.

Lenneberg and Roberts (1956) replicated a portion of this study among the Zuni, where they found a comparable relationship between codability and recognition. However, since Zuni uses a single term for yellow and orange, subjects had difficulty distinguishing between the two. This difficulty was not found to occur among native speakers of English. However, bilingual speakers of Zuni and English made this error much less frequently than monolingual Zunis.

This latter point again reinforces the idea that codability affects performance. As we saw earlier with our Haitian and Zulu examples, the bilingual Zunis illustrate the argument that when simple terms are made available to individuals who previously lacked them, they learn to make discriminations more readily than when such terms are not available to them. This fact suggests that we are not dealing here with sensory differences, for if differences in color discrimination and recognition were due to such biological factors, the type of learning indicated in the behavior of bilinguals, or of more highly acculturated individuals, would be unlikely. Lenneberg and Roberts, of course, were not at all concerned with such possible physiological differences among groups. It will also be remembered that Bornstein's thesis, which was developed only later, does not deal with yellow and orange, the longer wavelengths in the color spectrum.

With the two studies we have just summarized, the concept of codability seemed well established. However, in the years following these researches, other investigators working in the same area obtained results that cast doubt on the relationship between codability and recognition. To resolve some of the contradictions that emerged from these newer investigations, Lantz and Stefflre (1964) developed the concept of *communication accuracy*, which, they claimed, was a better predictor of color recognition. This concept means that whether a short word or a long phrase is the best identifier in remembering, recognizing, and identifying a color to others, depends on the color involved. Moreover, which colors are best identified by short words and which by longer, more descriptive terms depends on the specific language. This latter point was also confirmed by Stefflre and associates (1966) in a study in Mexico, comparing Maya speakers to Spanish speakers.

These studies refined the understanding of the relationship between language and color recognition. However, the concept of linguistic relativity still was applied to color throughout this period.

Color Terms and Cultural Evolution Reexamined

A major challenge to linguistic relativity in the domain of color classification came in 1969 with the publication of *Basic Color Terms: Their Universality and Evolution,* by Brent Berlin and Paul Kay. As its title indicates, this ambitious study is a direct attack on the Sapir-Whorf tradition. The authors argue that they have discovered universals of color classification and also that there exists a clear-cut evolutionary sequence in the development of color terminologies. Specifically, Berlin and Kay claim that all languages have from two to eleven basic color terms, three of them referring to achromatic colors (black, white, grey), and eight to chromatic colors (red, green, yellow, blue, brown, purple, pink, orange). Basic color terms are said to be simple and not reducible to anything else. They are said to cover broad areas of reference, which subsume the range of nonbasic terms. For instance, in English *sea green* and *jade green* refer to subdivisions of the region covered by the broader basic term *green.* It is expected that basic terms will be used more frequently by speakers of the language than the nonbasic terms.

Berlin and Kay collected color vocabularies from speakers of twenty languages and from ethnographic and dictionary sources on another seventy-eight languages. They then asked their informants to choose the "best" examples of each color from an array of Munsell color chips. Next they asked them to indicate all the chips of varying colors that could be referred to by the same term. The ranges of the color terms varied widely, but the best choices, or "foci," clustered about the same area of the color space, as represented by the array of chips.

On the basis of these findings Berlin and Kay argue that although the boundaries of color areas vary from language to language, the central areas are constant; anthropologists, they claim, had previously been misled into thinking in relativistic terms because they paid attention to these varying boundaries rather than to the constant foci. Moreover, the eleven basic color terms represent an evolutionary series. All languages have two basic color terms, for black and white, and the simplest languages are those that have only these two terms. The second stage is represented by languages that have three terms, and these terms are always for black, white, and red. The third stage adds either green or yellow, and the fourth the other. Stage five adds blue, and stage six brown. The remaining stage involves the addition of terms for any or all of the remaining four basic colors: purple, pink, orange, and grey. In other words, growth of color vocabulary is orderly. There are no three-term languages that have terms for black, white, and green, or four-term languages that have terms for purple, pink, yellow, and brown.

This study involves two major theoretical propositions: 1) human visual perception is universally the same making a constant distinction between focal and peripheral colors; and 2) the development of color terminology has followed an orderly, consistent evolutionary sequence. The second proposition is documented from synchronic data, that is, from current languages with color vocabularies of varying sizes, not from diachronic, that is, historic or prehistoric sources.

Cultural Evolution Versus Physiological Adaptation: The Debate

Both of these propositions have been variously hailed and challenged in the lively debate that has followed the publication of this book. Bornstein (1975) for example, has acclaimed the test data produced by Berlin and Kay but considers their evolutionary theory "paradoxical." According to him the simpler, "deficient" color vocabularies appear in the tropics not because many of these people have socially and technologically less complex cultures, as Berlin and Kay argue, but because they are biologically adapted to their environments by dense optical pigmentation.

A number of elements in the research methods employed by Berlin and Kay in their original work have been questioned also. The first has to do with the use of informants. In the case of only one language, Tzeltal, was systematic fieldwork carried out, and tests were conducted with as many as forty informants. For the other nineteen languages, bilingual informants, living in the San Francisco Bay area, were used. As we have already seen in several examples, bilingualism and acculturation may affect test performance with regard to color discrimination. Also, although Berlin and Kay claim that all the "best" examples of the basic color terms, the *foci,* were closely clustered, their evidence shows that the precise amount of clustering varied from color to color. The translation of color terms raises another important and difficult question, and the use of dictionaries is not comparable to the systematic elicitation of terms from informants. Incidentally, the question of translation was already raised by Titchener (1916) in his critique of Rivers' work at the turn of the century.

There is also the fact that selecting chips from an array is an artificial situation. How comparable is it to situations in everyday life? Can color terminology and color selection obtained in such a situation be used as an indicator of classification, categorization, and experience of color in daily life?[4] Admittedly, this issue represents a somewhat different research problem, but it is important not to assume that the work by Berlin and Kay sheds any light on it. For example, in a modern industrial society such as the United States there are several different sociocultural domains of color: those of the optical physicist, the opthalmologist, the color chemist, the fashion designer, the homemaker, the rose fancier, and so on.[5]

By contrast, we may ask, how do people manage who have only two basic color terms, black and white? What does the world look like to them? Karl Heider (1970) describes the color terminology and its use among one such people, the

Dugum Dani of New Guinea (West Irian). The basic terms are *modla,* which he translates as "light or bright," and which includes red in its range, and *mili,* "dark or dull." These terms are used, among other things, to contrast the skin color of Europeans and of the dark-skinned Dani themselves. Yet the varieties of sweet potatoes that have darker flesh, ranging from yellow to orange, are referred to as *modla,* perhaps because these colors seem brighter. In addition to these basic terms, there are other terms, which are linked more specifically to certain animals, for example, but whose name may be used metaphorically as a color term: for example, *gut,* the name of the white heron, may be used to describe or refer to certain white clays.

In a more detailed discussion, E. R. Heider (1972) showed that *mili* also includes in its range blues and greens, "cool" colors, and *modla* also covers reds and yellows, "warm" colors. Such evidence on Stage 1, or two-term, languages has led to the recognition that "black" and "white" are not adequate translations for these two terms. As a result, terms with such broad coverage have more recently been referred to as "composite colors" or "macrocolors" (Kay and McDaniel 1975, Wittkowski and Brown 1977). In Stage 1 "macrowhite" and "macroblack" categorize not only the entire spectrum by two-part opposition, but also two other types of attributes of the color space. Macrowhite covers light and warm colors, whereas macroblack covers dark and cool colors. Wittkowski and Brown (1977) suggest, furthermore, that when a third term, "macrored," is added, the light/warm category is split. In Stage 2 languages, then, macrored is associated with warm colors, macrowhite with light colors, but macroblack still remains linked to both dark and cool.

A Test of Two Competing Explanations

We now have two competing evolutionary theories concerning the size of the color vocabulary. Bornstein's theory concerns biological evolution, and the theory of Berlin and Kay concerns cultural evolution. How can we decide between them?

Melvin Ember (1978) has shown for a sample of thirty-one cases, that societies with six or more basic color terms are more likely to be further distant from the equator than those with fewer terms. Naroll (1970), in an earlier study, had shown that societies with six or more color terms are more complex. On the basis of a control analysis, Ember then found that complexity and distance from the equator interact, both influencing the size of the color vocabulary. In other words,

high societal complexity does not predict size of the basic color lexicon in societies close to the equator, and ... light eye pigmentation [presumed to exist in higher latitudes] does not predict size of the basic color lexicon in less complex societies ... [This] suggest[s] that we have an example here of cultural and biological factors interacting as determinants of a semantic domain (Ember 1978:366–367).

Ember's findings may provide a significant contribution to a partial resolution of the puzzle.

A Color Vocabulary in Action

Descriptive intracultural analysis can give us insights that large-scale statistical studies cannot furnish. They can provide us with a better idea of how codes that include only a small number of basic color terms actually operate. Such a detailed study of the workings of a color code was published more than twenty years ago by Harold Conklin (1955). His study concerns Hanunóo, a language of the island of Mindoro in the Philippines.

Conklin tells us that Hanunóo has four basic color terms, on which there is complete agreement. These terms may be translated as "black," "white," "red," and "green." The focus of red is "orange-red," and that of green is "leaf-green," but each of the four terms has a broad range. Although Hanunóo has a term for green and lacks a separate term for blue, this fact does not mean, as one might infer from Bornstein, that they do not distinguish between the two. Blue, indigo, violet, dark green, dark grey, and other deep shades are grouped with black, whereas light green, mixtures of green, yellow, and light brown are grouped with green. Light blue, however, is grouped with other light tints under white.

These four basic color terms, however, are not only color terms. They also have a series of other referents. The terms for white and black also are paired opposites for light and dark, while another set of contrasts is made between dryness (red) and wetness or freshness (green). The terms for both black and red are also associated with "deep, unfading, indelible, desirable," while those for white and green are linked to "pale, weak, faded, bleached, colorless," hence, "undesirable." There is also a second level of nonbasic color terms, which allows a high degree of specificity.

Conklin concludes this discussion in the following words:

> This intracultural analysis demonstrates that what appears to be color "confusion" at first may result from an inadequate knowledge of the internal structure of a color system and from a failure to distinguish sharply between sensory reception on the one hand and perceptual categorization on the other (Conklin, 1955:343).

Further Studies of Focal Colors

As already mentioned, the 1969 study by Berlin and Kay has produced considerable discussion and also a number of attempts to use its findings in further research. A developmental psychologist, Eleanor Rosch Heider, has pursued research on the perceptual-cognitive importance of the focal colors. Working with young children, whose color vocabularies were as yet undeveloped, she found that three-year-olds preferred focal colors to nonfocal colors, and that four-year-olds were better at matching focal colors than nonfocal ones (Heider 1971).

Heider also worked with the Dani, who, as we have seen, lack terms for all the chromatic colors. Patterning her study after the original recognition tests developed by Brown and Lenneberg (1954), she taught the Dani color terms as part of the recognition tests. She found that they were able to remember focal colors better than nonfocal colors (Heider 1972). She concluded that the focal colors are remembered better than nonfocal colors even by people who lack words for them, whether they are small children or members of a language group that lacks the terms. Therefore, she argues,

> it would appear that the color space, far from being a domain well suited to the study of the effect of language on thought, is rather a prime example of the influence of underlying perceptual-cognitive factors on the formation and reference of linguistic categories (Rosch 1975:183).

Determinants of the Color Vocabulary: A Summary

We have taken quite a lengthy look at the subject of color categorization, because a consideration of its complex history touches on a number of important issues in the field of human perception and cognition. Moreover, the dominant point of view at each period of this history illustrates the prevailing views concerning differences among human groups.

Thus, as we have seen, to nineteenth century scholars from Gladstone to Rivers, who were classical evolutionists, "deficient" color terminologies reflected "deficient" color vision. Both the terminologies and the visual performances were considered to be indicators of racial inferiority. This inferiority was believed to be due to the "primitive," that is, "early," status of the groups involved, whether they were Homeric Greeks or contemporary Papuans.

To Bornstein, writing in the 1970s, deficient color vocabularies similarly reflect a lack of visual sensitivity to certain colors, specifically blue and green; however, this characteristic is interpreted not as a sign of biological inferiority, but as a result of biological adaptation to a particular geographic setting.

To Berlin and Kay, however, who also speak in evolutionary terms, vocabularies containing an "incomplete" list of basic color terms reflect not biological characteristics but low cultural complexity. Like the classical evolutionists before them, they rank both early and contemporary cultures on the basis of complexity, but unlike either their predecessors or Bornstein, they do not infer biological differences from their data.

EVOLUTION, UNIVERSALS, AND RELATIVISM

The explanation of differences in color terminologies offered by Berlin and Kay is based on a primary concern with universals. This concern is shown in their distinction between focal and nonfocal colors as well as in the regularities which underlie their evolutionary scheme. Their work represents a period in cultural anthropology and linguistics when there is a strong interest in uncovering species-wide universals that transcend culture and underlie cultural variability. That is, they recognize group differences within a framework of universal givens.

Such universalist and evolutionary approaches have generally been contrasted in the past with "relativistic" positions. Relativism, however, has meant different things in the history of anthropology. The work by Berlin and Kay has emerged from the most radical relativism of all. This approach has variously been called "the new ethnography," ethnoscience, ethnosemantics, or ethnographic semantics. Paul Kay (1970:20) has defined it as "the systematic study of the meaning of words and the role of these meanings in cognitive systems." We shall look at this subject in a little more detail presently.

We have referred several times to the contrasts between those who think in terms of a universal, constant human nature or human mind, and those who think that while there may exist such an underlying psychobiological principle, at the observational level of human behavior we see radical differences among varying cultural and linguistic groups. Culture, it appears, influences perception, cognition, affects, tastes, and values, ethics, and esthetics, and, in a feedback loop, physiology as well. In the present context, when we speak of relativism in regard to classification systems, such as the categorization of colors in our example, reference is usually made to the Sapir-Whorf hypothesis, also variously termed *linguistic relativism* or *linguistic determinism.* For example, in one of the strongest formulations of this point of view, Whorf (1956:214 [orig. 1940]) wrote:

> No individual is free to describe nature with absolute impartiality, but is constrained to certain modes of interpretation . . . We are thus introduced to a new principle of relativity, which holds that all observers are not led to the same picture of the universe, unless their linguistic backgrounds are similar, or can in some way be calibrated.

Thus, linguistic relativism states that the classification by which sensory input is organized is given for individuals by the specific languages in which they are socialized; moreover, not only do languages differ in respect to the categories they contain, but, it is implied, the categorizations are arbitrary. They are not given by the world of experience or by the structure of the experiencing organism, but by language and culture. Rosch (1975:177) notes that the social sciences, including anthropology, psychology, and linguistics, have, in fact, paid little attention to the source of the categories, to why given cultures and languages "cut up" the world of sensations as they do.

What we have done in the past is to document in more or less specific terms that languages and cultures differ to a considerable extent in the order they impose on this "world of sensations." This idea certainly was revolutionary in the writings of Sapir and Whorf (although it did have its predecessors). Their work, as we saw, grew out of the impressive contrasts between American Indian languages and European languages. Conklin, in his paper on Hanunóo color categories, furnished an example from a different linguistic stock and a different culture area. But are the differences arbitrary?

Segall, Campbell, and Herskovits (1966), in their study of group differences in susceptibility to optical illusions, not only documented that group differences exist, but also offered hypotheses about why they exist. Not only does culture affect perception, they suggested, but the effect is not an arbitrary or random phenomenon. Instead, they turned to both technological and ecological factors for explanations. It is important to remember that Herskovits' name is strongly associated with cultural relativism (see, for example Herskovits 1973), and that a relativistic position (perception is variable as a result of cultural differences), underlay this particular research undertaking. One may, then, be a relativist without holding to a concept of arbitrary or random variations.

Ethnoscience: From the Unique to the Universal

Berlin and Kay, as we have seen, placed their work within the framework of ethnoscience. This approach, both in its method and its theory, had its origin in structural linguistics. The linguist Kenneth Pike (1954, 1966) differentiated two standpoints for the study of human behavior, by analogy to two approaches used by linguists in the study of the sound system of a language: the phonetic and the phonemic. He termed these two standpoints the *etic* and the *emic*. The etic approach is universalist, using units of analysis and comparison that are thought to be culture-free. The emic approach, on the other hand, is culturally specific; the units or criteria it uses, like the phonemes of the linguists, are culturally specific. One cannot know in advance what emic units there are, for their discovery is one of the aims of the research. Therefore we must not assume that we know what units we will use to describe a system, or indeed, that we can phrase testable cross-cultural hypotheses in advance. The emic approach yields a description of a cultural system from the inside, not from the outside, from the point of view of the participant, not from that of the observer.

This approach in itself is not truly new to cultural anthropology, with its long-standing relativistic point of view. What is new is the specific definition of goals that ethnoscience set for itself. Culture is defined explicitly as a matter of shared (or agreed upon) cognition. The research therefore focuses on the discovery of this shared cognition of a group of people through the study of language. Generally, ethnoscientists study words to discover native systems of classification and the principles on which these systems are based. To do so, they have developed a rigorous system of interviewing or "eliciting of information" from informants. This type of research, too, is patterned after the manner in which linguists obtain their data. In particular—ethnoscientists have often been criticized for this fact—like linguists they are frequently satisfied to work with a small number of informants, because they assume cognition is shared and not individually variable.[6] Over the years, a series of studies has dealt with systems of classification of many different aspects of experience, or "domains." These domains range from what are sometimes considered to be trivial matters, such as the classification of firewood among the Tzeltal, to classifications of plants, animals, diseases, kinship terms, and as we have seen, colors.

For many years, this approach has produced statements of unique classification systems. Often, these data have been isolated from general ethnographic descriptions. Because they applied only to unique instances, their significance for anthropological theory has been questioned, and the work has been criticized as insignificant. For example, Melford Spiro, describing his own research in Burmese supernaturalism, distinguishes his orientation from that of the "new ethnography," as ethnoscientists have sometimes called their own approach:

> I am not interested . . . in Burmese supernaturalism *per se,* nor am I interested, as an end in itself, in "how the natives think" about their supernatural beliefs or in the criteria by which they classify and order them. For me these are intellectually trivial questions, "trivial" with respect to what I consider the main task of inquiry in the social sciences—*viz.* the discovery of regularities in social and cultural phenomena and of the causal laws by which they may be explained . . . My interest, unlike that of the new ethnography, is not in "reproducing" Burmese supernaturalism by means of Burmese categories (which in any event I believe to be impossible); rather I am interested in explaining it by means of theoretically relevant categories . . . The categories that are relevant for anthropological inquiry are not the categories through which the "natives" order the world, but those through which it is ordered by anthropological inquiry (Spiro 1967:5–6).

He goes on to say that the emic approach "leads to a descriptive and relativistic inquiry whose interest begins and ends with the parochial" (p. 6).[7]

In defending ethnoscience, however, its champions have argued that such attacks are unjustified, and that their approach will ultimately lead not only to comparison on the basis of truly significant units, but also to a revelation of universal structural principles of human cognition. They thus join Spiro in a search for a universal common "human nature," which is a constant and which underlies the wide variation in local forms. Berlin and Kay argue that their work in color classifications has revealed just such universal principles and, moreover, that it has done so within an evolutionary framework. Kay (1970) and Rosch (1975), furthermore, suggest that the contrast between focal colors and peripheral colors that they have discovered cross-culturally may reveal a more general principle of classification. Rosch calls it the "principle of salient prototypes," in which the "best example" or prototype (like the focal colors) is always surrounded by lesser examples of the type until one type shades into another.

With the work of Berlin and Kay, then, it would appear that ethnoscience has moved from a position of radical relativism to a universalist-evolutionist approach. In this respect, it seems to have followed the trend of the discipline from which it derives, structural linguistics. On the other hand, the other dominant tradition in cross-cultural studies of perception and cognition, the tradition of psychology, is basically universalist, whether we speak of laboratory-based studies in perception and cognition, or of developmental studies in the manner of Jean Piaget. The anthropological element in this research, if it can be called that, is that it is carried out among non-Western people and that the psychologists involved in it have gained, over the years, some appreciation of the importance of cultural factors for their methods and for their results.

PERCEPTION AND PERSONALITY

Our discussion so far has dealt with interrelations among sensation, perception, and cognition, all referring to the visual field. We now turn to a series of studies that have directed attention to a possible link between perception and personality, and also have raised the question of the relationship between visual perception and other sensory modalities.

The story begins with the publication by H. A. Witkin and associates (1954) of a first report on research testing hypotheses about the relationship between perception and personality. The study involved a series of laboratory experiments to investigate perception and of clinical tests to evaluate personality. The subjects were from the United States, and the sample was broken down by age and sex, but not by class or culture (ethnic group). The most important of the laboratory procedures were the Tilted-Chair-Tilted-Room Test, the Rod-and-Frame Test, and the Embedded Figure Test. In the first test, the subject is placed in a tilted field and is required to move into a position that seems upright. To do so, some people orient themselves by what they see, the visual field, whereas others rely on their body sensations, on when they "feel" upright. The Rod-and-Frame Test also investigates subjects' perception of the upright, this time of an object rather than of their own bodies. The subject is placed in a dark room where only a luminous frame is visible, surrounding a luminous rod. The frame is tilted, and the subject's task is to move the rod so that it will be in an "upright" position. Again, some people rely on the relationship they see between frame and rod, whereas others rely more on their own body sensations to decide when the rod is "upright." Subjects who base their judgment on visual cues are said to be "field-dependent," whereas those who do not are termed "field-independent."

In addition to tests of orientation, another series of perceptual tests was used. One of them is the Embedded Figure Test. Here the subject has to separate a form from a larger field in which it is "embedded" or incorporated. Although it is a paper-and-pencil test and requires a visual approach, its results correlate well with those of the orientation tests. To obtain personality data, the Rorschach and TAT were administered, and life history and interview materials were collected from the subjects.

The results showed significant differences between field-dependent and field-independent people. Children are generally more field-dependent than adults, and women are more field-dependent than men. Within age and sex groups, however, some personality differences were associated with field dependence. For example, field-dependent people showed greater passivity and less active coping with the environment than field-independent people. Also, they were less introspective and had greater difficulty in handling impulses of sexuality and aggression; they were more dependent and more anxious.

A whole series of studies among highly diverse groups has used this general approach, broadening its scope by introducing some new variables and some new procedures. Among the latter are the Draw-a-Person Test and the Kohs Block Test, both of which have shown high correlation with the orientation tests.

Going beyond his original research, Witkin developed the concept of "cognitive styles": "characteristic self-consistent modes of functioning found pervasively throughout the individual's cognitive, that is perceptual and intellectual, activities" (Witkin 1974:99). Field dependence and field independence are thus to be seen as aspects of different styles of perception called *global* and *articulated*. The *articulated* type of perception finds distinctions within a field and in a homogeneous field organizes the space by imposing structure on it. The global type does not. Witkin goes on to observe that cognitive styles are themselves manifestations of much wider regularities in the psychological activities of individuals and are reflections of socialization practices. On the personality level, as indicated by various tests, people with an articulated perceptual-cognitive style are more highly *differentiated* than those with a global style. Witkin furthermore comments that these "various indicators 'hang together' " in the course of individual development, and that this fact "suggests that they are not discrete achievements of separate channels of growth but rather diverse expressions of an underlying process of development toward greater psychological complexity" (Witkin 1974:101).

As the first in a series of empirical studies from which the above generalizations were later drawn, Witkin and his associates (1962) studied a sample of ten-year-old boys in New York City. Here field-independent boys were found to be more differentiated than field-dependent boys. They were more independent, with more of a sense of separate identity and better impulse control. Their mothers also were more differentiated than those of the field-dependent boys.

The relationship between children's level of differentiation and that of their parents was confirmed in a later study by Corah (1965), who also found that it is the level of differentiation of the parent of opposite sex (mothers for boys, and fathers for girls) that is more likely to be relevant.

This last finding was confirmed cross-culturally by Dawson (1963, 1967) in quite a different setting, two tribal groups in Sierra Leone (West Africa). In one part of his study , he found that field-dependent men were more likely to have had, according to their own reports, strict mothers, than field-independent men. The two groups Dawson compared are tradition-oriented Temne, who have severe socialization practices, and the more modern Mende, who are less likely to use physical punishment in rearing their children. Moreover, Temne families are reported to be more heavily dominated by the mothers than those of the Mende. Dawson found the Temne to be more field-dependent than the Mende.

J. W. Berry (1974, 1975, 1976) has carried on a series of studies in which he utilized the ecological model first developed by Barry, Child, and Bacon (1959). For this purpose he selected groups with different subsistence economies, living in different environmental settings. In the first of these studies, he compared the Temne of Sierra Leone and the Eskimos of Baffin Island. The Temne, who are primarily subsistence agriculturalists, live in tropical bush country. Their visual field, therefore, might be said to be highly complex and differentiated. As we have already seen, they are strict in their socialization practices. The Eskimos, on the other hand, live in a world of uniform snow fields; the landscape is visually highly homogeneous. They are hunters who travel widely in search of game and must learn to orient themselves in this highly undifferentiated setting. Berry notes that Eskimo language has a complex system of geometrical-spatial terms, and he suggests that these terms aid the growing child in learning to deal with such undifferentiated space. Eskimo socialization is lenient, and children have a great deal of freedom, as is typically the case among hunters.

Using paper-and-pencil tests (Kohs Blocks Test and Embedded Figure Test), Berry found the Eskimos to be more field-independent than the Temne. Berry also sought to control for acculturation, by testing both traditional and transitional (acculturated) groups among the Eskimos and Temne. Transitional Temne were more field-independent than traditional Temne; however, both traditional and transitional Eskimos were much more highly field-independent. Another interesting finding was that, among Eskimos, women as well as men are field-independent. This finding suggests that it is not the occupation of hunting, which is a male specialization, that leads to field-independence. This finding has been confirmed by MacArthur (1969) for another Eskimo group.

As a further step in his investigations Berry developed a more complex and refined research procedure. He summarized his argument in the following terms:

> Hunting peoples are expected to possess good visual discrimination and spatial skills, and their cultures are expected to be supportive of the development of these skills through a high number of "geometrical spatial" concepts, a highly developed and generally shared arts and crafts production, and socialization practices whose content emphasizes independence, and self-reliance, and whose techniques are supportive and encouraging of separate development (Berry 1974:133).

In this study, Berry used a total of ten samples, five rural/traditional and five urban/transitional. Temne from Sierra Leone and Baffin Island Eskimos represented the ecological extremes, supplemented by New Guinea natives, Australian Aborigines, and two groups of Scots, as controls. Adults and children and men and women were included in all the samples.

The findings support the hypothesis that "peoples will attain levels of visual discrimination appropriate to the ecological demands" (Berry 1974:139). Berry further suggests that the generally greater field independence of transitional groups, as seen in the perceptual tests, may be related to their greater degree of literacy. Interestingly, among both the traditional and the transitional Australians as among the two Eskimo groups, there is no significant difference between males and females. This finding is also true of the transitional New Guineans, but not of the traditional group. Nor, incidentally, is there any male/female difference among the rural Scots, although it does exist in the urban group.

Berry (1975) has also conducted an ambitious and complex study of traditional and transitional sections of three Canadian Indian tribes. Because his earlier work involved too broad a diversity of cultures, he now drew his groups from a more limited geographic area. The tribes selected were the Tshimshian (high accumulation coastal fishermen), Carrier (medium accumulation, with a substantial amount of hunting), and Cree (low accumulation hunters). In this research, Berry was interested in investigating the relationship between perceptual approach and cognitive, social, and emotional characteristics, by means of a variety of tests. He also wished to discover the effect of acculturative stress on these various characteristics.

This study again confirmed (by means of the Kohs Block Test) the existence of high field independence among hunting peoples. On the other hand, there is no clear association between cognitive style and emotional and social characteristics. These findings have led Berry to question Witkin's unitary concept of "differentiation." Instead, he suggests that the interrelationship of perceptual, cognitive, social, and emotional characteristics may depend on the specific "ecocultural" setting in which an individual grows up. In other words, the relationship of various aspects of psychological activity to each other may turn out to depend on ecology and culture, a suggestion that could have profound implications for psychological theory.

As far as acculturation is concerned, Berry and his coworkers found that high scores on measures of differentiation are associated with low scores on measures of acculturative stress when individuals within the same sample are compared. This relationship does not hold true between samples, however. The most highly differentiated group, the Cree, who are hunters and who are also the least acculturated, showed the highest stress and the greatest degree of cultural marginality. Berry interprets this finding to mean that the hunting societies, whose traditional ways are at greatest variance with those of the larger society to which they must adjust, suffer the greatest stress. On the other hand, on the individual level, those persons in any society who are highly differentiated, both in cognitive style and in personality characteristics—those who are the most self-reliant and independent—may have an easier time in the situation of culture contact and culture change.

Berry and his associates gathered materials on ten subsistence-level groups and two Western groups in the course of a ten-year period. The full report on these materials is presented by Berry (1976). As we have seen, the primary aim of this large-scale investigation has been to explore the relationship between ecological variables and differentiation on the one hand, and the relationship among acculturation, differentiation, and stress on the other hand. In this final report, Berry also turns to some possible practical applications of these findings. He suggests that ecological and cultural analyses of the kind he and his associates undertook apply only to people at subsistence level. In industrialized societies other factors affect personality diversity. However, he also notes that it takes more than one generation for the influence of the original ecocultural adaptation to cease to be effective and relevant to our understanding of the people in the contact situation. We shall consider Berry's important comments on culture change and adaptation to westernization and development in Chapter 9.

SENSOTYPES

As we saw earlier, Berry's research has led researchers to question one aspect of Witkin's theory of differentiation. Another question of great importance, concerning methods of investigation, has been raised by M. Wober (1966, 1975).

Wober (1966) began by attempting to replicate Witkin's experiments with a group of Nigerian workers, most of them Ibos. In contrast to most of the comparative studies on field dependence, including Berry's, Wober used not only a paper-and-pencil test, but also an orientation test. In contrast to Witkin, he found no correlation between the performances of his subjects on these two types of tests. In the orientation test (Rod-and-Frame Test) the Africans were more field-independent than Witkin's sample from the United States, but on the paper-and-pencil test (Embedded Figure Test) they were less so. Wober concludes that the types of tests demand different perceptual skills: the Rod-and-Frame Test requires attention to the sensations and orientation of the body, or "proprioception," whereas the Embedded Figure Test calls on visual skills. Wober also notes that in an earlier study by Gruen (1955) dancers in the United States who, through their training, had acquired proprioceptive skills, performed better on orientation tests than on paper-and-pencil tests.

Wober goes on to suggest the concept of "sensotypes"; cultures differ, he argues, in the emphasis they place on different sense modalities. Growing up in different cultures, children do not utilize the same sense modalities to the same degree to acquire and process information from the environment. African cultures stress dance and rhythm over the visual aspects of learning, as compared to Western cultures, with their stress on literacy. Thus, Western children are trained in visuality, whereas African children are trained in proprioceptivity. The implication of this approach is that perceptual performance is a result of varying "sensotypes," and we must beware of constructing theories on what may be artifacts of the types of tests used.

In quite a different context, A. Ombredane (1954, cited in Price-Williams 1975) had earlier characterized African cultures as "musico-choreographic." In a study of the relationship of pictorial depth perception and acculturation among the Baganda, Kilbride and Robbins (1969:288) come to a similar conclusion. They stress that their unacculturated subjects misidentified pictorial objects not because they were unable to " 'see' form or objects in pictures but rather through an inability to use cues to depth or to see spatial relationships between pictorial objects." They go on to point out that in Western societies visual perceptual skills are developed to deal with great quantities of "symbolic visual communication" to which the individual is exposed. In African societies, by contrast, there are "drum languages, elaborate speech making, tonal languages and a cultural focus on music." The Baganda, like other Africans, consequently may be expected to excel in "aural-proprioceptive abilities."

The existence of differences in "sensotypes" produced by different cultural styles remains to be explored further. However, the hypothesis of such difference is of major practical as well as theoretical importance. For example, different "sensotypes" appear to involve divergent sources of creativity and cultural elaboration, different kinds of cognitive approaches, and so on. If only one of these sensotypes were compatible with modernization and industrialization, it would imply profound perceptual as well cognitive transformations for many of the peoples of the world. The result might well be a great cultural as well as technological homogenization, and consequent cultural impoverishment of the world's peoples.

CROSS-CULTURAL STUDIES OF COGNITION: PROCESS, CONTENT, AND DEVELOPMENT

Cross-cultural studies in the area of cognition have involved two quite different aims. On the one hand, psychologists have desired to use alien cultures as a testing ground for hypotheses formulated in Western societies concerning the nature of cognition and its development in the course of the child's maturation. On the other hand, they have continued to debate whether or not "primitives" are "rational," or whether there is such a thing as "primitive mentality." In more recent times, this question is related to the modernization of traditional peoples and their capacity to "learn" Western culture. For the psychologist, this issue often entails practical questions about implementing Western schooling in Third World countries.

To the classical evolutionists, such as Tylor and Frazer, primitive people were rational in their thought processes but came to faulty conclusions due to inadequate information. Frazer, for example, argued that magic was primitive man's inadequate science. Tylor thought that religious beliefs, specifically a belief in souls, resulted from primitive man's interpretation of the experience of dreams, trances, visions, and death. If these beliefs were erroneous explanations of the phenomena, it was not due to an inability to reason.

The French philosopher, Lévy-Bruhl, on the other hand, held in his major writings that there were indeed differences between a primitive and a civilized "mentality." (He changed his mind later in life, as shown in his posthumously published *Carnets* [1949].) Lévy-Bruhl thought that primitive beliefs should not be treated as the result of individual psychological processes. Rather, beliefs are social facts, derived from "collective representations." These representations, however, at times are based on faulty premises, and the arguments involved may contain logical contradictions.

With the development of intensive ethnographic fieldwork by Boas and his students primarily among American Indians, and by British functionalists (Malinowski, Radcliffe-Brown, and their students) in Oceania, Australia, and Africa, a vigorous cultural relativism developed. Anthropologists increasingly took the position that all peoples are equally capable of logical thought, although their factual information might be insufficient. Moreover, they observed that Westerners, even sometimes highly technically trained individuals, were as irrational and illogical as any "primitives" in many situations outside their specialized fields. Prejudice, politics, and religion all offer ample evidence of irrationality.

As a result of their greater first-hand acquaintance with the daily lives of traditional peoples, anthropologists came to stress the effectiveness with which people everywhere solve their practical problems. They pointed out that reports

Solving practical problems: In the coastal plains, where land is at a premium, Haitian peasants make use of even the smallest plots of land to grow food crops.

of travelers, explorers, missionaries, and others stressing irrational beliefs tend to distort the overall picture of traditional people and cultures. For example, in his book on Haiti, M. J. Herskovits (1937a:viii–ix) attacks the descriptions of that country by sensationalist writers:

> Yet how are these descriptions of hysterical paranoid folk, ridden with fear of the dark forces of magic and the anger of vindictive gods, to be reconciled with the picture of the Haitian as he is shown in the second section of this book—of a man going about his affairs in matter-of-fact fashion, tending his crops, buying and selling, carrying on his amorous conquests, establishing and providing for his family?

Moreover, Western observers often assume, quite naïvely, that a self-evident connection exists between behavior patterns or ideas that are linked in their own cultures. Often such links are not perceived by other people, because they are not based on any logical necessity. Instead, such connections are the result of historical factors. For example, a Protestant missionary in Haiti was surprised to discover that some of his most faithful converts continued to believe in the existence of sorcerers with the power of turning human beings into animals. When he asked them how they could believe such things, now that they were Christians, they assured him that there was no relationship between this belief and Christianity. His incredulity concerning sorcerers, they explained to him, was simply due to his ignorance of the powers held by certain Haitians.

Another example concerns an assumed linkage between two types of behaviors. A U.S. psychologist, visiting Japan for the first time, was startled by the fact that, although Japanese men had adopted Western styles of clothing, they continued to urinate in public, simply stepping to the side of the road. To him, this type of behavior, which is traditional, fitted well with traditional clothing. Somehow, he had expected that once a different clothing style was accepted, this behavior would be abandoned automatically.

When observers have taken the trouble to investigate the knowledge that native populations possess concerning various aspects of their environments, they are often not only surprised but also impressed. Nicolas Blurton-Jones and M. Konner investigated the knowledge !Kung men have of animal behavior. On the basis of extensive discussions with these excellent hunters, they describe the !Kung's knowledge in the following terms:

> The sheer volume of knowledge is overwhelming ... The accuracy of observation, the patience, and the experience of wildlife they have had and appreciate are enviable. The sheer, elegant logic of deduction from tracks would satiate the most avid crossword fan or reader of detective stories.

Writing from the point of view of self-conscious specialists in animal and human behavior, they remark:

> The objectivity [of the !Kung] is also enviable to scientists who believe they can identify it and that the progress of science is totally dependent on it. Even the poor

theorizing of our !Kung left us uneasy; their "errors," the errors of "Stone Age savages," are exactly those still made today by many highly educated Western scientists (tautological theories of motivation, inadequate application of natural selection theory).

In their conclusions, there is evident surprise:

> We have gained little or nothing in ability or intellectual brilliance since the Stone Age ... We know more and we understand more, but our intellects are no better. It is an error to equate the documented history of intellectual achievement with a history of intellect ... Just as primitive life can no longer be characterized as nasty, brutish, and short, no longer can it be characterized as stupid, ignorant or superstition dominated (Blurton-Jones and Konner 1976:334).

Having discovered that traditional peoples have drawn a substantial amount of practical knowledge from observation and inference, anthropologists have tended to pay less attention to the irrational in belief and behavior. What appears irrational at first glance is often seen to have a practical and effective basis in experience. Even the linguistic relativists who argued that people classify the world of reality differently, depending on their particular language, did not argue that some people classify more effectively than others, or that some are incapable of classification or abstraction. In part, this concern with rationality and reality may have been responsible for a lengthy period in which there was little interest in the study of religion.

In recent years, there has been some renewed interest in religion and "irrationality," this time in the context of the study of symbolism. Dan Sperber, for example, has discussed his research on the subject among the Droze of Ethiopia. He observed behavior and heard explanations that appeared to him to be absurd. For example, he saw a group of dignitaries circling the marketplace in a counterclockwise direction. When he inquired he was first told that they do so because "it is the custom," and then, that they move in the direction of the sun, which is from right to left. He comments on the patent absurdity of this:

> I know ... that there are no more reasons, between the Tropic of Cancer and the Equator, for thinking that the sun turns from right to left rather than from left to right; that to turn "like the sun" leaves the sun completely indifferent; that to circle the market and to come back to one's point of departure without buying anything, or selling anything, saying or hearing anything is not economical ... (Sperber 1975:3).

Clearly, such behavior, if it is to be understood and not merely reported, must be interpreted in some framework other than inadequate rationality. Sperber considers it in the framework of symbolism, of hidden meanings for which an analysis in terms of rationality is inappropriate. Moreover, all of this behavior has nothing to do with the fact that the Droze, like all other peoples, have a series of techniques for growing crops, trading, building houses, making tools, and so on, just as do the Haitians, of whom Herskovits speaks in the remark cited earlier.

PSYCHOLOGY AND ANTHROPOLOGY: DIFFERENCES IN METHODS

Anthropologists have taken cultural data and have drawn inferences from them about human capacities for memory, classification, abstraction, inference, and other aspects of cognition. Psychologists have found this approach unsatisfactory and unconvincing, for, as Michael Cole (1975) has pointed out, so many intervening variables appear in a naturally occurring behavior sequence that such situations are ambiguous. Therefore, psychologists have preferred to work with controlled experiments, which are set up as problem solving situations. To do so, they have defined "thinking" in operational terms as "a new combination of previously learned elements" (Cole 1975:163).

On the other hand, it has long been known that there are important limitations on experimentation and testing in non-Western societies. For example, Otto Klineberg, writing in 1940, pointed out that for American Indian children, unaccustomed to working on a time schedule and taught to reflect carefully before making decisions, results on tests that reward speed are misleading. Sorenson (1976) says that the Fore were so unused to being asked questions, to the "interrogative mode" of interaction, that they were terrified and showed it by sweating and trembling. Fear of the investigator or experimenter, who is usually a stranger, is a factor generally to be reckoned with. There may also be a lack of incentive to work the problems or perform unfamiliar tasks, and there may be a lack of understanding of what is required. Moreover, some specific aspects of the task may constitute obstacles to the adequate solution of the problem, yet it may be difficult for the investigator to discern just what constitutes the obstacle.

For example, Cole (1975) reports on an experiment he carried out in Liberia with Kpelle children and young adults. To study their ability to draw inferences, subjects were presented with a device that had been widely used for similar purposes with children in the United States. This gadget consisted of three closed compartments, each with a panel and a button to be operated. The child first learns to push a button on the left-hand panel to obtain a marble, and then a button on the right-hand panel to obtain a ball bearing. By dropping these tokens into a hole in the central panel, the child can open it to obtain a piece of candy. The problem appeared virtually insoluble to the Kpelle; yet they did very well with a similar problem when they were given a device constructed of familiar materials. From his detailed analysis of the various stages in learning to deal with this task, Cole concluded that he can demonstrate (rather than merely assert, as is the habit of anthropologists), "that the people in question solve such problems under more familiar circumstances . . . [that] they can make inferences [and] that it is not just the presence of the funny device [but] a particular stage in having to work it that is the stumbling block" (Cole 1975:168). In other words, through dealing with experimental situations and their possible variations, one can locate the specific source of difficulty in the original performance. Inadequate performance does not by itself reveal incapacity, but it does require us to search out the exact obstacles. Anthropologists, Cole suggests, have been more dogmatic than helpful on this issue.

An interesting study by Rosalie Cohen and her associates also deals with difficulties on test performances. These investigators worked in the Pittsburgh area with children from low-income families of various ethnic origins. They discovered that two different cognitive styles that could be identified were linked to differences not in intellectual capacity but in the organization of primary groups. Children approached test items and group processes in a similar manner. An *analytic style,* similar to Witkin's articulated style, involves the abstracting of information from a situation, is stimulus-centered, and is field-independent. It was linked to the typical middle-class social organization, where important functions such as leadership, child care, and the handling of family funds are assigned to individuals by status positions within the group. Cohen (1969:830) contrasts this style with a *relational style,* which uses a descriptive mode of approach in which "only the global characteristics of a stimulus have meaning to its users and these only in reference to some total context." This relational cognitive style was associated with what are termed "shared-function" primary groups. Here such functions as those listed above are shared much more widely within the groups, so status positions are much less highly differentiated.

Children who perceived themselves as having relevance only as participants in their specific social groups, rather than as separate individuals of potential importance anywhere, saw test items as having significance only in specific contexts. As a result, so-called "culture-free" tests, which rigorously lack context (culture being generally thought to involve specific content and context, rather than cognitive style), left such children totally bewildered. Interestingly enough, there were children whose response style was inconsistent, and they were found to have had experience in both types of primary groups. This finding has a further implication: tests that show high correlations for one type of group may not do so for another. Wober, it will be recalled, has suggested that such a finding may be due to differences in sensotypes. For these different types of cognitive tests, Cohen argues that such inconsistency may be due to differences in group structures. In fact, Cohen's analysis suggests an analogy between tests of cognitive functioning and projective personality tests. Whereas the traditional projective tests link perception and personality, cognitive tests appear to link cognitive style and group experience.

These examples indicate some of the difficulties encountered in the cross-cultural testing of cognitive processes. It is therefore not surprising that many of the findings that have resulted from these researches are contradictory and difficult to interpret.

Basically, two principal approaches have been used in cross-cultural studies of cognitive development. One approach, the use of standardized tests, often has run into the various problems already indicated. Another approach, which has been more attractive to many, is based on the work of the Swiss psychologist, Jean Piaget and his associates.[8] According to Piaget, a series of logical structures develops in the child in succession as a result of the child's interaction with the environment. These logical structures are held to be universal, and the order in which they appear is thought to be invariable. However, as a result of cultural factors, the age at which each stage appears may vary. Piaget himself has expressed an interest in discovering to what extent these stages and their sequence are found cross-culturally.

A great deal of work has been done along these lines in various parts of the world, but the results have been, at best, equivocal. Dasen (1974), who has reviewed many of these studies, concludes that cultural influences may be greater than Piaget had originally thought. For example, the existence of Piaget's third and final stage of cognitive development, the stage of formal propositional reasoning, has been questioned for societies without formal schooling. Concrete operational thought, the middle stage on which most of the cross-cultural research has centered, apparently is reached in some societies somewhat earlier than in Europe and North America, in some at about the same time, and in many others somewhat later. Yet the studies have been so diverse that it is doubtful whether any valid comparisons can be made or whether any conclusions can be drawn from then.

Differences in test performance can be found readily, but how are they to be interpreted? Can they be considered evidence of differences in competence? The example from Cole (1975), cited above, suggests that they cannot. Moreover, at times tests show people to be intellectually slow and "backward," when ethnographic reports show them to have complex symbolic cultures. As Wober has put it in his critique of cross-cultural psychology as it has been practiced in Africa, research intended to investigate intellectual processes among Africans has frequently "been more informative about the test, or even about intelligence and adaptability among the testers themselves" (Wober 1975:160).

Expressing a frustration widespread among psychologists working in Third World societies, Cole and Scribner write:

> We believe the general failure of anthropologists and psychologists to share the same definitions, facts and theoretical constructs is a fundamental impediment to our understanding of the relationship between culture and the development of cognitive processes: all the more so because this failure goes unnoticed . . . Anthropologists and psychologists do not mean the same thing when they speak of cognitive "consequences"; they do not agree on the characteristics of culture that are potential "antecedents"; and they distrust each others' methods for discovering the link between the two (Cole and Scribner 1976:159).

They go on to say that "unless there is some agreement on what 'cognitive consequences' we are studying, there are no guidelines for deciding what aspects of culture are relevant to the search for 'critical socializing' experiences" (pp. 159–160). To get out of the present impasse, then, and to make a real collaboration between psychologists and anthropologists possible, it is necessary first to admit the present state of affairs, and then to develop a true "ethnography of cognitive activities." They point to three areas of generally unstated disagreements and divergences between members of the two disciplines. First, they distinguish between *content* and *process* in dealing with intellectual tasks, such as remembering. Psychologists think they are studying a culture-free process, whereas anthropologists tend to focus on content. Moreover, it is likely, as we saw earlier, that process itself may be affected by diverse cognitive styles that have their sources in cultural differences. Second, Cole and Scribner distinguish between the anthropologists' concern for studying behavior in a *natural* setting characteristic of a given culture, and the artifical or *contrived* situations used by psychologists. The error of the psychologists resides in the assumption that the contrived situation they set up "samples" the behavior of the subject, and that the findings in this situation can be generalized to the subject's everyday life. On the other hand, the natural setting of the anthropologist allows observation but only rarely experimentation to distinguish among hypotheses in attempting to understand what is observed. For example, are feats of memory of native genealogists due to rote learning or to other mental processes?

The substantive findings of the work among the Kpelle has been summarized by Cole and his associates in a notable volume entitled *The Cultural Context of Learning and Thinking* (1971). Cole provides a fascinating autobiographical glimpse of this work in a retrospective review, which terminates, however, with a look toward the future (Cole 1978). He and Sylvia Scribner are currently at work on what he calls "the ethnographic psychology of cognition." He describes this approach as an "ethnography that analyzes cognition as specific sets of activities engaged in on specifiable occasions." In such research "the psychologist will look to the effect of different organizations of activities of individual behavior. The ethnographer will concentrate on the ways larger social factors (economic activities, religion, family structure) organize different intellectual activities" (Cole 1978:630).

SUMMARY

Cross-cultural studies of perception and cognition by psychologists and anthropologists have involved different kinds of intellectual approaches, different assumptions and methods, and not surprisingly, different kinds of results. It has, however, become increasingly clear that cultural differences are far-reaching. They appear to involve not merely differences in informational content or the values placed on various types of skills and abilities, but also differences in the very processes by which cognitive activities take place. The current search for cooperative approaches, which is best shown by the work of Michael Cole and his associates, is therefore most welcome.

Cognitive activity, competence, and style are only imperfectly revealed by any kind of performance, particularly one contrived without adequate knowledge of the role of cultural factors. Although, in principle, this fact is increasingly recognized by specialists in psychology and education, it is less clear what cultural factors, other than those involving specific informational content, are relevant to an adequate evaluation of cognitive competence.

Our discussion has suggested that, as Berry (1976) has indicated in his model, relations of varying complexity exist between perception and cognition on the one hand, and language, ecology, subsistence economy, and socialization on the other. In Rosalie Cohen's view, primary group organization should be added here. These interrelated factors have a bearing on personality, according to H. A. Witkin and his associates. Research into the culturally constituted behavioral environment of any human group must take this complex of interacting factors into account.

While these subjects are of the greatest interest for anyone attempting to understand the organization and growth of cultural differences against a background of a basic common human nature, these researches also have immediate practical consequences. In the contemporary world situation, where peoples of highly diverse cultural backgrounds are moving rapidly into participation in modern industrial societies, acculturative stress and adaptation to new requirements are matters of crucial significance. Differences in cognitive styles and cognitive capacities also have important implications for intelligence testing in schools in this country, and for the debate about group differences in performance that has been raging for several years. As is clear from our discussion in this chapter, many complex aspects of cultural differences appear to be involved in cognitive development. *There is absolutely no evidence that any biological, or racial, factors are involved in performance differences among populations.*

Considering what has been achieved in the last two decades, we may be on the threshhold of a truly revolutionary transformation of cross-cultural psychology.

NOTES

1. The psychologist D. H. Owen (1978) has reviewed some of the experimental evidence of the influence of prior experience on perceiving. Although reference is made to animal experiments, the possible relevance of cultural differences is not considered.

2. Robert A. Hall (1953) lists both a word for blue and one for green in his dictionary of Haitian Creole. However, Creole speakers vary in the degree to which they introduce words from the French lexicon, depending both on their exposure to French and the context of word use.

3. Chippewa informants who were Catholic, and who had only limited knowledge of traditional practices, suggested that *ninəm* were second cousins. That is, they were cousins who could marry. The confusion here is between cross-cousins, who may be first, second, or third cousins (or even more distantly related), and second cousins, who may or may not be *ninəm*, —that is, in anthropological jargon, who may be parallel as well as cross-cousins. The two languages and societies do not offer comparable categories.

4. In subsequent fieldwork, among the Aguaruna Jívaro of Peru, Berlin and Berlin (1975) found it necessary to adapt their research methods. They used natural or artificial

objects of the appropriate colors instead of the plastic chips of the color array, which informants found to be puzzling.

5. Basic and nonbasic color terms appear to be used in different contexts. I note, for example, that basic terms seem to be avoided in fashion advertisements in the United States, where one sees reference to colors such as banana, tobacco, wine, rust, navy, and taupe.

6. The assumption that cognitions are universally agreed upon in a given culture, however, is questioned by further field research. For example, Pollnac (1975) found intracultural variability in color classification among the Ganda, who also show disagreement in other types of classifications, such as those of plants.

7. Spiro has elaborated on these points in a later publication. Presenting a "personality-oriented ethnography" of Burmese kinship and marriage, he describes his work as "unabashedly 'emic'; that is, it is concerned with ethnographic data in terms of what actors think, feel, believe, desire, and so on" (Spiro 1977:xii). He goes on to point out that his approach is not limited to "*how* natives think" but also concerns *what* they think and *why* they think it; that is, it involves not only cognitive but also motivational and affective aspects. Moreover, Spiro again stresses that personality-oriented ethnography goes beyond the emic dimensions to an etic study, a comparative science of humanity.

8. For summaries of Piaget's theories and work, see Piaget and Inhelder (1969), Ginsburg and Opper (1969), and Gruber and Vonèche (1978).

CHAPTER 7

Altered States of Consciousness

INTRODUCTION

Altered States of consciousness (ASC) are of great importance for psychological anthropology, for they can tell us a great deal about certain major dimensions of our common human nature and how it manifests itself in diverse cultural traditions. Such states exist in all human societies. They are known in many different forms and have been integrated into a variety of cultural patterns. They play different roles, are utilized in numerous diverse contexts, and are provided with a multitude of meanings. As we shall see, they represent characteristic types of responses to certain changes in the sensory, perceptual, cognitive, motivational, and affective relationship between indivuduals and their experience, responses that are to a great extent culturally patterned. In spite of their outward diversity and the variability of their cultural and social significance, altered states share a number of important common features. Yet surprisingly, they have, on the whole, been neglected by psychological anthropologists.

Historical Background

The subject of altered states of consciousness has had a curious history in anthropology. E. B. Tylor, as we saw in Chapter 2, considered trances, visions, and dreams among the basic factors that incited early human beings to develop theories of souls and spirits, in short, of religion. Students of primitive religion, a subject that includes shamanism, the American Indian vision quest, African and Afro-American possession rituals, and so on, found it necessary to deal with altered states. However, they generally studied beliefs and institutions and paid little attention to the psychological dimension. They saw shamans or possession trancers in ritual settings either as faking or as "hysterical." In fact, a lively debate developed in the field of Afro-American studies between various lay observers and psychiatrists, who thought that Haitians and Brazilians who become "possessed" on ritual occasions suffered from mental disorders, and M. J. Herskovits (1937a, 1948), who, in the tradition of cultural relativism, argued vigorously that because such behavior was acceptable and desirable according to the local cultural traditions, it was "normal" and should not be discussed in the language of psychopathology. Still, he left unexplained what happens to, or in, the individual, and why some people get to be "possessed" whereas others do not. Although Herskovits sought to explain Haitian and Brazilian possession trance as part of the Western African heritage of these societies, he does not tell us why certain societies of West Africa institutionalized altered states in a particular fashion. This theory also tends to limit our investigation to Afro-America and West Africa; yet, as we shall see, the problem is far more vast.

Clearly, altered states of consciousness represent a problem for psychological anthropology. Yet, although the anthropology of religion, as well as specific local enthnographies, had to take the existence of these states and their contexts of belief and ritual into account, psychological anthropology abstained from dealing with these matters for a long time. There are several reasons for this avoidance. One reason is a matter mentioned in Chapter 6: irrationality had dropped out of fashion with the development of cultural relativism. Visions, trances, and belief in possession were considered by Tylor and his contemporaries as hallmarks of the savage and the barbarian. Cultural relativism, rejecting such evaluations, emphasized the rational and, later, the adaptive nature of culture. One consequence of these orientations was to play down belief and behavior that seemed bizarre or exotic in terms of Western culture, and to emphasize ways in which "primitives" were, in fact, superior in their life-styles to "civilized" Westerners. It is also true that as long as emphasis was placed on the uniqueness of each culture, the differences rather than the underlying similarities were often stressed, and the common features of altered states tended to be overlooked. As a result, the information on which a general theory might have been built was not brought together.

One additional factor interfered: psychological anthropology has had no theory of its own. Instead, whether we deal with personality development, psychological testing, or psychopathology, anthropology has leaned heavily on psychoanalysis, clinical psychology, or psychiatry. For psychologists, the subject of "consciousness" had become taboo when nineteenth century psychological pioneers, under E. B. Titchener at Cornell, found that introspection as a research method yielded highly subjective results that could not be verified. As a result there was no theory for anthropologists to test or utilize that dealt with altered states, and their maintenance. There was some interest in hypnosis, but it did not provide an explanatory system, only a label of dubious usefulness. Even where drugs were used to induce their production, as among many American Indian tribes, the mechanism by which the drugs worked was not understood.

This situation has changed drastically in the last twenty-five years, when several research trends came together with a number of developments in Western society, especially in the United States. Psychologists here now have a lively interest in three types of altered states: dreams, drug-related states, and states of meditation and relaxation. As we shall see, there are other states of equal importance.

In this country, altered states of consciousness burst on the scene in the early 1960s with the burgeoning interest in psychedelic substances. At that time, Timothy Leary and a number of associates at Harvard not only experimented on themselves with LSD (lysergic acid diethylamide-25) but also founded the *Psychedelic Review* and the International Federation for Internal Freedom (IFIF). Somewhat later, Leary attempted to launch a religious movement, The League for Spiritual Discovery (LSD). These advocates associated the use of drugs, and the states produced by them, with mediation exercises based on various oriental traditions, particularly those of the Tibetan Book of the Dead. Hallucinogens, altered states of consciousness, and related matters rapidly drew great public attention and fascination, and since then a substantial literature has grown up in this area. Meanwhile a number of psychologists rediscovered "consciousness" as a field of investigation (see, for example, Ornstein 1972, Tart 1972, White 1972). It became necessary to distinguish between "normal waking" or "ordinary, personal" consciousness and altered states. These, it turned out, were numerous and varied and often perfectly unspectacular, not merely the much touted drug-induced hallucinatory states or religious ecstasies.

A Typology

Arnold Ludwig (1968) listed five major types of ASC, classifying them by the manner in which they are induced. For each of these five types he listed a dozen or more forms, so the total comes to more than sixty different forms of ASC, and the list is not complete. The five sets of causes of ASC are: 1) the reduction of exteroceptive stimulation and/or motor activity; 2) its opposite, the increase of exteroceptive stimulation and/or motor activity; 3) increase of alertness or mental involvement and 4) its opposite, decreased alertness or mental activity; and 5) a series of "somatopsychological" factors. This last group includes not only drug-induced states but states resulting from other changes in body chemistry, due to both internal and external causes, from hypoglycemia to hyperventilation and fevers.

The first two pairs of causal factors involve an increase or a decrease from a presumed preexisting "normal" level of stimulation or activity. When the level is altered, so is the state of consciousness. "Reduced stimulation and/or activity" includes not only such relatively familiar states as highway hypnosis, but also sensory deprivation produced either experimentally or as a result of solitary confinement. "Increased stimulation and/or motor activity" includes such conditions as mob contagion, religious conversion and healing trances in revivalistic settings, and "dance and music trance" in response to jazz, rock and roll, and other highly rhythmic music. Ludwig also includes here battle fatigue, hysterical conversion neuroses, dissociational states, and so on. Examples of the third type, "increased alertness and/or mental activity," include prolonged vigilance on sentry duty, watching a radar screen, or fervent prayer. The fourth type, "decreased alertness and/or mental activity," is illustrated by a relaxation of critical faculties in daydreaming, boredom, and profound relaxation, or in mediumistic trance and meditation states.

Notice the great diversity among the examples. In our society, some are fairly commonplace, others are unusual and striking events; some are religious in nature, others are pathological; some are socially constructive, others are dangerous and undesirable; some are cases of individual deviance, others are culturally patterned and institutionalized. They are grouped together because they share a limited set of causes.

As Ludwig further points out, these causes, which appear at times to be contradictory (for example, either increase or decrease of stimulation may produce an altered state), lead to states that share a number of important and distinctive features. He lists the following features: alterations in thinking, disturbed sense of time, loss of control, changes in the expression of emotions, changes in body image, perceptual distortion, changes in meaning and significance assigned to experiences or perceptions, a sense of the ineffable, feelings of rejuvenation, and hypersuggestibility. That is, *altered states of consciousness are conditions in which sensations, perceptions, cognition, and emotions are altered.* They are characterized by changes in sensing, perceiving, thinking, and feeling. They modify the relation of the individual to self, body, sense of identity, and the environment of time, space, or other people. They are induced by modifying sensory input, either directly by increasing or decreasing stimulation or alertness, or indirectly by affecting the pathways of the sensory input by somotopsychological factors. As a result, the rules of perception and cognition that cross-cultural psychology has been investigating (Chapter 6) do not necessarily apply to these states.

CULTURALLY STRUCTURED ASC

Three Examples

The social consequences of ASC, Ludwig notes, may be either maladaptive or adaptive. Indeed, their cultural contexts and contents are highly diverse. Let us consider some examples of ASC in action.

Here is an excerpt from my Haitian fieldnotes. They refer to a scene that took place in the countryside, when an elderly woman of some means was putting order into her affairs by having a *vodou* priest *(hungan)* and his followers perform a week-long series of rituals, which had been neglected for a number of years:

It is early afternoon and a group of men and women are seated under a roof of palmleaves. Two men are playing drums and a number of women are dancing, circling clockwise about the center pole of the structure. Several carry flags, and songs are being sung for Ibo-Lélé, the spirit to whom the ritual is addressed. While this is going on, two chickens are killed and their blood is collected in a clay pot. Suddenly, Ida, one of the women dancers, begins to tremble and sway on her feet. Several times she seems ready to fall, but each time one of the bystanders catches her, and she continues dancing. The others have stopped and all attention is on the woman who is entering trance, or, in local parlance, is being "mounted." Ibo-Lélé is possessing her, in response to the drums, the songs, the dances and the food, all calling him. Ida now dances more and more rapidly, with greater control over her movements. Now she is dancing more and more stiff-limbed, sometimes with her eyes closed. As she circles the center pole ever more closely, several women rush in to snatch away the dishes of sacrificial food that have been set out at the base of the pole, and which risk being turned over as she whirls about seemingly blindly. Finally, she falls on a mat at the edge of the structure, where several women are sitting, the *hungan's* wife among them, who catches Ida in her arms, as she lands on her knees. At that moment the drums stop and the possessed woman remains motionless. Then, as the drums start again, Ida begins to breathe more and more rapidly, raises herself up on her hands and knees and in two or three low jumps attacks the *hungan.* He is standing and she tries to get between his legs, and to cause him to fall; then raising herself up, she attempts to pull him down upon her. Now several people are seeking to restrain her, but she seems to have great strength. In the ensuing struggle her skirt begins to climb up and one of the other women pulls it down and tucks it between her legs. In the process, the possessed woman kicks over the jar with the blood and other offerings for Ibo-Lélé, and though it is caught quickly, some of the contents are spilled on the ground. As Ibo-Lélé's fury appears to increase, several women are waving kerchiefs at Ida to calm her (or him?) and finally the *hungan* succeeds in leading her away from the dance ground and into the nearby house. There she collapses on a chair and is not seen for the remainder of the day. The ritual is temporarily interrupted, and when the *hungan* returns he appears exhausted and disheveled. He explains that Ibo-Lélé had been angry because he had been called in the middle of the day, when the sun was too hot (Bourguignon, unpublished).

Quite a different example of ASC comes from a report by R. L. Carneiro on the Amahuaca Indians of the Amazon region of South America. In their dreams and in their ASC these people see spirits, called *yoshi.*

Every now and then the Amahuaca hold seances in order to interact with *yoshi* in greater numbers and for a longer time then they usually do in dreams. While many Amazonian tribes rely on tobacco narcosis to achieve spirit visions, the Amahuaca do not. They make use instead of an infusion made from the narcotic plant ayahuasa

Vodou drums are being prepared for baptism in a Haitian mountain community. They will have godparents and will receive names. The ritual drawings on the ground are made of flour. The drums are necessary to call the spirits.

(Banisteriopsis caapi), which has the power to produce extremely vivid and colorful hallucinations . . . the stronger the potion the more *yoshi* one will see. Before long, the drinkers begin to feel dizzy and start a very unusual kind of singing chant in a high-pitched tremolo in which the vocal chords are tightly constricted . . . Ayahuasa seances may last a long time. One session we witnessed began about eight o'clock at night and did not end until nearly six o'clock the next morning. Throughout its duration of nearly ten hours the men continued to sing virtually without interruption, pausing only a few seconds to drink some more or to vomit. As the drug takes effect, *yoshi* begin to appear, one or two at a time. They are said to drink ayahuasa, too, and to sing along with the men. The Amahuaca ask a *yoshi* where he has been and what he has seen, and he tells them. Unlike dreams, in which *yoshi* occasionally molest or injure a person, in ayahuasa seances they are generally friendly and tractable. It is just like when Amahuaca come to visit, we were told. A *yoshi* may stay an hour or two, and then he goes. But then another one comes, drinks with the Amahuaca, talks with them, and then he too departs. In this manner many *yoshi* may be seen and interrogated during the course of the night . . . Taking ayahuasa for the first time is apparently a rather frightening experience for a young man. Some of them reported seeing snakes crawling up their bodies. The *yoshi* of the jaguar is the one most often seen at this time, and it teaches the apprentice drinker all about *yoshi* (Carneiro 1964:8–9).

Our third example comes from North America, from the recollections of a Sioux medicine man by the name of John Lame Deer. When he was sixteen, he tells us, he went to seek his first vision. The vision quest, as it has been called, is a search for a personal guardian spirit, which was a widespread traditional practice in native North America. Before undergoing this experience, John says, he had never been alone in his life. The loneliness of the "vision pit" in which he spent four days fasting on an isolated hilltop added to his fear. As he explains it:

> I was still lightheaded and dizzy from my first sweatbath in which I had purified myself before going up the hill . . . The sweatbath had prepared me for the vision seeking. Even now, an hour later, my skin still tingled. *But it seemed to have made my brain empty.*

In this receptive state in the dark he felt that:

> Blackness was wrapped around me like a velvet cloth. It seemed to cut me off from the outside world, *even from my own body.* It made me listen to voices within me. I thought of my forefathers, who had crouched on this hill before me . . . I thought I could sense their presence right through the earth.

Finally comes the climax, after a time of fearful expectation:

> Suddenly, I felt an overwhelming presence. Down there with me in my cramped hole was a big bird . . . I felt feathers or a wing touching my back and head. *This feeling was so overwhelming that it was just too much for me.* I trembled and my bones turned to ice (Lame Deer and Erdoes 1972:14–15; italics added).

Terrified, the boy begins to sing and to pray, shaking the rattle he has brought with him. He goes on to hear voices and to see visions. The medicine man Lame Deer, who was his great-grandfather, speaks to him. At the end of four days, he is taken from the vision pit by the old man who had brought him there and who tells him that he is now a man. As a symbol of this transformation, he takes a new name, that of his ancestor.

Comparing Our Examples

In each of these examples, people seek to come into direct contact with spirits by means of ASC. They do so in the traditional fashion, which a young person, growing up in the society, must learn in order to behave correctly or to have the appropriate experiences. The ASC are not spontaneous or idiosyncratic, but fall into a cultural pattern. The spirits, at least in their broad outlines, are known, and to some extent the seeker is aware of what to expect. Moreover, in each case there are experienced and expert individuals who know what is to be done. Thus, cultural patterning, social practice, learning, and expertise all exist in the ASC situations that we find in these different cultures.

In spirt of these similarities, there are important contrasts among our three examples. To begin with the Amahuaca, they, like many American Indian groups, use a psychoactive plant substance to produce the ASC; the state is manifested by *seeing* and *hearing* things; that is, it is characterized by *altered perceptions.* Although several people sit together to sing and to drink, each sees and speaks with the *yoshi* as an individual. Each has a *private* trance experience.

For the young Sioux, the situation is, in some respects, similar. He, too, has his own private vision, he too hears and sees things. He, too, experiences altered perceptions. There are, however, some important differences: his trance is *not* induced by drugs but by the preparation of the sweatbath, the fear of isolation, darkness, the expectation of a vision, and the four days of hunger and cold, for he is naked and fasts during this period. Both psychological and physical stress prepare the boy for the experience that will transform his identity.

On most of these points, the Haitian case is quite different. ASC is induced neither through drugs nor through stress and deprivation, but through rhythmic drumming, rhythmic movement in dancing, and group expectations. It is true that in all three situations singing functions as prayer, as the mobilization of symbols and as a way of conjuring up the appropriate images and moods, but this role is different in each case. For the Haitians, unlike the Amahuaca and the Sioux, the ASC involves a public performance, not a private experience. Also, the Sioux vision seeker and the Amahuaca drug takers are men; among the Haitians, on the other hand, although both men and women participate, the individuals who are "possessed," like Ida in our example, are more likely to be women. The altered state among the Haitians may well consist of changes in perception, of seeing and hearing things, but we know little about it because people do not remember what happens to them during the time they are "possessed." They probably experience amnesia concerning these periods of time, reinforced by the belief, or cultural dogma, that when the spirit comes, it displaces one of the human being's souls (there are two), and therefore no memory is possible. In any event, Haitians like the Indians, actively invite the spirits to come, but the spirits do not appear as the hallucinations of individuals, but as personalities, to be observed by all present. The spirit, it is believed, takes over the body of a human individual, who for the time ceases to be herself or himself. The human being, during this time, is the "horse" that is "mounted" by the spirit. In the example we have described, this belief means that it is not a woman named Ida who attacks the *hungan* in a fit of rage, but rather the spirit Ibo-Lélé. Ida is not responsible for anything she does, and it will not be held against her. In fact as a personality, she is absent. When the scene was discussed by those present, and later by all those who were told about it, no one asked why Ida had behaved in this way on that particular day. The questions all centered about Ibo-Lélé and why he had been angered and whether or not he had rejected the sacrifice offered to him.

Inducing Altered States

As we consider our three examples, we find that ASC are used in each of these societies, but they are used in different ways and they are brought about by different means: The Amahuaca use psychotropic drugs, the Sioux primarily use isolation and fasting, and the Haitians use dancing and drums. All use expectations and traditions to help the desired results to come about, and all have some idea of what is to occur. Prelearning takes place before the event, and learning occurs during and as a result of the event. All three of these methods have been used in Western society in a nontraditional context, and comparisons between ASC occuring in such different contexts are instructive.

Wallace (1959) made a detailed comparison between the reactions of North American Indians who take peyote as part of their religious rituals and white subjects who took it as part of a clinical experiment. There were many striking differences both in the behavior and in the subjective experiences of the two groups. The Indians participated in a religious ritual, and they experienced feelings of reverence and frequently also relief from physical illness. The whites found themselves in an experimental setup, without cultural preparation providing special meaning. They experienced wide shifts of mood, ranging from agitated depression to euphoria. Moreover, the whites showed a breakdown of social inhibitions, behaving in various socially disapproved ways, whereas the Indians maintained proper decorum. Changes in perception of self and others were frightening to the whites; those occuring among the Indians fitted their religious expectations. Similarly, the Indians had visions that were in accordance with beliefs and that were culturally patterned, whereas the "visions" or hallucinations of the whites, which were formed without any cultural model, varied among individuals. Also, while the peyote experience led to changes in the Indians both in behavior and in psychological well-being, the whites, as far as the research determined, experienced no long-range changes and no therapeutic benefits.

The differences in the results of taking peyote, then may be related to the cultural differences between the two groups, the mental structure with which they approached the experience, the group context, and the symbolic meaning. The drugs, in other words, do not contain their own "content" but only modify human consciousness for a time. What happens during that time is largely dependent on what is brought to the experience by the individual who participates in it.

The methods by which the Sioux Indian boy acquires his vision is similar to that produced in the laboratory through sensory deprivation. Henney (1973, Henney in Goodman et al. 1974) has reviewed in detail reports of a series of sensory deprivation experiments conducted in this country and in Canada in the 1950s. She found striking similarities between these experiments, in which subjects hallucinated, and a ritual among the Spiritual Baptists on the Island of St. Vincent in the Caribbean. In this ritual, too, individuals are isolated, placed under conditions of restricted mobility and sensory input, and expected to have visions.

In ther review of sensory deprivation studies, Henney discovered that although the isolation and limitation of movement and sensory input were related to the production of hallucinations or "pseudoperception," other factors were of great importance as well. They include the way in which people react to others who have such experiences. Also relevant are the social cues and the explicit or implicit suggestions subjects receive concerning their experiences.

Henney concludes that:

> In addition to the physiological effects of sensory deprivation on the human organism, psychological and cultural factors appear to contribute significantly to the total phenomenon (Henney in Goodman et al. 1974:79).

Henney's comparison of sensory deprivation subjects and Spiritual Baptists seeking a supernatural vision parallels to a great extent that made by Wallace between experimental subjects and peyotists. Henney's analysis can be extended to a comparison between the Sioux youth and the sensory deprivation subjects as well. On the one hand, there is a traditional cultural content related to a transforming religious vision, and on the other, there is the cultural and social meaning of "laboratory experiments" participated in by volunteer college students. As in the case of peyote discussed by Wallace, the isolation and other limitations on physical and social action set up a condition favorable to the experience of pseudoperception. But *what* will be perceived and *how* it will be experienced is related to the cultural context and the traditional meanings provided to the individual.

Much the same can be said of the Haitians, or other possession trancers. This type of altered behavior has been likened to hypnosis, a subject the dynamics of which are little understood. In particular, in the ritual situation we have described there is no interaction between a hypnotist and a subject. One might suggest that the indivudual hypnotizes herself, as a result of previous experiences and expectations, or that the drums provide cues in a suggestive atmosphere. However, the specific behavior depends both on social and on individual factors. Again, we are dealing with a religious situation and not with the settings in which hypnosis is found in our own society: entertainment, experimentation, or medical healing (hypnosis is now widely used in this country in helping people to lose weight or to stop smoking, as well as to reduce fear and pain in dental work or in childbirth).

Where possession trance appears in a religious context, the behavior corresponds both to a learned model and to certain personal and/or group factors. In some societies, group factors are kept to a minimum, whereas in Haiti they are given great prominence. In the case we have described, Ida gave expression to a group tension specific to the particular series of ceremonies: the woman who was sponsoring them wanted her debts to the spirits settled through a variety of ceremonies, including sacrifices, but she was reluctant to have anyone go into possession trance, that is, to have spirits appear. Because this reluctance was very much against local habits and traditions, and because the prescribed dancing and drumming, which could not be avoided, did stimulate possession trance, Ida, under the pressure of these cues, was in conflict over succumbing to them. The result was an unusually violent possession trance. This is part of Haitian folk knowledge, the women say that there are ways of restraining the spirits, but if you use them and the spirits come just the same, they may come so violently as to kill you. In psychological terms, setting up a conflict between cues for and against possession trance is a dangerous procedure.

In our three examples, then, in addition to the specific manipulations (drugs, sensory-motor deprivation, hyperventilation in dancing, modification of balance, rhythmic drumming, and so on) there are major cultural factors that provide social support, traditional context, cultural content, and religious rewards for undergoing ASC. All our groups believe in invisible spirits who can be persuaded to appear and to interact with humans, but the nature of these interactions is quite different: whereas it is *private* in the American Indian cases, it is *public* in the Haitian case. Whereas it is an *experience* for the former, it is a *performance* for the latter. In all cases, however, we deal with *traditional* practices, not with idiosyncratic ones. And, most importantly, in all cases we deal with *ritual.*

Altered States and Ritual

Ritual is a central concept in the anthropological study of religion. In fact, A. F. C. Wallace (1966) has defined religion as "ritual rationalized by myth," that is, ritual explained and made meaningful by a sacred belief concerning natural beings or forces, for there may be secular non-religious rituals as well. Ritual has been variously defined, but there are a number of general points of agreement among anthropologists who have written on this subject. For one thing, it is distinct from "practical" or "rational" or "technological activities," such as hunting, planting and harvesting crops, fishing, cooking, housebuilding, and a myriad of other everyday activities. Second, it is stereotyped and repetitive: for example, there are fixed, traditional, learned ways to call the spirits. Third, ritual occurs in a separate place and time, often at night, or at periods specially set aside. It is thus separated from the ordinary, workaday world. Fourth, symbols of ritual present a different, generally unseen aspect of the world. In the process, the individual's relation to the world is modified. Wallace (1966), in particular, speaks of a "ritual reorganization of experience," a kind of learning, through which the world is simplified for the individual: the complex world of experience is transformed into an orderly world of symbols. At the same time, there is also a transformation of the individual, who acquires new understandings, or in Wallace's terms, "new cognitive structures," and a new transformed identity. In some cases, the identity is membership in a special group or a new status. In the rituals we have described, this change in identity particularly marks the Sioux youth, but also those who drink ayahuasca for the first time, or who are "possessed" for the first time.

For Wallace, the essence of ritual is communication; yet, because ritual is stereotyped and predictable, it tells us nothing new, conveys no information. What is conveyed, however, is meaning, particularly "the image of a simple and orderly world" (Wallace 1966:239). In the rituals we have described, moreover, communication between humans and spirits, as the people conceive of them, is the very purpose of the ritual. ASC, in each case, are the means by which this communication can be accomplished. On the one hand, among the Amahuaca the drug makes it possible to "see" and "hear" the spirits, to ask them questions. For the Sioux, it is the stress that leads to the visionary experience. On the other hand, the Haitians produce the physical presence of the spirits by having human individuals serve as their vehicles ("horses"). From the observer's point of view, we can say that, as a result of drug ingestion, the Amahuaca *hallucinate* the presence of the spirits, as do the Sioux. The Haitian situation is somewhat more complex: one or more persons are temporarily *deluded* into thinking, feeling, and perceiving themselves to be the spirits whose role they are enacting, while others in the group accept and encourage this role enactment.

As observers, we can also consider these rituals as communication among the participants. The principal aim and result of these three types of rituals are the *confirmation and elaboration of belief:* the spirits do exist, they come when they are properly called, they say and do certain things, and they have certain collective and individual characteristics. ASC rituals effectively confirm what tradition has said; moreover, because the spirits are heard and seen, their words and actions may be the basis for modifications of ritual, belief, or secular behavior. As such, they are contributors of major significance to the elbaoration of a culturally constituted behavioral environment. These are important considerations to which we shall return in Chapter 9.

In his analysis of factors producing altered states, Ludwig does not distinguish between individual, idiosyncratic states and culturally patterned, ritually structured ones. We may assume that certain individual states, such as fever delirium, auras preceding epileptic seizures, or trance resulting from drowsiness or boredom occur in all human societies. Anthropological interest focuses on cultural structuralization of altered states. We must distinguish also between altered states employed in the context of religious ritual and those that serve recreational purposes. In the words of Weston La Barre (1975:24), "There appears to be no human society so simple in material culture as to lack some sort of mood-altering drug as an escape from the workaday world."

There is reason to believe that the ritual uses of altered states have ancient roots in human history and prehistory. Ralph Solecki (1975) discovered a 60,000-year-old Neanderthal burial at Shanidar cave in Northern Iraq. The human remains had been placed on pine boughs, and there was evidence of a bouquet of flowers. When the pollen was analyzed, seven of the eight plant species represented were recognized as medicinal plants that are still used in the region, as well as elsewhere in Europe and Asia. Peter Furst (1976), in his broad survey of hallucinogens and their cultural uses, wonders whether the Shanidar Neanderthalers also had knowledge of the psychedelic plants that existed in their environment. The so-called "dead man" in the Upper Paleolithic cave painting at Lascaux, in France, probably represents a man in trance. The healing plants and the trancing relate well to the function of the shaman, which is so widespread in hunter-gatherer societies, and for which there are various other types of archaeological evidence, such as the painting representing a dancing "sorcerer" at another ancient French site, the cave of Les Trois Frères.

Weston La Barre (1972) has argued that hallucinatory "revelations" (visions, trances, dreams) are the source of all religions. The necessary requirement is that the visionary must be able to persuade others to accept the truth of the revelation and its applicability to them. If, as La Barre argues, the visionary's experience consists of an expression of unconscious wishes, these wishes must be shared by followers if they are to find their own meaning in the message. Many such cases have been known in modern times and in recorded history. On the other hand, we also have evidence of numerous instances in which the would-be prophet was unsuccessful in getting others to share that private world and a result not only failed as a religious leader but was rejected as heretical or mad.[2]

In an extensive study of the social and cultural patterning of ASC (Bourguignon 1973b), we found that such states exist in religious contexts in 90 percent of a sample of 488 societies. This sample, which was drawn from the *Ethnographic Atlas* (Murdock 1967), included all parts of the world and traditional societies at various levels of technological complexity. In fact, 90 percent represents a conservative judgment, for in the 10 percent of the cases for which no reports of such ritualized ASC were found, we could rarely be sure that we were not simply dealing with incomplete accounts. Moreover, for North American Indians, where the ethnographic studies are quite detailed and of high quality, we found reports of ASC in 97 percent of the sample societies!

Cultural Interpretations of Altered States

The cultural patterning of ASC involves beliefs or interpretations of what occurs during these states. We have distinguished several types of such explanatory systems (Bourguignon 1968a). On the one hand there are "naturalistic" or empirical explanations, of the kind provided by Ludwig. These explanations are formulated in terms of the normative world view of Western society, as expressed in medicine. They represent a etic approach, which can be applied whenever and wherever ASC are observed. This approach may be contrasted with an essentially emic one, which we identified in the societies in our sample, in a still larger group from which we collected additional data, and also in the history of Western societies (Bourguignon 1976). Two principal types of emic explanations appear over and over again: ASC are explained either as due to "possession" by spirit entities, or as involving experiences of one's soul or spirit, often as resulting from an encounter with the spirit. This encounter may happen by sending one's soul on a spirit voyage or "trip,"[3] or, as in the case of the Amahuaca and the Sioux, by having the spirits come to visit. We have called the first type "possession trance" (PT) and the second "trance" (T). The Haitians on the one hand and the Amahuaca and the Sioux on the other then represent the two basic types of culturally patterned, institutionalized ASC. Both of these emic types of explanations are essentially "supernaturalistic": they involve both ritual and what (Wallace 1966) has called a "supernatural premise." The etic explanation involves neither ritual nor supernaturalism.

Figure 2 divides supernaturalistic explanations of ASC into two basic categories, possession beliefs and nonpossession beliefs. Both are evaluated at some times and places as positive and in others as negative. In the Haitian example, we have a belief in a spirit presence during ASC rituals. The spirits are invited and the possession trance is desirable and positive. In the tradition of the Middle Ages, which has been somewhat revived and exploited in this country in recent years, we have a belief in demonic possession that requires a ritual of expulsion or exorcism. Possession trance is explained, in this context, as an invasion of the body and the will by evil forces, which must be driven out through religious ritual. In certain areas of the world, notably in East Africa, there exists a third alternative: manipulating or transforming the evil, illness-causing, possessing spirit into an ally. This approach appears in the zar cult, which has been reported for

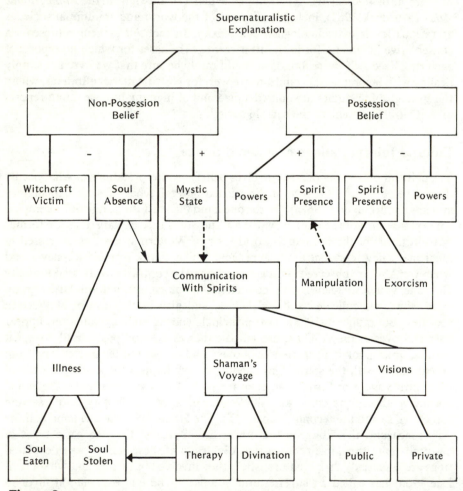

Figure 2
SUPERNATURAL EXPLANATIONS OF ALTERED STATES OF CONSCIOUSNESS (FROM BOURGUIGNON 1968).

the Amhara of Ethiopia (Leiris 1958, Messing 1959, Morton 1977), the Somali (Lewis 1971), and the Egyptians (Saunders 1977). Such beliefs and practices, in one form or another, are found throughout many parts of Europe, Africa, the Middle East, and the Far East, and among the descendants of these people in the New World, such as the Haitians.

Among American Indians possession trance also occurs, but it is not always associated with the concept of "spirit." Often, as in the case of the Yurok shaman (Kroeber 1925), it involves a belief in "powers" that take over the person of the shaman or shaman candidate. These powers, which deal with pain and with healing, are not personalized and anthropomorphized (or zoomorphized) as the spirits are.

Nonpossession beliefs that explain altered states appear to be more varied, although we may again distinguish between positive and negative evaluations of the ASC. On the positive side, we have mystic states that involve communication with spirits either by means of visions or by means of the shaman's spirit voyage. The visions may be experienced in a public setting or privately. The shaman's voyage, if it is not primarily concerned with visions, may have two specific practical applications. One is divination: diagnosing illness, discovering the causes of troubles, or foretelling the future. The other is the healing of patients. If the patient is ill, because his or her soul is absent, having perhaps been stolen by an enemy, the aim of the shaman's voyage may be to get the soul back. Trance may be explained also as due to the absence of the trancer's soul: either the shaman's, who is communicating with spirits, or the patient's, whose soul has been stolen or worse, eaten. Finally, trance may be due to bewitchment.

Although this list of emic explanations is not exhaustive, it does indicate a wide variety of beliefs linked to ASC. The particular ritualization of ASC will reflect the beliefs concerning this state. The state will be intentionally self-induced only if it is considered a positive good; it may be induced in others as part of therapy or group initiation, which, at times, may be synonymous. It should be noted that these emic explanatory systems say nothing about the manner in which ASC are induced, or even whether they occur spontaneously or are brought about intentionally.

Possession

Let us consider the concept of possession further. Figure 3 shows that possession beliefs may be linked not only to the ASC (trance behavior), but also to other kinds of behaviors, conditions, and cultural contexts. Again, there is both a positive and a negative evaluation of "possession," regardless of whether or not it is linked to an altered state. On the positive side, we find, particularly among American Indians, that a person may become inhabited by power (whether it is conceived of as in some way animate or inanimate). For example, the Havasupai shaman (Spier 1928) has a power in his body which he uses to locate illness in

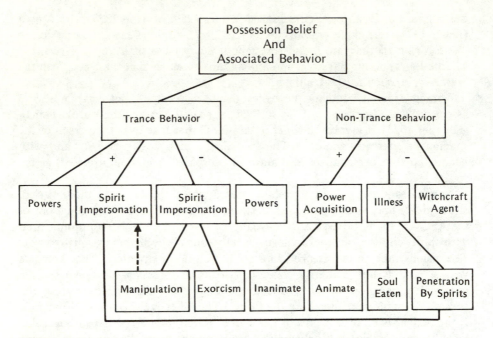

Figure 3
POSSESSION BELIEF AND ASSOCIATED BEHAVIOR (FROM BOUR-GUIGNON 1968).

his patient. Harner (1973a) tells us of the Jívaro that they hunt heads in order to acquire power, which becomes part of their own soul stuff.

Lienhardt (1954) describes the installation of the Nyikang, the King of the Shilluk, of the Upper Nile. The soul of the first king enters the body of the incumbent, who experiences a brief seizure (possession trance). Afterwards, the new king remains permanently "possessed" by the soul of his predecessor, though he returns to normal consciousness and is not expected to experience other ASC at later periods. Another combination of nontrance possession and possession trance occurs sometimes among the followers of the *zar* cult, where, in the emic view, the initial possession may be expressed as infertility or illness; only at a therapeutic ritual, which is an initiation, does possession trance occur (Lewis 1971). In etic terms, we would say that the patient experiences illness or infertility (or some other disorder) and this experience is *interpreted* as resulting from possession by a spirit.

It is clear from examples that possession that is not acted out in ASC behavior may coexist in a single society with possession trance. Similarly, in our analysis of ASC and their emic explanations, we find cases in which both trance and possession trance coexist in the same society.

In our examples we have seen that a belief in possession may be used to explain not only ASC, but also the acquisition of power or the presence of illness. Finally, there is the third case, which appears to be limited to Africa, in which possession explains witchcraft. Among many African peoples, such as the Azande (Evans-Pritchard 1937) or the Fang (Fernandez 1961), it is believed that certain individuals are inhabited by a witchcraft being, which leads them to cause harm to others, often without being aware of doing so. A strikingly similar belief exists among some New Guinea peoples, such as the Kaluli (Schiefflin 1976).

As this brief review shows, the broad concept of possession covers a great variety of specific beliefs. In one form or another, however, it occurs in all parts of the world. In our sample from the *Ethnographic Atlas,* referred to earlier, we found that 74 percent of our 488 societies had one or more forms of possession belief (Bourguignon 1973b). The fact that the concept is so widespread and that the context of the beliefs and their specific applications are so varied suggests that we are dealing with a very old idea, one that has been modified and fitted into various kinds of cultural patterns. Yet it is also striking that the possession concept is not found with equal frequency in all parts of the world. It has its highest incidence in the Insular Pacific and its lowest among the societies of aboriginal North America (52 percent) and South America (64 percent). The cultures of the New World, then, are significantly different with respect to these beliefs, as indeed in respect to much else, from those of the Old World.

Although we may be impressed with the extent to which possession has been used as an explanation, it is also striking how much less frequently it appears than the integration of ASC into the repertoire of religious rituals. This fact, together with the observation that possession belief is not always linked to ASC, suggest the hypothesis that they did not originate together and that ASC experiences did not give rise to the possession concept. Rather, possession belief and ASC appear to have independent histories, and to have been joined, perhaps on several occasions, under particular circumstances.

The emic theories that account for ASC and the various applications of possession belief represent a variety of "ethnopsychologies," psychological theories characteristic of various cultures, traditional ones for the most part. It should be stressed that the concept of "possession" is *not* synonymous with a type of ASC, although people frequently speak and write about "possession states" or "possession behavior." Strictly speaking, these terms apply only where an altered state is interpreted by both the actor and those in the actor's social environment as due to "possession" of some kind. Bear in mind also that what people believe about ASC affects their behavior. It is obviously impossible for possession trance to occur where a belief in possession is absent. In Haiti, for example, where spirits are believed in and each is characterized by particular types of behavior, food and drink preferences, and typical attributes, people must somehow learn to behave appropriately in their altered states in order to be recognized and accepted as possessed by a given spirit, whether Ibo-Lélé or some other well known entity. Such emic psychological theories account for behavior under various circumstances, and for different kinds of experiences, in waking life and in sleep, in health and illness, and so on. Some remnants of such traditional theories are still found in our own speech habits. For example, we may say that a man was "beside himself" with rage or grief, or "I don't know what got into her," or "I was not myself" (but someone else?), and so on. Even the Greek roots of "enthusiastic" (god within) and "ecstatic" (standing outside) reflect such ancient beliefs.

Trance Types

The distinction between trance (T) and possession trance (PT) however, is more than a device for classifying altered states in terms of types of emic explanations. When Bourgignon and Evascu (1977) focused on the societies in which these culturally institutionalized states occur, we discovered that our sample could be broken down into four types of societies or "trance types": 1) societies that exhibit T only, 2) those that have T but also PT, 3) those with PT only, and 4) the 10 percent that has neither form of ASC, as far as we can tell. Because this last group is so small and also because we could not really be sure that "no ASC" did not really mean "no report," we dropped this final group from our analysis. Examining regional distribution of the three types of societies (T, T/PT, PT), we found that T is highly correlated with North America and to a lesser, but still significant extent, with South America. In North America, the vision quest is an important factor, and in South America, the widespread use of hallucinogens is directly related to the high incidence of T. On the other hand, we found PT to be significantly correlated with sub-Saharan Africa, and to a somewhat lesser degree, with the circum-Mediterranean region. PT is so rare in North America that we have a statistically significant *negative* association between this type of ASC and North America as a major ethnographic area (Bourguignon and Evascu 1977).

These regional distributions are interesting, but they do not tell the whole story. What about cultural complexity? After all, North American Indians were predominantly hunter-gatherers, whereas the peoples of sub-Sahara African were traditionally horticulturalists (Bourguignon and Greenbaum 1973). In a first series of tests (Bourguignon 1973b) we found that our three types of societies showed statistically significant differences in twelve societal characteristics, six of them clearly related to differences in societal complexity. This finding encouraged us to pursue the matter further. Rather than merely asking whether our three types of societies were more or less complex, we selected four variables and broke them down into a series of steps. The variables were class stratification, jurisdictional hierarchy, the degree or percentage to which a society's subsistence economy is dependent on production (animal husbandry, agriculture, or a combination of the two), and finally, percentage of dependence on agriculture. The results showed clearly that the greater the societal complexity and the higher the level of subsistence economy, the more likely the soceity was to have PT rather T. However, many of our 488 societies were closely related either historically or geographically, and a test of diffusion showed that our results might be accounted for through these relationships. We therefore proceeded to select a much smaller sample of eighty-four societies, being careful to avoid possible causes of "contamination" through cultural diffusion. The results again con-

Mangé loa (Feasting of the gods), painting by the Haitian artist Wilson Bigaud (Collection Paul H. and Erika Bourguignon). Many phases of the ritual are shown in this picture. The woman at the right, supported by the man next to her, is in possession trance. The cross in the foreground is for Gédé the spirit of the cemetery. The snake in the tree represents an African spirit. (There are no large snakes in Haiti.)

firmed the relationship between societal and economic complexity and trance type (Bourguignon and Evascu 1977).

How can we account for this relationship? A closer look at how ASC are produced and the cultural role they play may help us in understanding these functional associations. To begin with, American Indians frequently used drugs to achieve altered states of consciousness. La Barre (1972, 1975) several times reviewed the extensive evidence for the existence of what he called a "New World narcotic complex," covering a great portion of the Americas, from the southern half of the United States to most of the region of the Amazon Basin and the Andes. Pointing out that the botanical sources of hallucinogens (in mushrooms, cacti, and vines, as well as in many seeds, barks, flowers, roots, and saps) are available in the Old World as well as the New, the botanist R. E. Schultes asked why eighty or more varieties of hallucinogens were known to American Indians, whereas the peoples of the rest of the world were familiar with only about six such substances. La Barre (1972:272) relates this greater knowledge of hallucinogens to a specialized interest in the subject resulting from "the ubiquitous persistence of shamanism among the aboriginal hunting peoples of the New World." The relationship between the two is explained by the observation that "ecstatic-visionary shamanism is, so to speak, *culturally programmed for an interest in hallucinogens and other psychotropic drugs"* (italics in original). La Barre points out that the old religions of shamanism of the hunting peoples of Eurasia and Africa were thoroughly transformed by the new traditions that resulted from the Neolithic Revolution. That is, the new relationship among humans, plants, and animals brought about by the domestication of plants and animals was expressed in new symbolic forms and new rituals.

All of this discussion is consistent with our findings, both with regard to the geographic distribution of trance and possession trance, and to the relationship between trance type and subsistence economy. It should be added that we found few cases of drug-induced ASC in sub-Sahara Africa, where PT is the dominant form of ASC. For a number of New World societies, combining data from both North and South America, we found (Bourguignon 1968b:20) that where drugs were used, trance (T) was much more likely than possession trance (PT). This relationship was highly significant statistically. As to the importance of the hunter-gatherer mode of life, which is typically associated with shamanistic religions, it must be stressed that when La Barre speaks of "aboriginal hunting peoples of the New World" he refers to the great majority of North American native societies and to a significant minority of the groups of South America. Of the North American societies coded in Murdock's *Ethnographic Atlas,* 77 percent had a heavy reliance on hunting, gathering, and fishing for their subsistence; and so did 28 percent of South American societies. By contrast, only 4 percent of the societies of sub-Saharan African depended heavily on these activities for food (Bourguignon and Greenbaum 1973: Table 6). Notable among this group, however, were !Kung, among whom visionary trance states play a significant role.

Visionary Trance.   Although the hallucinatory or visionary trance state is of such great importance in the Americas, it is not always induced by drugs. The case of the Sioux medicine man John Lame Deer illustrates the widespread guardian spirit complex. The solitary quest for a vision, the four days of isolation and fasting, occasionally, as among the Cheyenne (Gladwin 1957) various kinds of mortifications and self-tortures—these were essential parts of this pattern. Although in several tribes women or girls also sought visions, it was a predominantly male activity. Swanson (1973) noted that this North American practice served as a kind of puberty initiation but was notably different from the typical initiation ceremonies of Africa and Australia, with their group activities and initiation "schools." Swanson speaks of the guardian spirit quest as a rite of "empowerment" by means of which the seeker "inducts himself" into adulthood. The vision is a distinctive feature of this complex. By means of it, the spirit bestows power on the individual. This power is a gift that the recipient, as Swanson (1973:360) puts it, "on his own volition, might use or neglect." This idea receives support from La Barre (1972:274), who writes: "In this male-centered hunting society,[4] curiously a boy's manhood and manly prowess in hunting and war and sexuality *all came as gifts from the outside*—that is, as 'medicine power' imbibed from the outside, generalized, impersonal, mana-like, supernatural . . ."

(italics in original). Because this gift is acquired from spirits that must be approached in a fearful quest, Swanson argues that the guardian spirit complex is linked to individual initiative, requiring the individual's own need and desire for the power. The quest, then, constitutes an effective test of the boy's independence, his discretion, and the strength of his motives. Such personal characteristics are important in societies, says Swanson, in which, in addition to group goals and interests, individuals have a considerable degree of autonomy to pursue their own goals. Considering the findings of Barry, Child, and Bacon (1959), in a study to which we have referred a number of times, Swanson suggests, that a substantial but not complete dependence on hunting, gathering, and fishing will produce the type of socialization pressure toward self-reliance and achievement consistent with such a religious pattern. Swanson's statistical analysis of data on forty-two societies of Native North Americans confirms this hypothesis.

A study by D'Andrade (1961) on the use of dreams to seek and control supernatural powers also has bearing on the present discussion. D'Andrade himself points out that, on the basis of the ethnographic literature, it is not always possible to distinguish among dreams, drug states, visions induced by other means, and related conditions. The similarity between trance states and dreams, both of which are private, internal experiences, is great, and in cultural terms, they are often either interchangeable or used together in some way. For example, the Diegueño Indians of California used the drug *toloache* (*Datura stramonium*) in the initiation of their "dream doctors" or shamans. As one of them explained:

> *Toloache* puts you into a kind of dream state of mind that stays with you the rest of your life, and you never forget what you have learned. It helps you to keep on learning and gives you real power in everything. Without it you aren't a real doctor (Toffelmeier and Luomala 1936:201).

D'Andrade coded a worldwide sample of sixty-four societies for the use of dreams to seek and control supernatural powers; those with this cultural complex are, in fact, more likely to be societies where visionary trance is present than where it is not (Bourguignon 1972). It was D'Andrade's purpose to test the hypothesis that using dreams in this fashion—to acquire a spirit helper in fantasy—results from anxiety about being alone, on one's own, and under pressure to be independent. He tested this hypothesis by means of two indicators, suggesting that societies that use dreams to seek and control supernatural powers are more likely to be 1) those where the son moves away from the parental home, local groups, or village after marriage, than where he does not, and 2) those in which socialization pressures for independence and self-reliance are great. D'Andrade, basing his work on the work of Barry, Child, and Bacon (1959), expected societies heavily dependent for their subsistence on hunting, gathering, and fishing to use dreams in this manner. Both of these hypotheses were confirmed.

There are some interesting points of agreement and of difference between the approaches of Swanson and D'Andrade. Swanson says that where the individual boy is pushed to be independent and self-reliant, he must make himself a man and not expect a group to do it for him. He must demonstrate his fortitude by the rigors of the quest for a guardian spirit, from whom he acquires power, which is then his own. Yet, as La Barre (1972) notes, the power is conceived of as coming to the boy from the *outside,* it is not a natural part of his own development. Indeed, he may well be afraid in the process of acquiring it; moreover, spirits are called by showing them dependence, weakness, and humility. They give the boy power because they take pity on him. D'Andrade says that where the boy must leave his parents and be on his own, and where he is pushed to be self-reliant, he will be anxious; unable to be dependent on human support, he will seek supernatural help, or one might say, fantasize such support to bolster his self-confidence.

This analysis suggests a possible line of explanation for the association between trance (T) and hunting, gathering, and fishing economies. Pushed to be self-reliant early in life, and required to achieve as self-reliant and independent individuals as adults, boys in such societies are exposed to special kinds of anxieties. On the one hand, the vision, the guardian spirit, and the power so acquired compensate for the stresses arising from unsatisfied dependency longings in childhood, and on the other, they give the young man support in his enterprises. Trance, then, not only *gives expression* to this situation but also *provides a remedy.*

We have been speaking not only about certain kinds of societies, but also certain individuals, specifically men. Visionary trance, whether part of the guardian spirit complex or drug-induced in other settings, is far more frequently reported as practiced by men than by women. Certainly the socialization pressure for independence is consistently greater for boys than for girls, and hunting is a much more independent and risk-laden activity than gathering. However, there may be other factors, in somewhat different settings, which also make trance (T) primarily a male experience. Among them are the social context and symbolic content, of the use of hallucinogenic drugs such as *ayahuasca* (also called *shori, yajé*, or *caapi*) reported for a number of Amazonian tribes.

Janet Siskind (1973) describes the ritual of drinking *shori (Banisteriopsis caapi)* among the Sharanahua in the jungle of Eastern Peru. The men drink the prepared hallucinogenic as a group, but each man sings his own songs, calling his own spirits. Through the songs and through the mythology associated with *shori,* as well as through the telling of their visionary experiences, young men must "learn to shape the visual illusions and the physiological sensations into the mold and form of the spirits . . . Men sing of what they see and their singing calls the visions" (pp. 136–137). Furthermore, the taking of *shori* is frightening, and this fear is linked, in Siskind's view, not only to the sensations and visions produced by the drug but also to the group:

> When the Sharanahua first take *shori* they are frightened. The [hallucinated] snakes that encircle them are only slowly transformed, after months of taking part in the ritual, into beautiful images. This transformation of terror into euphoria . . . is a

significant part of the ritual. The terror of *shori* for a Sharanahua is the terror of strangers, the very men with whom one takes *shori.* For most young men these are not his (sic) kinsmen, but [strangers] in whose village or household he has found a wife. As the young men continue to take part, their fears fade, the snakes are beautiful, and they begin to learn to call the spirits and to "know" (Siskind 1973:137).

Among these matrilocal people, a boy seeks a wife in the family of his father's sister. The men of the village, therefore are unrelated to each other. *Shori* ritual, Siskind believes, functions as a ritual of solidarity for the men. The women, being related to each other, do not require such a ritual. However, beyond the establishment of solidarity, there is another level, that of fantasy and regression, which relates to mastery:

> The terrors of *shori* are childhood terrors, and the experience of trance is one of helplessness. Like an infant one is in the control of *shori* and the spirits. By giving up the cultural role of adulthood, as the man [in the myth] gives up his being a hunter to imitate the tapir [by copulating with Snake-Woman] one again experiences desires long buried for freely given satisfaction, sex without antagonism, friendship without rivalry ... The intense pleasure of *shori* lies in these moments of connection ... (Siskind 1973:141).

The author suggests (p. 147) that the true meaning of the ritual is a repeated "hallucination of social unity" where none exists in reality. The dynamics of the ritual, says Siskind (p. 145), involve "a feeling of communality between the men achieved through their shared desire and antagonism toward women. There is no other basis for male solidarity at Marcos." The myths and some of the songs are evocative of sexual images, and at least some of the visions involve women as well as snakes. Some men liken *shori* to sex and feel sexual desire under its influence.

The ritual and the symbolic meanings associated with the same drug are reported by Reichel-Dolmatoff (1971, 1972) for the Tukano Indians of the northwestern Amazon region of Colombia. Summarizing the myth that describes the origin of the drug, he states:

> Therefore, in the context of Tukano mythology, *yajé* [the drug] has a marked sexual character. Hallucination and coitus are equivalent, not in the sense of procreation or gratification but rather as an experience full of anxiety, because of its relationship to the problem of incest (1972:96).

Various sexual associations link the plant, the making of the drink, the vessel in which it is macerated, and various other ritual elements. The pot with its decorations represents the uterus, and while drinking from it the men may insult it, as they would insult "a female being who had defied them, presenting a danger they are ready to confront" (Reichel-Dolmatoff 1972:101). Men take the drug in order to return to the uterus, to begin at the beginning of the universe and of humanity, and to encounter the tribal divinities. The creation of the universe is associated with the establishment of the social order and of the laws of exogamy:

On the other hand, a return to the womb is considered an incestuous act, since the person becomes identified with a phallus which enters into the maternal cavity, where he now passes through an embryonic stage of rebirth. . . . For the Indian the hallucinatory experience is essentially a sexual one. To make it sublime, to pass from the erotic, the sensual, to a mystical union with the mythic era, the intra-uterine stage, is the ultimate goal, attained by a mere handful, but coveted by all . . . In the words of an Indian educated by missionaries . . . "To take *yajé* is a spiritual coitus; it is the spiritual communion which the priests speak of" (Reichel-Dolmatoff 1972:103–104).

A full analysis of these citations and of the rich data presented by Reichel-Dolmatoff would take us far afield. For now, the masculine, sexual symbolism associated with trance and hallucination as it appears among these Amazonian peoples is to be stressed.

Although these Amazonian groups do not depend for their subsistence primarily on hunting, gathering, and fishing, La Barre's reference to "male-centered hunting societies" does apply to them. For example, Siskind tells us of the Sharanahua that although they depend for 60 percent of their subsistence on agricultural products, their society is strongly focused on meat, which is obtained by hunting. Hunting, indeed, is the principal occupation of men, and it is also an exclusively male occupation.

The relationship between hunting, men, and trance is not limited to the Americas. The !Kung of Botswana furnish an excellent example from Africa. According to several authors (Marshall 1965, Lee 1968, Katz 1976) half or more of the men are "medicine owners." Trance results not from drugs but from rhythmic dancing, autosuggestion, hyperventilation, and concentration, and its purpose is to cure or to avert illness and misfortune. Lorna Marshall says that "the dance is one concerted religious act of the !Kung and brings people into such unison that they become like one organic being" (1965:270). Dances occur in the evening and last throughout the night, or longer. A fire is built and women sit around it, forming a circle. Their singing helps the male dancers go into trance. The !Kung say that trance is brought about by heating up the medicine substance in their stomachs by means of dancing. Medicine is transferred to others, either to cure them or to make them into medicine men, by the trancers rubbing their bodies. Illness is said to come from ghosts, or from an evil spirit. According to Marshall, medicine men may rush out into the darkness and scream at these spirits, and when they then fall unconscious into deepest trance, it is believed that their spirits leave their bodies and go out to meet these evil beings.

This pattern is quite different from the ones we have discussed so far. Trance is induced by the means we have come to associate with possession trance, rather than by drugs or by solitary deprivation, fasting, and mortifications. It is, however, limited to men. It is linked to curing, as is trance among curing specialists in the South American groups, where, however, others also may seek the trance experience. Although !Kung medicine men come together to dance, each has his own visionary experience and each does his own curing. The collective behavior fits well with the image of the !Kung as cooperative and focused on sharing. Yet it is interesting that among such peaceful, nonaggressive people, the spirits of the dead are thought to be so hostile to the living as to send them illness and harm![5]

Possession Trance.   Having explored the pattern of interrelationships among trance, hunting, and men, let us look at possession trance (PT) and explore the social context and cultural and symbolic content of this pattern. As we reported earlier, possession trance is widespread in sub-Saharan Africa, and to a somewhat lesser extent in the circum-Mediterranean area. It also appears with a certain frequency in Eurasia and the Insular Pacific. It is frequent in Afro-America among the descendants of African peoples who have maintained the religious tradition of their ancestors to a significant extent. Haitian *vodou* is a case in point.

As mentioned earlier, PT is more likely to be found in societies with heavy dependence on agriculture and food production, as opposed to hunting, gathering, and fishing. A value system in which agricultural production is given prominence is also of importance here. Following Barry, Child, and Bacon (1959) again, we expect in such societies greater emphasis on obedience, reliability, and nurturance—in a word, compliance. Moreover, Barry, Bacon, and Child (1957) have shown that regardless of economy, nurturance, reliability, and obedience rank higher in the socialization of girls than in that of boys. Therefore, it might be said that in contrast to hunting and gathering societies, high accumulation societies stress the "female" values of obedience, responsibility, and nurturance.

Haitian teenager in a carnival mask, made of orange and grapefruit peels. As with trance states, representational masks are much more frequently used by men, than by women in all parts of the world. Like possession trance, they produce a temporary change of identity.

Possession trance appears to be a typically female phenomenon. Although we have no hard statistical evidence to support this claim, numerous ethnographers and others describing possession trance rituals report that a majority of those going into possession trance are women, or that possession trance cult groups are composed exclusively of women (see also Lewis 1971). For example, most of the detailed case histories of possession trancers reported in Crapanzano and Garrison's (1977) volume deal with women, and all come from complex societies. Moreover, possession trance typically occurs in group rituals and is supported by cult groups. This fact, in itself, is an interesting and noteworthy phenomenon. Among other things, it raises a question about the possible relation between the group nature of the PT behavior and the greater field-dependence of women— the lesser differentiation of women as separate individuals, reported by Witkin (1966), which we discussed in Chapter 6.[6]

We shall take a brief look at some examples of societies in which women are active in possession trance rituals, and consider some of the surrounding circumstances. J. D. Gussler (1973) presents a review of the literature on possession trance among a number of South African tribal groups, among them the Zulu, the Swazi, and the Xhosa. One of the most important contexts of possession trance in the traditional life of these societies appears in the cult of diviners, most of whose members are women. A woman joins such a cult as a result of having fallen ill, if her illness is diagnosed as due to spirit possession. The diviner who discovers this cause will then initiate the woman into her cult group, in order to produce a cure. As in the East African *zar* cult, mentioned earlier, the spirit causing the illness is not driven away but turned into an ally. Some former patients eventually become cult leaders themselves. Gussler points out that among these several Bantu groups—societies that have strict hierarchies— women have generally a low status. Although they may have warm attachments to their natal family, at marriage they move to live among strangers, where they have a lowly position and even may have to compete with co-wives for the attention of a husband.

The woman's new life is hemmed in by a great many taboos, and her range of activities is severely restricted. Among these taboos are limitations on various foods rich in animal proteins and vitamins A and B. They are imposed on women in particular when they are thought to be in periods of ritual vulnerability, such as at menstruation, at marriage, and after childbirth. These are also times, however, when the human body is especially in need of these food substances. Gussler relates the high incidence of spirit possession, or *ukuthwasa* illness, in women in these societies to the social, psychological, and nutritional stresses to which they are exposed. The high maize diet, with its lack of animal protein and vitamins A and B, leads to a high incidence of pellagra in Southern Africa, and this disease, as Gussler documents, has many symptoms that resemble the *ukuthwasa* illness of the Zulu and their neighbors. During the initiation-cure rituals cattle are slaughtered as sacrifice to the ancestors, and as Gussler notes, established diviners may have a good and regular supply of beef. Thus, joining the cult of diviners may improve the symptoms *both* as a result of nutritional changes and because the woman now has much greater freedom and prestige.

Lenora Greenbaum (1973a) found a strong statistical association among African societies between "fixed internal status distinctions" (slavery and social stratification) and the pressure of possession trance. She suggests (1973b) that possession trance is related to the existence of a rigid social structure, and proposes the hypothesis that "in a rigid society, . . . one where the social structures deny the individual freedom for achievement and personal control over his daily life activities, possession trance is likely to be widespread" (Greenbaum 1973b: 59). By having a "possessed" medium make decisions for the individual, and thus letting the spirits assume the responsibility for these decisions, the individual is given a degree of elbow room. By defining spirit possession somewhat more narrowly as spirit mediumship, Greenbaum finds strong support for her hypothesis in a review of data on fourteen African societies. The Zulu and their neighbors, whom Gussler has considered in greater detail, represent a good example of a rigid society with fixed status distinctions, and it is the women who are the most tightly controlled in these male-dominated societies.

A situation quite different from that of the South African Bantu, such as the Zulu, and the Somali and others among whom we find the *zar* cult, is found in West African societies such as the Yoruba of Nigeria and the Fon of Dahomey. These two groups, incidentally, are also important because much of their religious heritage has been maintained in the Americas, from Cuba to Brazil, by people who were brought there as slaves. In West Africa, possession trance cults are organized to worship clan ancestors or the principal gods of the tribes. People join the cults for various reasons, including illness and infertility, but such disturbances are not considered to be evidence of possession. The majority of the possession trancers in these cults, although not often their leaders, are women.

Possession trance cults in which women predominate are not limited to Africa and Afro-America. For example, Clive Kessler (1977) reports such cults in the Malay state of Kelantan. Although the healers are men, the majority of the patients, he notes, are women, a fact that he relates to the stress inherent in their social position. Another example comes from the United States, where, according to June Macklin (1977), two and one-half times as many women as men are spirit mediums licensed by one of the major spiritualist organizations.

I. M. Lewis (1971) interprets Zulu possession cults, like the *zar* cult from which most of his first-hand data come, as expressions of the war between the sexes. Illness is a tool that women use to manipulate their menfolk, in particular their husbands and their kin, into paying for initiation-cures, and then permitting the patient, or temporarily cured patient, to join a society of women and thus to acquire a degree of freedom. Generalizing more broadly, Lewis argues that these cults deal with peripheral amoral spirits, which reflect the peripheral social position of women. They are not the "main morality cults" of the society, an observation that as we have seen, does not hold true, for example, for the ancestor cults of the Fon, which also have a majority of female members. Lewis claims, moreover, that those men who join the cults, where this option is available to them, also suffer from social disabilities. Lewis expands his thesis to say that possession cults—except in certain small-scale societies, where they are the main morality cults and are dominated by men—are expressions of social protest for the depressed and despised categories of people. He suggests that Haitain *vodou* can be understood in such terms as well.

An analysis of Haitian *vodou,* however, shows some of the difficulties of Lewis' thesis. First of all, *vodou* reflects a strong syncretism of African and Catholic beliefs. The spirts of African or local origin are identified with saints of the Catholic church. Even more importantly, God, or as the Haitians say, *Bon Dieu,* is the central figure of their beliefs, even though ritual, for the most part, deals with the spirits, variously called *saints* or *loa.* The spirits, moreover, are not amoral; although they may be either good or evil, they enforce the central moral values of the society. *Vodou* is the folk religion of the peasants and the urban masses, representing 90 percent of the population. The women in the *zar* cult may be able to manipulate the men, who are their oppressors, by mystical means, for the men, too believe in the spirits. The Haitian lower class, however, cannot use religious power in its dealings with the dominant minority. Lewis' argument tells only part of the story, for although social deprivation applies not only to women, but also to most of the men, the women still represent a majority of the possession trancers.

It is undoubtedly true that possession trance cults provide for some measure of social manipulation, as Lewis, Gussler, and Greenbaum point out. This manipulation, however, is surely not the whole story, if we are to understand the frequent observation of the predominance of women in possession trance cults. A comparison with visionary trance (A), which we discussed earlier, should be of some help here. Let us recapitulate: trance is more likely to be found in small-scale, relatively simple societies dependent on hunting, gathering, and fishing for most of their subsistence; it is experienced primarily by men. It may be induced through mortification and isolation, as in the vision quest, where it is part of the initiation into manhood. Or it may be induced through hallucinogens. At least in some cases, it may be related, as Siskind (1973) has shown, to a social structure based on matrilocal residence, in which men live among strangers. This reminds us of D'Andrade's hypothesis that the practice of using dreams to seek and control supernatural power is associated with male anxiety about being alone and required to be independent and self-reliant.

If we contrast this group of features with those linked to possession trance, some striking differences appear. Possession trance, it will be recalled, is more likely to occur in more complex societies, those dependent to a greater extent on agriculture or a combination of agriculture and animal husbandry. They also are more likely to be societies with social stratification and more complex political structures. Such societies, as Greenbaum (1973b) has suggested, are also more likely to be rigid. As we saw among the Zulu (as well as such other groups mentioned earlier as the Somali or the Malay), woman leave their natal families to live among strangers. These, then, are not societies in which one might expect *men* to experience anxieties about having to be alone. It is the *women* who are exposed to the threats of an alien social environment. Yet, if we go back to the findings of Barry, Child, and Bacon (1959), these are societies in which people, and women in particular (Barry, Bacon, and Child 1957), are reared to be compliant, obedient, reliable, and nurturant, rather than independent and self-reliant. They will not seek spirit help to augment their own powers to be able to deal with a hostile group. Instead, the call on powerful, authoritative spirits to *act in their place.* It may well be the least compliant, most strong-willed of the women who find adaptation to their new lives most difficult and who may therefore be most in need of the escape mechanism provided by the possession trance cults. Note, too, that whereas the North American vision quest, where it exists, is obligatory for young men, the possession trance cults always exist only for a minority. Each type of ASC, in its own way, reveals sources of stress within these different types of societies.

Comparing Trance Types.   On the basis of what has been said so far, let us now compare these two types of ASC in two regards: their characteristic patterns of interaction, and their imagery and symbolism.

Trance characteristically involves interaction with one or more other personalities, beings, or forces through hallucinatory experience, whereas possession trance involves the impersonation of another personality. The trancer sees, hears, feels, perceives, and *interacts* with another; the possession trancer *becomes* another. Trance, in short, is an experience; possession trance is a performance. An experience is an end in itself, although it may be lived through before others or for others. A performance is carried out in front of an audience; indeed, it requires an audience, for possession trance typically is followed by amnesia, so without an audience no memory of the event is recorded. In fact, the audience may have to report the actions and words of the spirit to the impersonator. The trance experience is remembered, and without this memory the experience is often incomplete. The trance experience must be reported to others to be effective (as in the case of the diviner who returns from a spirit trip with information for clients), or it must be remembered for one's own sake. The visionary must remember the instructions of the guardian spirit, the power that has been acquired.

The trancer is typically (though not always) a man; the possession trancer is typically (though not always) a woman. Trance, generally, is induced by hypoglycemia due to fasting, sensory deprivation, mortification, or drugs. The experience is preceded by learning what to expect and how to interpret what is perceived or felt. Possession trance is induced by drumming, singing, dancing, crowd contagion, or more rarely by drugs. Here learning involves the behavior appropriate to each possible spirit visitor to be impersonated.

The trance experience is intrapsychic and essentially passive on the part of the trancer though it may lead to actively curing patients. The passivity and helpless dependency is particularly true of the initiatory experiences of the vision quest. The possession trancer, on the contrary, acting out a role before an audience, is involved in an *active* performance. The *physically passive* visionary interacts with the spirits; the *psychologically passive* possession trancer's body is used as a vehicle by means of which the spirits interact directly with her audience, while she is psychologically absent.

We now turn to a comparison of the imagery, the symbolism, and the fantasy linked to each of our two states. In each case, the imagery concerns two basic themes: mastery and sexuality. Note that the physically *passive* trance is linked to an *active* imagery: the trancer sends his soul on a trip, a spirit journey; he speaks with spirits or even struggles with them to bring back the soul of a patient. He obtains a boon from them, be it a cure, some special power, or knowledge. *Active* possession trance, on the other hand, is represented by a dependent, *passive* imagery. The possession trancer is the spirit's wife, his mount (horse, mule, or camel), his vehicle or vessel. She is mounted, ridden, or entered, indeed possessed by the spirit. The trancer remains himself and gains power by interacting with another entity, whether through the pity of that other, as in the vision quest, or through struggle, as in the shaman's journey. By contrast, the possession trancer ceases to be herself; she becomes another through identification and for a time loses her own identity, becoming the passive instrument of that other.

In both instances, however, the theme of mastery is striking: the trancer achieves mastery by having power, knowledge, success, or special gifts bestowed by a supernatural entity. The possession trancer achieves it by abdictating her own self, identifying with or making room for a more powerful self who takes over her body and who performs powerful acts while residing in that body. It is striking that the altered state typical of women involves an active performance linked to a passive fantasy, whereas the altered state typical of men involves a passive experience frequently linked to an active fantasy.

These types of states and experiences appear to "make sense" in terms of the socialization practices of the societies in which they occur, of the typical roles assigned to men and women, and of the stresses that are given relief in these ritualized states. We have already noted that socialization of women typically emphasizes obedience and lack of independence. In possession trance, obedience and dependency are given ultimate expression. Yet it also shows how this very obedience, by reaching a maximum, becomes a means for manipulating life situations. One ceases to be oneself, one identifies with and impersonates a more powerful other. And it is as that other that the apparently obedient and passive individual may not only ventilate suppressed or repressed feelings but also initiate changes in her own life as well as in the lives of others.

The male who is taught to be an independent and self-reliant hunter seeks the protection of an imaginary helper in the person of the hallucinated spirit in visions as well as in dreams. The woman's problem is quite different. She cannot deal with it directly but must use the hierarchical features of her social structure to work for her, getting a powerful ally, sometimes an ancestor, to work on her behalf.

This situation explains in part the observation that has been made frequently that possession trance appears to be a self-serving process, in which the spirits appear to express the wishes of the possessed individual without much disguise. This observation has led to the charge, probably justified in some instances, that an altered state does not actually occur but is merely simulated. However, simulation is by no means always the case.

It must be remembered that the pressures of a rigid and hierarchical social structure cannot, by themselves, explain the institution of possession trance cults, or the psychological transformation of individuals. We need another element, a personality structure that involves a certain type of self-perception as well as characteristic ways of dealing with interpersonal and intrapersonal conflicts. Social norms and values, mediated by the socialization process, are key elements in this situation. The imagery and symbolism of ASC rituals can provide further insights. We considered earlier the sexual imagery involved in many of the hallucinatory trance rituals. Let us now consider the corresponding imagery of possession trance, as expressed in this case not through what is seen and heard but through what is acted out and the way in which it is explained in mythological themes.

We have already mentioned the widespread use of the metaphor of "mounting" for spirit possession, in which the possession trancer is the spirit's horse, mule, or camel. The possessed individual may also be called the spirit's wife. The Fon of Dahomey, for example, use both of these expressions, and a cult initiate is called a *hunsi* (wife of spirit), a term that has survived in Haitian *vodou*. There, a male spirit, impersonated by or "possessing" one individual, may address a woman as "my wife." Also, female spirits may insist on marrying a human man, who must then set aside a special room in his house for this spirit wife, who comes to him in his sleep. Crapanzano (1977) has described and analyzed the relationship between a Moroccan husband and wife and their spirit spouses. Zempleni (1966) has reported at some length on the possession trance rites of the Lébou and Wolof peoples of Senegal. These rites are part of, primarily, women's cults. Among the ailments are reproductive disorders of women, which are said to be due to the spirit fiancés or spirit husbands, who must be exorcized. Many of the possessing spirits, however, are ancestral spirits, and the symbolism of the ritual is basically one of submission. Nonetheless, initiation is referred to as marriage between the possessed woman and her possessing spirit. During ritual dances, overt sexual behavior may be mimed, including rape, and it is said that some women experience orgasm during possession. This situation is made more complex by the observation that women may be possessed by female as well as male spirits, that women possessed by male spirits may mime sexual interactions with other women, and so on.

The whole symbolism of the relationship between humans and spirits as love and marriage is not limited to Africa, Afro-America, and the Mediterranean region. For example, Spiro (1967:212) reports the marriage of Burmese female shamans to their spirits. There are, indeed, also certain striking Christian parallels, such as the marriage of Catholic nuns to Christ. In her book on the south Italian village of Torregreca, Ann Cornelisen (1969) offers a striking description of such a ceremony. One is also reminded of the various Judeo-Christian interpretations of the Song of Songs.[7]

In comparing the sexual imagery of possession trance, as it appears primarily in African and Afro-American cults, with that of Amazonian Indians described earlier, several differences are immediately obvious: The Amazonian men, as we have seen, engage in fantasies under the action of the drugs, while the African and other women possesion trancers act out fairly complex roles. The men's fantasies are directed toward women, and also at a reduction of the anxiety and the hostility they feel towards both their sexual partners and their kinsmen. The women's behavior in possession trance, on the other hand, frequently involves a degree of male impersonation. Also, the fantasies of the Amazonian men involve a degree of regression, a feature which appears to be absent from possession trance behavior. Because the Indian men engage in fantasies, these experiences are complete in themselves. The possession trance, as behavior, however, may have considerable social consequences, not only for the woman herself but also for her group.

Summary.   We may now summarize briefly some of the salient points reviewed in this discussion: Institutionalization of altered states of consciousness is virtually universal in human societies. However, the types of states, their method of induction, and their ritualization and interpretation vary from society to society.

We have distinguished two broad types of ritualized altered states of consciousness: trance and possession trance. They are linked to differing levels of societal complexity and ultimately, to different levels of subsistence economies. They are also differentially distributed geographically; the Americas, predominantly hunting societies, have trance, and Africa, primarily agricultural societies, has possession trance. These two subsistence types are distinguished also by differential patterns of socialization.

Patterns of socialization also distinguish the sexes, with males—particularly in hunting societies—being socialized for independence and self-reliance, and women—particularly in agricultural societies—being socialized for obedience and compliance. In view of the differences in socialization associated both with subsistence differences and sex differences, it is not surprising to find differences in altered states by sex as well as by type of society. We have suggested, on the basis of some evidence, that hallucinatory trance, often induced by drugs, is more characteristic of males, particularly in hunting societies, whereas possession trance is more characteristic of women, particularly in agricultural societies.

The type of altered state institutionalized and the nature of the institutionalization itself reveal points of stress within a society. These typical points of stress vary from society to society, from subsistence level to subsistence level. The stresses relate to socialization patterns and sex roles, and to the positions in the social system that are under greatest pressure, such as young men or newly married women. Young men feel pressure to perform and achieve as independent individuals, often in hostile settings (as in hunting, warfare, or sex), young women feel the shift from natal home to the control of a mother-in-law, conflict with co-wives, or the need to produce offspring. *I wish to suggest that it is this variation in types of stresses, together with differences in socialization goals and practices, that leads to a society's "choice" of a "female type" of altered state (possession trance) as prototypical or of a "male type" (hallucinatory trance).*

Mythology and World View

The drug-induced fantasies of the American Indians are linked to elaborate transcendent mythological and cosmological systems, whereas the mythic "range" of the African women's cults is much more limited. We shall consider these more limited schemes first. In societies where possession trance is practiced, the ritual behavior involves the acting out of certain mythic themes. The possession trance reveals the identity and characteristics of the spirits: they are largely anthropomorphic, and often they are ancestors. They are then, in some sense, part of the human group, which they enlarge in time and space. Their demands are those of powerful humans: obedience, food, and sex. Like powerful chiefs or heads of families, they punish the disobedient.

The American Indian myths are by far more elaborate. Harner (1973b:134) says of the Jívaro that "the normal waking life is explicitly viewed as 'false' or 'a lie'." The supernatural world is the "real" world for them, and this world can be entered through the use of hallucinogens. To what extent can the construction of this "real" world be explained on the basis of characteristic responses to certain drugs? This is an interesting question to which answers exist at present only in rudimentary form. La Barre (1975) points to the need to distinguish between *psychophysiological* constants in the hallucinatory process resulting from the use of certain drugs, and constants in the *symbolic* content of hallucinations. For example, certain drugs appear to "promote a feeling of flying through the air" (La Barre 1975:13). Some produce "macropsia", the enlargement of what is perceived—which may explain myths of giants—and others lead to "micropsia," the reduction in size of what is seen. This condition may be the basis of stories of "little people." Both of these legendary forms are widespread. Some drugs also modify the subjects' perception of the size of their own bodies. They are reminiscent of Alice in Wonderland, who found a bottle labelled "drink me," which had dramatic effects on her size.

Siskind (1973:136) makes the distinction between psychophysiological and symbolic factors explicit:

> The small scrolls and rope-like images may be produced directly by the chemical acting on the nerves, but the visions that the Sharahuana seek are learned from other men and from the beliefs they share . . . Jaguars, snakes and beautiful women cannot be found in a vegetable substance or located at nerve endings . . . The young men must learn to shape the visual illusion and the physiological sensations into the mold and the form of the spirits.

The greater elaboration of hallucination-supported mythologies, is striking, and it requires more detailed study. For the moment, we may say that where the dream world of hallucinations is given cultural support and is defined as "true" reality, with the waking world merely its reflection if not an outright "lie," motivations for waking behavior must be sought to a considerable extent in this hallucinatory dream world. It becomes itself a dimension of culture, which has generally been neglected in analyses of the interaction between culture and personality.

Siskind speaks of the cultural beliefs that shape hallucinatory images. In fact, we may distinguish between cultural and personal symbolism, and the constant interaction between the two.[8] The mythological content, which is culturally shared and to a degree prescribed, arose out of personal expressions of unconscious fears and desires of individuals, and new modifications from this personal source are always possible. On the other hand, personal, idiosyncratic content in hallucinations or in possession trance behavior, which deviates to a considerable extent from the cultural model, is more likely to occur when individuals are disturbed or in some way out of step with their peers. In Chapter 8, when we deal with ethnopsychiatry, we shall consider some of these deviant or pathological positions.

ALTERED STATES AND SOCIALIZATION

What enables people to experience altered states? The question is not asked as often as it should be, for it generally assumed that anyone who takes drugs or is hypnotized will enter an altered state. In fact the subject is more complex, as we have already seen. It is important to stress again that ASC of the types we have been discussing are culturally patterned to a high degree, and so is the expectation that appropriate individuals will experience these states when they are supposed to do so, but not at other times and places.

Because the states are so highly patterned, they entail several kinds of learning. One kind is the acquisition of the apppropriate personality dispositions. We have already referred several times to the different sorts of socialization imposed on boys and girls, and to the differences among societies of different subsistence types. There are also, of course, characteristics of socialization that apply specifically in individual societies. For example, Gregory Bateson (1976) speaks of certain components of socialization for ASC in Bali, where there are many different kinds of possession trance. Balinese socialization is highly kinesthetic: for example, when children learn to dance, individual limbs are manipulated, in contrast, for example, to Western dance instruction, in which the child is expected to follow a model. There is, moreover, a great concern for balance. The disruption of balance is basic to the kind of disorientation, of separation of the self from the body, as it is perceived, that underlines the induction of an altered state. At the other extreme is Harner's report (1973b:90) that the Jívaro administer a strong hallucinogen to a disrespectful boy, in order for him to "see the supernatural world" in his trance. This experience, it is expected, will teach him that his father has knowledge and consequently is to be respected. Siskind (1973) for the Sharahuana and Carneiro (1964) for the Amahuaca tell of learning to see the correct things. On the other hand, Lame Deer has given us a description of how the puberty fast of the Sioux is both a learning experience and an experience of identity transformation. Katz (1973) has shown how, among the !Kung, trance constitutes a type of socialization. In Haiti, children play at possession trance to the amusement of their elders, and first possession trance experiences often occur among adolescents in such play situations.

Learning, then, operates at several levels: First, the child acquires the basic personality dispositions, such traits of independence and dependence and attitudes toward the self and the body. Next, the child learns the basic structure of the universe, the existence of spirits and their behavior, and the manner in which their presence may be perceived or induced: This prelearning is requiste before a ritual ASC may be experienced successfully. What has been learned previously can be called upon when a stressful situation arises or a personal crisis develops. The process of facing the problem with the resources available constitutes a further level of learning. At a fourth level is the ritual itself, which, as we discussed earlier, is itself a type of learning process. At each stage, the attitude and behavior of others supports and authenticates what is learned, considers it desirable and rewards it, or to the contrary, considers it inappropriate and provides ritual means for dealing with the situation. This second response arises particularly when personal symbolism takes precedence over the cultural one. Finally, the ASC experience itself affects the further development of the individual, the individual's place in society, and the world view that is informed, in some basic sense, by the experience of, at least, some members of a society, of extraordinary events in relation to self and spirit others.

Because ASC provide an avenue for the expression of both social and personal stresses, we return to them not only in our discussion of mental health and illness (Chapter 8) but also in our consideration of the psychological dimensions of social and cultural change (Chapter 9).

ALTERED STATES IN OUR OWN SOCIETY

In our discussion so far most of the examples of altered states have been drawn from traditional societies, with only occasional references to modern societies. As we look around, however, it is clear that altered states play an important role in our own society as well. In the 1960s there were veritable drug cults, many of which attached religious or mystical meanings to experiences with hallucinogens. At the same time, there has been a growth of new religions, as well as the revival of old forms, in which emphasis was placed on more or less complex altered states. Most prominent among these old forms have been evangelical Christian groups emphasizing intense conversion experiences, gifts of the spirit such as speaking in tongues (*glossolalia*), and healing. Many of these practices have moved from backwoods traditional groups and tent revivals to modern electronic missions. The Catholic Church has seen the development of a Neo-Pentecostal or Charismatic movement, and so have some of the Protestant churches. A second type of religious group stressing and encouraging altered states of consciousness has come from the Orient, from India and Japan primarily. A third type has come from Latin America: spiritism from Puerto Rico and various Afro-Caribbean forms from Cuba, Haiti, Trinidad, and elsewhere.

Not only have these groups attracted large numbers of followers, but there has also been a major interest in books dealing with altered states and related experiences. The success of the writings of Carlos Castaneda is a case in point, and readers may have wondered why no references to this author have appeared in our discussion so far. There is every reason to believe, as Richard de Mille (1976) has carefully documented, that Castaneda's writings are fiction rather than documentary reports of the author's experiences with the Yaqui medicine man Don Juan and the witch Doña Soledad. Passing novels off as field reports constitutes a hoax on a credulous public. The enormous popularity of Castaneda's writings, then, appears to tell us more about his readers and their fantasies than about Yaqui beliefs and rituals.

While many have looked for religious experiences, probably an even larger number have sought out altered states in ways largely stripped of their original religious meanings: Transcendental Meditation and Yoga, for example, have been widely advertised as means of stimulating physical and psychological well-being, or, particularly in the case of TM, of achieving success as that word is ordinarily understood in the United States: in terms of money and career.

In secular contexts, altered states of various kinds, especially drugs and relaxation (meditation) have been used in therapeutic settings by medical practitioners. Together with a disenchantment with many aspects of traditional psychotherapies, the drugs and the Oriental methods of approach to mental healing have led to renewed research concerning human consciousness. Science, in this case, appears to have followed popular culture, rather than the other way around.

The counterculture of the 1960s has gone, but the interest in religious experiences and in altered states has remained as its heritage, together with a skeptical stance concerning rationality, technology, and a society based on them. The skepticism has been reinforced by the energy crisis and the new scarcity of the 1970s. The traditional churches have not filled the void, but electronic evangelism has done so to a remarkable degree.

Weston La Barre has written that religion is "the response of society to problems the contemporary culture failed to solve" (La Barre 1970:44). The flourishing of the new and revived religions suggests the failure of other institutions in our society to meet major needs of many people.

NOTES

1. See especially Benedict (1923).

2. See Appendix I: "The False Messiahs," in La Barre (1970). For the detailed study of one specific, fascinating case, see Scholem (1973).

3. A. F. C. Wallace (1969) traces the wide cross-cultural distribution of the image of the trip as a cultural scheme for interpreting hallucinatory and mystical experiences. He concludes that "every real trip brings heightened awareness of the real world" (p. 155). It is perhaps no accident that every example he cites, whether actual or from television drama, involves male protagonists.

4. Although hunting large game is universally a male specialty, we now know that with the exception of the Eskimo, the vegetable food collected by women actually forms the major basis of subsistence in "hunting" societies. Nonetheless, prestige is centered on the men's activity and their success in their frequently unrewarded efforts.

5. It is interesting that another nonaggressive group, the Ifaluk, as reported by Spiro (1953), also have hostile spirits of the dead who cause evil, including illness and madness through possession.

6. The widespread existence of such groups represents an interesting contradiction to L. Tiger's claim, in his book *Men in Groups* (1969), that there exists a biological basis for "male-bonding," the tendency to form exclusively male groups. A comparable female tendency is said to be absent because women lack the underlying biological characteristics. See also Nancy Leis' article on women's associations among the Ijaw of West Africa (1974).

7. The phenomenon is, of course, much more widespread, and many more examples could be cited. The theme is represented in somewhat attenuated form in such familiar lines from Protestant hymns as: "And he walks with me and he talks with me and he tells me I am his own," and "Jesus, lover of my soul."

8. This distinction between the chemical effect of the drugs and the cultural and personal content of visions is graphically shown in the following quotation from Gordon Wasson, who with his wife and several other investigators rediscovered several important psychotropic species of mushrooms in southern Mexico in the 1950s. The most important of these species is *Psilocybe mexicana.* He writes:

> All my visions had a pristine quality: when I saw choir stalls in a Renaissance cathedral, they were not black with age and incense, but as though they had just come, fresh carved, from the hand of the Master . . . (Wasson 1961 [orig. 1959]:319).

Clearly, personal and cultural experiences contribute to the content of drug-induced hallucinations.

CHAPTER 8

Mental Illness in Comparative Perspective

INTRODUCTION: THREE CASE REPORTS

Aneitin, a male in his early forties, shows many symptoms of schizophrenia. [He] not only lives alone but takes no part in Ifaluk society. In the past he had been dangerous. Periodically he became violent, shouted and screamed at people, and physically attacked them when they came near him (Spiro 1959:154).

Sadiya, a woman of about 35, had been a case of apparent schizophrenia. Shortly after the death of her mother [ten years prior to the report] Sadiya awoke screaming one morning and ran from the house. Her father caught her and beat her, but to no avail. The neighbors brought gifts and tried to calm her, but her speech remained meaningless and jumbled and she would run frantically through the village laughing wildly. She remained in this hopeless incapacitated condition for several months (Kennedy 1977 [orig. 1967]:380).

Juanita, a 14-year-old girl, came home from high school one day extremely agitated and then fled to a nearby town, pursued by her parents. . . . She was apprehended by the police [eventually and had to be] forcibly subdued and held . . . During the following weeks similar episodes were repeated. Eventually she had to be restrained by ropes in her house. [She was then hospitalized for one year and treated with electric shock.] Shortly after her return [home] she became violent again, attacking family members, ripping at her clothes, running in the street, insulting townspeople, and stealing from stores. . . .

Was Juanita really schizophrenic? . . . Juanita showed bizarre behavior of a relatively sudden onset that persisted at home, in the hospital, and at home again for several years. Her behavior seemed like that one sees in others who are called schizophrenic (Guthrie and Szanton 1976:147, 160).

The first of these case reports deals with a man on the atoll of Ifaluk in Micronesia, the second with a young woman in Nubia (Southern Egypt), and the third with a teenage girl in the Philippines. Similar accounts have been reported by anthropologists, psychiatrists, and others from all parts of the world. The implication is clear: mental disorders are to be found everywhere, in all societies and cultures, among all races, and in all geographic zones.

How have peoples everywhere dealt with this phenomenon? Are mental illnesses recognized? How are they explained? How are they treated? The reports from which the three examples are taken indicate that both Sadiya and Juanita were treated successfully by traditional healers. Are there disorders that exist only in certain societies? How frequent are mental disorders? These are some of the questions that will concern us in this chapter.

BACKGROUND

As we saw at the beginning of this book, culture and personality as a field of anthropology grew up in close contact with psychiatry, particularly with psychoanalysis. For example, Freud attempted to compare the complexes of neurotic patients with the ritual practices and beliefs of primitive peoples. In the early years of the century, too, questions were raised about whether mental illnesses existed in "Stone Age" populations, or whether they are a phenomenon of "civilization." The very question suggests a theory of mental disease: it was attributed to the fact that modern complex societies impose severe limitations on the satisfaction of individual impulses, which are subordinated to the social order. To the contrary, primitive societies, it was thought (on the basis more of imagination than information), allow the individual greater freedom for personal expression, and as a result, disorders that are seen in Western society would be absent.

Anthropological fieldwork soon revealed the erroneous character of these views. At present there exists a field of *cultural psychiatry* or *psychiatric anthropology,* and also a neighboring and partially overlapping field of *transcultural psychiatry.* Like cross-cultural psychology, which we dealt with in Chapter 6, transcultural psychiatry is largely a product of the second half of the twentieth century, when psychiatrists confronted unfamiliar situations in the developing areas of the world. For example, when the Australian physician B. G. Burton-Bradley went to Papua New Guinea, in 1959, he was that territory's first psychiatrist, and for most the following decade and a half he was the only psychiatrist serving a population of two and one-half million people. His book, *Stone Age Crisis* (1975), describes what he found and how the life of the people of that territory changed in the period of his observation.

Social, cultural, and economic changes in the developing countries have created a need for psychiatric services for a number of reasons. Principal among them is the fact that disruptions of traditional life patterns have produced stresses leading to psychiatric illness in significant numbers of people. Among these stresses is the loss of the support of families or village communities by individuals who have moved to urban centers or who have gone to work in Western enterprises, such as mining centers or plantations. Also, as a result of the breakdown of traditional institutions under the impact of acculturation or westernization, traditional resources for dealing with disturbed individuals have become less available. At the same time, few psychiatrists have been working in developing areas, and they have frequently found themselves faced with an overwhelming task. On the one hand, there was the need to establish mental health services where none had been in existence, and often to do so with limited resources and inadequate personnel. On the other hand, there was the recognition that the cultural circumstances of patients must be understood in order to be able to provide a service that consisted of more than merely housing disturbed individuals who could not remain in the community. Psychiatrists in this situation developed means of communication with each other and also with anthropologists, who were often relied upon to provide information on the relevant cultural dimensions. In particular, two journals have grown up that play an important role in this network of communications: the *Transcultural Psychiatric Research Review,* published in Montreal, and *Psychopathologie Africaine,* published in Dakar (Senegal).

A series of topics have been at the core of debate and research in this area. On the one hand, there are questions concerning the definition, nature, and frequency of mental disorders, and the cultural factors relevant to them, as seen by psychiatrists and anthropologists using an absolute, or etic, approach. On the other hand, there are questions about the traditional systems of explanation and treatment of disturbances recognized as such in the various societies. Much of the research here centers on the activities of traditional healers and on possible explanations for their success. A third approach asks what roles certain emotional and cognitive states play in cultural life; we have taken a partial look at this question in our review of altered states of consciousness (Chapter 7). These researches are of both theoretical and practical interest. They affect the procedures used by specialists trained in Western medicine, and particularly psychiatry, in the developing areas and in at least some segments of our own society as well.

Although psychiatric anthropology is historically an outgrowth of culture and personality, it is now an integral part of the newer field of medical anthropology, which itself has largely grown out of culture and personality. It should be emphasized that when we consider traditional healing methods and theories, the distinction that is made in Western medicine between psychiatry and other branches of medicine is likely to be absent, and whatever the ailment, psychological dimensions appear to be relevant to a great many, if not all, treatment methods.

THE RELATIVITY OF THE "NORMAL"

Writing in 1934 for an audience of psychologists, Ruth Benedict remarked:

> It does not matter what kind of "abnormality" we choose for illustration, those which indicate extreme instability, or those which are more in the nature of character traits like sadism or delusions of grandeur or of persecution, there are well described cultures in which these abnormals function with ease and with honor and apparently without danger or difficulty to the society (Benedict 1959 [orig. 1934]:263).

She goes on to illustrate how many traditional societies accept and pattern trance states that are considered abnormal in the West. At the same time she observes:

> Western civilization allows and culturally honors gratifications of the ego which according to any absolute category would be regarded as abnormal. The portrayal of unbridled and arrogant egoists as family men, as officers of the law, and in business has been a favorite topic of novelists ... Such individuals are probably mentally warped to a greater degree than any inmates of our institutions ... They are extreme types of those personality configurations which our civilization fosters (Benedict 1959 [orig. 1934]:279).

In Benedict's view, then, neither social adequacy nor any absolute standards of normalcy are satisfactory criteria for mental health.

Almost half a century has passed since Benedict wrote this article. We have acquired a great deal of first-hand information on personality functioning and cultural patterns in all parts of the world. Yet the debate over criteria for mental health and mental illness has continued to rage. With some variations these two positions, decked out in ever new vocabularies, have continued to be defended.

Taking Benedict's findings into account, the historian of medicine, Erwin Ackerknecht (1943), distinguished between "autonormal" and "heteronormal," and between "autopathological" and "heteropathological." The "autonormal" individual is one who is considered normal in terms of his or her own society, as the "autopathological" individual is one who is considered abnormal or sick in these terms. On the other hand, the "heteronormal" individual is one who appears healthy to the foreign, scientific observer, and the "heteropathological" individual is one judged abnormal by these scientific standards. In other words, the psychiatrist, using universal standards of health, may arrive at a picture other than that of the individual's fellows, whose criteria for judging "normality" and "abnormality" may well be different.

This distinction raises another question: what if the standards of the society are themselves pathological? For example, Margaret Mead, in her autobiography, recalls her periods of research among several New Guinea peoples, and how she "loathed the Mundugumor culture with its endless aggressive rivalries, exploitation, and rejection of children" (1972:205). As a result of their complex kinship system and social structure, among these people,

Women wanted sons and men wanted daughters, and babies of the wrong sex were tossed into the river, still alive, wrapped in bark sheath. Someone might pull the bark container out of the water, inspect the sex of the baby, and cast it away again . . . It seemed clear to me that a culture that so repudiated children could not be a good culture, and the relationship between the harsh cultural prescribed style and the acts of individuals was only too obvious (Mead 1972:206).

Is it possible that a culture might be "wrong" and that, under such circumstances, the deviant individual, who does not conform to the social rules, might be less pathological than his peers? In the case of small, isolated, homogeneous societies, where individuals have little opportunity of being influenced by alternative models and few exposures to other ways of dealing with interpersonal relations, such a question may be idle. However, when we speak of large-scale, heterogeneous, complex societies it is quite another matter. The question was posed most acutely in the late 1930s and the years of World War II in regard to Nazi Germany. Had all the Germans gone mad? Could one claim that the sadomasochistic individual, at ease in this murderous regime, was a "normal" individual? Or, if normal in a statistical sense, could such a person be said to be healthy and well-adjusted? Such a situation clearly called for a closer look, for which cultural relativism was not enough.

A number of approaches to this problem have been suggested. Based on Clyde Kluckhohn's 1944 study of Navaho witchcraft, G. A. DeVos has proposed a distinction between "adaptation" and "adjustment." According to his usage, adaptation refers to social structure, and adjustment to "an ideal progression of maturation which is potential for all human beings. It is not culturally or situationally relative, but . . . may be culturally fostered or deformed" (DeVos 1976a:4). *Adjustment,* then, refers to personal maturation, in contrast to *adaptation,* which concerns behavioral responses to the social situation by individuals, and by groups through the development of special institutions. Witchcraft beliefs and possession trance cults may be examples of adaptive institutions that reveal tensions and stresses within the social fabric, which they are designed to ease.

Although psychiatrists have tended to view individuals in terms of adjustment and personal maturation, they also increasingly have become aware of the social context in which individuals function. Thus Rudolf Kaelbling (1961) could suggest that in any society there will be psychopathology when the individuals are unable to conform to the expectations of the community or to their own expectations. As DeVos has indicated, there is a great difference in diagnosis whether we focus on behavior as either conforming or deviant, or on personal maturation and development. By focusing on behavior, a group of sociologists has developed what has come to be known as "labeling theory," which claims that in Western society a person to whom the label of mental illness is attached is made to learn a special stigmatized role. In part, this view can be traced back to Ruth Benedict, for in the article quoted earlier she points out that in the United States homosexuality "exposes an individual to all the conflicts to which aberrants are always exposed"; yet these conflicts are matters of our culture, not universal and inherent in the tendency to homosexuality, as comparison with American Indian cultures shows. The psychological conflicts of the homosexual are, it is argued, *added* to the deviant behavior tendency. In the terminology of Lemert (1967), homosexuality would be termed a "primary deviance," and the neurotic conflicts many homosexuals experience would be termed "secondary deviance."

Because of the cultural relativist implications of labeling theory, Jane Murphy (1976) has sought to test it on the basis of data on mental illness from her research among the Eskimo of Alaska and the Yoruba of Nigeria. The information for these studies was collected by means of interviews and participant observation. In both of these cultures she found that there was a word, or label, for insanity. Descriptions of insane persons included reference to hallucinations, delusions, disorientation, and bizarre types of behavior, and resembled what would be called schizophrenia in Western societies. Murphy is careful to point out that the Eskimo and the Yoruba make a distinction between insane persons and those with special gifts or aptitudes to hear and see things that others do not perceive, to divine, to look into the future, and so on. Although there is occasional confusion among Westerners between pathological and visionary states, between madness and shamanism, such confusion does not appear to exist among the local people or their healing specialists. Murphy cited the example of the Eskimo shaman who is, temporarily, thought to be "out of his mind," something that can be learned and over which a certain control is exercised. As a result, the shaman's behavior is appropriate to his role and is executed only at appropriate times and places, and not continuously or spontaneously. The insane person lacks such control.

Relating her own data to the literature on mental illness in different cultures, Murphy concludes that the processes that produce disturbances of thought, feeling, and behavior in schizophrenia not only exist in most (if not all) cultures, but also are everywhere recognized and labeled. These constant underlying processes may be associated with culturally variable content. On the other hand, neither Yoruba nor Eskimo has a single word to cover what are called "neuroses" in Western psychiatry. They do, however, have large vocabularies dealing with specific forms of emotions, upsets, and disturbances. In both of these societies most emotional problems are considered to be types of illnesses that can be treated by a shaman or medicine man.

As far as the incidence of mental illness is concerned, statistics on schizophrenia in various societies show the rates to be very similar, ranging between 4.4 and 6.8 per 1000 population.

On the basis of these several findings, Murphy judges that labeling theory is off the mark:

Rather than being simply violations of the social norms of particular groups, as labeling theory suggests, symptoms of mental illness are manifestations of a type of affliction shared by virtually all mankind (Murphy 1976:1027).

Murphy's findings are consistent with those of an earlier study carried out by R. B. Edgerton among four East African tribes. He discovered (Edgerton 1966) not only that all four tribes had a concept of psychosis, but also that there was a high degree of agreement among them on the behaviors ascribed to "psychosis." Also, these behaviors are similar to those that are listed in Western countries, especially for schizophrenia. At the same time, Edgerton also found some inter-tribal differences. For example, the Kamba and the Hehe, who hold that psychosis is due to witchcraft, magic, or anger of the ancestors, also believe that psychosis can be cured and that patients therefore should be given treatment. The Sebei and the Pokot, on the other hand, who consider the condition to be an illness that comes about for no reason, hold that it is incurable and that patients should be treated harshly: tie them, let them starve, let them wander about, or even kill them. These responses, which were elicited by questionnaires among samples of the four tribes, indicate a relationship between beliefs about the causes of psychotic behavior, the expected outcome, and the attitudes toward treatment of patients.

CULTURE AND MENTAL DISORDERS

In view of Edgerton's and Murphy's findings, it may well be that labeling theory, at least in its strongest formulations, does not account for mental illness. There is, moreover, an increasingly accepted view according to which schizophrenia results from biological causes (Himwich 1971, Frohman and Gottlieb 1974). What, then, is the relationship between culture and mental disorder? Several such relationships have to be considered.

From the point of view of the psychiatrist, it is important to understand what kind of behavior is culturally patterned and what kinds of ideas are socially shared. It is easy to consider certain ideas "bizarre" because they are alien to the psychiatrist's own cultural background. We have already encountered a number of ideas that are widely accepted in certain societies but that seem strange to us: that it is desirable under certain circumstances to hallucinate or to believe that one is someone else ("possessed"), that some people can transform others into animals, and that dead people can be partially revived *(zombis),* to cite only a small number of examples. Whether or not an idea is "bizarre," then, will depend to a considerable extent on whether it is a unique and "deviant" personal product, or whether it is a socially shared belief. Moreover, beliefs influence actions, and to understand whether actions are bizarre, we must know how they are related to local beliefs, as well as to the personal, perhaps deviant, views that the individual may hold. At this point, however, the elaborations of beliefs, which may give rise to "secondary deviance," in the terminology of labeling theory, become relevant. Clearly, an individual can be said to be "possessed" *only* when the cultural group believes in possession and when, consequently, associates, seeing certain behavior, "recognize" the individual to be possessed. Where such beliefs do not exist as a social tradition, the individual has developed a personal pathological delusion, which results from emotional disturbance, not from learning the doctrines of a particular religious group.

For example, some years ago, the psychologist Milton Rokeach (1964) found that at the Michigan State Hospital in Ypsilanti there were three patients, each of whom claimed to be Christ. No one else shared their conviction, and their delusions were not matters of religious belief. The only cultural aspect in their personal madness was their acquaintance with Christianity and with the identity and the life of Jesus as told in the Gospels. This situation is quite different from certain other cases in which delusional individuals of forceful personality, and under appropriate circumstances, convert others to their views of reality, and as a result become cultural innovators. Mother Ann Lee, who founded the Shaker sect in England in the eighteenth century, was such a person. As a result of some difficulties with the authorities, she was in prison, and there she had a vision of Jesus, who revealed to her, she said, the duality of God as both male and female. Jesus, according to this account, incorporated the male aspect of the deity, or the Christ spirit, while Ann Lee was anointed by him to receive and incorporate its female aspect. According to White and Taylor (1904:21–22), who were themselves members of the Shaker sect, "henceforth Ann Lee was recognized among the humble band of 'poor in spirit,' 'pure in heart' . . . as the visible Head, the one in whom dwelt the Divine Mother." While we might consider her case in the context of psychopathology, her opponents in England considered her to be a sinner and a heretic. Like her followers, her opponents did not question the reality of her vision, they only questioned the source and the truth of the revelation. In doing so, however, they, as much as her followers, strengthened her own convictions. Leaving England with a small group, Ann Lee came to America where she founded a flourishing religious community, in spite of the fact her beliefs scandalized most Christians, and that she also imposed strict rules of celibacy and of communal property on all the converts. By all indications, she appears to have been a highly effective leader and organizer. Her own delusions were made the cornerstone of the group's beliefs.

A comparison among the Haitian possession trancer, the Christs of Ypsilanti, and Mother Ann Lee is quite instructive. The Haitian possession trancer is playing out a socially acceptable role on a ritual occasion, a role which she has learned and which includes both culturally stereotyped and personally idiosyncratic features. The role allows her to express certain personal stresses and some tensions in the group. Ann Lee, whose delusions had a basis in her personal history as well as in the troubled social conditions of her country, became a highly revered founder of a religious movement, who received respect, obedience, support, and love from her followers. In contrast to the clinical cases, she did not become a patient in a state hospital, and she was not made to give up her faith in the truth of her personal convictions. Instead, she converted others, who joined her in her view of herself and of the universe. The hospital patients were, in effect, punished for their convictions, whereas Ann Lee was rewarded for hers. The great difference between Ann Lee and the Haitians, however, is that she invented and developed a world view, a new culture, for herself and others on the basis of her own emotional and cognitive distortions. Personal adaptation, then, may be, for certain exceptional individuals, not *conformity* to cultural standards but *transformation* of these standards. We shall come back to this problem in Chapter 9.

Another way in which cultural factors interest the psychiatrist concerns the nature of the stresses that members of a society experience, and that may be relevant to the occurrence of mental disorders in certain individuals. In this connection, it is important to identify individuals who, as a result of their social positions, are particularly vulnerable and experience greater pressures than others. For example, in speaking of the Zulu, we noted the highly stressful situation of young, newly married women; this special stress exists in many other societies as well, such as India or Japan. In many societies, too, high value is placed on a woman's having children, particularly male children. Inability to have children, or the death of young children, may precipitate illness in women who feel these pressures in addition to personal grief and loss.

An example comes from M. J. Field (1960), who reports that among the patients who came for help to possessed healers at shrines in rural Ghana, she saw numerous women who accused themselves of being witches. Most of them were middle-aged women whom Field, a psychiatrist, considered to be suffering from involutional depression. Although this ailment is not unknown in this country and in Europe, it has a special social and cultural background among the Akan-speaking peoples of Ghana. Here menopause is traumatic not only because, as everywhere, it indicates the end of child-bearing, but because of the social implications of this biological fact. Among these people, the production of children is the primary and continued purpose of marriage; since plural marriages are common, the cessation of child-bearing in one woman may well encourage a husband to take a new young wife to continue to father children. He may shower wealth as well as attention on such a young woman, to the disadvantage of the older wife. On the other hand, there is a shared belief in the existence of witches and in the possibility of being a witch without knowing it. That is, one may have the capacity to cause harm without conscious will or concrete action. Such women then accuse themselves of having caused illness or death or other disasters to their own children and to other kin. They explain their depression, restlessness, and inability to work, to eat, or to sleep as supernatural punishment for being a witch. Such patients rarely are seen in Western-style hospitals, so it often has been reported that depression as a mental disease does not exist in Africa. The reason, however, that such patients are not usually hospitalized is twofold: on the one hand, they are not troublesome or agitated, so they do not come to the attention of authorities, and they can be dealt with and maintained at home. On the other hand, there is the social opinion that holds, and that the patients share, that they are not mentally ill, but are punished sinners. Therefore it is the shrines, and not Western-style psychiatric facilities, that can help them. Because they are witches they must confess their sins.

Although Field does not offer any statistics, it appears from her information that in many instances such patients recover. Two factors seem to be relevant to this observation. First of all, in the United States, too, involutional depressions frequently show spontaneous remissions; that is, in time, whether or not anything special is done, patients often recover from this disorder. Secondly, in cases where the shrine priests (or their spirits) impose substantial fines in the form of sacrificial animals, they often must be paid by the patients' relatives. The willingness to make serious monetary sacrifices is a sign of positive support for the patient, which, in itself, may be therapeutic and help to reestablish the woman in a normal home situation.

Field sees a direct connection between witchcraft beliefs and depression, saying that witchcraft

> is kept alive [by depression] and the fantastic delusions of sin and guilt which beset the patients. Witchcraft meets . . . the depressive's need to steep herself in irrational self-reproach and to denounce herself as unspeakably wicked (Field 1960:38).

Cultural belief and personal distortion thus tend to reinforce each other. That is, the culture provides a belief in witchcraft, and the patient applies the model to herself. In so doing, it should be added, she in turn becomes a model for others and also provides verification of the traditional belief for those who might be tempted to doubt its truth.

A further point, which Hallowell (1939) stressed with regard to public confession of sins among the Saulteaux, applies here as well, and indeed in all cultures where public confession of sin is required as part of the treatment of illness: The patient acts as a support of public morality. The confession makes the connection between sin and sickness evident to all those who hear the confession, showing that the wages of sin are, indeed, death or at least danger of death if pardon is not sought. In traditional societies, then, illness is not merely a problem of medicine but also a problem of the social order. The anthropologist, in contrast to the physician, therefore must understand the social control function of illness as well as the context of medical practice and belief. The two are often inseparable.

Uses of a Cross-Cultural Approach

On the basis of Western studies, numerous claims have been made concerning causes of mental disorders, stress-related diseases, and the reflection of such stresses in social pathologies, such as crime and interpersonal violence. Non-Western cultures may provide situations in which several factors that appear together in the West are separated. We have encountered several cases of this approach: Margaret Mead's early research on girls' adolescence in Samoa, Benedict's distinction between homosexuality among American Indians and in the United States, and our discussion of the Oedipus complex.

An example of such a cross-cultural test of direct relevance to mental health concerns the subject of residential crowding. Students of mammalian behavior as well as urban sociologists have argued that crowding produces stress and stress-related diseases such as essential hypertension, as well as juvenile delinquency and high rates of crime. Patricia Draper (1973) provides a test of this hypothesis in her work with the !Kung. Although these hunter-gatherers live in an arid and sparsely populated region, they construct their temporary settlements in such a way that they are as closely packed together as possible, with an average of less than 190 sq. ft. per person. This figure should be compared with the 350 sq. ft. per person recommended by the American Public Health Association. Furthermore, !Kung settlements are so constructed that the thirty to forty people who make up a group live in a single "room," the central area of a circular campsite. The individual grass huts that form the outside "wall" of this site, face inward toward the living area and serve primarily for storage. Virtually all activity is public and occurs in a space shared by the camp community. The majority of the group is present in the camp at all times, and children are never alone. None of the dire consequences predicted for such conditions of human press appear among the !Kung, whose blood pressure is low and does not rise with age.

There are, of course, important differences between the !Kung and people who live in urban ghettoes. One difference is that the !Kung, whether they stay in a given group or move to another one, are among relatives and friends, and have few occasions to encounter strangers. The context of the larger society in which urban crowding occurs is of major significance for an understanding of its effects. Crowding, identified simply in terms of a ratio of people to space, clearly appears to be inadequate as an explanatory variable.

Culture-Bound Syndromes

There long has been a debate among psychiatrists on whether or not there are mental disorders that exist only in certain specific societies. These disorders have been referred to as "culture-bound," "exotic," or "culture-reactive" syndromes or culture-specific disorders (see, for example, Yap 1969). We find description of diseases such as *amok, arctic hysteria, imu, koro, latah, malgri, possession, windigo* (or *witiko*) *psychosis,* and many more. For the most part, these are local terms, employed in a specific group or region. The question that they pose is whether the patients' behavior represents a specific syndrome (or group of symptoms) unknown elsewhere, or whether these are disorders familiar in other parts of the world, appearing exotic because of some specific elements of cultural content and local belief associated with them.

The problem may be illustrated by the example of *amok,* a Malay term that has entered the English language with a broader range of meaning. We may speak of someone as running amok when we wish to describe wild, aggressive behavior. Among Malay speakers, in a wide area of Southeast Asia (Western and Eastern

Malaysia, Indonesia, and parts of the Philippines), it refers to a more highly stylized behavior. It is believed to occur typically among middle-aged men, following a period of brooding over an insult, and is characterized by a violent series of murderous attacks. The man suddenly seizes one of several traditional weapons, such as a *kris* (a jagged dagger), a spear, or a machete, and attacks any person or animal in his path. If he is not killed in an attempt to stop him, the attack will be followed by prolonged exhaustion and amnesia. The *amok* attack represents a response to shame and insult and thus a vigorous expression of male self-assertion; as such, it is a face-saving behavior. In terms of traditional belief, it may be accounted for by spirit possession or by magic; the community reacts to it with both fear and respect. In the medical literature, we find a variety of attempted explanations of *amok,* ranging from epilepsy, liver disorders, and infections to schizophrenia, hashish poisoning, and sunstroke.

Tan and Carr (1977) report on twenty-one cases classified as *amok* in a hospital in Western Malaysia. Ten of them were Malay men, who were familiar with the concept of *amok,* and whose *amok* attack fitted the cultural pattern closely. The remainder were non-Malays (Chinese and Indians), who were also hospitalized as a result of a fit of murderous rage; they, however, were not familiar with the concept, and their behavior was more idiosyncratic and variable. They had been classified as *amok* because the arresting policemen had been Malays and had so labeled them.

The majority of the older Malay men, who were the true *amok,* had longer hospital stays and remained symptom-free in spite of the fact that they received no treatment. Tan and Carr conclude:

> Amok is a culturally (Malay) prescribed form of violent behavior, sanctioned by tradition as an appropriate response to a given set of conditions. It is not, *per se,* a disease, but a behavioral sequence that may be precipitated by any number of etiological factors, among them physical, psychological, and socio-cultural determinants (Tan and Carr 1977:65).

They question whether these untreated, nonrelapsing, long-term patients are, or ever were, psychotic. Since these patients were older men and had been hospitalized for a long time, these authors find support in their study for the claim by H. M. B. Murphy (1973), that classical cases of *amok* are decreasing in frequency, and that *amok* as a syndrome has undergone a variety of changes, with new social conditions producing new forms of deviant behavior.

The so-called culture-specific disorder that has created the most discussion is that referred to as the "possession syndrome." Wallace (1959) has spoken of possession as "that perennial flower of confusion." The confusion is due to several causes. The first among them is that, unlike the other syndromes in our list, possession is a concept that is familiar in the Judeo-Christian tradition. The cases cited in the New Testament, in which Jesus drove demons out of various kinds of sufferers, have long served as models for pathological behavior of a hysterical type. The similarity between such cases of "possession" and hysterical patients in a clinical context was recognized by the nineteenth century French psychiatrist Charcot and his students, who took a great interest in the literature of the past that described cases of possession. The Christian churches have continued to admit the possibility of demonic possession and exorcism, and there has been a certain revival of interest in this subject in recent years, encouraged in part by spectacular movie productions.[1]

A second source of confusion lies in the fact that, as we saw in Chapter 7, belief in some form of possession is widespread. Consequently, we are dealing not with a local phenomenon, but with a multiform notion with a virtually worldwide distribution. The unfortunate result is that people often erroneously think that what they recognize as possession is likely to be the same condition that someone else, in another part of the world, means by that term.

L. L. Langness (1976) has proposed that all the so-called culture-bound syndromes, including "possession," regardless of their local trappings, be considered as manifestations of a single type of disorder, for which he suggests the term *hysterical psychosis.* Moreover, he argues that the term "possession" should be used only for intentionally induced, ritual states (of the type we discussed at length in Chapter 7), and not for psychiatric disorders. He points out that psychiatric disorders, by whatever name they might go locally, are considered abnormal by the people themselves, whereas intentionally induced ritual possession is an institutionalized form of ritual behavior. Ritual possession is a sacred part of religion, and hysterical psychoses are profane. So far this suggestion is uncontroversial. However, Langness further argues that hysterical psychoses and positive, ritually induced possession are "functionally equivalent," serving the same purpose, so we should expect to find that when one is present in a given society, the other will be absent.

The ritual states Langness speaks of, and for which he wishes to reserve the term "possession," are well illustrated by possession trance as it occurs in the context of Haitian *vodou.* The negative, pathological cases are illustrated by a report from Northern India, published by Stanley Freed and Ruth Freed (1964). The patient was a fifteen-year-old girl, recently married, who was "possessed" by a ghost. The Freeds consider her condition a hysterical attack, involving temporary loss of consciousness, shivering and convulsions, and complaints of various physical symptoms. The precipitating cause of the incident appears to have been her new role as a wife, which caused a separation from her family, entry into a large group of strangers from whom she could expect little support, and her conflicts over sexual relations. The Freeds, following the psychiatric literature, distinguish between two kinds of "gains" the patient obtains from hysterical attacks: a "primary" gain is the relief of the unconscious psychic tensions; the "seconardy" gains involve a modification and manipulation of the situation in which the patient finds herself, to increase the sympathy and support she receives from her new relatives.

The Freeds' patient was treated by local curers. In some cases such cures fail, and patients are brought to hospitals. Teja and his associates (1970) saw fifteen such cases in two Indian hospitals. According to them, the typical "possession" case is a woman in her twenties, of low education and low income. Of the thirteen who were women, the psychiatrists diagnosed six as hysteria, five as schizophrenia, and two as mania. Nonetheless, they argue for a category of "hysterical possession states" because of the cultural content and context, which very closely parallels that described by the Freeds.

These reports support Langness' argument that the term "possession syndrome" tells us little about the psychodynamics of such cases but only identifies something about the local belief system. Indeed, one might go further, for the precise local content of beliefs varies considerably. Thus, in their comparison of their own case with cases reported from other parts of Northern India, the Freeds note a number of differences both in the actual symptoms and in the beliefs concerning the possession. In an area they call Shanti Nagar, the Freeds found that spirit possession always involves individuals who are close relatives, whereas in Uttar Pradesh, another area of Northern India, studied by Opler (1958), they are frequently nonrelatives. Cases of possession in Uttar Pradesh typically involve accusations of witchcraft and aggressive behavior. More important, in Uttar Pradesh a great variety of illnesses and misfortunes are attributed to spirit possession, and not merely possession trance attacks or seizures. However, the shaman may induce such an attack in order to question the spirit who is supposed to be causing the trouble.

This comparison suggests that even in Northern India there is no single concept of possession illness, but regional variations in the beliefs, the associated behavior, and most importantly, in the disorders that reference to possession by ghosts covers. In other words, *in any area where a "possession" illness is reported, we have an emic category of illness, which may well cut across Western categories of disease.* This fact is an important limitation on Langness' suggestion, for where barrenness is attributed to spirit possession we are likely to be dealing with something other than a hysterical psychosis.

In India we also find a great many different types of ritual, institutionalized possession trance cults with possessed curers (or shamans) playing a large role (for example, Harper 1957, Montgomery 1975, Prince 1976). Some of these rituals in honor of the goddess Kali even have been maintained in Guyana by Indian immigrants (Rauf 1965, Singer et al. 1975). This fact suggests that the hypotheses concerning the functional equivalence of hysterical psychoses and ritualized possession trance should be reformulated.

Moreover, the negatively evaluated, spontaneous, pathological type of so-called possession, is not easily and rigorously separated from the positive, intentionally induced ritual states. In a large number of societies a negative, apparently pathological state, interpreted as due to possession by a spirit, precedes initiation into a therapeutic cult, after which the "possession" occurs only at appropriate times, during rituals when the spirit specifically is invited to become manifest. We referred earlier to the widespread *zar* cult, and the cult of diviners among Zulu women. In other words, in many instances a pathological "possession" of the type that might well fit the definition of a hysterical psychosis is *transformed into* a ritualized possession trance as a result of a therapeutic initiation.

This connection may apply also to certain culture-bound syndromes that are not labeled "possession" in the ethnographic and psychiatric literature but are known by various local names. Kerry Stroup (n.d.) has reviewed the reports on one such syndrome, called *imu*. *Imu* is a hysterical disorder among the Ainu of Northern Japan, most of the cases reported occurring among women. Imu is similar to *latah*, which is a Malay term, and also to certain forms of *arctic hysteria* reported from Asiatic Russia. All of these disorders have a number of features in common: compulsive copying behavior, including repeating or echoing the speech of others *(echolalia)* and the actions of others *(echopraxia),* and the compulsive use of filthy speech *(coprolalia)*. Such individuals also are characterized by great suggestibility; they are easily startled and often teased by others, thus provoking an attack, which is considered to be amusing. In addition, in *imu,* according to local belief, there is some connection with snakes: a snake spirit is thought to possess the woman, and an image of a snake is used in an exorcistic healing ritual. Among the Ainu there are also female mediums, who serve as diviners to identify causes of illness, and who are the assistants of male healers. They are women who suffered from *imu* in their youth and were put through special healing rituals (Kitigawa 1960). Thus this particular dissociational illness may, for some individuals, be a first stage in the acquisition of a valued cultural role, open only to a few women in this male-dominated society.

A radical distinction between ritualized possession trance and the hysterical psychoses, such as that suggested by Langness, would also imply that, upon individual evaluation, one would find participants in the cults to be well-adjusted individuals. Such evaluations have been carried out relatively rarely. Before we turn to some of this information, it might be useful to consider several distinctions among the ways in which possession trance is used in ritual contexts. For example, one might expect to find differences between cultures in which possession cult roles are highly stereotyped and those in which they allow a good deal of room for the expression of individual needs through the supposed voice and behavior of the spirits. This latitude includes the number of spirits a person may be possessed by, or in psychological language, the number of alternate personalities an individual may develop and the degree to which they may be differentiated.

An example of a highly stereotyped possession is presented by Robin Horton (1969) from the Kalabari region of Nigeria. Here male priests of the cult of the founding heroes are possessed during a special annual festival. Horton notes that the men who are the priests had been identified by diviners when the position had fallen vacant. They had not received a "call" either through illness or spontaneous possession trance or in some other manner. Individuals might be reluctant to accept the charge because of the many restrictions and difficult duties associated with the office, but they would accept when illness or misfortunes were interpreted as the result of such reluctance. Moreover, there was no training for the role. The behavior of possession trance was highly stereotyped and, in a way, dangerous. Seeking to evaluate the psychological elements in this situation, Horton concludes that in this case it

> is more a matter of society imposing its will on an individual, than of an individual using peculiar behavior to adjust to society. [To obtain] intermittent dramatic appearances of its guardian spirits [the community] commandeers the bodies of certain of its members. It does so without any obvious reference to the psychic suitability of the individuals concerned. [Yet] it seems able, despite these apparently unpropitious conditions, to force genuine dissociation upon those whom it selects (Horton 1969:24–25).

At the other extreme, there is the case of Haitian *vodou,* in which individuals may be possessed by several different personalities, and in which they have a good deal of latitude in what they say and do, which permits them, in many instances, not only to act as healers or diviners, but also to further their own ends. For example, I have reported elsewhere (Bourguignon 1965) how a young woman was possessed by a female spirit who demanded that the young woman's common-law husband marry both the possessing spirit (in a *vodou* ceremony) and the spirit's "horse," the young woman herself (under Haitian law), in order to be healed of a psychotic episode. Clearly, the "horse's" personal wishes were relevant to this therapeutic method; she was able to give expression to her unconscious wishes, through the voice of a possessing spirit. Individuals, in this way, can use possession by spirits to manipulate their social environments. In that sense, it has positive value for an individual living in a socially highly restrictive environment. I have referred to possession in this context as "regression in the service of the self."

The Brazilian psychiatrist, René Ribeiro (1956), who has spent many years studying Xangô cult groups in Recife, Pernambuco (Brazil), reports that the psychiatric status of individual participants in these cults varies widely. He notes that for some individuals participation in the cults is therapeutic and helps them in dealing with their problems, whereas for others it is an expression of their disorders.

There are also differences between individuals who join such groups in order to be cured and those who join for other reasons, if the cult is so organized that various reasons exist for seeking admission. Even among those who come for cures there will be differences in psychological status related to the progress of the cure. Furthermore, there are likely to be important differences between leaders of such groups and rank-and-file members. We have more detailed individual psychiatric evaluations of cult leaders or shamans than on cult members. Joan Koss (n.d.) points out that Puerto Rican spiritist healers vary considerably in personality adjustment. The same is reported by Yuji Sasaki (1969) for Japanese shamans. Boyer (1962, Boyer et al. 1964) on the basis of Rorschach tests and other data, found shamans among the Mescalero Apache to be healthier and more creative than other members of their society.

Some Possible Causes of Culture-Bound Syndromes.   The psychological mechanism that is involved in possession trance is dissociation. M. J. Field defines it as "a mental mechanism whereby a split-off part of the personality temporarily possesses the entire field of consciousness" (1960:19).

Such dissociation is characteristic of hysteria, which, however, has other features as well. Some psychiatrists who have worked among people where possession trance specialists are found, such as Field (1960) and Pfeiffer (1971), emphasize that dissociation is not necessarily pathological. However, even though learning is sometimes obviously involved in the development of this type of behavior, there is good reason to think that individuals who have a propensity for dissociational reactions are characterized by hysteroid personalities. As La Barre (1975:41) has pointed out,

> psychodynamically, "possession" is not so much an invasion by an alien psyche as it is the *overwhelming of conscious ego functions* by ego-alien primary-process mentation . . . (italics in original).

In other words, the secondary personality, which is believed to be a spirit entity, is a part of the individual's own personality that is not recognized or faced. In the context of shamanism or of possession trance cults, the person's ego, the rational practical aspects of the personality, can make use of these split-off tendencies in support of the individual and of the community. On the other hand, we must not lose sight of the fact that even in individuals who suffer from hysterical psychoses, there will be a substantial cultural content and a cultural context that structures both the patient's behavior and the response with which the social group meets this aberrant behavior.

It is possible that at least some of the culture-bound syndromes have organic or ecological origins. This kind of cause may at least constitute one aspect of arctic hysteria in North America. Wallace (1972) has suggested that the behavior may be due to a calcium deficiency, and Foulks (1972), who has pursued the matter in the field in Alaska, has pointed to the drastic annual variation in daylight as a possible ecological factor relevant to these behavioral and emotional disturbances. Similarly, as we have seen, Gussler (1973) has suggested a convergence of ecological and psychocultural factors in the development of possession trance illness among Zulu women.

Summary.   A survey of the literature on the so-called culture-bound syndromes suggests three important points. First, in many instances we are dealing with a traditional, or native, concept of illness, which includes what to a Western, medical observer are a number of diverse ailments or disturbances. It is helpful to understand these categories if we wish to understand how emic medical systems work. However, they are not helpful if we wish to diagnose ailments in terms of a supracultural scientific diagnostic system, in order to understand whether the same psychodynamic processes are at work in all human groups.

Second, at least some of the ailments covered by the term "culture-bound syndromes" share the characteristics of hysterical psychoses. However, in any specific case this similarity cannot be assumed; the diagnosis must be verified clinically.

Third, ailments that are recognizable in an absolute diagnostic system are nonetheless likely to have some specific local "coloring," that is, to have cultural features that modify the clinical picture of a disorder. We have noted this modification, for example, in the case of involutional depression in Ghana.

TRADITIONAL HEALERS AND HEALING SYSTEMS

We have seen that the so-called culture-bound syndromes started out as emic disease categories, and through contact with Western medicine, have been turned, at times, into special diagnostic categories. Native categories such as *latah* and *amok* may indeed be only fragments of complex traditional medical systems.

The most complete description of a traditional system of classification, explanation, and treatment of mental disorders has been published by George Devereux (1961), for the Mohave Indians. He himself speaks of it as a "kind of 'Mohave textbook of psychiatry'," dictated to him by Mohave specialists. The Mohave shamans recognize a great range of disorders and often explain the difference between their views and those of Mohave laymen. Some disorders may be due to various kinds of aggression; others are disorders of the sexual impulse and what Devereux calls "mood disturbances"; there are also disorders caused by such external agents as witches and ghosts. Traditionally, the Mohave were hunters and warriors, so disorders resulting from aggression interestingly reveal the unconscious guilt such behavior produces. Members of war parties, for example, were believed to be exposed to dangerous influences, which might cause insanity, emanating from new scalps, prisoners, and aliens. This notion of danger even was expanded in more recent times to include Mohave Indians who have served in the U.S. Armed Forces. Anxiety over killing, however, might also appear in hunters who had eaten their own kill, as well as in individuals who had killed witches to free the community from them. Contacts with aliens and enemy ghosts also were considered dangerous. Mohave psychiatry is both supernaturalistic and psychological. It is part of a world view in which various supernatural beings and forces (ghosts, witches, dreams) are active and dangerous; it is psychological in seeking to understand individual emotions and motivations.

Theories of disease, and specifically, mental disease, are related to a general world view, to the beings and forces that are believed to exist and to their supposed connections with human beings and their state of health and prosperity. As such, in traditional societies, medical systems are part of larger religious systems. Moreover, therapeutic systems are related to theories of disease. Thus, if disease is due to infractions of taboos or social rules, it is punishment for such infractions, and the appropriate therapy will involve confession. La Barre (1964) has discussed at some length how confession works as cathartic therapy among many American Indian tribes. As these tribes have undergone drastic cultural changes, confession has taken on new forms, appearing in the context of the Peyote Cult and the Native American Church. Hallowell (1976 [orig. 1963b]) has shown how confession serves not only to relieve the guilt of sinners, but also to maintain social sanctions among the Saulteaux, a society without chiefs, judges, and courts. A. F. C. Wallace (1958) has discussed how psychotherapy through catharsis worked among the Iroquois by interpreting dreams as "wishes of the soul" and of supernaturals who appeared in, or sent, the dreams. Every effort was made to satisfy these wishes, as they were understood. In the eighteenth century, Iroquois society underwent great disruptions, resulting in demoralization, drunkenness, and social disorganization. They were rescued from this state by a new religion founded by Handsome Lake, a visionary prophet, himself a former alcoholic. In this new system, Wallace tells us, emphasis was placed on control, and confession of sins was used in this context. On the basis of his historical research, Wallace has proposed a more general hypothesis that should be important for cross-cultural studies:

> in a highly organized sociocultural system, the psychotherapeutic needs of individuals will tend to center in catharsis (the expression of suppressed or repressed wishes in socially non-disturbing ritual situations); . . . in a relatively poorly organized system, the psychotherapeutic needs will center in control (the development of a coherent image of self-and-world and the repression of incongruent motifs and beliefs) (Wallace 1958:94).

Anthropologists have long attempted to account for the successes of traditional healers. They have observed cures, and they have noted people's confidence and faith in these practitioners. Indeed, it often has been reported that shamans and other healers consult their own colleagues in times of sickness, which suggests that they themselves have confidence in the techniques they practice. For the most part, anthropologists have dealt with specific societies, often with specific episodes of illness and curing, and only rarely have they attempted to make broader generalizations.

For example, in a fascinating paper, Victor Turner (1964) describes in some detail the illness and cure of a man among the Ndembu of Zambia. Turner points out that among these people the illness of a single individual often is seen as expressing disharmony not only within the patient, but also within the patient's group, and it is the task of the diviner to rearrange the group, to restore harmony to it. In the specific case, the illness was explained, through divination, as resulting from the anger of an ancestral spirit. There was a good deal of conflict among the relatives of the patient, and a major portion of the healing ritual was devoted to the confession of ill feelings toward the patient by various persons and to his own expression of grudges against others. In addition, much magical ritual was carried out, including the sleight-of-hand extraction from the patient's body of a tooth, which, supposedly, the afflicting ancestor had sent into the patient to trouble him. After the sequence of rituals, which apparently improved the patient's condition, moreover, certain individuals moved away from the village, so the social group was reorganized. As Turner points out, "the sick individual . . . is reintegrated, into his group, step by step, as members are reconciled with one another in emotionally charged circumstances" (Turner 1964:262). The social group is rebuilt, and relations among its members are modified. In a larger scheme of things, relations between the living and the dead ancestors are also altered. At the same time, there is not only social manipulation but also a dramatic manipulation of the emotions, through the confessions that "clear the air" and through the various symbolic, ritual actions. Both the patient and the body politic are healed.

Among the many diverse elements in the curing process that have been reported from societies in all parts of the world, several common features stand out. They may be summed up in two terms: "symbols" and "rituals." In a famous paper, Claude Lévi-Strauss (1963) has spoken of the "effectiveness of symbols," comparing the procedures used by the shaman among the Cuna Indians of Panama to those of the psychoanalyst. The shaman uses a special telling of a myth to help a woman in a difficult delivery. The myth follows the birth process in great detail, and Lévi-Strauss suggests that it is helpful in that it guides the woman, focusing her attention on her body and increasing her awareness of what is going on within her. The psychoanalyst, similarly, helps the patient become conscious of what is going on within, psychologically rather than physiologically. More recent relaxation techniques are even more similar to that of the Cuna shaman.

A. F. C. Wallace (1966), as mentioned earlier, considered ritual as a process of unlearning and relearning; indeed, he speaks of a "ritual transformation of experience" and thus of a transformation of the individual. Kiefer and Cowan (n.d.) more recently have looked to psychological experiments for analogies with rituals. Experiments that use drug-induced altered states of consciousness have shown that alterations of consciousness have an effect on the storing and remembering of information. (This effect has been referred to as "state-dependent learning.") Also, the total context in which information is acquired has a great effect on ability to recall it.[2] Rituals are situations that provide special contexts of behavior, with heightened meaning and emotional intensity. Awareness or consciousness is modified in such settings, even if no altered state is specifically induced. Ritual, therefore, provides an ideal setting for the unlearning of faulty forms of adjustment and for the learning of more adjustive forms. Ritual situations heighten patients' suggestibility by the great attention that is paid to them, the use of symbols, the support of supernatural authorities, and so on.

The British psychiatrist, William Sargant, basing his work on the work of the Russian physiologist Pavlov, has defended the thesis that extreme emotional excitement helps the individual to unlearn and forget old ways of feeling and, again in the setting of heightened suggestibility, to learn new desired responses. He has applied this thesis to political conversion ("brainwashing") and to religious conversion ("possession") (Sargant 1959 [orig. 1957], 1974).

A number of comparisons have been made also between the procedures used by native healers and by modern psychiatrists. For example, the Canadian psychiatrist, Raymond Prince, has reported the different kinds of Yoruba healers and healing methods in an article (1964) and in a documentary film.[3] He speaks of traditional healers in charge of treatment centers, diviners, possession trance cults, and men's secret societies (or "masquerade cults"). Both physiological and psychotherapeutic elements are used in the healing process. Both are generally employed in a magico-religious context that involves beliefs in the activities of witches, ancestor spirits, and gods. A great deal of ritual is employed. Among the physiological elements is the drug rauwolfia, a powerful tranquilizer, which has been known in West Africa for hundreds of years. However, a species of rauwolfia was introduced into Western medicine, from India, only in the last quarter century. Prince identifies a series of psychotherapeutic elements in Yoruba practice: suggestion on many different levels, from the most symbolic and metaphorical to direct commands; the use of sacrificial animals, which may contain a "sacramental" element (the identification of the patient with the animal and the substitution of the animal for the patient in the "paying off" of angry spirits); manipulation of the environment, (such as an order to move to a different neighborhood or to change occupations); and "ego-strengthening elements" (such as the requirement to join the ancestor cult, which might provide the patient with greater self-confidence by offering assurance of the spirits' protection). Prince also sees parallels to Western group therapy in the possession trance cults and in the men's secret societies; by joining them, the patient gains the support of a group of peers. Also, as we mentioned earlier, such cult groups provide sanctions for behavior that is prohibited under ordinary circumstances. As a result, it becomes possible for the patient to act out personality aspects that normally have to be repressed, or whose expression is punished in ordinary life situations. For example, women temporarily may act out roles of men, and men those of women. Tabooed aggressive and sexual behavior may be engaged in, because responsibility for it is assigned to the spirits.

Although Prince points to a number of similarities between Western psychiatry and the methods of the native healers (the use of drugs, sometimes of intentional suggestion and command, and more generally of suggestion and command as part of the total medical setting), he also points to one major difference: Western psychotherapies attempt to help the patient gain "insight"—understanding of the unconscious strivings that influence behavior—and to help integrate repressed elements, such as those expressed in dissociational states, into the personality. The Western psychotherapist's aim, then, is not merely to reduce symptoms and to help the individual to function in society, but to reach greater emotional health and maturity. There is little evidence that any of the traditional therapies seek to do so.

How Successful Are Traditional Healers?

This difference in aims between Western psychotherapists and traditional healers raises a number of interesting questions. Foremost is the question of just how successful traditional healers actually are. Anthropologists and psychiatrists, as we have seen, have considered at some length how traditional healers work and how their actions may alleviate the sufferings of the patient. However, there is little hard evidence of their rate of success. Moreover, as Prince (1979a) has pointed out, we have little reliable data to show that Western psychotherapies "work" either. In this context there are at least two different problems: on the one hand, how do we define a "cure"? As we have just seen, there is quite a difference among the goals therapists set for themselves: the removal of symptoms, the reintegration of the patient into the community, and emotional growth and maturation are just some of these goals. On the other hand, adequate statistics are hard to come by. Even in industrialized societies the most readily available statistics, hospital admissions and discharges, are open to a variety of interpretations.

When we ask the patients about their cures, we sometimes discover another aspect of the problem. J. Monfouga-Nicolas (1972) studied the Bori possession trance cult among the Hausa people of Niger, West Africa. This is a cult of women, who join because of various kinds of illnesses. Although the cult leaders distinguish fifteen kinds of "madness," patients suffering from them are only a small minority, with others coming to the cult because of frequent miscarriages, sterility, and various other troubles. Because the author had no medical diagnosis available to her, the precise nature of illnesses and the relative contributions of psychological and organic elements to the complaints are not known. She says that members are considered "cured"; however, this claim has to be understood in their sense. For them, illness is related to guilt, and initiation permits the externalization of this guilt and thereby the removal of the self-destructive tendencies associated with guilt. Consequently, even if physical symptoms continue to exist, their meaning has changed. This outcome is remarkably similar to what a U.S. sociologist, E. Mansell Pattison (1974), found among patients who were converts to fundamentalism: they felt "healed" even though they might not have lost their disease symptoms, and even might continue to seek medical treatment at the same time. The faith healing increased the strength of their religious beliefs, so Pattison concludes: "Faith healing is not an exercise in the treatment of organic pathology, but an exercise in the treatment of life style" (1974:451). Like the Bori adepts studied by Monfouga-Nicolas, and like members of possession cults around the world, these U.S. Protestants belonged to groups that gave them intense emotional support. Also, like the other cultists, they experienced altered states of consciousness, which found their expression in glossolalia ("speaking in tongues") and other ecstatic states, referred to as "gifts of the Spirit."

As far as the Hausa women are concerned, the French psychiatrist J. Broustra (1972) suggests that the Bori cult treats individuals suffering from neuroses and psychosomatic symptoms. True insanity, by contrast, is the specialty of healers who rely on an extensive knowledge of plant remedies. One of these specialists who, according to Broustra, probably treated no more than one hundred cases in a career spanning a period of twenty years, reported that he had better success with some types of cases than others.

As mentioned before, we have limited information on the actual success rate of native healers. However, it appears that the greatest success occurs in cases with physical symptoms that have a strong element of emotional involvement. For example, Vincent Crapanzano studied the Moroccan curing cult called Hamadsha. He says of their healers that they are able to produce, "often dramatically, the remission of symptom—paralysis, mutism, sudden blindness, severe depression, nervous palpitations, paraesthesias, and possession" (1973:4). According to this author, many of the disorders treated successfully by making the patient a member of the cult represent bodily expressions of guilt reactions. Once the patient has joined, it is believed that a failure to obey the command of the spirits will cause a relapse, and conversely, if a relapse does occur it will be explained as punishment for a transgression. This situation is similar to that in the Bori cult of the Hausa and in the *zar* cult of Ethiopia, Somalia, the Sudan, and Egypt.

In spite of the reports of successes of this type, some other accounts suggest that such treatments may not be without their dangers. B. Lewin (1957) presents an interesting case history from his psychiatric practice in Egypt. The patient was a woman who was brought to him suffering from a severe depression. She was childless, and concerned over her condition, she had sought the help of a *zar* cult leader. This specialist explained that a spirit was causing the patient's infertility and that to satisfy him it would be necessary for her to join the cult. Once she had joined and was assured that the spirit would no longer keep her from having children, she began to show signs of pregnancy. However, when she was examined at a prenatal clinic, she was told that she was not pregnant. The patient refused to believe this diagnosis, and her false pregnancy continued for the full term. When she did not have a baby, however, she again returned to the *zar* specialist, who said that the spirit *(jinn)* had been jealous and had stolen the child. At this point she came to the psychiatrist.

There are several interesting aspects in this situation. We do not know why the woman was infertile, but clearly this fact represented a cause not only of sadness and disappointment to her, but also of great fear. It must be remembered that under Moslem law a husband may divorce a wife for failure to have children. In this state of mind she came to see the *zar* healer. Here she received not only a meaningful explanation but also a method of dealing with her problem. The ritual process and the strong suggestion from the healer, together with her own great desire to have a child, led her, however, not to conceive a child, but to a hysterical pregnancy. The ritual cure, instead of solving the problem, had, in fact, created a new one! The *zar* healer, however, was not at a loss to account for the strange situation, and offered another supernatural explanation consistent with the first. "Cures," then, may produce positive results, but, as this case shows, they also may be dangerous.

Another interesting aspect of this case is that we are dealing with a woman in a developing country, where several different kinds of services are available: on the one hand, there is the traditional sector represented by the *zar* healer, and on the other hand, there is the modern sector represented by the prenatal clinic and the psychiatrist. Depending on their specific difficulties, patients may use services in both of these sectors, either at the same time or in succession.

This is an exceptional case, in that there is not only a dramatic failure of the healing process, but also information available through a psychiatrist. To evaluate the procedures of traditional healers, we need medical diagnoses and long-term follow-up studies, not merely descriptions of what the healer does and accounts of short-term remissions in a few cases.

One such detailed study has been published by W. G. Jilek (1974), who worked as a psychiatrist and physician among the Coastal Salish Indians of British Columbia for some six years. Among these people, an ancient spirit cult has been revived in recent years, in modified form, and has become a healing cult. According to Jilek, there are among the Coastal Salish numerous individuals who suffer from what he calls "anomic depression," that is, depression linked to social and cultural disruption. This depression is shown in aggressive and antisocial behavior, alcoholism, drug addiction, depression, anxiety, and various bodily complaints. Jilek links these disorders directly to the marginal status of the Salish in white society, and to the social and personal conflicts produced by acculturation. The Salish speak of such cases as resulting from "spirit illness," for which white medicine has no proper cure. The guardian spirit ceremonials have become rituals of identity change. As often happens in initiation rites, the novice is ritually, symbolically, slain and reborn. In this process he loses his old identity as a marginal individual and is revived with a proud new Indian identity.

This ritual process, which lasts several days, includes a number of different stages, some public and some private. It includes inducing altered states of consciousness, fasting, having a vision of the guardian spirit, and acquiring a spirit song and spirit dance. These activities are followed by a period of indoctrination and finally, by a great, strenuous, public dance. Afterwards, the new members continue to participate in the ceremonials during each winter season. That is, they join the group on a permanent basis.

Jilek reports that of twenty-four patients, all but three showed varying degrees of improvement either in their symptoms or in their behavior. Some of these individuals had long-term problems; they had received unsuccessful medical treatment, or in the case of the aggressive individuals, punishment by the local authorities, which had not prevented them from being chronically in trouble. In

Jilek's view, moreover, the renewed institution of the guardian spirit ceremonials is helpful not only to specific troubled individuals, but to the community as a whole, which is recovering its Indian identity.

Howard Stein (1977), in his review of Jilek's book, again raises the question: what do we mean by "cure"? He wonders whether by joining this cult, the patients do not simply substitute one form of "addiction" (the cult) for an older one, such as alcoholism or drugs. Also, he asks whether it is useful for these people to reaffirm an Indian identity, instead of seeking to make their way in the "real" world of white industrial Canadian society. The difference between this situation and, for example, that of the Bori cult members among the Hausa, seems to be that the Indians seek to *reconstruct* the old ways, when they actually may have an alternative. The Hausa simply continue, for the time being, to live in their traditional society.

The problem is an interesting and difficult one, and it has many practical implications. In some ways, the case of the Salish Indian cultural revival and the psychotherapeutic identity changes it brings about in individuals is reminiscent of the great religious ferment that has been in existence in the United States for a number of years. This ferment has involved a variety of Eastern religions, as well as vigorous pentecostal and charismatic movements within and outside of a great many Christian churches. There have been numerous reports claiming that such religious conversions have brought about personal transformations, including the rehabilitation of drug addicts and alcoholics. The questions raised by Stein are similar to those brought up by Prince with regard to the need for patients to gain insight into their underlying unconscious emotional conflicts.

Some Practical Applications

Because Western-trained psychiatrists have discovered at various times and in various places that they have not been successful among culturally different, traditional, populations, and also perhaps because they are few in numbers, several have undertaken striking and bold experiments. The first Nigerian psychiatrist, T. A. Lambo (1964), began to experiment in 1954 with village-based community psychiatry. This experiment included cooperation among the psychiatrist, the hospital staff, and traditional healers or "witch doctors," an idea that was shocking to most Western physicians.

Both the community-based treatment facility and the collaboration with folk healers have since gained widespread acceptance in many parts of the world. In Dakar, Senegal, such cooperation has been developed by French and French-trained African physicians and folk healers among several local ethnic groups. In the United States, Cornell University has established a project among the Navajo Indians incorporating many of the features of Lambo's work.[4] Harwood (1977), Garrison (1977), and Koss (n.d.) are anthropologists who have worked with Puerto Rican spiritists either in Puerto Rico or in New York City, while they were associated with community health projects. In these and in many other cases around the world, anthropologists have worked as cultural interpreters; they have studied the local social system and the local beliefs and practices concerning disease and healing, and have assisted psychiatrists in understanding the behavioral world of their patients. On the other hand, in many instances they have also explained the world of the psychiatrists to the folk healers and to the local community. This work is now a major activity for those involved in the growing field of medical anthropology.

As we have seen, cultural factors must be taken into consideration in seeking to understand mental disorders, and in the types of treatments to which members of different societies are likely to respond. When the therapist and the patient belong to the same society and share the same view of the forces that shape health and illness, the therapeutic process is furthered; when they approach the problem with different perceptions and different interpretations, the therapeutic process is complicated by this fact. This difficulty is increasingly being recognized in many developing areas of the world, and perhaps, to a lesser extent, in the United States. Here, too, there are many ethnic groups with their own systems of religious healing, and it is possible that their efforts might be mobilized for cooperation with mental health specialists. As Allan Harwood (1977) notes, in concluding his book on Puerto Rican spiritists in New York:

> In this period of United States history, when many of the values and norms of the society are being called into question and a more relativistic ethical system is apparently emerging, it seems appropriate for those in the helping professions to reevaluate their premises and techniques. . . . Many workers are increasingly open to new forms of treatment and to view people in their sociocultural context before instituting traditional [current U.S. medical] forms of psychotherapy (Harwood 1977:217).

Under these circumstances, an anthropological understanding of sociocultural systems clearly seems to have practical applications.

SUMMARY

In this chapter we have considered a number of related questions concerning the area of overlap between psychological anthropology and psychiatry. As so often before in this book, we have been faced *both* by evidence of universal human characteristics and by the importance of cultural differences and variability.

We noted at the outset that major psychiatric disorders, such as schizophrenia, appear to exist in all human societies, that they exhibit the same basic features, and that they are recognized as disorders by people everywhere. However, there are important differences in the ways in which these disorders are explained and in which patients are treated, not only differences between traditional and modern societies, or among traditional societies, but even differences between modern industrial societies. For example, J. M. Townsend (1975) studied matched samples of one hundred mental patients in a U.S. and a German psychiatric hospital.

He found statistically significant differences between these two samples of patients in how they viewed themselves and their illness. Whereas the German patients thought of mental illness as biologically caused and generally incurable, U.S. patients held that they were themselves partially responsible for their own conditions and that they could therefore improve, given proper motivation and help. The author points out that this notion of "behavioral free will"—the idea that one can shape one's own destiny—has been noted by many observers as a major theme of U.S. ideology. The concept of mental illness that people in the United States hold, then, is not arbitrary but is part of a larger picture that they have of their culturally constituted behavioral environment and of their own place within it. It stands in sharp contrast to that of the Germans, who see their society as having much more highly fixed status assignments.

What kinds of behavior will be considered deviant in any given culture? The consideration of this question led us to a discussion of the relativity of normalcy. Following this section, we turned again to the issue of the complex relationship between culture and mental disorders. Here we found evidence of variations in the roles that disturbed individuals may play, in theories of illness, and in therapeutic methods. Illness, we emphasized, is often defined as punishment for the infraction of sacred social rules, and therefore public announcement of the sin, as in confession, may serve to bolster the rules and uphold the social system. Under these circumstances, medical practice may fulfill some of the functions of the legal system.

There is also some evidence that certain deviants may show us, by means of their behavior and their preoccupations, what some of the stress points are in a social system. We have mentioned this idea several times in connection with spirit possession illness, but it is true of other disorders as well. A particularly fine demonstration of this point is offered by P. J. Wilson (1975) in his account of Oscar, an "extraordinary person" whom he came to know in his fieldwork on the island of Providencia, in the southern Caribbean. In this sensitive study Wilson shows how Oscar, in his madness, highlights the conflicts inherent in the value system of his society by violating its rules, especially the rules concerning privacy.

Next, we again saw how the cross-cultural approach allows us to test hypotheses derived from a single culture; specifically, societies of a different type allow us to discover unexpected implications of hypotheses derived from conditions in modern Western societies. We had earlier considered this issue in connection with Margaret Mead's study of adolescents, and we now consider it in reference to stress and crowding.

Pushing the issue of cultural variability a step further, we reviewed discussions about the possibility that there might be mental disorders that are unique or specific to certain cultures. This question led us to yet another problem, the relative merits of emic and etic approaches to mental illness.

Since mental illness occurs universally, most, if not all, societies have developed healing systems, and research has shown that at least some of them are effective. Their success presents a challenge to Western medicine. To account for it, often observers have compared traditional and Western systems, producing a double-barrelled conclusion: effective traditional methods are found to contain many features that seem to make them similar to modern medicine. Are native healers therefore really psychiatrists who differ from their modern counterparts only in their jargon? Or are modern psychiatrists really witch doctors who use magical means in curing their patients, regardless of whether they are aware of doing so?

This discussion finally has led us to consider the possible practical applications of the knowledge anthropologists have acquired concerning traditional societies and their healing systems. Under certain circumstances, the anthropologist may act as an interpreter of traditional ways to the psychiatrist and of the psychiatrist's ways to the people. In a number of places, in recent years, traditional healing methods have been used in collaboration with modern medicine, and such cooperation has appeared to produce better results than have been obtained when the two systems have worked as competing or mutually hostile institutions.

NOTES

1. In April 1978 a German court convicted two Catholic priests and the parents of a young woman, Anneliese Michel, of having contributed to her death. According to medical testimony, the patient had suffered from epilepsy and had died of starvation. The priests had carried out a prolonged series of exorcistic rituals, "driving out" a great number of evil spirits, Adolf Hitler among them. These demons, they believed, were causing the girl's illness by possessing her. The patient died after she attempted to live only on holy water for a time, refusing all food.

2. In his great novel, *Remembrance of Things Past* (1932–1934), Marcel Proust, in a famous passage, describes how his narrator gropingly rediscovers forgotten memories, when vague hints of recollections are stirred up in his mind by the eating of a fine pastry, called a *madeleine*, which he had not tasted in a long time. Ernest Schachtel (1959) in a justly famous paper entitled "On Memory and Childhood Amnesia" discusses this case and some other examples in detail.

3. *Were Ni (He Is a Madman): The Management of Psychiatric Disorders by the Yoruba of Nigeria*, Raymond Prince and Frank Speed. This excellent film is available from Professor Prince through the R. M. Bucke Memorial Society for Religious Experience, in Montreal, Canada.

4. Prince (1979b) discusses the relationship between the psychiatrist and the folk healer as a partnership. In this article he notes the fact that in 1977, the World Health Organization, in an editorial in its journal *World Health*, was advocating cooperation between physicians and health personnel and native specialists, including herbalists and midwives. Prince shows how this attitude represents a drastic reversal of a long-standing position of Western specialists, who saw in folk healers only ignorance compounded by charlatanism.

⑨

Culture Change: Transformation and Continuities

INTRODUCTION: THE SIGNS OF CHANGE

Item: In the Spring of 1978 the Select Committee on Population of the U.S. House of Representatives conducted two weeks of hearings on population and development assistance. Expert witnesses presented testimony on a broad variety of topics, among them:

Population, North–South Relations (between developed and developing countries), and the United States' stake
Population Growth, Poverty, and Development: U.S. Interests, Programs, and Policies
Developing Country Perspectives on Population and Development (Mexico)
The South View of North–South Relations
Population Growth—Stimulus for U.S. Production and Markets
The Need for Agricultural Expansion in Developing Countries
World Energy Prospects
The Impact of Development Programs on Population Dynamics (with emphasis on the roles and status of women)

Item: In Brazil, the First Assembly of Indigenous Chiefs was called together by a Catholic Missionary group at Diamantina in the state of Mato Grosso on April 17, 1974. The representative of the Tapirapé addressed the group in the following terms, as translated by the American anthropologist Charles Wagley:

The ranches are surrounding us. The [land companies] are taking away all of our land. Why did the whites want to pacify us? Afterwards what is going to happen to us in the middle of whites working for the whites who want to take away our land? Is it meant that the Indians should have nothing and to put an end to the Indians?

... The Tapiraguaia Company wants to take all of our land. It wants to give us a small piece of bush ... which is not worth anything. Where we plant is good forest. The whites say, "Look, the Indian is not equal to us. Let's take away their land because they do not have guns nor machine guns, nor bombs, nor money. All they have are bows and arrows and clubs. Only these are for the Indians to use ..." (Wagley 1977:125).

Item: A psychologist has written recently about development:
Development, as a concept in the social sciences, has often been used in the popular sense of simply becoming bigger, wealthier, and, at the extreme, more like the western world. The ethnocentric usage has been dismissed by many in the past few years ... If education is to serve the "development" of an individual, group, or nation, it must start with the present state of affairs and work toward some valued future state. Imposed educational systems that make incorrect assumptions about initial behaviour and culture or choose non-valued states as the eventual goal cannot possibly contribute to "development." [Therefore] an accurate description of a wide variety of traditional behaviour is required, a clear statement of individual and cultural goals must be articulated, and a programme of moving between the two must be worked out ...

The old assumptions about "cultural deprivation" cannot survive a framework in which education is viewed as development. Groups, armed with information about their own characteristic patterns of skills, may opt for a number of goals. If they choose to build upon the strengths they already possess ... then such "reinforcing education" is development; and if they choose to strengthen those skills which are not high in relation to other groups, then such "compensatory education" is development. (Berry 1976:225–226, 227).

Item: A travel advertisement received in the mail says:
The Orient: Thailand/ Hong Kong/ the South Pacific Islands. Imagine the Orient of your dreams. Places with the most romantic names. Places that, not so very long ago, only truly intrepid travelers ever had a chance to see.

Distant places and different cultures. Silent, robed monks worshipping unknowable gods in temples of incalculable age ... Women jostling by with great burdens balanced on their heads (How do they *do* that?) Children climbing, scampering, carrying on like children anywhere ...

Waves caressing a Polynesian shore. Dancers prancing under the moon to the music of hollow-log drums. This is Paradise! ...

New Guinea. A dark and mysterious island where Stone Age tribes survive, their rituals unchanged. You'll travel ... to see the fearsome dance of the Mud-Men, to get a feeling for the South Pacific as the First European explorers found it centuries ago. You'll relax at some of the world's grandest hotels ... We took your dreams to the most creative people in the travel business ... and they conjured up a stupendous trip.

These four items, picked virtually at random from a variety of sources, allow us a glance at some of the many aspects of the dramatic social and cultural changes that are going on all around us. For example, development assistance is a major issue in the foreign policy of the United States. Public hearings by

Congressional Committees, where numerous expert witnesses are questioned, serve not only to provide information for legislators but also to educate the public on matters of concern. In the titles of these hearings we see that development is perceived as related to population growth, and both are considered to have implications for the U.S. economy: its production, its markets, its raw materials, and its energy supply. The United States, like other industrial countries, has sought for many years to influence development in countries that are variously called "underdeveloped," "developing," or more recently, "South." The Agency for International Development (AID) and the Peace Corps probably stand for "development" in the minds of most Americans, but there are a variety of other ways in which direct aid from the United States—including weapons, technical experts, and money—has had a major impact on the countries of the South.

Brazil is a major "developing" country that currently is experiencing rapid economic growth and social and economic dislocations associated with that growth. The Tapirapé are one of a number of small tribes of Brazilian Indians. In the 1940s they almost died out when their total population dropped to forty-seven persons. Unlike many other such tribes, however, they have come back from the brink of extinction as a result of the efforts of Catholic missionaries, so that in 1976 they numbered 130 people. Yet the Tapirapé, and others like them, are in the path of the last great land boom in the interior of Brazil. S. H. Davis (1977) has called the Indians "victims of the miracle" of the economic development of the Amazon region. The expansion that now is taking place involves both Brazilian and multinational companies who are seeking to bring land under intensive cultivation, raise livestock, exploit timber resources, and so on. For example, Georgia Pacific Company was granted a concession of 1,250,000 acres by the Brazilian government. To exploit their vast holdings, these companies import laborers from other parts of the country, so that a great movement of people is taking place.

Moreover, the Indians are not the only ones facing difficulties in the current situation. As Charles Wagley has noted:

> The Brazilian Indian problem is basically a political problem. The future of the remaining tribes depends upon political decisions and political support . . . Given the enormous problems which Brazil as a nation faces today, among them illiteracy, transportation, sources of energy, the sprawl of great cities, the production of basic foodstuffs, and the unequal distribution of income between the poverty stricken, and the middle and upper classes, it is doubtful whether the Brazilian government will give the Indian cause the support it deserves (Wagley 1977:303–304).

The Tapirapé are aware of some of the difficulties and dilemmas. They know that some Brazilians are worse off than they. They have begun to learn Portuguese and to acquire some of the skills of a modern society.

When we look at the situation of the Brazilian Indians, it is clear that Berry's concept of development is not being applied. The ends are not those of the people themselves, but are established by larger historical, economic, and social forces.

Indeed, the decimation and reduction of the Brazilian Indian population reported in the world press in recent years represents only the last act in a drama begun in the 1500s. Clearly, only in the minority of cases is there likely to be a situation in which "a clear statement of individual and cultural goals [is] articulated."

Finally, what is one to say of a situation in which "traditional culture" and "underdevelopment" become the exotic attractions offered to tourists from the industrialized countries by "the most creative people in the travel business"? Tourism not only despoils the very attractions it seeks to present, it is also a singularly hazardous form of "development," for it provides few new skills and goods to the people. Indeed, it may create a situation in which the "natives" who are employed by the tourist enterprises are seen as servants, and those who are not face the inflation that results from the influx of the money the tourists spend. At the same time, contrary to the illusions of many travelers, no understanding of traditional cultures is brought about, nor meaningful cultural exchanges, nor better relationships. For instance, tourists may be offered a theatrical version of rituals, which are emptied of traditional meanings, for the sacred is not acted out on cue for a foreign audience.

Implications for Psychological Anthropology.   Psychological processes of all kinds are involved in sociocultural change, both as causes and as effects. Innovations that are introduced into a society require learning of the new and often also some unlearning of old ways. If learning is to be effective, there must be motivation, and often the motivation for learning the new ways is rooted in the traditional society. Transformations of culture and society, whether resulting from contacts among societies or from innovations arising within a society, may bring about significant and often dramatic changes in the attitudes and behaviors of individuals. They may also involve modifications in people's sense of identity. Cultural transformations of the type illustrated in our examples undoubtedly create stresses of various kinds. Yet they also may bring opportunities, for some individuals, for the greater development of their potentials and greater expression of their personal qualities.

In this chapter we take a closer look at the psychological processes that are involved in sociocultural change, both as causes and as effects. The subject of social, cultural, and psychological change has appeared over and over again in this book. We have referred to it in a variety of contexts. Let us reconsider some of the topics that we explored earlier from the special perspective of this chapter.

CULTURAL EVOLUTION AND INNOVATION

In Chapter 2 we discussed the psychological evolution of humanity and the emergence of culture. We saw that culture was made possible by the growth of a *capacity for culture,* which included the potential for complex learning, for the development of language, and more generally, for the symbolic transformation of experience. Hockett and Ascher (1964) referred to this radical and dramatic series of modifications as the "human revolution."

In seeking to understand our uniquely human manner of living, anthropologists often have placed great stress on the observation that culture is *learned.* Perhaps even more important is the fact that what is learned has first to be *discovered* or *invented* by someone and then to be *transmitted* to and shared by others. Every item in our cultural repertory is built on an initial act of innovation and then on a series of modifications in the course of time. Here it is interesting to realize that very early in the development of culture those artifacts that are related to the basic practical aspects of living, such as tools and weapons, reflect only a portion of the total culture.

Like utilitarian culture, symbolic cultures has very ancient roots. Alexander Marshak (1976) has analyzed an engraved ox rib found by the French prehistorian François Bordes. It dates from Acheulian times, some 300,000 years ago. The individual who made markings on this piece of bone lived in France before our species existed. Marshak describes the designs as "a series of connected festooned double arcs" forming a type of serpentine image. In later Mousterian artifacts he finds not one but a variety of symbol systems in different types of symbolic artifacts, including pendants and carved plaques with characteristic design patterns. These symbols reveal the existence of a complex cognitive capacity together with an ability for abstracting, for creating models, and for making objects that are quite different from those used in practical pursuits. Also, they required skills distinct from those needed to make tools for hunting or gathering, for butchering or building, and so on. The symbolic artifacts were *nonutilitarian;* that is, they were evidently not directly applied to practical ends. They may well have had symbolic significance and ritual uses meant to further economic activities, human health, or human and animal fertility. If so, they were applied to practical ends in what appear from our own perspective to be indirect ways.

The nonutilitarian, symbolic artifacts of the Upper Paleolithic reveal early evidence both of magico-religious practices and of art. The artistic value of these objects is evident in the great skill needed to produce them, in the splendid observation of nature they reveal, and in the striking transpositions of this observation that they exhibit. The magico-religious uses of these artifacts, however, can only be inferred from our knowledge of how such objects are used among recent ethnographic groups, or more ancient ones of whose actions and beliefs we have documented accounts.

Great creative capacity and innovative vision are shown in these ancient symbolic artifacts. Yet in focusing on cultural change we must not lose sight of the important elements of tradition and continuity. Marshak points out, for example, that serpentine designs represented a durable design tradition throughout the Upper Paleolithic, a tradition practiced by many generations of artists.

In considering the evolution of culture in our earlier discussion we stressed the differences between the ways of life of small bands of hunter-gatherers and those of larger populations who raise crops and domesticated animals. Contrasts between groups at these different levels of subsistence economy and sociocultural complexity involve not only differences in livelihood and group organization but also in child-training practices, typical personalities, and certain characteristic aspects of the culturally constituted behavioral environments. In our earlier review of these materials we were concerned with establishing contrasts among types of contemporary groups. Essentially, we drew a set of static pictures, because we did not ask one crucial question: how can we account for the change from one level to another?

Prehistorians do not, as a rule, study culture change as a psychological problem. They do not have access to the kind of evidence that would allow them to do so. Yet it is clear that in each instance some individual man or woman did something new. Someone accidentally discovered the possibility of doing something differently and then—and this step is crucial—exploited and built on this discovery. Or else someone experimented, by trial and error, finding new ways of doing tasks that had to be done.

In other words, to get from the state in the prehistory of humanity when all groups were foragers to the stage in which some moved on to other types of ecological adaptations, we must deal with the cognitive processes that are involved in innovations. These processes include discovery and invention, learning and borrowing, and acceptance, or rejection of newly introduced deviations from old ways. Anthropologists studying modern groups have given some attention to this subject, but the earliest and most significant innovations have not been available to us for direct investigation. For example, virtually all species of plants that are cultivated at present and all animal species that are raised now were domesticated a very long time ago. Although new breeds and strains have been developed, no additional wild species have been domesticated. At present, we are able to study how additional groups of foragers take over patterns of horticulture or pastoralism, or how they resist such transformations. We are not able to study the old discoveries being made anew. That is to say, we know more about the circumstances involved in *adopting* new ways by acquiring them from other societies, than about how the original dramatic innovations took place.

However, we may be sure that among the significant elements were cognitive processes that concerned the application of familiar knowledge to new situations. It is then not surprising to think that the simplest horticulture was, as it is often now, in the hands of women, for as gatherers women acquired detailed and important knowledge of plants, which could be used in modifying the conditions under which root plants, for example, could be propagated. On the other hand, it is also to be expected that men are everywhere involved in working with large animals, for as hunters they acquired knowledge that could be useful in the domestication of the animals.

The subject of early innovations has received serious consideration by scholars other than prehistorians. The French cultural anthropologist Claude Lévi-Strauss, in his book *La Pensée Sauvage* (1962), translated into English as *The Savage Mind,* distinguished two forms of human thought: a "wild" or "undomesticated" form, which is primary in all human beings, and a "domesticated" or civilized form, which is the special product of civilization and which has given rise to science. This form is secondary, and, in a sense, artificial. It is also quite recent. The radical innovations of the Neolithic, for example, must be understood as resulting from the workings of the primary or "wild" form of thought. As Lévi-Strauss points out, the many specific inventions of that age are still basic to our own way of life. They involved transforming wild plants into cultivated varieties, wild animals into domesticated breeds, clays into pottery, and countless other highly technical innovations. The inventions and discoveries that made such transformations possible required a particular series of psychological characteristics, among which he lists the following:

> A truly scientific attitude, an assiduous and always wide awake curiosity, an appetite for knowledge for the pleasure of knowledge, since only a small fraction of observations and experiments (of which we must suppose that they were inspired first and foremost by a taste for knowledge) could give practical and immediately useful results (Lévi-Strauss 1962:23, translated by Bourguignon).

Such an attitude is still the basis of contemporary folk knowledge, including folk remedies for human and animal ailments, the observations of hunters (as we saw among the !Kung), and the traditional skills of generations of mothers, cooks, handymen, and artisans. (Jacks-of-all-trades are called *bricoleurs* in French, and this term has come to be associated with Lévi-Strauss' "wild" variety of thought). Although, then, this "wild" approach permits innovations, it is also linked to a good deal of traditionalism and conservatism, for innovation involves risk, and only under certain circumstances can societies, as well as individuals, afford to take risks.

The contrast between the "wild" and "domesticated" mind points to important differences between two types of thought, but an approach that stresses oppositions does not help us to understand how the one could have evolved from the other. The British social anthropologist Jack Goody, in *The Domestication of the Savage Mind* (1977), attempts to do precisely that. He argues that to understand contrasting types of thought it is necessary to consider differences in the *means* of thought and of communication. For Goody, the crucial change that led to a transformation of thinking was the development of writing and literacy. He argues that writing has transformed not merely communication but, more importantly, thought itself, altering "what we can do with our minds and what our minds can do with us" (Goody 1977:160). Rather than contrasting "traditional" and "modern" societies, he speaks of "oral" and "literate" ones. Although the role of writing in communication has often been stressed, Goody notes a neglect of "the role of the inner ear and the contribution of writing in clarifying one's thought." This observation is strikingly related to our earlier discussion of the evolution of language, where we emphasized the role of language in thought and in the development of an image of the world, in contrast to those who see the primary significance of language as a system of communication.

Goody's analysis is important because of the insight it provides into the cultural basis of the evolution of human cognition. His argument points to the revolutionary significance of the invention and development of nonbiological means by which cognitive processes have been modified. It is the type of analysis that, one suspects, could have been made only by an anthropologist who not only had worked in a nonliterate society, but also had seen at first hand the spread of literacy and its impact on the people of West Africa.

In contrasting oral and literate societies, Goody observes that

the *essential* difference . . . is . . . the accumulation (or reproduction) of skepticism. Members of oral . . . societies find it difficult to develop a line of skeptical thinking about, say, nature, or man's relationship to God simply because a continuing critical tradition can hardly exist when skeptical thoughts are *not* written down, *not* communicated across time and space, *not* made available for men to contemplate in privacy as well as to hear in performance (Goody 1977:43, italics in original).

He goes on to remark that " 'Traditional' societies are marked not so much by an absence of reflective thinking as by the absence of the proper tools for constructive rumination" (Goody 1977:44). Goody sums up his argument with the statement that writing

encourages special forms of linguistic activity associated with developments of particular kinds of problem-raising and problem-solving, in which the list, the formula and the table played a seminal part. If we wish to speak of the "savage mind," these were some of the instruments of its transformation (Goody 1977:162).

PERCEPTION, COGNITION, AND CULTURE CHANGE

Much of the literature we reviewed in Chapter 6 deals with differences between traditional and Western or westernized, groups. This literature includes a broad range of investigations, and concerns such diverse matters as color sorting and color vocabularies, field dependence and field independence, susceptibility to optical illusions, and so on. In this connection some researchers, for example G. Jahoda, have pointed to the advantage that subjects have who are literate and who have acquired familiarity with graphic representations.

One example we did not discuss in detail earlier refers to differences in depth perception. Following up a number of earlier studies, Kilbride and Robbins (1969) tested several groups of people among the Baganda of Uganda. Subjects were presented with drawings, which they were asked to interpret. Both urban individuals and somewhat acculturated rural people were found to make a larger number of correct identifications than traditional, rural individuals, that is, they were more likely to use cues to depth in pictorial representations. The process of acculturation, in other words, includes a new-found skill in interpreting two-dimensional representations of three-dimensional objects. A survey of the new urban or urbanized environment will show quickly how widespread graphic representations are in this setting, ranging from signs and billboards to movies, and from labels to tracts and newspapers. Under these circumstances the new skills have strong survival value in what is, in fact, a new culturally constituted behavioral environment. Literally, this new world looks different to the acculturated Baganda than to his traditional brother![1]

If Wober is correct and we may indeed speak of different *sensotypes* in accounting for the differences in the perceptual skills of human groups, then westernization, or acculturation to a Western life style, appears to require, or to bring with it, a modification of sensotypes for many of the peoples of the world. This transformation takes place, as Goody argues, by means of the introduction of new modes of communication, especially literacy and other forms of graphic representation, such as drawings, photographs, films, and television programs. Schooling plays a major role here. These new modes of communication also bring about changes in interpersonal and intergroup relations. For example, it is now possible for a man who leaves his village to remain in touch with his relatives by means of letters; he is no longer lost to his community, perhaps suddenly to reappear at some distant point in time. Relations with the past and, potentially, with the future are also modified. Consequently, altered conceptions concerning distances in space and time are brought about by the new means of communication.

Part of the process of westernization or modernization involves the learning of new information and new skills. Moreover, as individuals acquire new ideas they must find ways of coming to terms with them, either integrating them into their

Boys looking for work in a Peruvian market center. Children who must work have little time for school.

existing world picture or reworking their world picture to accommodate them. In the process, they may modify the new material, or both the old and the new, in order to arrive at some coherent behavioral environment. M. J. Herskovits (1948) has referred to the cognitive processes involved here as *retention, reinterpretation,* and *syncretism.* Retention involves the maintenance of an old cultural trait or pattern, such as an object, religious belief, or practice, in a new cultural context. For example, the type of house found in rural Haiti is identical with that seen in many parts of the West African countryside. Reinterpretation, however, involves a transformation of some kind.

Let us consider, for instance, what happened when people from a number of different West African societies were brought to many parts of the Americas as slaves. In Haiti, they quickly were taught some rudiments of Catholicism. They were able to make sense of these new teachings only in terms of what they already knew, their own traditional beliefs and rituals: Thus, they interpreted or reinterpreted baptism as a kind of protective rite. On the other hand, African gods and Catholic saints were identified with each other or "syncretized." Because St. Patrick was said to have chased the snakes out of Ireland, he was thought to be associated with snakes and therefore identified with the Dahomean snake spirit, Damballah; because St. James the Elder was said to be a great warrior, he was identified with Ogun, the warrior spirit of the Yoruba; and so a great number of other spirit entities were paired with saints. From the contributions of the two religious traditions, those of West Africa and those of Europe, there arose the hybrid religion of Haitian *vodou.* A similar process occurred in other parts of the Americas, in Cuba, and Jamaica, Trinidad, and various parts of Brazil. On the other hand, Europeans, who observed these emergent religions, interpreted them in the light of their own tradition and saw in them the work of the Devil. For instance, the French eighteenth century missionary Father Labat (1724) describes some cases of Afro-American spirit possession trance that he observed on the Caribbean island of Martinique. He tells us not what he saw, however, but what *he thought* he saw, with the observations filtered through his own culturally conditioned perceptions: these people, he says, are so fearful of the Devil that when he appears to them they fall into convulsions like epileptics. Clearly, understanding among people of different cultural backgrounds is severely handicapped!

DIFFUSION AND ACCULTURATION: TRANSFORMATIONS OF OBJECTS AND IDEAS

Innovations consist to a large extent of transformations of preexisting objects, practices, or ideas. They are either elaborations or modifications of materials available within a given cultural tradition or, perhaps more frequently, modifications of cultural elements acquired through contact with other groups. This fact has long been known to anthropologists, and it has frequently been rediscovered.

Peruvian Indian women in their characteristic brightly colored wool skirts and hats. Their clothing shows cultural diffusion of styles. On the church steps.

Shopping for cloth.

For example, Edward Sapir pointed out as long ago as 1916 that, "properly speaking, no [cultural] element originates at a specific point in time, but is imperceptibly connected by a process of gradual change, with another element or with other elements lying back of it" (Sapir 1949 [orig. 1916]:413). He notes, furthermore, a matter of great psychological relevance: when groups borrow from each other, cultural elements vary in what he terms their "conceptual detachability." For example, the maximum detachability might be found in a tool or implement; the detachability of a myth plot might be greater than that of the ideological system of which it is a part, and so on. Cultural elements that are thus separated from their traditional context will acquire new meanings and significance when they are embedded within a new context. That is to say, in psychological terms, they will be "understood" differently.

We may illustrate such transformations at the simplest level, that of material objects. For instance, Indian women of the Andean highlands wear long full woolen skirts in bright colors, which were introduced by the Spaniards in the sixteenth century. They also wear felt hats, worn in Europe by men, introduced in the nineteenth century. However, such borrowing with transformation is a two-way street, for these Indians were also taught to knit, and among the things they make are white knit dance masks that are used to satirize Europeans. These woolen masks, with slight modifications, have been introduced into the United States as a commercial item; they are sold as ski masks!

Under certain circumstances, however, the object that moves from one society to another is modified less than the society itself. In a well-known and frequently cited and reprinted paper, Lauriston Sharp (1974 [orig. 1952]) traced the radical effects of the introduction of steel axes on the lives of the Yir Yoront of Northern Australia. Among other effects, as a result of the indiscriminate handing out of steel axes by missionaries to one and all, women as well as men, the relations between men and women were modified, as were those among traditional male trading partners through whom stone axes formerly had been acquired. Alfred Métraux (1959b), in a paper entitled "The Revolution of the Ax," has shown how equally drastic changes were brought about by this one tool in a number of the world's other traditional nonmetallurgical societies. Because a culture is a system of interrelated parts, modifications in technology have repercussions in psychology, in such areas as interpersonal relations, self-respect and self-perception, value systems, and motivation.

Material objects, however, are only one aspect of innovation and the transformations that are associated with it. We considered the modification of Christian elements in contact with African cultural features earlier, when we spoke of Haitian *vodou* and similar Afro-American religions. Let us take a closer look at what has happened to some of the African elements that were maintained in Haiti. Remember that this situation has peculiar features: whereas many tribal peoples were exposed to European influences in their own countries, Afro-Americans are descendants of people who were uprooted from their homelands and transported thousands of miles away, under the harshest conditions of slavery. There they were brought together not only with European masters, but also with Africans from other tribal groups, with different languages and variant cultural traditions. Nevertheless, a remarkable number of the African ways survived. In Haiti, they survived in aspects of the language, in the types of houses built in the countryside, and in the music, but foremost in the religious beliefs and practices.

Unlike Cuba and Brazil, for example, where the slave trade continued until close to the end of the nineteenth century, Haiti became independent in 1804, and its contacts with Africa, as well as Europe, were broken off at that time. Among the changes we find in the Haitian religious tradition is that, compared with West Africa, there are few myths. That is, few full-length stories are told about spirits, their history, their exploits, about the origins of the world and of things as they are today, and so on. The spirits are known primarily through their behavior during rituals, when they are invited to appear and to possess individuals among the faithful. Each spirit has one or more names, a particular type of clothing, music, dance steps, and tastes in food and drink, as well as various special powers and interests. When we compare the names and attributes of the spirits of Haitian *vodou* with those of their West African counterparts, we see what changes have taken place in the ways in which the spirits are conceived and in the roles they play.

One of the most powerful spirits, both in Haiti and in Dahomey (West Africa), is Legba. In Africa he is the seventh and youngest son of Mawu-Lisa, the androgynous creator spirit. As the youngest, he is said to be the spoiled child. He is both a divine trickster and the messenger of the gods. Because he is a trickster, he sometimes gets the messages mixed up. Because of his special position, humans must address him first when they wish to speak to the gods. Legba also has strong sexual associations: persons possessed by this spirit dance with a large wooden phallus and mime intercourse with female bystanders during their dance.

In Haiti, too, Legba is a very important spirit. There, also, he must be approached before any of the other spirits can be called. Worshippers sing a song in which they ask, "Legba, open the gate for me!"—that is, open the gate so that the other spirits may come. However, he is no longer the youngest of the spirits, and he no longer dances with a wooden phallus. Instead, he is a very old man who hobbles about, and though he has a wooden stick, it is a crutch. As Alfred Métraux (1959a:360) has put it: "out of this most potent of the gods the Voodooists have made an impotent old man who walks on crutches."

We cannot understand this drastic transformation if we look at Legba in isolation. In Haiti, the role of the phallic trickster still exists, but it now is found in a different context. It has been taken over by a spirit, or indeed a group of spirits, called Gédé. This name also exists in Dahomey, but there it refers to the mythical first ancestor of the people who originally lived at the place that later became the capital of the kingdom of Dahomey. In Dahomean mythology and ritual, however, Gédé does not play a significant role. The Gédé spirits in Haiti are associated with both fertility and death, with childbirth, with magic, and with means of warding off magic. They are represented as disreputable and poor, indeed the poorest of all. They live in the cemetery, and the dead are, in some sense, under their control.

It is tempting to speculate on the differences the beliefs about these spirits have undergone, and how they reveal what has happened to the people. Why is it that the young, spoiled child of the creator has become a lame old man? Why is death now linked so closely with fertility? And why is the trickster now a corpse and the representative of the poor?

To approach any understanding of these transformations we must remember that beliefs and rituals can be understood only within the total cultural and societal context, certain aspects of which they represent in symbolic terms. We must look at other gods, not only Legba and Gédé, and we must look at the society in which the beliefs and rituals function.

Some features of the changes are clearer. For example, there is no trace in Haitian belief of Mawu-Lisa, the androgynous Dahomean creator. At the head of the universe, as the Haitians see it, is *Bon Dieu*, the Christian God, of whom the missionaries speak, and who has little relationship to the African spirits, although they too are known by Christian names. Legba may be represented by St. Lazarus, who walks on crutches, or St. Anthony the Hermit, who is an old man. Gédé may be linked to a female saint, St. Radegonde, and all the spirits of the Gédé group are said to be the godchildren of St. Brigitte. Because Gédé is both Death and the dead, his feast day is All Saint's Day (November 1) and the day before, which we know as Halloween. Gédé impersonators dress in black frock coats and stovepipe or bowler hats, and wear dark glasses, to cover the eyeless sockets of the dead. Their appearance parodies that of the wealthy. In the marketplace, they demand food and money, in a variation of what we recognize as "trick or treat." They joke and behave in a provocative, rude, and lewd manner.

Vodou, then, accommodates both Christian ideas, and African ideas from numerous tribal backgrounds. For example, earlier we saw a reference to Ibo-Lélé of Ibo origin; Ogou, the Haitian god of war, is of Yoruba origin, and so on. There are also a number of Haitian spirits who are of local origin and who belong to a group called Pétro. Legba has a Pétro counterpart, called Carrefour, who is in charge of the crossroads, which are dangerous places, and who presides over powerful magic.

In part, then, *vodou* integrates European, African, and local elements. On the other hand, there is also a reflection in *vodou* of Haitian social reality. The major gods, such as Legba, Ogou, and many others are seen not only as powerful gods, but also in some sense, as similar to powerful people within human society. They may be light in skin color, have "good"—that is, non-negroid—hair, speak French, and have expensive tastes. Gédé, on the other hand, speaks the native Créole, drinks cheap liquor, eats from a gourd dish, is rough and vulgar in his

Catholic religious procession in a Peruvian Indian village, a tradition brought by the Spaniards: Men carry a statue and paper flowers through the village streets.

Women, children, and men crowd about the man who carries the image of the child Jesus.

manners, and in many other respects reflects the self-image of the poor. He also may ridicule the pretensions of the rich, and so express class attitudes.

The universe of *vodou,* then, as represented in belief and ritual, integrates a variety of historical influences, and holds up an image of the world that is patterned on the realities of a drastically stratified Haitian society. In this world, the Haitian lower-class individual, however poor and downtrodden, is personified in the character of a powerful spirit, the spirit of death and life, of magic and fertility, of fate and lighthearted mockery. Whereas in Dahomey, Legba is associated with fate, fate is not a separate entity in the Haitian pantheon of spirits. Gédé seems to have taken over that role, for as Death he alone can determine, for example, whether or not magic used against a victim will be effective. In the end, it is he who has the last word. In comparing Haiti and Dahomey, then, we see that certain specific beliefs and rituals have been maintained, yet their context has been altered so radically that the overall picture is quite new and distinctive.

HOW PERSONALITY AFFECTS CULTURE CHANGE

Robert LeVine (1976) has attempted to sketch a picture of personality characteristics typical of the agricultural peoples of sub-Saharan Africa and to show how these personality features are relevant to the adaptations Africans make to social and cultural change.

LeVine bases his discussion on three claims. First he claims that in spite of the diversity of local and regional cultures, societies throughout the African continent share a common "profile" of characteristics. Second, this common profile of cultural characteristics makes it possible to establish a generalized picture of certain common traits in African personality, because cultural rules become psychologically relevant when they reveal what kinds of behaviors and expectations people are "comfortable" with. That is, expectations that might appear stressful in our own society might seem appropriate to Africans. Our rules of behavior, to the contrary, might put them under stress. Third, LeVine claims that preexisting personality trends predispose the ways in which people respond to change.

LeVine lists seven psychologically relevant societal characteristics: social distance between persons of different age and sex; age and sex hierarchy; emphasis on material transactions in interpersonal relationships; functional diffuseness of authority relations; the tendency to blame and fear others when under stress; the relative absence of separation anxiety and related affects; and concreteness of thought. He shows how these characteristics have played important roles in the adaptations Africans have made to certain aspects of social change. For example, primary group relations are formal and structured by social distance between persons of different age and sex, so there is little of what we might call "closeness" between parents and children and between husbands and wives. Consequently there is little separation anxiety when men go off to cities to work for prolonged periods of time, or when boys and young men go away to school. These absences have been accepted as reasonably tolerable and have caused relatively little family disruption, particularly when they have been accompanied by the fulfillment of traditional material obligations among kin. As LeVine states, "Families do not have to be residentially intact in order to remain socially and psychologically real for their members" (1976:132). Moreover, because material transactions have been traditionally important to the fulfillment of social roles, LeVine argues, Africans have responded positively to economic incentives. Also, intergenerational differences in degree of acculturation have not been disruptive as they have been in many parts of the world, because the social distance that exists among members of different generations has made agreement on values and life-styles not a primary requirement for family harmony and cohesiveness; what matters a great deal more is that material obligations be met and deference to elders be offered. On the other hand, the stresses that have been caused by economic, cultural, and social change have led to increases in accusations of witchcraft and magical beliefs, consistent with the traditional tendency to blame and fear others when under stress. Finally, concrete patterns of thought have represented an obstacle to the success of Western schooling.

In this interesting discussion, LeVine omits two important psychocultural features that are widely characteristic of sub-Saharan Africa and that have had important repercussions among Afro-Americans: the widespread possession trance pattern and certain aspects of the position of women. Both of these features are relevant to change in Africa as well. We shall take a brief look at some examples.

Peter Fry, in his book *Spirits of Protest* (1976), reports on spirit mediumship among the Zezuru of Rhodesia (Zimbabwe) among whom he worked in the 1960s. Here, as in many parts of Africa, spirit mediums play a significant role. They are possessed, at formal séances, by spirits of ancestors and ancient heroes, who reveal causes of illness, perform cures, and most importantly, identify witches. Historically, spirit mediumship in this area has had important connections with the political situation. Shortly after the arrival of the British, in the 1890s, the mediums supported and directed a rebellion. When it was defeated, the mediums lost much of their prestige, and the way was opened for the Christian missions. The rise of African political nationalism in the 1960s, which was accompanied by a rise in cultural nationalism, also involved an increasing rejection of Christianity. According to Fry, there was great popular optimism at that time concerning the imminent coming of majority rule in Rhodesia, and this hope he says, was manifested by "the spontaneous emergence of new spirit mediums" (p. 120). However, when African political parties were banned and when Ian Smith declared the independence of Rhodesia from Britian, a great reaction set in. Africans started to look for "sell-outs," who were suspected of taking sides with the whites. This response was not all: now witches were being searched out and accusations were being made against them. Fry comments,

It seems that the battle with witchcraft was an attempt to control a situation which had got out of control; the conflict between white and black had been transmuted into a conflict between the ancestors and witchcraft (Fry 1976:121).

The ancestors here were represented by the spirit mediums, through whom they spoke. Fry goes on to say: "Now that political activity had been effectively repressed religion remained as an outlet for pent up hostilities generated by the colonial situation" (Fry 1976:122).

Spirit mediumship is an old institution, and as we have seen, it is widespread in Africa. It has taken on a variety of forms and has played important roles in numerous situations. Its use in a modern political situation is an indication of its viability and adaptability. Moreover, it has a significant psychological dimension: it taps the capacity for possession trance; it allows a supposed communication with ancestors, thus stressing continuity; it channels hostilities. We also see here the importance of a feature observed by LeVine: in a period of crisis, blame and fear are directed at others, and the witch and the "sell-out" are the perfect targets. Fry also notes that about half the spirit mediums he encountered were women, which points to the important religious, and in this case also political, role of African women.

In spite of their long separation from Africa in time and space, Afro-Americans have maintained a significant number of the psychocultural features LeVine lists. For Haiti, we may note the social distance among generations, and the deference offered by the young to the old. Material obligations play a crucial role in interpersonal relations, and even in relations with supernaturals, the material is of primary significance. For example, ancestors and other spirits must be fed, and those who do so acquire some degree of power over them in this manner. The tendency to assign blame to others and to fear them, in situations of stress, is evident in a great concern with witchcraft and sorcery, *zombis* and werewolves, and other such powerful nefarious beings. *Vodou* represents a clear continuation of African possession trance cults; it uses and encourages the traditional psychological capacity to experience possession trance. It shows the great role of women in such cults, to whom it also offers visible significant leadership roles. As the dominant force in the retail trade, women lead independent and self-reliant lives, for the money they earn is their own and they decide how to utilize it. This fact, too, represents a continuity of African—especially West African— patterns.

There are significant class differences in Haiti, which apply to the role of the African heritage, as to everything else in the economic, social, and cultural life of the society. As we say earlier (p. 184), Western-educated upper-class individuals, unlike the poor, are strongly aware of the multiple sources of the country's heritage. For many individuals this represents a source of conflict; we have referred to this difficulty as "socialized ambivalence." such ambivalence is not unique to Haiti, however, but affects westernized individuals in many parts of the world, because they must make choices among their multiple traditions.

HOW CULTURE CHANGE AFFECTS PERSONALITY

LeVine, as we have seen, presents an analysis of an African culture profile and draws a picture of African personality from it. He then asks how the personality traits that he infers have affected the adaptations Africans have made under circumstances of social and cultural change. This approach is only one of several psychocultural perspectives on the study of change.

Another approach asks how the typical personality of a group has been affected *by change,* rather than how it has affected the reaction *to change.* We touched on this subject briefly in Chapter 5, when we discussed methods for assessing adult personalities typical of certain cultural groups. We reported there that Hallowell (1974 [orig. 1951]) had compared three levels of acculturation among Ojibwa Indians at different localities, using the Rorschach test for this purpose. He found clear psychological differences in the composite psychological portraits of the people at each of these three levels. Yet he also found evidence of continuities in the personality structure among the three levels. For example, at Level 2, he found that important readjustments in personality had taken place as a result of the new situation, and he suggested that such positive readjustments had been possible because economic and social change in this area had taken place relatively slowly, over an extended period of time. On the other hand, at Level 3, among the most "Americanized" of these Ojibwa, there remained little of the old way of life. Hardly anyone spoke the old language, and there was much psychological maladjustment to be seen in the Rorschach test and in the behavioral data that we were able to obtain. Level 3 is the group to which my informant Nelly belongs, whose life history I cited in Chapter 5. The Rorschach findings indicated that the elements of the old personality structure that remained in this group were not functional and did not permit the people to cope with the new situation. Specifically, children were brought up to be independent, in a way that befitted the old hunting way of life and that did not facilitate the type of cooperation necessary for life in the settled community on the reservation. Hallowell speaks of the typical personality structure of this group as showing a "kind of frustration of maturity" (Hallowell 1974 [orig. 1951]:352).

Adaptive Strategies

Hallowell, as we have seen, presented a single personality picture for each of the levels of acculturation he studied among the Ojibwa (or Chippewa) Indians. These pictures are, in fact, composites made up of test scores and interview materials. In this way, we see the predominant type that characterized each of the separate local groups. The differences between them are explained by the history of acculturation at each location and its impact on the people.

In their long-term study of another group of American Indians, the Menomini of Wisconsin, George and Louise Spindler found a highly differentiated population living on the reservation. Using sociocultural and economic criteria, they

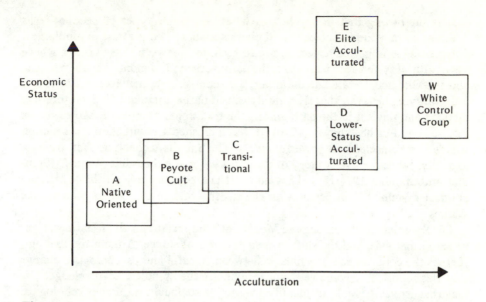

Figure 4
ACCULTURATIVE CATEGORIES. (FROM GEORGE AND LOUISE SPIN-
DLER, *DREAMERS WITHOUT POWER*. COPYRIGHT 1971 BY HOLT,
RINEHART AND WINSTON, P. 5).

were able to identify five different groups or "acculturative categories" during the
research period between 1948 and 1961 (G. D. Spindler 1955, L. S. Spindler 1962,
G. D. Spindler and L. S. Spindler 1971). The five categories are: a native-oriented
group; the Peyotists; transitionals; and the acculturated people, divided by occupation into an elite and a low-status group. These five groups also occupy somewhat different positions on the economic ladder. During the period under
discussion the native-oriented group maintained traditional religious rituals and
many of the ways of the past. The Peyotists, members of the Native American
Church, practiced a syncretic religion that combined many Christian and native
elements, in addition to the use of the hallucinogen, peyote. In spite of the
religious differences between them and the native-oriented group, and the antago-
nisms that derived from these differences, in many aspects of their culture the
Peyotists were similar to the native-oriented. The transitionals, on the other hand,
were a heterogeneous category of people. For the most part, they had a traditional
background but were moving toward non-Menomini society, and in many ways
they resembled "poor whites" in their life-style. The acculturated people were a
great deal more like the surrounding whites, of either the working class or middle
class. As Louise Spindler (1977:80) puts it:

> The life styles within these five sociocultural categories must be seen as coping
> strategies—as ways of getting along in a conflicted world. These coping strategies are
> changing as the world changes.

It is interesting that in psychological terms the five types of people are as different as they are in sociocultural characteristics. The greatest psychological differences, as might be expected, are to be found between those groups whose sociocultural systems are least alike, the native-oriented Menomini at one extreme and the elite acculturated at the other. The competitive, achievement oriented, self-gratifying behavior that is so highly valued in the dominant U. S. culture was tabooed and deviant in the past, among the traditional Menomini. Moreover, as Louise Spindler has shown (1970), it was punished by witchcraft, a sanction wielded by respected and powerful elders. The Spindlers conclude that, psychologically, "the adaptive strategy of the elites has made them like Whites" (Spindler and Spindler 1971:187). They add: "It is a commentary on the Whiteman cultural system that in order to 'make it,' the Menomini had to become like Whites . . ." (p. 189).

The Spindlers' work among the Menomini is important for their findings, their research methods, and the shift in their theoretical stance. Among the findings, there is the confirmation of a linkage between cultural and psychological change that was reported by Hallowell, whose influence the Spindlers acknowledge. The fact that it was possible to identify five major sociocultural and psychological groupings in a single reservation community constituted a genuine discovery. Clearly, the impact of white culture was not the same on all the people on the reservation.

Here a further important research result must be mentioned: Louise Spindler (1962) found that significant differences exist between the adaptations of men and of women, in each of the five categories. Women experience less conflict and turmoil in the acculturation process than men do, as shown in life history interviews and test data. Combining the data for men and women distorts the picture. The Rorschach data for the Menomini also reveal this difference (Spindler and Spindler 1967). Because women continue to play traditional roles to a much greater extent than men, their roles and values are much less directly challenged by the acculturation process. In contrast, the men must, to a significantly greater extent, acquire new skills and new value orientations. Moreover, among the Menomini, even under traditional conditions, the roles of women were much more flexible than those of men. As a result, in the new situation they experienced much greater continuity in the expectations placed on them than was true for the men. This situation in turn often has resulted in a difference in degree of acculturation among spouses, which has heightened the conflicts experienced by the men.

The discovery of important sex differences in the acculturational experience of the Menomini helped the Spindlers to understand, if not to anticipate, an event that occurred in 1974. At that time, "a group of women . . . gained control of most of the leadership positions in the newly created reservation" (L. S. Spindler 1977:108). The Menomini reservation had been "terminated" by the federal government in 1961, but as a result of a long struggle, which was headed by a vigorous, well-educated woman, the community was given reservation status again in 1974. This woman, once elected chairperson of an important governing committee, appointed other women to key positions. L. Spindler suggests that the flexible role structure and the egalitarianism of the traditional society was conducive to, or provided the "conducive base" for, the modern development.

One of the implications of these findings is that, when we look at the psychological consequences of cultural and social change, we must ask more specifically: consequences for whom? There may be no reason to believe that the impact will be the same for all members of a community, and there is every reason to think that there will be differences for men and women. Another implication is that it is possible for more than one type of adaptation to exist in a given community. It may also be, as seems to be the case among the Menomini, that more than one type may be "successful," that is, not maladjusted. In the 1950s the acculturated and the native-oriented appear to have made the most successful adjustments. The transitionals seem to have had the greatest difficulties. It is interesting that in some respects the transitionals appear to resemble the dominant type found among the Lac du Flambeau Chippewa in 1946.

Considering the five acculturative categories as "coping strategies" means viewing the behaviors of the people not as the results of forces impinging on them, but as due to choices and decisions made by individuals who are confronted with practical problems. Louise Spindler (1978) has traced the evolution of this theoretical orientation, which focuses on what people do as opposed to what happens to them. It is interesting that this reorientation has come at a time when various movements in this country and around the world have given expression to a similar idea in political as well as social terms. The Woman's Movement represents one example. We hear of goals and strategies, of options and resources.[2] Among American Indians, the 1970s have seen the development of a Red Power Movement and a reassertion of the value of traditional ways. Some of this movement has taken the form of political action, of lawsuits concerning treaty rights and land claims, and of demonstrations and pressures on a Congress that, responding to a white backlash, would abolish all treaties. Another type of response has involved the revival of traditional religious rituals. Particularly in urban situations and in some of the areas of the Southeastern United States, some part-Indians have decided to assert their Indian identities. Such observations support the view expressed by the Spindlers that in situations of culture change, individuals are not merely on the receiving end, as it were, but are themselves actors who may, more or less explicitly, select "adaptive strategies."

As we observe acculturation going on before our eyes, then, we not only see the outcome, but we watch individuals making choices. This important level of analysis has been ignored when the stress was placed on the impact of change (or more generally, of culture) on the individual. A balanced picture must include both approaches, so that we can see, as for example in the life history materials the Spindlers presented for the Menomini, how some individuals come to be in a situation that enables them to make certain choices.

Another important point must be stressed here: research findings are necessarily affected by how the investigator conceptualizes the problems to be studied.

What we want to learn about will influence the methods of investigation we use, the questions we ask, and the types of answers we get. If we consider culture change a situation in which people are confronted not only with new problems but also with new options, we will want to look at the kinds of choices they make and the factors that influence the decision-making process. We shall then use research methods that give us information on these matters. For example, when Louise Spindler (1962) wanted to know about the roles Menomini women play and about the values they held, she developed a new tool, the expressive autobiographic interview technique (EAI), which was more structured than a full spontaneous chronological autobiography. The fact that different conceptualizations lead to the use of different tools and thus to different results means, strictly speaking, that we cannot make full comparisons between groups that have not been studied by the same methods.

How Much Continuity?

In spite of the comments we have just made about differences in research results that are produced by the use of diverse methods, there is ample evidence in the great quantities of psychocultural research that has been carried out over the past forty years to show that continuity exists even in the midst of change. The Spindlers have shown both change and continuity in a study that is in many ways different from their work among the Menomini. They investigated schooling in the German village of Schönhausen in 1967–1968 and then again ten years later.

In this research they used a technique they designed, called the Instrumental Activities Inventory (IAI). It consists of a series of line drawings showing people in a great variety of activities. These drawings can be presented in contrasting pairs, such as working in a vineyard versus working in an office, so that expressions of preferences between urban and traditional village occupations and activities can be observed. It is interesting that the choices children made on this test correlated strongly with those they made in their actual life histories, when these were reviewed after a ten-year period. Moreover, the choices made on the tests in the 1977 study showed the same patterns as those discovered in the earlier investigation, in spite of the fact that there had been a sweeping reform of curriculum and textbooks in the intervening years. Moreover, both among rural children and those living in a more highly urbanized environment, there is a "romantic idealization of village-land-traditional life" (Spindler and Spindler 1978:5) "There appears to be a regional cultural complex . . . that is persistent through time and that tends to homogenize the perceptions and evaluations by children, with the aid of the school" (Spindler and Spindler 1978:7).

Working in quite a different part of the world, Rhoda Métraux (1976) also has pointed to a phenomenon of psychocultural continuity. In her study, which was carried out in New Guinea, she addressed herself to a different level of personality structure, and she formulated her research problem in different terms. Her investigation was conducted among the Iatmul from 1967 to 1973; this group had been studied by Gregory Bateson and Margaret Mead in 1938. A great many changes had taken place in this area during the intervening period, beginning with the Japanese occupation during World War II. This event halted much of the ceremonial life of the people, including male initiation rites. Since the early 1950s, children have been sent to school, and there has been some introduction of foreign ideas and objects. Yet, although there has been change in the Iatmul way of life, it has not been characterized by total rejection of traditions or total acceptance of the new.

In her research, Métraux used the Lowenfeld Mosaic Test, which consists of 256 small plastic tiles in five shapes, each in six colors. Subjects are asked to use these tiles in making designs of their own, and both the process of making the design and the end product are analyzed. Among the Iatmul, Métraux found important age differences in responses to this test. The young people used a naturalistic and experimental approach, whereas the old men used traditional ceremonial themes in working with the tiles. As experienced woodcarvers, they were used to visualizing a complicated design, producing it without a model or preliminary sketch. The process whereby both adults and children constructed the designs, says Métraux, was

> based in and reflected the dualistic handling of symmetry and complementarity, the principles that integrate Iatmul interpersonal relations, ceremonial themes, artistic production and world view at a deep level of cultural personality ... This is one precondition for the survival of the social and cultural identity of the Iatmul ... (Métraux 1976:215).

New Guinea is particularly interesting for anyone wishing to study the psychological impact of social and cultural change. Many of its peoples were isolated until very recently, and they have been brought into intensive contact with the outside world in a short period of time. Perhaps the most detailed information is available on the Manus of the Admiralty Islands, on the edge of New Guinea. These people were first studied by Margaret Mead and Reo Fortune in 1928. They have been restudied several times by Mead and a number of other investigators. In her 1953 restudy of Manus, reported in *New Lives for Old* (1956), Mead had the opportunity of seeing people she had known as children at her first visit, twenty-five years earlier. In the old-style Manus society, they had been happy, carefree, nonanimistic youngsters. However, under the traditional system, such a positive childhood typically was followed by a period of stress and strain that followed the arranged marriages, which entailed severe financial obligations and debts for the young men. For the young women, living in the homes of their new husbands' families imposed great restraints, for they were poorly prepared for the rules of propriety that they now were expected to respect. Because of their debts and the scarcity of resources, the young men fell into the typical patterns of hostile competition, which made enemies of childhood friends.

As a result of World War II and its aftermath, Manus society underwent profound transformations. Among the changes were the abandonment of the system of arranged marriages and the financial obligations associated with them. The concerns with property and guilt, which had made the Manus veritable prototypes of the Protestant Ethic, also were gone. Mead was interested to discover that the youngsters she had known, now grown to adulthood, had not acquired the typically harsh and unpleasant personalities she had been acquainted with in members of their parents' generation. No longer forced into competitive positions with their agemates, they had been able to maintain their childhood friendships and their open and pleasant personalities.

Manus culture had been changed in part under the impact of foreign (U.S. and Australian) influences, and in part under the forceful charismatic leadership of one man, Paliau. The new social arrangements were based on a rejection of much in the traditional culture, including beliefs in severe and punishing ghosts and a morality of scarcity. The outside world had impressed on the Manus a notion of plenty, and interestingly, a morality of sharing. The picture of modern society that had served the Manus as a model for the reconstruction of their own is a curious one. It is, one might say, not U.S. and Australian culture, but only an "export" variety of it, for it was presented to the Manus by their contact with U.S. Navy personnel, and with life on Australian-owned and managed plantations. The Manus therefore now lived in barrack-style housing, days began with flag raisings and roll call, property was widely shared, and so on. In some respects the competitive, striving, property-conscious, traditional Manus had been a great deal more "Western" in their outlook on life than this collectivistic noncompetitive society that developed out of the contact situation.

One aspect of this restudy of the Manus, then, concerns the sources of the ideas the Manus used in restructuring their society. Their image of industrial or Western society was mediated by specific types of contacts and by Western products. These sources were a great deal more important in effecting changes than the actual conditions in the industrialized societies that sent out the products and the emissaries. This statement applies not only to the Manus but also to the great number of peoples around the world whose ways of life are altered under the impact of Western influences.

There is also another important implication here, which concerns a theory of personality development. Mead's restudy of the Manus suggests that adolescence is a crucial period in individual development. Presumably, the parents whom Mead knew as adults in 1928 had had childhood experiences similar to those Mead was able to observe at that time. As a result of the drastic disruptions they experienced at marriage, we are told, they were transformed into quarrelsome and competitive, striving individuals. Their childhood, as seen through the evidence of their own children, did not make such personalities inevitable. Indeed, when the next generation of young people did not have to go through the same kind of disruptions they had experienced at marriage, the harsh personalities did not develop. A single type of childhood, consequently, may give rise to different kinds of adult personalities, depending on what follows this childhood. The importance of this finding cannot be exaggerated.

In spite of the appearance of radical discontinuity between the old culture and the new among the Manus, as described by Mead, more recent work has shown that, in fact, the situation was more complex. Theodore Schwartz, who first went to Manus with Mead in 1953, returned to the area for further research several times over the following twenty years. Somewhat to his surprise, he discovered that the break was not so complete after all. He found that access to the new culture was blocked in part by economic factors, and for those who remained in the villages, by social factors. Even among the generation most exposed to westernization, Schwartz found significant continuities in beliefs and attitudes. As he puts it:

> In spite of their having been kidnapped by an alien culture, perhaps the early years, the afternoons, and the school holidays sufficed for their induction at the deeper levels of their culture (Schwartz 1976a:230).

Culture Change and the Life Cycle

Culture change may have an impact on psychological development at various points of the individual development cycle. In Mead's restudy of the Manus, there is evidence that changes in adult role requirements had their most important effect on the transition from childhood to adulthood, leading to a new typical adult personality. In other cases, we have evidence concerning different points in the life cycle at which important changes are introduced. For example, as we saw earlier, Draper (1975) notes the difference in the work load of women among sedentary and foraging groups of !Kung. This difference, in turn, had an effect on the work assigned to young children, and on the pressures toward responsibility and obedience that were placed on them as a result. Leiderman and Leiderman (1977) report on the effects of economic change on both infants and young children among the Kikuyu of highland Kenya. Traditionally, women were aided in child care by female relatives, including their younger sisters, or their own children. Nowadays, Kikuyu are eager to send both girls and boys to school, so that child nurses, when they are used, tend to be very young (below seven). Whether or not such youngsters are used as infant caretakers will depend on the economic level of the family, the size of the family, and the mother's responsibilities. The community under study was divided into several economic levels, and these levels were seen to be related to the mental and motor development of infants. Moreover, for the second half of an infant's first year of life, its mental development is also statistically significantly related to the age of the caretaker. We find then that social and economic change affect not only the role of women, but also, through the emphasis on schooling, the roles of children. These two roles together, in turn, affect the differential development of infants.

There are some cases, however, in which changes in child training are part of a total planned revision of a way of life. The most clearly controlled example is the Israeli kibbutz (Spiro 1958). In this instance, young people at the turn of the century set out to plan a totally new way of living and working, and among the new elements of their society was the residential separation of children from their parents. In contrast to the other groups we discussed, this change was not the secondary result of economic and social changes, but a primary aim of the founders of the kibbutz movement. Nonetheless, such drastic voluntary changes are possible only on a relatively small scale. Changes in the early years of the Soviet Union and in Communist China were quite different in character; there the development of child-care facilities resulted from the need for women to work in fields and factories, rather than from the initial plans for social transformation.

CRISIS CULTS AND REVITALIZATION MOVEMENTS

Observers of the dramatic impact that contact with Western societies has had on traditional peoples have been impressed with a certain type of widespread response: the frequent development of vigorous and, at times, aggressive ecstatic religious movements, seeking to resolve the pressing problems of a harsh present.

Probably the first anthropological study of a phenomenon of this type was James Mooney's (1965 [orig. 1896]) report, *Ghost Dance Religion and the Sioux Outbreak of 1890*. The Ghost Dance of 1890, and an earlier form of the same movement in 1870, represented a reaction of the Indians of the Plains, and regions further to the West, to the destruction of their way of life as a result of white settlement of the area. The Ghost Dance religion, propagated in 1890 by the prophet Wovoka, held that the Indian dead would return, and they would bring back the old way of life, while the whites and their culture would be destroyed. The Indians had to undertake various rituals, principally ritual dances, to promote this coming of the end of the current state of affairs. In the dances, people went into trance states during which they had the experience of speaking with their dead relatives. As the religion spread among the tribes over large distances, new features and elaborations were added to its basic pattern. Even after the defeat of the Sioux at Wounded Knee, the Ghost Dance survived in modified form among various Indian groups and gave rise to a number of later movements.

Mooney himself recognized that the Ghost Dance religious movement had resulted from oppression, proverty, and dissatisfaction. In the years since Mooney wrote his historic report, hundreds of religious movements in response to acculturative pressures have been described. La Barre (1971), who has published an extensive review of the vast literature concerning these movements, speaks of them as "crisis cults." He says that they are "new projective sacred systems" that result from "culture shock and the strains of acculturation" (La Barre 1971:4). In fact, La Barre sees such reactions to distress as a basic source of the development of all religions, and he therefore called his book on the origin of religion *The Ghost Dance* (La Barre 1970). Among the most frequently cited examples of crisis cults are the so-called "cargo cults" of Melanesia, in which the people believe that the whites, again, will disappear and the ancestors will bring the people wealth, in the form of trade goods or cargo. Other well known examples are the religion of Iroquois prophet Handsome Lake, and the Ras Tafari Movement of Jamaica. Historians speak of "millenarian" or "chiliastic" movements (Lanternari 1963, Thrupp 1970). Their studies range from the Middle Ages and the Age of Reformation to the religious background of the Taipei Rebellion of China in the middle of the nineteenth century.

One of the most systematic approaches to such cults is that of A. F. C. Wallace, who coined the term "revitalization movements." He defines these cults as "deliberate, organized attempts by some members of a society to construct a more satisfying culture by rapid acceptance of a pattern of multiple innovations" (Wallace 1970:188). Notice that there is no reference to religion here; indeed, Wallace considers some secular revitalization movements, such as the Communist Revolution and the development of the social system of the Soviet Union. However, his principal interest has been the religious revitalization movement that he studied among the Iroquois Indians.

According to Wallace, every revitalization movement is preceded by a state of social and personal disorganization and intense dissatisfaction. Such conditions prevailed among the Iroquois of New York State at the end of the eighteenth century. They had suffered military defeat by supporting the losing side in the American Revolution. They had lost much of their land, and they had suffered social as well as economic disaster. Their old ways, in which men were warriors and women horticulturalists, were no longer viable. There was much drinking and great arguing and factionalism among them.

The new religion was launched by Handsome Lake, a Seneca chief who himself had become a drunkard. He had had a vision, which proclaimed that he and his people must give up their evil ways, and stop drinking, quarreling, and practicing witchcraft. Following this vision, over a period of time, a complex code of life for a new society was revealed to him. It included such revolutionary, shocking innovations as the acceptance by men of agricultural work, which traditionally had been the responsibility of women. It is remarkable that as a result of his visions, Handsome Lake himself reformed and, as the phrase has it, became "a new man," and equally remarkable that the message was received with enthusiasm by the Iroquois, whose way of life was drastically and profoundly altered by it.

Considered as cultural innovation, the Code of Handsome Lake, and the society that resulted from it, clearly do not consist of totally new elements, but rather represent a regrouping of both old and new features. It is important to recognize, for example, the great influence exerted by a group of Quakers who were then living among the Iroquois, and whose way of life helped to provide a model for some of the new patterns.

On the individual level, Wallace believes the prophet experienced the visions as the direct result of his personal crisis. The visionary trance state, for Wallace, is a "mazeway resynthesis," that is, a spontaneous, stress-induced reorganization of the individual's total pattern for living, including both his personality and an individual version of the culture. Wallace's view of the prophet's transformation is influenced by a psychophysiological model of stress and also by case histories of spontaneous cures of individuals who experienced psychotic episodes. In fact, such cures constitute dramatic resolutions of conflicts and experiences of maturation and psychological transformation.

In some respects, Wallace's view is similar to that of certain specialists who speak of the significance of "conversion" experiences. For example, the British psychiatrist, William Sargant, considers what he calls "possession" (that is, altered states of consciousness) to be transforming, healing experiences on the individual level, and he sees such transformations being used for religious or political ends in both conversion and brainwashing (Sargant 1959). Of course, on the group level, there can be "revitalization" only when a potential prophet or leader, having experienced a private crisis, is able to attract a significant number of followers; that is, the prophet's vision of a new way of life must correspond closely enough to that of other members of the group, and the prophet's need to lead and reveal the truth must correspond to the group's willingness to follow. Revitalization then is not merely, or even always, a religious process, but it is always a significantly political one.

Wallace's analysis has been questioned by Theodore Schwartz (1976b) on the basis of his own studies of Melanesian cargo cults and, specifically, cults among the Manus. He argues that even though such a theory is plausible there is no direct evidence of heightened levels of stress among people who engage in cult behavior. In fact, for the Melanesians he knows, Schwartz suggests that stresses —at least, certain kinds of stresses—have been reduced since the time of their grandparents, prior to massive culture contact: native warfare has come to an end, new means of settling conflicts and disputes exist, and modern medical services deal with diseases that caused fear and danger in earlier times. He also argues that in order to understand the cults, more attention must be paid to the followers, and not simply to the cult leaders. Schwartz observes, moreover, that the apparently sudden "revelations" are actually a long time in the making; presenting them as sudden communications from supernaturals should be seen primarily as a cultural way of phrasing matters to maximize the chances of getting support for what appear to be radically new ideas. In the case of the Manus, Schwartz says, it is the "contact culture"—the mixture of the old and the new that resulted from contacts with other societies—and not the traditional culture, that represented the context in which the prophecies and revelations had to be meaningful and acceptable.

Schwartz goes on to suggest that cult behavior does not involve pathological states such as coma and convulsive seizures during which visions are received. Rather, cult behavior *mimics* these states; it uses them as models for means of communication with the supernatural. Therefore, he says, cult behavior, including visionary states, is properly speaking, *pathomimetic* rather than *pathological*. However, he does not explain *why* such pathological states are chosen as models for communication with supernaturals.

The question Schwartz raises requires some further distinctions. To Wallace, the prophet Handsome Lake was a man in a state of personal disorganization who cured himself through a sudden transforming experience. This experience, it would appear, was successful largely because he was able to acquire followers and achieve the status of prophet and respected leader. It may well be that not all prophet-leaders go through such crises, although many apparently do. Mother Ann Lee, who founded the Shakers, and of whom we spoke in Chapter 8, represents a somewhat different example of a similar pattern. However, gaining followers is a crucial element in the process of self-actualization. The history of mental illness is strewn with the wrecked lives of unsuccessful prophets. On the other hand, there may be shrewd political leaders whose behavior is merely patterned on that of "true" visionaries.

Two further important distinctions must be made: if, following Wallace, we see the first visionary trance experience as a genuine reorganizing, resynthesizing, transforming psychic event, it cannot truly be termed pathological; indeed, it should be more properly spoken of as *therapeutic*, although it is, admittedly, part of a sequence of pathological states. In other words, hearing voices is pathological only for the failed messiah, not for the successful one, if the future career of the prophet is to be taken into consideration. Furthermore, Schwartz' concern is not with the leaders and their original inspiration but with followers. However, Wallace, too, distinguishes between the mazeway resynthesis of the prophet and what he terms "hysterical conversion" of the followers (Wallace 1970). Still, the trances and visions the followers repeatedly experience during cult rituals may be something else, for here the patterning and routinization of what may originally have been a unique personal event already has set in. Suggestion, expectation, and ritual methods of trance induction all play their role here, and there is no need to postulate acute social and personal stresses to account for the institutionalized occurrence of ritual trance states. To the extent that they are patterned on coma and convulsions it may well be appropriate to speak of such states as "pathomimetic." Jilek (1974), in his discussion of the revival of the guardian spirit ceremonial among the Salish, similarly makes a distinction between a pathological and a *pathomorphic* state, a term which corresponds closely to Schwartz's *pathomimetic.*

Both Schwartz and Jilek consider psychiatric disorders as models for ritualized altered states of consciousness. Gussler (1973) has suggested that an ecologically produced nutritional deficiency disease also may play such a role. She has pointed to the striking similarity of symptoms exhibited by sufferers of pellagra and sufferers from a disease that the Southern Bantu say is caused by spirit possession.

Two Examples.

In the present context, it is interesting that conditions in which society and culture require dramatic reorganizations frequently are associated with cults and movements that have a number of common characteristics. Among these features are strong leaders, whose authority may be bolstered by claims to supernatural

support, and whose personal histories often reflect the stresses and transformations of the group in which they seek their followers. Part of the process of
winning followers may properly be called conversion: a vigorous personal emotional upheaval, which leads to great faith in the leader and his or her mission.
The initial conversion experience often involves a substantial personal reorganization, as well as a personal validation of the new faith. This validation may come
through the experience of a cure, the solution of personal problems, a confirmation of a prophecy, and so forth.

Crisis cults vary greatly in scope, duration, and needless to say, success. Those
that are most fully successful eventually lose their emotional intensity, and what
were once true personal transformations and reconfirmations of these transformations may become merely routine, ritual gestures. In the present period, many
such groups have sprung up in this country and in many other parts of the world.
Zaretsky and Leone (1974) have shown that there are literally hundreds of such
groups in the United States. In Latin America, the two most rapidly growing
religions are Pentecostalism and Spiritism. However, they are not unified movements, but appear in numerous local groups and in many varied forms. We shall
consider briefly an example of each.

F. D. Goodman (1973, 1974) has reported on what she terms a "religious
upheaval" in a Maya village in Yucatan, Mexico. Goodman had the rare luck of
coming into the community at the very beginning of this "upheaval," and through
periodic visits, she was able to observe its full course and aftermath. At her first
visit to the village, the small apostolic church had a new minister, who "spoke
in tongues" and who encouraged his flock to accept this practice of ecstatic
prayer. He was a successful leader, and the group rapidly began to grow in
numbers. In the minister's vigorous preaching there was much concern with the
Second Coming and the imminent end of the world. He urged the faithful to
repent and to be baptized in the Holy Spirit, which is manifested in glossolalia
(speaking in tongues). Over a period of several months, he increased the membership of the group and raised its emotional involvement to a high pitch of excitement. Women as well as men now made major religious commitments and spoke
in tongues. The Second Coming was felt to be close at hand. Miracles of healing
and conversion were reported and healing through prayer and laying on of hands
took on great importance. The closer the end of the world was felt to be, the
greater the level of anxiety; people begin to have visions of the Devil, and there
was great fear. At the same time, tension developed between the minister and the
flock. After a great peak of excitement, periods of continuous prayer, accusations
by individuals in trance against others, and so on, exhaustion set in, and with the
help of emissaries from the central religious body, the group was set right and
told that they had been misled by the Devil. A disintegration of the group
followed.

Goodman, who offers an account of these events in fascinating detail, suggests
that the physiological arousal of the ecstatic state follows a clear curve of augmen-

tation and attenuation, which can be observed through the analysis of individual ecstatic utterances. The upheaval, as a group movement, follows a similar sequence. She accounts for this parallel through the observation that most of the participants learned to produce glossolalia at about the same time, reached a maximum excitement at the same time, and felt the letdown simultaneously as well. The emotional and physiological arousal that had powered the upheaval was exhausted.

Quite a different situation is represented by the Umbanda cult of Brazil. Here we observe a type of religious movement that has its basis in a syncretism of a variety of religious traditions: Catholicism, Afro-American cults, the Spiritism of Allen Kardec imported from France, and some ideas of American Indian origin. The specific contribution of each of these elements appears to vary among cult centers and perhaps in different regions of Brazil, as described for example by Pressel (1973, 1974) for São Paulo and by Lerch (1978) for the city of Porto Alegre, in the southern state of Rio Grande do Sul. In Umbanda there appears to be a gradual modification and evolution to integrate many divergent elements into the patterns of belief and practice. Central to these beliefs and practices are possession trance experiences of mediums, who are consulted by clients about various types of problems. The cult plays somewhat different roles for the mediums, who are mostly women, for the leaders, some of whom are men, and for the clients who may be potential mediums. Pressel sees Umbanda as a Brazilian folk religion that expresses the basic themes and values of this developing society.

One of the most interesting aspects of this religion is that many beliefs of African origin, including some of the identities of the possessing spirits, have been taken over by Brazilians of other ethnic origins. Spirits include a category known as "old blacks," that is, spirits of dead slaves. These spirits are known for their great wisdom and patience and their willingness to help with long-term problems. Others are spirits of Indians, and still others spirits of wicked persons, who are often foreigners. Finally, there is the category of child spirits, which, Pressel (1973) suggests, represent an emergence of a new Brazilian identity.

Umbanda is not a rapid, short-lived movement of revitalization or crisis, in spite of the fact that it has a good deal in common with such cults and movements, particularly its use of possession trance states. It lacks a prophet or leader, and a well organized program or series of revelations. Rather, it attempts to resolve the daily problems of health and family harmony, of livelihood and personal autonomy. For many women, it provides an area of legitimate independence and activity outside the home, as well as means of personal advancement (Lerch 1978). Finally, it represents a symbolic statement of a new Brazilian identity in terms of a truly local world view and religious synthesis.

Spiritism of a type similar to Umbanda in many respects also flourishes in Puerto Rico and among Puerto Ricans in New York. As we saw in Chapter 8, it has become a major source of help for Puerto Ricans in distress, particularly in the area of mental health.

Some Implications

Considerations of crisis cults and revitalization movements have brought us back to subjects treated earlier, altered states of consciousness and problems of mental health. These three themes are intimately linked. Revitalization movements play an important role not only in the reconstitution of distressed and disrupted societies in periods of rapid change, but also in the reorganization and reintegration of disturbed individuals.

How we understand such religious movements will depend on the conceptual scheme we use to study them. We spoke earlier of La Barre's concept of "crisis cults." For him, they are responses to an acute or chronic problem that is unresolved by secular means. Moreover, he sees religion in general as an adaptation "to the inner world of man, his unresolved problems and inner needs" (La Barre 1970:44). The cults, in his view, do not deal directly with practical problems but transpose the issues of the "real" world to the realm of fantasy. On the other hand, if we look at the same activities within Wallace's scheme and approach them as revitalization movements, we shall be concerned with their political intents and results, as well as with the psychological starting points and dynamics, with regard to both leaders and followers. Yet both La Barre and Wallace will require us to look at the state of the society in question just prior to the beginning of the crisis cult or revitalization movement. Why does the society have to be reorganized? Why does a more satisfying way of life have to be created? What constitutes the crisis? Why is it that the previously operating safety valves, such as witchcraft accusations or periodic wars, no longer suffice to prop up the social order?

Such cults or movements, then, may be said to constitute "adaptive strategies" for entire societies, as well as for their leaders and their individual members. In addition to asking why such cults appear in certain societies at given points in time, we also want to know why certain individuals join and others do not, and why some appear to select a religious solution to their problems, whereas others seek direct economic or political action.

In our own society, where there has been a rapid growth of diverse religious groups and where a variety of religiously based alternate life-styles have been launched, young people seeking solutions to problems of identity often "shop around" among several such groups over a period of time. For example, oriental derived religions, such as Krishna Consciousness (Daner 1976) or Meher Baba (Robbins and Anthony 1972), as well as Neo-Pentecostalism (McGuire 1976) often have been reported to act as halfway houses for young people trying to break drug habits. Yet by the time many of these people have reached their late twenties, they have settled down to a job and a family, and leave drugs, communes, gurus, and vigorous religious exercises behind as part of the process of growing up in U.S. middle-class society.

IDENTITY: ETHNICITY, RELIGION, SEX, AND CHOICE

In this chapter our emphasis has been on change resulting from culture contact and acculturation, especially on the impact of Western industrial society on the psychological adjustment of people in the developing world. American Indians represent a somewhat special case, for they constitute enclaves of traditional or semi-traditional cultures within one of the world's most highly industrialized societies. Ours is also a society that, in spite of its multiple heritage and its verbal emphasis on freedom of choice, offers a single model of success, a single set of values and goals. As we saw earlier, in the Spindlers's discussion of the Menomini, American Indians, to be "successful," at least in terms of the white society, must, in a sense, abandon their Indian identity. This loss of identity has long been the fate of immigrant groups in the United States. Yet the model does not always work, for not all minority members are able to take on the identity that is proposed to them. For example, Berreman has noted that Aleuts have adopted many of the values proposed by white society, many of its perspectives and behaviors, yet they are prevented from reaping the rewards these bring to whites "because they are ineligible for membership in their reference group" (Berreman 1978:30). Aleuts would have to become members of white society, not merely persons following its patterns or striving for its goals.

Perhaps in response to the civil rights struggle of blacks in the 1960s and to their efforts at revaluing their ethnic and racial identity, there has developed in this country a great concern with ethnicity. In the 1970s, ethnicity and ethnic identity have become significant social and political issues, and subjects of scholarly interest (for example, De Vos and Romannucci-Ross 1975). As a result our concerns in this country parallel those that have come to the fore in other parts of the world.

In the past for most people everywhere ethnic, religious, and sexual identity were ascribed statuses. People knew who they were. In a world of rapid change, great transformations, and great migrations, this is no longer so. Group membership and ethnic, religious, and even sexual identity have become problematic, matters of choice, reaffirmation, or redefinition. The American Indian Movement, with its pan-Indian emphasis, tends to reduce the great cultural differences among the great variety of tribal units and to create a single American Indian identity in contrast to that of the white.

Nation states traditionally have been built up through the unification of regions, the centralization of governments, and the absorption of immigrants. These processes have included the development and imposition of a single national language at the expense of local variants or minority languages, disparagingly called "dialects." In Africa, for example, we still see this process of nation-forging at work. How long will it be before one is a Nigerian rather than an Ibo, a Yoruba, or a Hausa? Yet at the same time, in the old nations of Europe, we see that regional languages are being revived, and old customs fostered. People fear the loss of their traditions; even when the traditions have been transformed into ceremonial observances and rituals into performances, they acquire a special value as symbols of group identity.

A word must be said about sexual identity. As a result of medical technology it is now possible for some to opt for a change of sex, to decide to be a woman rather than a man, or a man rather than a woman. Also, it is possible nowadays in the United States to assert one's identity as a homosexual or "gay" and to speak of "sexual preference" as others speak of "religious preference" or another type of choice. In this context, homosexuality is treated as a matter of life-style, not as a biological or psychological necessity. In addition to such variants on sexual identity, we also find a redefinition of roles of the sexes. This redefinition is a broad social process, with many significant social, economic, and political implications, as well as psychological aspects. Of particular interest is a process used by the Women's Movement, termed "consciousness raising." This concept derives from Marxism, and in important respects it resembles religious or political conversion. It involves a change of one's perception of oneself, and of one's life experience, needs, and goals, as well as a reappraisal of others. Conscious choices of ethnic, religious, or political identities often follow along similar lines.

Identity choices, changes, redefinitions, and reevaluations are crucial elements of the process of culture change. Sometimes they are clear outcomes of previous changes; sometimes they are best understood as leading to further changes. In either case, they are links in a long causal chain, not single independent events. Furthermore, individuals do not shape their identities simply by making rational decisions, weighing alternatives and their advantages and disadvantages. Unconscious and irrational processes are likely to be at work, of which the individuals themselves are likely to be unaware, as well as practical factors. Some of the psychological aspects can be studied best when we compare persons who have basically similar backgrounds yet who make different choices of group affiliation. A choice that may be full of potential for self-realization for one individual may constitute an irrational, self-defeating attempt at resolving internal conflicts in another.

Ethnic, religious, or even sexual identity may be a matter of individual affiliation and transformation, or it may involve minority groups within a larger society. When groups are involved, we may be dealing with social, political, or religious movements. In that case, we must ask about the difference in the perspectives of the leaders and the followers: what needs are to be satisfied, what ends are to be gained, what means are to be used? For the leaders, and often for members as well, the drive for power, for authority, or for financial gain must not be overlooked.

The problems of personal identity that we have touched on briefly in these pages are major issues in the present-day world. They involve powerful symbols about which social and political forces cluster. They deserve our serious attention and careful study; we must consider their psychological dimensions as well as their economic and political aspects, which may appear to be more obvious. They are clearly relevant to the subject of development: the Amazonian Indians, of whom we spoke earlier in this chapter, find that their identity is destroyed as tribal lands are transformed into large corporate holdings and groups are dispersed; rural migrants become urban shanty town dwellers on the margins of large cities in Third World countries; migrants from the countries of Southern Europe and Africa to the industrial centers of the North, find their identities challenged and transformed.

Summary

In this chapter we have focused on the psychological implications of culture change. However, this very large subject has not been restricted to this chapter. Rather, it appears throughout the book for most of our topics deal with social and cultural change, in one context or another. Even when the topic is not mentioned explicitly, it must be remembered that most of the societies studied by anthropologists in the twentieth century have had their traditional ways of life modified through contacts of various kinds—even the most isolated societies, and even those groups who have attempted to resist change or, in extreme cases, to reverse its direction. Consequently, whether the topic of the chapter was socialization, personality assessment, or perception and cognition, to mention just three, the data, for the most part, could have served for our final chapter on change. The selection of the research reports for review in any of these contexts, as opposed to that of change, is necessarily arbitrary. There has been therefore also some overlap and partial repetition of materials in the various chapters.

In the present chapter we began by returning to our earlier discussion of cultural evolution and of innovation in its psychological dimension. Innovation, as we saw, may be the result of inventing or discovering objects or behavior patterns, or borrowing them from other groups. In either case, cognitive processes are involved. Acceptance of new patterns entails motivation and learning, and often the unlearning of old ways as well. Innovations, whatever their source, create both opportunities and stresses, because they require a reorganization of habits and of understandings, and also because we are dealing with social systems, not with a simple inventory of traits. One change leads to another, and the simple introduction of one element, such as the steel axe among the Yir Yoront of Australia, may have far-reaching consequences for the total way of life of the group, and indeed, for its very existence. This idea of the entanglements of cultural elements carries a clear lesson for those who would engage in planned change or "development," for the planning rarely goes far enough, and the remote repercussions of a single "simple" change rarely are evaluated fully in advance of decision making.

When we look at the place of innovation in the context of cultural evolution, of the distance we have come from small hunting and gathering bands of a rare

The presidential palace in Port-au-Prince, Haiti, as seen from a hillside slum. In developing countries, central cities are surrounded by slums into which newcomers from rural areas are crowded.

animal species to the teeming billions of humans in the single interrelated world of the final quarter of the twentieth century, we appreciate the implications of human creative capacity to construct novel culturally constituted behavioral environments.

In the context of such considerations we looked at the contrast made by Claude Lévi-Strauss between the "savage" and the "civilized" mind, and at Jack Goody's incisive analysis of the importance of literacy in the process he terms "the domestication of the savage mind." This analysis has great significance, for it sheds important light on the differences between traditional (oral) and modern (literate) societies, and on the transition from the one to the other. From a psychological perspective, it means that literacy is an important aid in thinking, or better, in the development of characteristic thinking processes.

In the course of what is variously called "development," "westernization," or "modernization" schooling plays an enormous role. It is one of the ways in which perception and cognition are altered significantly when peoples of different cultures meet. There are other important factors as well. One of the most important is religious conversion. A third factor, often historically the first, is the introduction of new goods. All of these factors contribute to the restructuring of culturally constituted behavioral environments. Among the cognitive processes at work are reinterpretation and syncretism, which lead to the emergence of contact cultures, selective combinations of the old and the new.

Culture contact leading to large-scale modifications in ways of life, most particularly those of a dominated group, is spoken of as *acculturation*. What has been the impact of acculturation, as a special form of culture change, on the typical personalities of people at the "receiving end"? Wherever this subject has been studied, it has been shown that there is both change and continuity. On the one hand, the preexisting cultural and personality patterns have influenced the reaction of people to cultural change. Africans, as LeVine suggests, have reacted to change in ways that might have been predicted from pre-change patterns. Change, for them, often has not been disruptive; indeed, it often has been highly positive. In our chapter on methods we referred to another study by LeVine, in which he compared children's dreams in three West African cultural groups. The dreams related interestingly to pre-change cultural differences among the three groups, revealing differences in their need for achievement and in their actual realization of upward mobility and striving. LeVine's investigation was based on the work of the psychologist David McClelland (1961, McClelland et al. 1971), who sees the need for achievement as a major driving force for economic development.

In addition to asking how pre-existing patterns have affected people's reactions to change, we have also received some evidence of what has happened to people as a result of change, that is, how the impact of change has modified typical personality patterns in certain societies. A third approach to the relationship between change and personality patterns is illustrated by the work of the Spindlers among the Menomini. Here we reported that they found different types of results in a single reservation community. Rather than speaking simply of the effect of change and perceiving individuals as passive recipients, they came to view people as using different "adaptive strategies" in their responses to change. They also found that sex was an important variable to be considered in studying cultural change and its consequences.

Yet another approach to the study of personality patterns and culture change that we reviewed stresses the continuity that exists in the midst of change. Often we are misled by external appearances into seeing more transformation in the attitudes, values, life orientations, and thinking of people than has actually occurred. In this connection it is important to ask at what point in the life cycle changes affect individuals. What are the implications of changes in the mother's work loads, not only for the mother but also for her children? What are the implications of schooling, not only for the children who are sent to school, but also for other members of their families?

A major theme, of which we have become aware as a result of the developments in our own society in the 1960s and 1970s, has been that of religious responses to social change: crisis cults, revitalization movements, and the like. They, too, may be seen as adaptive strategies, ways of seeking solutions to troubling problems. In religious conversion, a solution may be sought not by changing society, but by transforming the self. By changing one's identity, by being "reborn" in the United States, or by developing one's mediumistic capacities in the Umbanda cults of Brazil, one changes one's relationship not only to the universe, but also to members of one's own society and family. On the other hand, where society is to be reorganized as well as the individual, we may, in fact, be dealing with political movements of renewal and transformation.

Our final subject in this chapter concerned the relationship between sociocultural change and definitions of identity in ethnicity, religion, and sex. We have touched on this general subject elsewhere in this book. For example, in Chapter 5 we spoke of the "socialized ambivalence" among upper-class Haitians, who are torn between various possible sources of identity definition. In Chapter 8 we discussed Jilek's study of modern spirit dancing among the Salish Indians. This movement has revalued their Indian identity for these people and as a result has provided them with a powerful psychotherapeutic system to deal with "anomic depression," a disturbance related to their conflicts over being Indians.

Redefinitions and reevaluations of ethnic, religious, and sexual identity are at the heart of many social movements in the contemporary world. Their psychological implications deserve serious attention and study.

NOTES

1. There is no question here of a biological deficiency; it is merely a matter of learning. More acculturated individuals show that this learning is within reach of those who undergo some exposure to graphic representations with perspective.

2. Loring and Otto (1976) suggest how women in the United States can make rational decisions about the choices—or adaptive strategies—that are open to them.

An Overview and a Look Ahead

We began this book by asking: what is psychological anthropology? We have covered a lot of ground in this volume, both literally and figuratively speaking. We have referred to a large number of cultures, and we have reviewed a long span of time. Although most of the peoples we have spoken of were studied within the last fifty years, we also took a broad, panoramic view of human behavioral and cultural evolution. In terms of theory, we have dealt with the history of psychological anthropology, from its modest beginnings as culture and personality in the 1920s and 1930s to its present greatly enlarged scope. It is to be hoped that this book, as a whole, has offered an answer to our original, deceptively simple question.

What does psychological anthropology have to offer, and to whom? Have we discovered anything? Are there some lessons to be learned? And taking stock, can we say where we are headed in psychological anthropology? What new turns is our complex and lively field taking?

As we look back from the present multitude of questions, it appears that the earliest problems were phrased narrowly: what relationship is there between "culture" and "personality"? This question derived in part from the discovery of culture, from the realization of the great role it plays in human life, and from the dawning appreciation of its enormous diversity. In part also it derived from the impact of psychoanalysis and personality theory on the thinking of U.S. anthropologists. Cultures were palpably different, and so, it seemed, were the personalities associated with them.

The impact of this discovery still is not established fully, although "anthropology" has become a household word in the United States, and persons identified as "anthropologists" have been known to figure in TV scripts. For example, G. A. Miller writes: "Unfortunately, most psychologists are poorly prepared by education or acculturation to understand the mental processes of people living in relatively static, traditional cultures . . ." (1971:ix). Commenting on American efforts to contribute to the development of Third World countries, George Foster remarks:

> The enthusiasm of many technical specialists and of the equally numerous less well-trained professional do-gooders sometimes terrifies me. The blind ethnocentrism of many Americans . . . takes my breath away. When I see an earnest American greeting a foreigner with a bone-crushing fraternity-type hand-shake, meanwhile fixing him with a beady stare, under the assumption that he thereby connotes sincerity, I blanche (Foster 1962:260).

Psychological anthropology has taught us that there is a very broad range of differences among cultural groups in attitudes, values, perceptions of the world and of themselves, and ways of dealing with, and experiencing emotions. Cultural patterning extends to personality and interpersonal relationships. Relativity is not merely skin-deep. We cannot assume that what psychologists have learned in this country holds true of people in other cultures, without testing that assumption. Psychological anthropology, then, has acted as a testing ground for psychological theories developed in the West. The result has been that our concept of cultural relativity has been confirmed, but we have also learned to place it in perspective. There is a common human nature that underlies the variations we observe.

Because psychological anthropologists have restudied some of the same groups over a period of many years, we have been able to discover what happens in the course of time, when there have been major social and cultural changes. The Manus, first studied by Mead in 1928, and restudied periodically since 1953, have presented us with a fine example of the interrelationship of psychological and sociocultural changes. We no longer need speculate about such relationships by attempting to reconstruct the culture and society of the past; we see it going on before our eyes.

We also have gained in methodological sophistication. We now have long-term studies, restudies, replications, simultaneous coordinated studies of several carefully selected societies, cross-cultural statistical (holocultural) investigations, and some studies that combine complex intracultural analysis with holocultural techniques. Our generalizations are now in the nature of hypotheses that have been tested, rather than descriptive or intuitive assertions.

Psychological anthropology, then, has contributed to psychological and psychiatric theory. It has contributed also to our understanding of our own society and of developments within it. Most notably, cross-cultural studies of altered states of consciousness have made it possible to place the burgeoning cults and movements and the U.S. fascination with getting "high" into a comparative context.

We can recognize still another gain of a more practical nature. Medical anthropology and educational anthropology, two applied fields that have developed over the last few years and are gaining in importance, have derived to a significant extent from the earliest work in culture and personality, which dealt with socialization and with mental health and its cultural implications.

In theoretical terms, there have been other changes. The field has expanded enormously. Many of the topics treated in this book, such as behavioral evolution, perception and cognition, and altered states of consciousness, were not significant concerns in 1954, when J. J. Honigmann published the first textbook in this area. In addition, we have become aware of the importance of variables we did not dream of then: in particular, the biological and ecological factors that appear to play an important role in psychocultural development. For example, we now have studies that link aggression with hypoglycemia (Bolton 1978) or possession trance with nutritional deficiency disease (Gussler 1973). It is such novel experiments in the formulation of problems that bode well for the future of our speciality.

For a number of years, psychological anthropology was overshadowed by the growth of new interests and new subdisciplines in anthropology, ranging from ecological anthropology to symbolic anthropology. In the meantime, however, rather than witnessing a decline of interest in our field, we have seen a great diversification of concerns and of approaches. The field has now emerged with renewed force and vigor. A Society for Psychological Anthropology was formed in 1977, with its journal, *Ethos;* the *Journal of Psychological Anthropology* was launched in 1978; and in that same year, *The Making of Psychological Anthropology* (G. D. Spindler 1978) was published. Spindler's volume presents a major assessment of the field in the words of a number of its long-term practitioners, who review their own contributions, shedding light on the growth and development of their thinking. The impact of this book on anthropology and neighboring disciplines, and on students considering a career in anthropology, may be considerable.

At the end of our introduction to psychological anthropology, we see that it is a field of challenge and importance, concerned with real people confronting the problems of living in the contemporary world. Psychological anthropology, after some fifty years, is alive and well and looking forward to a prosperous future.

References

Aberle, D., 1960. "The Influence of Linguistics on Early Culture and Personality Theory." In G. E. Dole and R. L. Carneiro, eds., *Essays in the Science of Culture, in Honor of Leslie A. White.* New York: Crowell.

——, 1967 (orig. 1951). "The Psychosocial Analysis of a Hopi Life History." In R. Hunt, ed., *Personalities and Cultures.* Garden City, N.Y.: Natural History Press.

——, U. Bronfenbrenner, E. H. Hen, D. R. Miller, D. M. Schneider, and J. N. Spuhler, 1963. "The Incest Taboo and the Mating Patterns of Animals." *American Anthropologist* 65:253–265.

Abraham, K., 1913. "Dreams and Myths: A Study in Race Psychology." *Nervous and Mental Disease Monograph Series,* 15.

Ackerknecht, E. H., 1943. "Psychopathology, Primitive Medicine and Primitive Culture." *Bulletin of the History of Medicine* 14: 30–67.

Ainsworth, M. D. S., 1967. *Infancy in' Uganda.* Baltimore: The Johns Hopkins Press.

——, 1977. "Attachment Theory and Its Utility in Cross-Cultural Research." In P. H. Leiderman, S. R. Tulin, and A. Rosenfeld, eds., *Culture and Infancy: Variations in the Human Experience.* New York: Academic Press.

Allen, G., 1879. *The Colour-Sense: Its Origin and Development.* London: Trübner; Boston: Houghton. Reprinted as "second edition," London: Kegan, Paul, Trench, & Trübner, 1892.

Allen, M. G., 1967. "The Development of a Criterion for the Measurement of Mental Health in a Society." *Journal of Social Psychology* 57:363–382.

Ardrey, R., 1963. *African Genesis.* New York: Delta Books.

Ayers, B., 1968. "Effects of Infantile Stimulation on Musical Behavior." In A. Lomax et al., eds., *Folk Song Style and Culture.* American Association for the Advancement of Science.

Bandura, A., 1973. "Social Learning Theory of Aggression." In J. F. Kuntsar, ed., *The Control of Aggression.* Chicago: Aldine.

Barash, D. P., 1977. *Sociobiology and Behavior.* New York: Elsevier.

Barkow, J. H., 1978. "Social Norms, the Self, and Sociobiology: Building on the Ideas of A. I. Hallowell," with C. A.* comment. *Current Anthropology* 19:99–118.

Barnouw, V., 1950. *Acculturation and Personality Among the Wisconsin Chippewa.* Memoir 22, American Anthropological Association.

——, 1973. *Culture and Personality,* rev. ed. Homewood, Ill.: Dorsey.

Baron, R. A., and R. M. Liebert, eds., 1971. *Human Social Behavior: A Contemporary*

View of Experimental Research. Homewood, Ill.: Dorsey.

Barry, H., III, 1957. "Relationship Between Child Training and the Pictoral Arts." *Journal of Abnormal and Social Psychology* 54:380–383.

———, M. K. Bacon, and I. L. Child, 1957. "A Cross-Cultural Survey of Some Sex Differences in Socialization." *Journal of Abnormal and Social Psychology* 55: 327–332.

———, I. L. Child, and M. K. Bacon, 1959. "Relation of Child Training to Subsistence Economy." *American Anthropologist* 61:51–63.

———, L. Josephson, E. Lauer, and C. Marshall, 1976. "Traits Inculcated in Childhood: Cross-Cultural Codes 5." *Ethnology* 15:83–114.

Bastide, R., F. Morin, and F. Raveau, 1974. *Les Haïtiens en France.* Paris and The Hague: Mouton.

Bateson, G., 1976. "Some Components of Socialization for Trance." In T. Schwartz, ed., *Socialization as Cultural Communication: Development of a Theme in the Work of Margaret Mead.* Berkeley: University of California Press.

———, and M. Mead, 1942. *Balinese Character: A Photographic Analysis.* Special Publication 2. New York: New York Academy of Sciences.

Bayley, N., 1965. "Comparisons of Mental and Motor Test Scores for Ages 1–15 Months by Sex, Birth Order, Race, Geographic Location, and Education of Parents." *Child Development* 36:379–411.

Bell, D., 1968. "National Character Revisited: A Proposal for Renegotiating the Concept." In E. Norbeck, D. Price-Williams, and W. M. McCord, eds., *The Study of Personality: An Inter-disciplinary Approach.* New York: Holt, Rinehart and Winston.

Benedict, R., 1923. "The Concept of the Guardian Spirit in North America." *Memoirs of the American Anthropological Association* XXIX.

———, 1934. *Patterns of Culture.* Boston and New York: Houghton Mifflin. (Paperback reprint, 1961).

———, 1938. "Continuities and Discontinuities in Cultural Conditioning." *Psychiatry* 1:161–167.

———, 1946. *The Chrysanthemum and the Sword: Patterns of Japanese Culture.* Boston: Houghton Mifflin.

———, 1959 (orig. 1934). "Anthropology and the Abnormal." In M. Mead, *An Anthropologist at Work: Writings of Ruth Benedict.* Boston: Houghton Mifflin.

Bennett, J. W., 1956 (orig. 1946). "The Interpretation of Pueblo Cultures: A Question of Values." In D. S. Haring, ed., *Personal Character and Cultural Milieu,* 3rd ed. Syracuse: Syracuse University Press.

———, and M. Nagai, 1953. "Echoes—Reactions to American Anthropology: Japanese Critique of Benedict's *Chrysanthemum and the Sword.*" *American Anthropologist* 55:404–411.

Berlin, B., and P. Kay, 1969. *Basic Color Terms: Their Universality and Evolution.* Berkeley: University of California Press.

———, and E. A. Berlin, 1975. "Aguaruna Color Categories." *American Ethnologist* 2:61–87.

Berreman, G. D., 1978, "Scale and Social Relations." *Current Anthropology* 19:225–245.

Berry, J. W., 1974 (orig. 1971). "Ecological and Cultural Factors in Spatial Perceptual Development." In J. W. Berry and P. R. Dasen, eds., *Culture and Cognition: Readings in Cross-Cultural Psychology.* London: Methuen.

———, 1975. "Ecology, Cultural Adaptation, and Psychological Differentiation: Traditional Patterning and Acculturative Stress." In R. W. Brislin et al., eds., *Cross-Cultural Perspectives on Learning.* New York: Sage Publications, Wiley.

———, 1976. *Human Ecology and Cognitive Style: Comparative Studies in Cultural and Psychological Adaptation.* New York: Halsted Press.

Bettelheim, B., 1969. *Children of the Dream: Communal Childrearing and American Education.* New York: Macmillan.

Biesheuvel, S., 1974. Foreword. In J. W. Berry and P. R. Dasen, eds., *Culture and Cognition: Readings in Cross-Cultural Psychology.* London: Methuen.

Blass, T., ed., 1977. *Personality Variables in Social Behavior.* New York: Halsted Press.

Blurton-Jones, N., and M. Konner, 1976. "!Kung Knowledge of Animal Behavior (or: The Proper Study of Mankind Is Animals)."

In R. Lee and I. DeVore, eds., *Kalahari Hunter-Gatherers*. Cambridge, Mass.: Harvard University Press.

Bolton, C., R. Bolton, L. Gross, A. Koel, C. Michelson, R. L. Munroe, and R. H. Munroe, 1976. "Pastoralism and Personality: An Andean Replication." *Ethos* 4:4631–4681.

Bolton, R., 1973. "Aggression and Hypoglycemia Among the Qolla: A Study in Psychobiological Anthropology," *Ethnology* 12:227–259.

———, 1976. "Hostility in Fantasy: A Further Test of the Hypoglycemia Aggression Hypothesis." *Aggressive Behavior* 2:251–274.

———, 1978. *Aggression and Hypoglycemia in Qolla Society*. New York: Garland STMP Press.

———, and C. Bolton, 1975. *Conflictos en la Familia Andina: Un Estudio Antropológico entre los Campesinos Qolla*. Cuzco, Peru: Centro de Estudios Andinos.

———, C. Michelson, J. Wilde, and C. Bolton, 1975. "The Heights of Illusion: On the Relationship between Altitude and Perception." *Ethos* 3:403–424.

Bonté, M. L., 1960. "Contribution à l'Étude des Illusions Optico-géométriques: Essais de Mésure de l'Illusion de Müller-Lyer chez les Bashi et les Bambuti (Pygmées) du Congo Belge." Unpublished M.A. Thesis, Université Catholique de Louvain (cited in Segall et al., 1966).

Bornstein, M. C., 1973. "The Psychophysiological Component of Cultural Difference in Color Naming and Illusion Susceptibility." *Behavior Science Notes* 8:41–101.

———, 1975. "The Influence of Visual Perception on Culture." *American Anthropologist* 77:774–99.

Bourguignon, E., 1954. "Dreams and Dream Interpretation in Haiti." *American Anthropologist* 56:262–268.

———, 1956. "A Life History of an Ojibwa Young Woman." In B. Kaplan, ed., *Microcard Publications of Primary Records in Culture and Personality 1*. Madison, Wisc.: The Microcard Foundation.

———, 1959. "The Persistence of Folk Belief: Some Notes on Cannibalism and Zombis in Haiti." *Journal of American Folklore* 72: 36–46.

———, 1965. "The Self, the Behavioral Environment and the Theory of Spirit Possession." In M. E. Spiro, ed., *Context and Meaning in Cultural Anthropology. In Honor of A. I. Hallowell*. New York: Free Press.

———, 1968a. "World Distribution and Patterns of Possession States." In R. Prince, ed., *Trance and Possession States*. Montreal: R. M. Bucke Memorial Society.

———, 1968b. "A Cross-Cultural Study of Dissociational States: Final Report." Columbus, Ohio: Ohio State University Research Foundation.

———, 1969. "Haïti et l'Ambivalence Socialisée: Une Reconsidération." *Journal de la Société des Américanistes* 58:178–205.

———, 1972. "Dreams and Altered States of Consciousness in Anthropological Research." In F. L. K. Hsu, ed., *Psychological Anthropology*, new ed. Cambridge, Mass.: Schenkman.

———, ed., 1973a. *Religion, Altered States of Consciousness, and Social Change*. Columbus: Ohio State University Press.

———, 1973b. "Introduction: A Framework for the Comparative Study of Altered States of Consciousness." In E. Bourguignon, ed., *Religion, Altered States of Consciousness and Social Change*. Columbus: Ohio State University Press.

———, 1976. *Possession*. Corte Madera, Calif.: Chandler and Sharp.

———, and T. L. Evascu, 1977. "Altered States of Consciousness Within a General Evolutionary Perspective: A Holocultural Analysis." *Behavior Science Research* 12: 197–216.

———, and L. S. Greenbaum, 1973. *Diversity and Homogeneity in World Societies*. New Haven: HRAF Press.

Bowlby, J., 1952. *Maternal Care and Mental Health*, 2nd ed. Monograph Series, 2. Geneva: World Health Organization.

Boyer, L. B., 1962. "Remarks on the Personality of Shamans, with Special Reference to the Apaches of the Mescalero Indian Reservation." *The Psychoanalytic Study of Society* 2:233–254.

———, et al., 1964. "Comparisons of the Shamans and Pseudoshamans of the Apaches of the Mescalero Indian Reservation: A Rorschach Study." *Journal of Projective Tech-*

niques and Personality Assessment 28:173–180.

Brim, J. A., and D. H. Spain, 1974. *Research Design in Anthropology.* New York: Holt, Rinehart and Winston.

Bronfenbrenner, U., 1970. *Two Worlds of Childhood: U.S. and U.S.S.R.* New York: Russell Sage Foundation.

Brosin, H. W., 1952. "A Review of the Influence of Psychoanalysis on Current Thought." In F. Alexander and H. Ross, eds., *Dynamic Psychiatry.* Chicago: University of Chicago Press.

Broustra, J., 1972. "Présentation d'un Guérisseur de la Folie au Niger." *Actualités Psychiatriques* 5:33–37.

Brown, R., 1958. *Words and Things.* Glencoe, Ill.: Free Press.

———, and E. H. Lenneberg, 1954. "A Study in Language and Cognition." *Journal of Abnormal and Social Psychology* 49:454–462.

Bruce, R. D., 1975. *Lacandon Dream Symbolism: Dream Symbolism and Interpretation among the Lacandon Mayas of Chiapas, Mexico.* Vol. I, *Dream Symbolism and Interpretation.* Mexico, D.F.: Ediciónes Euroamericanas Klaus Thiele.

Burton-Bradley, B. G., 1975. *Stone Age Crisis.* Nashville, Tenn.: Vanderbilt University.

Campbell, B., 1974. *Human Evolution,* 2nd ed. Chicago: Aldine-Atherton.

Campbell, D. T., and R. Naroll, 1972. "The Mutual Methodological Relevance of Anthropology and Psychology." In F. L. K. Hsu, ed., *Psychological Anthropology,* new ed. Cambridge, Mass.: Schenkman.

Carneiro, R. L., 1964. "The Amahuaca and the Spirit World." *Ethnology* 3:6–11.

———, 1970. "Scale Analysis, Evolutionary Sequences, and the Rating of Cultures." In R. Naroll and R. Cohen, eds., *A Handbook of Method in Cultural Anthropology.* Garden City, N.Y.: Natural History Press.

———, 1973. "The Four Faces of Evolution: Unilinear, Universal, Multilinear and Differential." In J. J. Honigmann, ed., *Handbook of Social and Cultural Anthropology.* Chicago: Rand McNally.

Caudill, W., 1972. "Tiny Dramas: Vocal Communication Between Mother and Infant in Japanese and American Families." In W. Lebra, ed., *Transcultural Research in Mental Health.* Honolulu, Hawaii: University of Hawaii Press.

———, 1976. "Social Change and Cultural Continuity in Modern Japan." In G. A. DeVos, ed., *Responses to Change: Society, Culture and Personality.* New York: Van Nostrand.

———, and C. Schooler, 1973. "Child Behavior and Child Rearing in Japan and in the United States: An Interim Report." *Journal of Nervous and Mental Disease* 157:323–338.

Childe, V. G., 1942. *What Happened in History.* Harmondsworth, England: Penguin.

———, 1951 (orig. 1936). *Man Makes Himself.* New York: Mentor Books, New American Library.

Clark, D. L., 1977. "Vestibular Stimulation Influence on Motor Development in Infants." *Science* 96:1228–1229.

Cohen, R. A., 1969. "Conceptual Styles, Culture Conflict and Nonverbal Tests of Intelligence." *American Anthropologist* 71:828–856.

Cohen, Y., 1964. *The Transition from Childhood to Adolescence.* Chicago: Aldine.

Cole, M., 1975. "An Ethnographic Psychology of Cognition." In R. W. Brislin et al., eds., *Cross-Cultural Perspectives on Learning.* New York: Sage Publications, Wiley.

———, 1978. "Ethnographic Psychology of Cognition—So Far." In G. D. Spindler, ed., *The Making of Psychological Anthropology.* Berkeley: University of California Press.

———, J. Gay, J. A. Glick, and D. W. Sharp, 1971. *The Cultural Context of Learning and Thinking: An Exploration in Experimental Anthropology.* New York: Basic Books.

———, and S. Scribner, 1974. *Culture and Thought: A Psychological Introduction.* New York: Wiley.

———, 1976. "Theorizing About Socialization of Cognition." In Theodore Schwartz, ed., *Socialization as Cultural Communication.* Berkeley: University of California Press.

Colson, E., 1976. "Culture and Progress." *American Anthropologist* 78:261–271.

Conklin, H. C., 1955. "Hanunóo Color Categories." *Southwestern Journal of Anthropology* 11:339–344.

Cooley, T., 1976. *Educated Lives: The Rise of*

Modern Autobiography in America. Columbus, Ohio: Ohio State University Press.

Coon, C. S., 1965. *The Living Races of Man.* New York: Knopf.

Corah, N. L., 1965. "Differentiation in Children and Their Parents." *Journal of Personality* 33:300–308.

Cornelisen, A., 1969. *Torregreca: Life, Death, Miracles.* Boston: Little, Brown.

Crapanzano, V., 1973. *The Hamadsha: A Study in Moroccan Ethnopsychiatry.* Berkeley: University of California Press.

———, 1977. "Mohammed and Dawia: Possession in Morocco." In V. Crapanzano and V. Garrison, eds., *Case Studies in Spirit Possession.* New York: Wiley.

———, and V. Garrison, eds., 1977. *Case Studies in Spirit Possession.* New York: Wiley.

D'Andrade, R. G., 1961. "Anthropological Studies of Dreams." In F. L. K. Hsu, ed., *Psychological Anthropology.* Homewood, Ill.: Dorsey.

Daner, F., 1976. *The American Children of Krsna: A Study of the Hare Krsna Movement.* New York: Holt, Rinehart and Winston.

Dart, R. A., 1959. *Adventures with the Missing Link.* London: Hamish Hamilton.

Darwin, C., 1871. *Descent of Man.* London: Murray.

———, 1872. *Expression of Emotion in Man and Animals.* London: Murray.

———, 1958 (orig. 1859). *On the Origin of Species by Means of Natural Selection.* New York: New American Library.

Dasen, P. R., 1974 (orig. 1972). "Cross-Cultural Piagetian Research: A Summary." In J. W. Berry and P. R. Dasen, eds., *Culture and Cognition: Readings in Cross-Cultural Psychology.* London: Methuen.

Davis, S. H., 1977. *Victims of the Miracle: Development and the Indians of Brazil.* New York: Cambridge.

Dawson, J. L. M., 1963. *Psychological Effects of Social Change in a West African Community.* Unpublished Manuscript, Department of Social Anthropology, University of Edinburgh.

———, 1967. "Cultural and Physiological Influences upon Spatial-Perceptual Processes in West Africa." *International Journal of Psychology* 2:115–128; 171–185.

de Mause, L., ed., 1974. *The History of Childhood.* New York: The Psychohistory Press.

de Mille, R., 1976. *Castaneda's Journey: The Power and the Allegory.* Santa Barbara: Capra.

Devereux, G., 1961. *Mohave Ethnopsychiatry and Suicide: The Psychiatric Knowledge and Psychic Disturbances of an Indian Tribe.* Bureau of American Ethnology, Bulletin 175. Washington, D.C.: Smithsonian Institution.

DeVos, G., 1961. "Symbolic Analysis in the Cross-Culture Study of Personality." In B. Kaplan, ed., *Studying Personality Cross-Culturally.* Evanston and White Plains: Row, Peterson.

———, 1973. *Socialization for Achievement: Essays on the Cultural Psychology of the Japanese.* Berkeley: University of California Press.

———, 1976a. "Introduction: Change as a Social Science Problem." In G. DeVos, ed., *Responses to Change: Society, Culture and Personality.* New York: Van Nostrand.

———, 1976b. "Conclusion: Responses to Change: Recurrent Patterns." In G. DeVos, ed., *Responses to Change: Society, Culture and Personality.* New York: Van Nostrand.

———, 1978. "The Japanese Adapt to Change." In G. D. Spindler, ed., *The Making of Psychological Anthropology.* Berkeley, Calif.: University of California Press.

———, and L. Romannucci-Ross, eds., 1975. *Ethnic Identity.* Palo Alto: Mayfield.

Divale, D. T., and M. Harris, 1976. "Population, Warfare and the Male Supremacist Complex." *American Anthropologist* 78:521–538.

Dodds, E. R., 1951. *The Greeks and the Irrational.* Berkeley: University of California Press.

Dollard, J., L. W. Doob, N. E. Miller, O. H. Mowrer, and R. R. Sears, 1939. *Frustration and Aggression.* New Haven, Conn.: Yale University Press.

Domarus, E., 1944. "The Specific Laws of Logic in Schizophrenia." In J. S. Kasanin, ed., *Language and Thought in Schizophrenia.* Chicago: University of Chicago Press.

Doob, L. W., 1957. "The Effect of Language on Verbal Expression and Recall." *American Anthropologist* 59:88–100.

———, 1960. *Becoming More Civilized: A Psy-*

chological Exploration. New York: Holt, Rinehart and Winston.

Douglass, W., 1969. Death in Murelaga. Seattle: Washington University Press.

Draper, P., 1972. A !Kung Bushman Childhood. Ph.D. Dissertation, Harvard University, Cambridge, Mass.

———, 1973. "Crowding Among Hunter-Gatherers: The !Kung Bushmen." Science 182:301–303.

———, 1975. "!Kung Women: Contrasts in Sexual Egalitarianism in Foraging and Sedentary Context." In R. R. Reiter, ed., Toward an Anthropology of Women. New York: Monthly Review Press.

———, 1976. "Social and Economic Constraints on Children Among the !Kung." In R. Lee and I. DeVore, Kalahari Hunters and Gatherers. Cambridge, Mass.: Harvard University Press.

DuBois, C., 1937. "Some Anthropological Perspectives on Psychoanalysis." Psychoanalytic Review 24:246–273.

———, 1941. "Attitudes Toward Food and Hunger in Alor." In L. Spier, A. I. Hallowell, and S. Newman, eds., Language, Culture, and Personality: Essays in Memory of Edward Sapir. Menasha, Wisc.: Sapir Memorial Publication Fund.

———, 1960 (orig. 1944). The People of Alor: A Social-Psychological Study of an East Indian Island. Minneapolis: University of Minnesota Press. (Paperback reprint.)

Edgerton, R. B., 1966. "Conceptions of Psychosis in Four East African Societies." American Anthropologist 68:408–425. Reprinted in D. Landy, ed., Culture, Disease, and Healing: Studies in Medical Anthropology. New York: Macmillan, 1977.

———, 1971. The Individual in Cultural Adaptation: A Study of Four East African Peoples. Berkeley and London: University of California Press.

Efron, D., 1941. Gesture and Environment. New York: King's Crown Press. Reprinted as Gesture, Races and Culture. The Hague: Mouton, 1972.

Eggan, D., 1955. "The Personal Use of Myths in Dreams." In T. Sebeok, ed., Myth: A Symposium. Journal of American Folklore 68:445–453.

———, 1961. "Dream Analysis." In B. Kaplan, ed., Studying Personality Cross-Culturally. Evanston, Ill.: Row, Peterson.

———, 1966. "Hopi Dreams in Cultural Perspective." In G. E. von Gruenebaum and Roger Callois, eds., The Dream and Human Society. Berkeley and Los Angeles: University of California Press.

Ember, M., 1978. "Size of Color Lexicon: Interaction of Cultural and Biological Factors." American Anthropologist 80:364–367.

Engels, F., 1972 (orig. 1884). The Origin of the Family, Private Property and the State, E. Leacock, ed. New York: Internation Publishers.

Erikson, E. H., 1963. Childhood and Society, 2nd ed. New York: Norton.

Ervin, S., 1964. "Language and TAT Content in Bilinguals." Journal of Abnormal and Social Psychology 68:500–507.

Estes, W. K., 1975. "Human Behavior in Mathematical Perspective." American Scientist 63:649–655.

Evans-Pritchard, E. E., 1937. Witchcraft, Oracles and Magic Among the Azande. Oxford: Clarendon Press.

———, 1940. The Nuer: A Description of the Modes of Livelihood and Political Institutions of a Nilotic People. Oxford: Clarendon Press.

Fernandez, J. W., 1961. "Christian Acculturation and Fang Witchcraft." Cahiers d' Études Africaines 2:244–270.

Field, M. J., 1960. Search for Security: An Ethno-Psychiatric Study of Rural Ghana. Evanston, Ill.: Northwestern University Press.

Fischer, J., and A. Fischer, 1966. The New Englanders of Orchard Town, U.S.A. New York: Wiley.

Foster, G. M., 1962. Traditional Cultures and the Impact of Technological Change. New York: Harper & Row.

Foulks, E., 1972. "The Arctic Hysterias of the North Alaskan Eskimo." Anthropological Studies 10, American Anthropological Association.

Frazer, J. G., 1911–1915. The Golden Bough, 3rd ed. (12 vols). London: Macmillan.

Freed, S. A., and R. S. Freed, 1964. "Spirit Possession as Illness in a North Indian Village." Ethnology 3:152–171.

Freedman, D. G., C. B. Loring, and R. M. Martin, 1967. "Emotional Behavior and Personality Development." In Y. Brackbill and G. G. Thompson, eds., *Behavior in Infancy and Early Childhood: A Handbook and Guide to Human Development,* 2nd ed. New York: Free Press.

Freeman, D., 1970. "Human Nature and Culture." In R. O. Slater, et al., eds., *Man and the New Biology.* Canberra: The Australian National University Press.

French, D., 1963. "The Relationship of Anthropology to Studies in Perception and Cognition." In S. Koch, ed., *Psychology: A Study of a Science,* vol. 6. New York: McGraw-Hill.

Freud, S., 1950 (orig. 1912–1913). *Totem and Taboo.* New York: Norton.

Frohman, C., and J. Gottlieb, 1974. "The Biochemistry of Schizophrenia." In S. Arieti, ed., *American Handbook of Psychiatry,* vol. 3.

Fromm, E., 1948. "The Oedipus Complex and the Oedipus Myth." In R. N. Anshen, ed., *The Family: Its Function and Destiny.* New York: Harper & Row.

Fry, P., 1976. *Spirits of Protest.* London: Cambridge.

Fujisawa, S., 1953. "A Psychological Study of the Formosan Aborigines." *Japanese Journal of Ethnology* 18(1–2) (in Japanese). Cited in Y. Huzioka, "The Personality of the Hadzapi." *Kyoto University African Studies* 2(1968):147–210.

Furst, P., 1976. *Hallucinogens and Culture.* Corte Madera, Calif.: Chandler and Sharp.

Gardner, R. A., and B. T. Gardner, 1975. "Early Signs of Language in Child and Chimpanzee." *Science* 187:752–753.

Garrison, V., 1977. "The 'Puerto Rican Syndrome' in Psychiatry and *Espiritismo.*" In V. Crapanzano and V. Garrison, eds., *Case Studies in Spirit Possession.* New York: Wiley.

Géber, M., 1956. "Développement Psychomoteur de l'Enfant Africain." *Courrier* 6:17–29.

———, 1961. "Longitudinal Study of Psychomotor Development Among Baganda Children." *Proceedings, 14th International Congress of Applied Psychology.*

———, and R. F. A. Dean, 1967. "Precocious Development of Newborn African Infants." In Y. Brackbill and G. G. Thompson, eds., *Behavior in Infancy and Early Childhood,* 2nd ed. New York: Free Press.

Ginsburg, H. and S. Opper, 1969. Piaget's Theory of Intellectual Development: An Introduction. Englewood Cliffs, N.J.: Prentice-Hall.

Gladwin, T., 1953. "The Role of Man and Woman on Truk: A Problem in Personality and Culture." *Transactions of the New York Academy of Sciences,* Series II, 5:305–309.

———, 1957. "Personality Structure in the Plains." *Anthropological Quarterly* 30:111–124.

———, and S. Sarason, 1953. *Truk: Man in Paradise.* Viking Fund Publications in Anthropology, 20. New York: Wenner-Gren Foundation for Anthropological Research:

Goldfrank, E., 1945. "Socialization, Personality, and the Structure of Pueblo Society." *American Anthropologist* 47:516–539.

Goldschmidt, W., 1976. "Absent Eyes and Idle Hands: Socialization for Low Affect Among the Sebei." In T. Schwartz, ed., *Socialization as Cultural Communication.* Berkeley: University of California Press.

Goldstein, K., 1948. *Language and Language Disturbances: Aphasic Symptom Complexes and Their Significance for Medicine and Theory of Language.* New York: Grune & Stratton.

———, 1960. "Concerning the Concept of 'Primitive'." In S. Diamond, ed., *Culture in History: Essays in Honor of Paul Radin.* New York: Columbia University Press.

Goodale, J. C., 1971. *Tiwi Wives.* Seattle: University of Washington Press.

Goodman, F. D., 1973. "Apostolics of Yucatán: A Case Study of a Religious Movement." In E. Bourguignon, ed., *Religion, Altered States of Consciousness, and Social Change.* Columbus, Ohio: Ohio State University Press.

———, 1974. "Disturbances in the Apostolic Church: A Trance-based Upheaval in Yucatán." In F. D. Goodman, J. H. Henney, and E. Pressel, *Trance, Healing, and Hallucination.* New York: Wiley.

Goody, J., 1977. *The Domestication of the Savage*

Mind. New York: Cambridge University Press.

Gorer, G., 1943. "Themes in Japanese Culture." *Transactions of the New York Academy of Sciences,* ser. 2, 5:106–124.

———, and J. Rickman, 1949. *The People of Great Russia: A Psychological Study.* London: Cressett.

Gould, S. J., 1977. *Ontogeny and Phylogeny.* Cambridge, Mass: Belknap.

Goulet, J., 1975. *Oh's Profit.* New York: Morrow.

Greenbaum, L., 1973a. "Societal Correlates of Possession Trance in Sub-Saharan Africa." In E. Bourguignon, *Religion, Altered States of Consciousness, and Social Change.* Columbus, Ohio: Ohio State University Press.

———, 1973b. "Possession Trance in Sub-Saharan Africa: A Descriptive Analysis of Fourteen Societies." In E. Bourguignon, ed., *Religion, Altered States of Consciousness, and Social Change.* Columbus, Ohio: Ohio State University Press.

Gruber, H. E., and J. J. Vonèche, eds., 1978. *The Essential Piaget: An Interpretive Reference and Guide.* New York: Basic Books.

Gruen, A., 1955. "Dancing Experience and Personality in Relation to Perception." *Psychological Monograph* 14, 69:399.

Gussler, J., 1973. "Social Change, Ecology and Spirit Possession Among the South African Nguni." In E. Bourguignon, ed., *Religion, Altered States of Consciousness, and Social Change.* Columbus, Ohio: Ohio State University Press.

Guthrie, M. G., and D. C. Szanton, 1976. "Folk Diagnosis and Treatment of Schizophrenia: Bargaining with the Spirits in the Philippines." In W. P. Lebra, ed., *Culture Bound Syndromes, Ethnopsychiatry and Alternate Therapies.* Honolulu: University Press of Hawaii.

Hahn, E., 1978. *Look Who's Talking!* New York: Crowell.

Haley, A., 1976. *Roots.* Garden City, N.Y.: Doubleday.

Hall, K. R. L., 1963. "Tool-Using Performances as Indicators of Behavioral Adaptability." *Current Anthropology* 4:479–494.

Hall, R. A., 1953. *Haitian Créole: Grammar,*

Texts. Memoir 74, American Anthropological Association.

Hallowell, A. I., 1939. "Sin, Sex, and Sickness in Saulteaux Belief." *British Journal of Medical Psychology* 18:191–197.

———, 1942. *The Role of Conjuring in Saulteaux Society.* Philadelphia: University of Pennsylvania Press.

———, 1954. "Psychology and Anthropology." In J. Gillin, ed., *For a Science of Social Man.* New York: Macmillan.

———, 1956a. "The Structural and Functional Dimensions of a Human Existence." *Quarterly Review of Biology* 31:88–101.

———, 1956b. "The Rorschach Technique in Personality and Culture Studies." In B. Klopfer, ed., *Developments in the Rorschach Technique.* Vol. 2, *Fields of Application.* Yonkers, N.Y.: World Book Co.

———, 1960. "Self, Society and Culture in Phylogenetic Perspective." In S. Tax, ed., *Evolution after Darwin,* vol. 2, *The Evolution of Man: Mind, Culture and Society.* Chicago: University of Chicago Press.

———, 1961. "The Protocultural Foundations of Human Adaptation." In S. L. Washburn, ed., *Social Life of Early Man.* Viking Fund Publications in Anthropology, 31. New York: Wenner-Gren Foundation for Anthropological Research.

———, 1974 (orig. 1939). "The Recapitulation Theory and Culture." In *Culture and Experience.* Philadelphia: University of Pennsylvania Press.

———, 1974 (orig. 1940). "Aggression in Saulteaux Society." In *Culture and Experience.* Philadelphia: University of Pennsylvania Press.

———, 1974 (orig. 1950). "Personality Structure and the Evolution of Man." In *Culture and Experience.* Philadelphia: University of Pennsylvania Press.

———, 1974 (orig. 1951). "Acculturation and the Personality of the Ojibwa." In *Culture and Experience.* Philadelphia: University of Pennsylvania Press.

———, 1974 (orig. 1954). "The Self and Its Behavioral Environment." In *Culture and Experience.* Philadelphia: University of Pennsylvania Press.

———, 1976 (orig. 1963a). "Personality, Culture and Society in Behavioral Evolution." In R. D. Fogelson et al. eds., *Contributions to Anthropology: Selected Papers of A. I. Hallowell.* Chicago: University of Chicago Press.

———, 1976 (orig. 1963b). "Ojibwa World View and Disease." In F. D. Fogelson et al., eds., *Contributions to Anthropology: Selected Papers of A. I. Hallowell.* Chicago: University of Chicago Press.

———, 1976 (orig. 1965). "The History of Anthropology as an Anthropological Problem." In F. D. Fogelson et al., eds., *Contributions to Anthropology: Selected Papers of A. I. Hallowell.* Chicago: University of Chicago Press.

Hamburg, D. A., 1963. "Emotions in the Perspective of Human Evolution." In P. H. Knapp, ed., *Expression of the Emotions in Man.* New York: International University Press.

Harlow, H. F., 1977. "Review of *Intelligence in Ape and Man,* by David Premack." *American Scientist* 65:639–640.

Harlow, N., 1975. *Sharing the Children: Village Child Rearing in the City.* New York: Harper & Row.

Harner, M. J., 1973a. "The Sound of Rushing Water." In M. J. Harner, ed., *Hallucinogens and Shamanism.* London: Oxford.

———, 1973b. *Jívaro: People of the Sacred Waterfall.* New York: Doubleday-Anchor.

———, ed., 1973. *Hallucinogens and Shamanism.* London, Oxford, New York: Oxford.

Harper, E. B., 1957. "Shamanism in South India." *Southwestern Journal of Anthropology* 13:267–287.

Harris, M., 1968. *The Rise of Anthropological Theory.* New York: Crowell.

———, 1970. "Referential Ambiguity in the Calculus of Brazilian Racial Identity." In N. E. Whitten, Jr., and J. F. Szewd, eds., *Afro-American Anthropology: Contemporary Perspectives.* New York: Free Press.

Hart, C. W. M., 1963. "Contrasts Between Prepubertal and Postpubertal Education." In G. D. Spindler, ed., *Education and Culture: Anthropological Approaches.* New York: Holt, Rinehart and Winston.

Harwood, A., 1977. *Rx: Spiritist as Needed, A Study of a Puerto Rican Community Mental Health Resource.* New York: Wiley.

Hayes, C., 1951. *The Ape in Our House.* New York: Harper & Row.

Heider, E. R., 1971. " 'Focal' Color Areas and the Development of Color Names." *Developmental Psychology* 4:447–455.

———, 1972. "Universals in Color Naming and Memory." *Journal of Experimental Psychology* 93:10–20.

Heider, K., 1970. *The Dugum Dani: A Papuan Culture in the Highlands of New Guinea.* Viking Fund Publication 49. New York: Wenner-Gren Foundation for Anthropological Research.

Henney, J. H., 1973. "The Shakers of St. Vincent: A Stable Religion." In E. Bourguignon, ed., *Religion, Altered States of Consciousness and Social Change.* Columbus, Ohio: Ohio State University Press.

———, 1974. "Spirit Possession Belief and Trance Behavior in Two Fundamentalist Groups in St. Vincent." In F. D. Goodman, J. H. Henney and E. Pressel, *Trance, Healing, and Hallucination: Three Field Studies in Religious Experience.* New York: Wiley.

Henry, J., 1959. "Culture, Personality and Evolution." *American Anthropologist* 61:221–226.

———, 1964 (orig. 1941). *Jungle People.* New York: Vintage Books.

Herskovits, M. J., 1937a. *Life in a Haitian Valley.* New York: Knopf.

———, 1937b. "African Gods and Catholic Saints in New World Negro Belief." *American Anthropologist* 39:635–643.

———, 1948. *Man and His Works: The Science of Cultural Anthropology.* New York: Knopf.

———, 1966 (orig. 1945). "Problems, Method, and Theory in Afro-American Studies." In F. S. Herskovits, ed., *The New World Negro.* Bloomington, Ind.: Indiana University Press.

———, 1973. *Cultural Relativism,* F. S. Herskovits, ed. New York: Random House.

———, and F. S. Herskovits, 1958. *Dahomean Narrative.* Evanston, Ill.: Northwestern University Press.

Hewes, G. W., 1973. "Primate Communication and the Gestural Origin of Language." *Current Anthropology* 14:5–24

Hicks, D., 1976. *Tetum Ghosts and Kin.* Palo Alto: Mayfield.

Himwich, H. E., 1971. *Biochemistry, Schizophrenia and Affective Illness.* Baltimore: Williams & Wilkins.

Hockett, C., 1960. "The Origin of Speech." *Scientific American* 203:88–96.

———, 1973. *Man's Place in Nature.* New York: McGraw-Hill.

———, and R. Ascher, 1964. "The Human Revolution." *Current Anthropology* 5:135–147.

Holtzman, W. H., 1964. "Recurring Dilemmas in Personality Assessment." *Journal of Projective Techniques and Personality Assessment* 28:144–150.

Honigmann, J. J., 1954. *Culture and Personality.* New York: Harper & Row.

———, 1961. "The Interpretation of Dreams in Anthropological Fieldwork." In B. Kaplan, ed., *Studying Personality Cross-Culturally.* Evanston, Ill.: Row, Peterson.

Horton, R., 1969. "Types of Spirit Possession in Kalabari Religion." In J. Beattie and J. Middleton, eds., *Spirit Mediumship and Society in Africa.* New York: Africana.

HRAF, 1978. *A Guide to Social Theory: Worldwide Cross-Cultural Tests,* 5 vols. New Haven, Conn.: HRAF Press.

Hsu, F. L. K., 1948. *Under the Ancestors' Shadow: Chinese Culture and Personality,* rev. 1971. New York: Columbia University Press.

———, 1953. *Americans and Chinese: Two Ways of Life,* rev. 1970. New York: Abelard-Schuman.

———, 1963. *Clan, Caste, and Club: A Comparative Study of Chinese, Hindu and American Ways of Life.* Princeton, N.J.: Van Nostrand.

———, 1969. *The Study of Literate Civilizations.* New York: Holt, Rinehart and Winston.

———, 1971a. "Psychosocial Homeostasis and *Jen:* Conceptual Tools for Advancing Psychological Anthropology." *American Anthropologist* 73:23–44.

———, 1972a. "Kinship and Ways of Life." In F. L. K. Hsu, ed., *Psychological Anthropology,* new ed. Cambridge, Mass.: Schenkman.

———, 1972b. "Introduction: Psychological Anthropology in the Behavioral Sciences." In F. L. K. Hsu, ed., *Psychological Anthropology,* new ed. Cambridge, Mass.: Schenkman.

———, 1975. *Iemoto: The Heart of Japan.* Cambridge, Mass: Schenkman.

———, 1978a. "The Art of Teaching the Human Science." Report on Teaching, 5. *Change: The Magazine of Learning* 10:6–7.

———, 1978b. "Passage to Understanding." In G. D. Spindler, ed., *The Making of Psychological Anthropology.* Berkeley: University of California Press.

———, ed., 1971b. *Kinship and Culture.* Chicago: Aldine.

Huzioka, Y., 1968. "The Personality of the Hadzapi: An Approach to the Evolution of Personality." *Kyoto University African Studies* 2:147–210.

Inkeles, A., 1972. "National Character and Modern Political Systems." In F. L. K. Hsu, ed., *Psychological Anthropology,* new ed. Cambridge, Mass.: Schenkman.

———, and D. J. Levinson, 1968. "National Character: The Study of Modal Personality and Sociocultural Systems." In G. Lindzey and E. Aron, eds., *Handbook of Social Psychology,* 2nd rev. ed., vol. 4. Reading, Mass.: Addison-Wesley.

Jahoda, G. 1958a. "Child Animism: I. A Critical Survey of Cross-Cultural Research." *Journal of Social Psychology* 47:147–212.

———, 1958b. "Child Animism: II. A Study in West Africa." *Journal of Social Psychology* 47:213–222.

———, 1966. "Geometric Illusions and Environment: A Study in Ghana." *British Journal of Psychology* 57:193–199.

———, 1971. "Retinal Pigmentation, Illusion Susceptibility and Space Perception." *International Journal of Psychology* 6:99–208.

Jerison, H. J., 1973. *Evolution of the Brain and Intelligence.* New York: Academic Press.

———, 1975a. Author's Precis and Reply, C. A.* Book Review of *Evolution of the Brain and Intelligence. Current Anthropology* 18:403–404; 415–426.

———, 1975b. "Fossil Evidence of the Evolution of the Human Brain." *Annual Review of Anthropology* 4:27–58.

———, 1976. "Paleoneurology and the Evolution of Mind." *Scientific American* 234:90–101.

Jilek, W. G., 1974. *Salish Indian Mental Health and Culture Change: Psychohygienic and*

Therapeutic Aspects of the Guardian Spirit Ceremonial. Toronto: Holt, Rinehart and Winston of Canada.

Johnston, T. F., 1977. "Auditory Driving, Hallucinogens, and Music-Color Synesthesia in Tsonga Ritual." In B. M. Du Toit, ed., *Drugs, Rituals, and Altered States of Consciousness.* Rotterdam: A. A. Balkema.

Jolly, A. 1972. *The Evolution of Primate Behavior.* New York: Macmillan.

Jones, D. E., 1972. *Sanapia: Comanche Medicine Woman.* New York: Holt, Rinehart and Winston.

Kaelbling, R., 1961. "Comparative Psychopathology and Psychotherapy." *Acta Psychotherapeutica* 9:10–28.

Kaffman, M., 1977. "Sexual Standards and Behavior of the Kibbutz Adolescent." *American Journal of Orthopsychiatry* 47:207–217.

Kanters, R. M., D. L. Clark, L. C. Allen, and M. F. Chase, 1976. "Effects of Vestibular Stimulation on Nystagmus Response and Motor Performance in the Developmentally Delayed Infant." *Physical Therapy* 56:414–421.

Kardiner, A., 1939. *The Individual and His Society: The Psychodynamics of Primitive Social Organization.* With foreword and two ethnological reports by R. Linton. New York: Columbia University Press.

———, 1945b. "The Concept of Basic Personality Structure as an Operational Tool in the Social Sciences." In R. Linton, ed., *The Science of Man in the World Crisis.* New York: Columbia University Press.

———, 1963 (orig. 1945a). *The Psychological Frontiers of Society.* With collaboration of R. Linton, C. DuBois and J. West. New York: Columbia University Press (paperback reprint).

Katz, R., 1973. "Education for Transcendence: Lessons from the !Kung Zhu/Twasi." *Journal of Transpersonal Psychology* 2:136–155.

———, 1976. "The Painful Ecstasy of Healing." *Psychology Today* 1976:81–86.

Kay, P., 1970. "Some Theoretical Implications of Ethnographic Semantics." In A. Fischer, ed., *Current Directions in Anthropology, Bulletin of the American Anthropological Association* 3(3, part 2). Washington, D.C.: American Anthropological Association.

———, and C. K. McDaniel, 1975. *Color Categories as Fuzzy Sets.* Working Paper 44, Language Behavior Research Laboratory. Berkeley: University of California.

Kennedy, J. G. 1977 (orig. 1967). "Nubian Zar Ceremonies as Psychotherapy." In D. Landy, ed., *Culture, Disease and Healing: Studies in Medical Anthropology.* New York: Macmillan.

Kessler, C., 1977. "Conflict and Sovereignty in Kelantanese Malay Spirit Seances." In V. Crapanzano and V. Garrison, eds., *Case Studies in Spirit Possession.* New York: Wiley.

Kiefer, C. W., and O. Cowan, n.d. *State/Context Dependence and Theories of Ritual.* Unpublished Manuscript.

Kilbride, J. E., M. C. Robbins, and P. L. Kilbride, 1970. "The Comparative Motor Development of Baganda, American White and American Black Infants." *American Anthropologist* 72:1422–1428.

Kilbride, P. L., and M. C. Robbins, 1969. "Pictorial Depth Perception of Acculturation Among the Baganda." *American Anthropologist* 71:293–301.

Kimball, L. A., 1970. "First Words of a Brunei Child." *Brunei Museum Journal* 2:67–86.

———, 1972. "First Phrases of a Brunei Child." *Brunei Museum Journal* 2:173–182.

———, 1975. *The Enculturation of Aggression in a Brunei Malay Village.* Ann Arbor: University Microfilms.

Kitigawa, J. M., 1960. "Ainu Bear Festival (Iyomonte)." *History of Religions* 1:95–151.

Klaus, M. H., and J. H. Kennel, 1970. "Mothers Separated from Their Newborn Infants." *Pediatrics Clinics of North America* 17:1015–1037.

Klineberg, O., 1940. *Social Psychology.* New York: Henry Holt.

Kluckhohn, C., 1944. "The Influence of Psychiatry on Anthropology in America During the Past 100 Years." In J. K. Hall, G. Zilborg, and H. A. Bunker, eds., *100 Years of American Psychiatry, 1844–1944.* New York: Syracuse University Press.

———, and W. M. Morgan, 1951. "Some Notes on Navaho Dreams." In G. B. Wilbur and W. Muensterberger, eds., *Psychoanalysis and Culture, Essays in Honor of Géza Róheim.* New York: International University Press.

———, 1967 (orig. 1944). *Navaho Witchcraft.* Boston: Beacon.

Konner, M. J., 1976. "Maternal Care, Infant Behavior and Development Among the !Kung." In R. Lee and I. DeVore, eds. *Kalahari Hunter–Gatherers.* Cambridge, Mass.: Harvard University Press.

Koss, J., n.d. "Social Process, Healing, and Self Defeat Among Puerto Rican Spiritists." *American Ethnologist* (forthcoming).

Kortlandt, A., 1973. "Comment on *Primate Communication and Gestural Origin of Language,* by G. W. Hewes." *Current Anthropology* 14:13–14.

Kroeber, A. L., 1925. "The Yurok," *Handbook of Indians of California.* Bureau of American Ethnology, Bulletin 78.

———, 1972a (orig. 1920). "Totem and Taboo: An Ethnologic Psychoanalysis." In W. A. Lessa and E. Z. Vogt, eds., *Reader in Comparative Religion,* 3rd ed. New York: Harper & Row.

———, 1972b (orig. 1939). "Totem and Taboo in Retrospect." In W. A. Lessa and E. Z. Vogt, eds., *Reader in Comparative Religion,* 3rd ed. New York: Harper & Row.

Kroeber, T., 1961. *Ishi in Two Worlds.* Berkeley: University of California Press.

La Barre, W., 1945. "Some Observations on Character Structure in the Orient: The Japanese." *Psychiatry* 8:319–342.

———, 1956 (orig. 1947). "The Cultural Basis of Emotion and Gesture." In D. G. Haring, ed., *Personal Character and Cultural Milieu,* 3rd ed. Syracuse: Syracuse University Press.

———, 1964. "Confessions as Psychotherapy in American Indian Tribes." In A. Kiev, ed., *Magic, Faith and Healing.* New York: Free Press.

———, 1970. *The Ghost Dance: The Origins of Religion.* New York: Doubleday.

———, 1971. "Materials for a History of Crisis Cults: A Bibliographic Essay." *Current Anthropology* 12:3–44.

———, 1972. "Hallucinogens and the Shamanic Origins of Religion." In P. T. Fürst, ed., *Flesh of the Gods.* New York: Praeger.

———, 1975. "Anthropological Perspectives on Hallucination and Hallucinogens." In R. K. Siegel and L. J. West, eds., *Hallucination: Behavior, Experience and Theory.* New York: Wiley.

Labat, P., 1724. *Nouveau Voyage aux Isles de l'Amérique,* 2 vols. The Hague.

Lambert, W. W., 1974. *A Study of Children's Aggressive Action in Six Cultures.* Ann Arbor: University Microfilms.

———, L. Triandis, and M. Wolf, 1959. "Some Correlates of Beliefs in the Malevolence and Benevolence of Supernatural Beings: A Cross-Cultural Study." *Journal of Abnormal and Social Psychology* 58:162–168.

Lambo, T. A., 1964. "Patterns of Psychiatric Care in Developing African Countries." In A. Kiev, ed., *Magic, Faith, and Healing.* Glencoe, N.Y.: Free Press.

Lame Deer, J., and R. Erdoes, 1972. *Lame Deer, Seeker of Visions.* New York: Simon & Schuster.

Langness, L. L., 1965a. "Hysterical Psychosis in the New Guinea Highlands: A Bena Bena Example." *Psychiatry* 28:258–277.

———, 1965b. *The Life History in Anthropological Science.* New York: Holt, Rinehart and Winston.

———, 1976. "Hysterical Psychoses and Possessions." In W. P. Lebra, ed., *Culture-Bound Syndromes, Ethnopsychiatry and Alternate Therapies.* Honolulu: University Press of Hawaii.

Lanternari, V., 1963. *The Religion of the Oppressed: A Study of Modern Messianic Cults.* New York: Knopf.

Lantz, D., and V. Stefflre, 1964. "Language and Cognition Revisited." *Journal of Abnormal and Social Psychology* 69:472–481.

Lawick-Goodall, J. van, 1968. "The Behavior of Free-Living Chimpanzees in the Gombe Stream Reserves." *Animal Behavior Monographs* 1:165–311.

———, 1971. *In the Shadow of Man.* Boston: Houghton Mifflin.

Lebra, T. S., and W. P. Lebra, eds., 1974. *Japanese Culture and Behavior.* Honolulu: University of Hawaii Press.

Lee, R. B., 1968. "The Sociology of the !Kung Bushman Trance Performances." In R. Prince, ed., *Trance and Possession States.* Montreal: R. M. Bucke Memorial Society.

Le Gros Clark, W. E., 1967. *Man-Apes or Ape-Men? The Story of Discoveries in Africa.* New York: Holt, Rinehart and Winston.

Leiderman, P. H., and G. F. Leiderman, 1977. "Economic Change and Infant Care in an East African Agricultural Community." In P. H. Leiderman, S. E. Tulkin, and R. Rosenfeld, eds., *Culture and Infancy: Variations in Human Experience.* New York: Academic Press.

Leiris, M., 1958. "La Possession et ses Aspects Théâtraux chez les Ethiopiens de Gondar." *L'Homme, Cahiers d'Ethnologie, de Géographie et de Linguistique,* nouvelle série, 1, Paris.

Leis, N., 1974. "Women in Groups: Ijaw Women's Associations." In M. Z. Rosaldo and L. Lamphere, eds., *Women, Culture, and Society.* Stanford, Calif.: Stanford University Press.

Lemert, E., 1967. *Human Deviance, Social Problems and Social Control.* Englewood Cliffs, N.J.: Prentice-Hall.

Lenneberg, E. H., and J. Roberts, 1956. "The Language of Experience, A Study in Methodology." Memoir 13. *International Journal of American Linguistics* 22.

Lerch, P., 1978. *The Role of Women in Possession Trance Cults of Brazil.* Unpublished Doctoral Dissertation, Ohio State University. Ann Arbor, Mich.: University Microfilms.

LeVine, R. A. 1966. *Dreams and Deeds: Achievement Motivation in Nigeria.* Chicago: University of Chicago Press.

———, 1973. *Culture, Behavior, and Personality.* Chicago: Aldine.

———, 1976. "Patterns of Personality in Africa." In G. DeVos, ed., *Responses to Change: Society, Culture, and Personality.* New York: Van Nostrand.

———, and B. LeVine, 1966. *Nyasongo: A Gusii Community in Kenya,* New York: Wiley.

Lévi-Strauss, C., 1962. *La Pensée Sauvage.* Paris: Plon. Translated as *The Savage Mind.* New York: Praeger, 1966.

———, 1963. "The Effectiveness of Symbols." In C. Lévi-Strauss, *Structural Anthropology.* New York: Basic Books.

Lévy-Bruhl, L., 1949. *Les Carnets de Lucien Lévy-Bruhl.* Paris: Presses Universitaires de France.

Lewin, B., 1957. "Die Konfliktneurose der Mohammedanerin in Ägypten." *Zeitschrift für Psychotherapie und medizinsche Psychologie* 8:98–112.

Lewis, I. M., 1971. *Ecstatic Religion: An Anthropological Study of Spirit Possession and Shamanism.* Baltimore: Penguin.

———, 1977. Introduction. In I. M. Lewis, ed., *Symbols and Sentiments: Cross-Cultural Studies in Symbolism.* London, New York, and San Francisco: Academic Press.

Lewis, O., 1959. *Five Families: Mexican Case Studies in the Culture of Poverty.* New York: Basic Books.

———, 1961. *The Children of Sánchez.* New York: Random House.

———, 1964. *Pedro Martínez.* New York: Random House.

———, 1965. *La Vida: A Puerto Rican Family in the Culture of Poverty/San Juan and New York.* New York: Random House.

———, 1966. *A Death in the Sánchez Family.* New York: Random House.

———, R. Lewis, and S. M. Ringdon, 1977. *Four Women: Living the Revolution. An Oral History of Contemporary Cuba.* Urbana, Ill.: University of Illinois Press.

Lienhardt, G., 1954. "The Shilluk of the Upper Nile." In D. Forde, ed., *African Worlds.* London: Oxford.

Lifton, R. J., 1971. *History and Human Survival.* New York: Vintage Books.

Lindzey, G., 1961. *Projective Techniques and Cross-Cultural Research.* New York: Appleton-Century-Crofts.

Livingstone, F. B., 1978. "Biological and Cultural Determinants of Human Behavior." Paper read at the Symposium on Sociobiology, Annual Meeting of the American Association for the Advancement of Science.

Lorenz, K., 1966. *On Aggression.* New York: Harcourt, Brace.

Loring, R. K., and H. A. Otto, 1976. *New Life Options: The Working Woman's Resource Book.* New York: McGraw-Hill.

Lowie, R. H., 1937. *The History of Ethnological Theory.* New York: Farrar & Rinehart.

Ludwig, A. M., 1968. "Altered States of Consciousness." In R. Prince, ed., *Trance and Possession States.* Montreal: R. M. Bucke Memorial Society.

Lurie, N. O., 1961. *Mountain Wolf Woman, Sister of Crashing Thunder: The Autobiography of a Winnebago Woman.* Ann Arbor, Mich.: University of Michigan Press.

MacArthur, R., 1969. "Sex Differences in Field Dependence for the Eskimo: Replication of Berry's Findings." In D. R. Price-Williams, ed., *Cross-Cultural Studies.* Baltimore: Penguin.

Macklin, J., 1977. "A Connecticut Yankee in Summer Land." In V. Crapanzano and V.

Garrison, ed.; *Case Studies in Spirit Possession.* New York: Wiley.

Madariaga, S., de, 1969. (orig. 1928) *Englishmen, Frenchmen, Spaniards.* New York: Hill & Wang.

Malinowski, B., 1927. *The Father in Primitive Psychology.* New York: Norton.

———, 1955 (orig. 1927). *Sex and Repression in Savage Society.* New York: Meridian.

Mandelbaum, D. G., 1973. "The Study of Life History: Gandhi." *Current Anthropology* 14:177–206.

Maretzki, T. W., and Maretski, H., 1966. *Taira: An Okinawan Village.* New York: Wiley.

Mars, L., 1947. *La Lutte contre la Folie.* Port-au-Prince, Haiti: Imprimerie de l'Etat.

Marshak, A. 1976. "Some Implications of Paleolithic Symbolic Evidence of the Origin of Language." *Current Anthropology* 17:274–281.

Marshall, L. 1965. "The !Kung Bushmen of the Kalahari Desert." In J. L. Gibbs, ed., *Peoples of Africa.* New York: Holt, Rinehart and Winston.

McClelland, D. C., 1961. *The Achieving Society.* New York: Van Nostrand.

———, J. W. Atkinson, R. Clark, and E. Lowell, 1953. *The Achievement Motive.* New York: Appleton-Century-Crofts.

McGuire, K. 1976. *People, Prayer, and Promise: An Anthropological Analysis of a Catholic Charismatic Covenant Community.* Ann Arbor, Mich.: University Microfilms.

Mead, M. 1928. *Coming of Age in Samoa.* New York: Morrow.

———, 1935. *Sex and Temperament in Three Primitive Societies.* New York: Morrow.

———, 1952. "Some Relationships Between Social Anthropology and Psychiatry." In F. Alexander and H. Ross, eds., *Dynamic Psychiatry.* Chicago: University of Chicago Press.

———, 1953. "National Character." In A. L. Kroeber, ed., *Anthropology Today.* Chicago: University of Chicago Press.

———, 1954. "The Swaddling Hypothesis: Its Reception." *American Anthropologist* 56:395–405.

———, 1956a. "Some Uses of Still Photography in Culture and Personality Studies." In D. Haring, ed., *Personal Character and the Cultural Milieu,* 3rd ed. Syracuse: Syracuse University Press.

———, 1956b. *New Lives for Old.* New York: Morrow.

———, 1961. Preface in R. Benedict, *Patterns of Culture.* Boston: Houghton Mifflin.

———, 1963. "Socialization and Enculturation." *Current Anthropology* 4:184–188.

———, 1964. *Continuities in Cultural Evolution.* New Haven: Yale University Press.

———, 1967 (orig. 1932). "An Investigation of the Thought of Primitive Children with Special Reference to Animism: A Preliminary Report." In Robert Hunt, ed., *Personalities and Cultures: Readings in Psychological Anthropology.* Garden City, N.Y.: Natural History Press.

———, 1972. *Blackberry Winter: My Earlier Years.* New York: Simon & Schuster.

———, 1975. "Review of R. B. Edgerton, *The Individual in Cultural Adaptation: A Study of Four East African Peoples.*" *American Anthropologist* 77:638–639.

———, 1978. "The Evocation of Psychologically Relevant Responses in Ethnological Field Work." In G. Spindler, ed., *The Making of Psychological Anthropology.* Berkeley: The University of California Press.

———, and R. Métraux, eds., 1953. *Studies of Culture at a Distance.* Chicago: University of Chicago Press.

Messing, S. D., 1959. "Group Therapy and Social Status in the Zar Cult of Ethiopia." In M. K. Opler, ed., *Culture and Mental Health: Cross-Cultural Studies.* New York: Macmillan.

Métraux, A., 1959a. *Voodoo in Haiti.* London and New York: Oxford.

———, 1959b. "The Revolution of the Ax." *Diogenes* 25:28–40.

Métraux, R. 1976. "Eidos and Change: Continuity in Process, Discontinuity in Products." In T. Schwartz, ed., *Socialization as Cultural Communication: Development of a Theme in the Work of Margaret Mead.* Berkeley: University of California Press.

Miller, G. A., 1971. Foreword. In M. Cole, J. Gay, J. A. Glick and D. W. Sharp, *The Cultural Context of Learning and Thinking.* New York: Basic Books.

Minturn, L., and Hitchcock, J. T., 1966. *The Rajputs of Khalapur, India.* New York: Wiley.

———, and W. W. Lambert, 1964. *Mothers of*

Six Cultures: Antecedents of Child Rearing. New York: Wiley.

Miyadi, D., 1967. "Differences in Social Behavior Among Japanese Macaque Troops." In D. Starck, R. Schneider, and H. J. Kuhn, eds., *Neue Ergebnisse der Primatologie.* Stuttgart: Fischer.

Monfouga-Nicolas, J., 1972. *Ambivalence et Culte de Possession.* Paris: Editions Anthropos.

Montgomery, E. 1975. "Trance Mediumship Therapy in Southern India: A Transcript of a Session." *Ethnomedizin* 3:11–26.

Mooney, J. 1965 (orig. 1896). *The Ghost Dance Religion and the Sioux Outbreak of 1890.* Abridged and with an Introduction by A. F. C. Wallace. Chicago: Phoenix Books, University of Chicago Press.

Moore, F. W., ed., 1961. *Readings in Cross-Cultural Methodology.* New Haven: HRAF Press.

Morgan, L. H., 1877. *Ancient Society.* New York: World.

Morton, A., 1977. "Dawit: Competition and Integration in an Ethiopian Wuqabi Cult." In V. Crapanzano and V. Garrison, eds., *Case Studies in Spirit Possession.* New York: Wiley.

Mounin, G. 1976. "Language, Communication, Chimpanzees," with C. A.* comment. *Current Anthropology* 17:1–22.

Munroe, R. L., R. H. Munroe, and R. A. LeVine, 1972. "Africa." In F. L. K. Hsu, ed., *Psychological Anthropology,* new ed. Cambridge, Mass.: Schenkman.

Murdock, G. P., 1957. "World Ethnographic Sample." *American Anthropologist* 59:664–687.

———, 1963. *An Outline of World Cultures.* New Haven, Conn.: HRAF Press.

———, 1967. *Ethnographic Atlas.* Pittsburgh: University of Pittsburgh Press.

———, C. S. Ford, A. E. Hudson, R. Kennedy, L. W. Simmons, and J. W. M. Whiting, 1965. *Outline of Cultural Materials,* 4th rev. ed. *Behavior Science Outlines,* vol. 1. New Haven: Human Relations Area Files.

Murphy, H. M. B., 1973. "History and the Evolution of Syndromes: The Striking Case of Latah and Amok." In M. Hammer, K. Salzinger, and S. Stutton, eds, *Psychopathology: Contributions from the Social, Behavi-*

oral and Biological Sciences. New York: Wiley.

Murphy, J. 1976. "Psychiatric Labeling in Cross-Cultural Perspectives (Yoruba and Eskimo)." *Science* 191:1019–1028.

Nadel, S. F., 1952. "Witchcraft in Four African Societies." *American Anthropologist* 54:18–29.

Naroll, R. 1970. "What Have We Learned from Cross-Cultural Surveys?" *American Anthropologist* 72:1227–1288.

———, and R. Cohen, 1970. *Handbook of Methods in Cultural Anthropology.* Garden City, N.Y.: Natural History Press.

Nissen, H. W. 1931. "A Field Study of the Chimpanzee: Observations of Chimpanzee Behavior and Environment in Western French Guinea." *Comparative Psychology Monographs* 8:1–122.

Norbeck, E., D. Price-Williams, and W. M. McCord, eds., 1968. *The Study of Personality: An Interdisciplinary Approach.* New York: Holt, Rinehart and Winston.

Nydegger, W. F., and Nydegger, C., 1966. *Tarong: An Ilocos Barrio in the Philippines.* New York: Wiley.

Ombredane, A., 1954. "L'Exploration de la Mentalité des Noirs Congolais au Moyen d'une Epreuve Projective, la Congo T.A.T." Institut Royal Colonial Belge.

Opler, M. K., 1958. "Spirit Possession in a Rural Area of Northern India." In W. A. Lessa and E. Z. Vogt, eds., *Reader in Comparative Religion.* Evanston, Ill.: Row, Peterson.

———, 1967 (orig. 1960). "Cultural Evolution and the Psychology of Peoples." In *Culture and Social Psychiatry.* New York: Atherton.

Ornstein, R. E., 1972. *The Psychology of Consciousness.* New York: Viking.

Ortigues, M., and E. Ortigues, 1966. *Oedipe Africain.* Paris: Plon.

Owen, D. H., 1978. "The Psychophysics of Prior Experience." In P. K. Machamer and R. G. Turnbull, eds, *Studies in Perception: Interrelations in the Philosophy and History of Science.* Columbus, Ohio: Ohio State University Press.

Parker, S., 1976. "The Precultural Basis of the Incest Taboo: Toward a Bio-Social Theory." *American Anthropologist* 78:285–305.

Parsons, A., 1967 (orig. 1964). "Is the Oedipus Complex Universal? A South Italian 'Nuclear Complex'." In R. Hunt, *Personalities and Cultures: Readings in Psychological Anthropology.* Garden City, N.Y.: Natural History Press.

Pattison, E. M. 1974. "Ideological Support for the Marginal Middle Class: Faith, Healing and Glossolalia." In I. I. Zaretsky and M. P. Leone, eds., *Religious Movements in Contemporary America.* Princeton, N.J.: Princeton University Press.

Paul, R. A., 1976. "Did the Primal Crime Take Place?" *Ethos* 4:211–248.

Pfeiffer, W. M., 1971. *Transkulturelle Psychiatrie: Ergebnisse und Probleme.* Stuttgart: Georg Thieme Verlag.

Piaget, J., 1928. *Judgement and Reasoning in the Child.* New York: Harcourt, Brace.

———, and B. Inhelder, 1969. *The Psychology of the Child.* New York: Basic Books.

———, and S. Opper, 1969. *Piaget's Theory of Intellectual Development: An Introduction.* Englewood Cliffs, N.J.: Prentice-Hall.

Pike, K. 1954. *Language in Relation to a Unified Theory of the Structure of Human Behavior,* Part I. Glendale: Summer Institute of Linguistics.

———, 1966. *Language in Relation to a Unified Theory of the Structure of Human Behavior.* The Hague: Mouton.

Pollack, R. H. 1970. "Müller-Lyer illusion: Effect of Age, Lightness, Contrast and Hue." *Science* 170:93–94.

Pollnac, R., 1975. "Intracultural Variability in the Structure of the Subjective Color Lexicon in Buganda." *American Ethnologist* 2:89–109.

Powdermaker, H., 1945. "Review of *People of Alor* by Cora DuBois." *American Anthropologist* 47:160.

Precourt, W. E., 1975. "Initiation Ceremonies and Secret Societies as Educational Institutions." In R. W. Brislin, S. Bochner, and W. J. Lonner, eds., *Cross-Cultural Perspectives on Learning.* New York: Wiley.

Premack, D., 1976a. *Intelligence in Ape and Man.* Hillsdale, N.J.: Halsted Press.

———, 1976b. "Mechanisms of Intelligence: Preconditions for Language." Conference on the Origins and Evolution of Language and Speech. *Annals of the N.Y. Academy of Sciences* 280:544–561.

Pressel, E. 1973. "Umbanda in São Paulo: Religious Innovation in a Developing Society." In E. Bourguignon, ed., *Religion, Altered States of Consciousness, and Social Change.* Columbus, Ohio: Ohio State University Press.

———, 1974. "Umbanda Trance and Possession in São Paulo, Brazil." In F. Goodman, J. Henney, and E. Pressel, *Trance, Healing and Hallucination.* New York: Wiley.

Price-Williams, D. R., 1975. *Explorations in Cross-Cultural Psychology.* San Francisco: Chandler and Sharp.

Prince, R., 1964. "Indigenous Yoruba Psychiatry." In A. Kiev, ed., *Magic, Faith, and Healing.* Glencoe, N.Y.: Free Press.

———, 1976. "Psychotherapy as the Manipulation of Endogenous Healing Mechanisms: A Transcultural Survey." *Transcultural Psychiatric Research Review* 13:115–134.

———, 1979a. "Variations in Psychotherapeutic Procedures." In H. C. Triandis, R. Brislin, and J. Draguns, *Handbook of Cross-Cultural Psychology,* vol. 5. Boston: Allyn and Bacon.

———, 1979b. "The Psychiatrist and the Folk Healer: Interface and Partnership." In G. G. Meyer and K. Blum, eds., *Herbal Medicine and Folk Healing.* Austin, Texas: University of Texas Press.

Proust, M. 1932–1934. *Remembrance of Things Past,* trans. by C. K. Scott-Moncrieff. New York: Random House.

Rabin, A. I., 1965. *Growing Up in the Kibbutz.* New York: Springer.

———, 1968. *Projective Techniques in Personality Assessment.* New York: Springer.

———, and Bertha Hanzan, eds., 1973. *Collective Education in the Kibbutz from Infancy to Maturity.* New York: Springer.

Radin, P. 1925. *Crashing Thunder: the Autobiography of a Winnebago Indian.* New York: Appleton-Century-Crofts.

Rauf, M., 1965. Personal Communication.

Read, M., 1960. *Children of Their Fathers: Growing up among the Nguni of Malawi.* New Haven: Yale University Press.

Reichel-Dolmatoff, G., 1971. *Amazonian Cosmos: The Sexual and Religious Symbolism of the Tukano Indians.* Chicago: University of Chicago Press.

———, 1972. "The Cultural Context of an Aboriginal Hallucinogen: Banisteriopsis caapi." In P. T. Fürst, ed., *Flesh of the Gods.* New York: Praeger.

Ribeiro, R., 1956. "Possessão: Problema de Etnopsicologia." *Boletim do Instituto Joaquim Nabuco* 5:5–44.

Rivers, W. H. R., 1901. "Introduction and Vision." In A. C. Haddon, ed., *Reports of the Cambridge Anthropological Expedition to the Torres Straits,* vol. 2, pt. 1. London: Cambridge.

Robbins, T., 1969. "Eastern Mysticism and the Resocialization of Drug Users: The Meher Baba Cult." *Journal for the Scientific Study of Religion* 8:308–317.

———, and D. Anthony, 1972, "Getting Straight with Meheir Baba." *Journal for the Scientific Study of Religion* 11: 122–140.

Roberts, J. M., M. J. Arth, and R. R. Bush, 1959. "Games in Culture." *American Anthropologist* 61:597–605.

———, and B. Sutton-Smith, 1962. "Child Training and Game Involvement." *Ethnology* 1:166–185.

———, and A. Kendon, 1963. "Strategy in Games and Folk Tales." *Journal of Social Psychology* 61:185–199.

Róheim, G., 1932. "Psychoanalysis of Primitive Culture Types." *International Journal of Psychoanalysis* 13:1–224.

———, 1934. "The Study of Character Development and the Ontogenetic Theory of Culture." In E. E. Evans-Pritchard, R. Firth, B. Malinowski, and I. Schapera, eds., *Essays Presented to C. G. Seligman.* London: Paul, Trench, Trübner and Co.

———, 1947. "Dream Analysis and Field Work in Anthropology." *Psychoanalysis and the Social Sciences* 1:87–130.

———, 1976. *Children of the Desert: The Western Tribes of Central Australia.* Edited and with an introduction by W. Muensterberger. New York: Harper.

Rohner, R. P., 1975. *They Love Me, They Love Me Not: Worldwide Study of Parental Rejection.* New Haven: HRAF Press.

Rokeach, M., 1964. *The Three Christs of Ypsilanti.* New York: Knopf.

Roman, K. G., 1952. Handwriting. A Key to Personality. New York: Pantheon.

Romney, K., and R. Romney, 1966. *The Mixtecans of Juxtlahuaca, Mexico.* New York: Wiley.

Rosch, E., 1975. "Universals and Cultural Specifics in Human Categorization." In Brislin et al, eds., *Cross-Cultural Perspectives on Learning.* New York: Wiley.

Rowell, T., 1972. *Social Behavior in Monkeys.* Baltimore: Penguin.

———, 1976. "Growing Up in a Monkey Group." In T. Schwartz, ed., *Socialization as Cultural Communication.* Berkeley, Calif.: University of California Press.

Rumbaugh, D., ed., 1977. *Language Learning by a Chimpanzee: The Lana Project.* New York: Academic Press.

———, and J. V. Gill, 1976. "Language and the Acquisition of Language-Type Skills by a Chimpanzee *(Pan).*" *Annals of the New York Academy of Sciences* 270:90–123.

Sapir, E., 1938. "Why Cultural Anthropology Needs the Psychiatrist." *Psychiatry* 1:7–12.

———, 1949 (orig. 1916). "Time Perspectives in Native North America." In D. Mandelbaum, ed., *Selected Writings of Edward Sapir in Language, Culture and Personality.* Berkeley, Calif.: University of California Press.

———, 1949 (orig. 1934). "Emergence of a Concept of Personality in a Study of Cultures." In D. Mandelbaum, ed., *Selected Writings of Edward Sapir in Language, Culture and Personality.* Berkeley, Calif.: University of California Press.

Sargant, W., 1959 (orig. 1957). *The Battle for the Mind.* Baltimore: Penguin.

———, 1974. *The Mind Possessed.* Philadelphia: Lippincott.

Sasaki, Y., 1969. "Psychiatric Study of the Shaman in Japan." In W. Caudill and T. Lin, eds., *Mental Health Research in Asia and the Pacific.* Honolulu: East-West Center Press.

Saunders, L. W., 1977. "Variants in Zar Experience in an Egyptian Village." In V. Crapanzano and V. Garrison, eds., *Case Studies in Spirit Possession.* New York: Wiley

Schachtel, E. 1959. "On Memory and Childhood Amnesia." Chap. 12 in *Metamorphosis: On the Development of Affect, Perception, Attention and Memory.* New York: Basic Books.

Schachter, S., 1964. "The Interaction of Cognition and Physiological Determinants of Emotional States." In L. Berkowitz, ed., *Advances in Experimental Social Psychology.* New York: Academic Press.

Schiefflin, E. L., 1976. *The Sorrow of the Lonely and the Burning of the Dancers.* New York: St. Martin's.

Schneider, D., and L. Sharp, 1969. *The Dream Life of a Primitive People: The Dreams of the Yir Yoront of Australia.* Anthropological Studies, 1, American Anthropological Association. Ann Arbor, Mich.: University Microfilms.

Scholem, G., 1973. *Sabbattai Sevi: Mystical Messiah.* Princeton, N.J.: Princeton University Press.

Schultes, R. E., 1963. "Botanical Sources of the New World Narcotics." *Psychedelic Review* 1:145–166.

―――, 1966. "The Search for New Native Hallucinogens." *Lloydia* 29:243–308.

Schwartz, T., ed., 1976a. *Socialization as Cultural Communication: Development of a Theme in the Work of Margaret Mead.* Berkeley, Calif.: University of California Press.

―――, 1976b. "Relations Among Generations in Time-Limited Cultures." In T. Schwartz, ed., *Socialization as Cultural Communication: Development of a Theme in the Work of Margaret Mead.* Berkeley, Calif.: University of California Press.

Sears, R. R., E. E. Maccoby, and H. Levin, 1957. *Patterns of Child Rearing.* Evanston, Ill.: Row, Patterson.

Segall, M. H., D. T. Campbell, and M. J. Herskovits, 1966. *The Influence of Culture on Visual Perception.* Indianapolis: Bobbs-Merrill.

Seligman, C. G., 1924. "Anthropology and Psychology: A Study of Some Points of Contact." *Journal of the Royal Anthropological Institute* 54:13–46.

Service, E., 1976. "Leslie Alvin White (1900–1975)." *American Anthropologist* 78:612–617.

Sharp, L., 1974 (orig. 1952). "Steel Axes for Stone-Age Australians." In J. P. Spradley and D. W. McCurdy, eds., *Conformity and Conflict,* 2nd ed. Boston: Little, Brown.

Shostak, M., 1976. "A !Kung Woman's Memories of Childhood." In R. Lee and I. DeVore, eds., *Kalahari Hunter-Gatherers.* Cambridge, Mass.: Harvard University Press.

Sillitoe, P., 1977. "Land Shortage and War in New Guinea." *Ethnology* 16:71–81.

Silverthorne, H., 1951. *Haitian T.A.T. Protocols.* Unpublished manuscript.

Simmons, L. W., 1942. *Sun Chief: The Autobiography of a Hopi Indian.* New Haven, Conn.: Yale University Press.

Singer, P., E. Araneta, and J. Naidoo, 1973. "Learning Psychodynamics, History, Diagnosis, Management, Therapy, by a Kali Cult Indigenous Healer in Guyana." Paper presented at the 9th International Congress of Anthropological and Ethnological Sciences. (Abstract: *Transcultural Psychiatric Research Review* 1975 [12]:71–73.)

Sipes, R. G., 1973. "War, Sports, and Aggression: An Empirical Test of Two Rival Theories." *American Anthropologist* 75:64–86.

Siskind, J., 1973. *To Hunt in the Morning.* New York: Oxford.

Slater, P. E., and D. A. Slater, 1965. "Maternal Ambivalence and Narcissism: A Cross-Cultural Study." *Merrill Palmer Quarterly of Behavior and Development* 11:241–259.

Slocum, S., 1975. "Woman the Gatherer: Male Bias in Anthropology." In R. R. Reiter, ed., *Toward an Anthropology of Women.* New York: Monthly Review Press.

Solecki, R., 1975. "Shanidar IV, a Neanderthal Flower Burial in Northern Iraq." *Science* 190:880–881.

Sorenson, E. R., 1976. *The Edge of the Forest: Land, Childhood and Change in a New Guinea Protoagricultural Society.* Washington, D.C.: Smithsonian Institution.

Southall, A., 1975. "Ecology and Social Change in Madagascar: Linton's Hypothesis on the Tanala and Betsileo." *American Anthropologist* 77:603–608.

Spain, D., 1972. "On the Use of Projective Tests for Research in Psychological Anthropology." In F. L. K. Hsu, ed., *Psychological Anthropology,* new ed. Cambridge, Mass.: Schenkman.

Sperber, D., 1975. *Rethinking Symbolism,* trans. by A. L. Marton. London: Cambridge.

Spier, L., 1928. "Havasupai Ethnography." *American Museum of Natural History. Anthropological Papers* 29:81–392.

Spindler, G. D., 1955. *Sociocultural and Psychological Processes in Menomini Acculturation.* University of California Publications in Culture and Society, vol. 5 Berkeley, Calif.: University of California Press.

———, ed., 1974. *Education and Cultural Process: Toward an Anthropology of Education.* New York: Holt, Rinehart and Winston.

———, 1978a. Introduction to Part 1, in G. D. Spindler, ed. *The Making of Psychological Anthropology.* Berkeley, Calif.: University of California Press.

———, 1978b. Personal Communication.

———, 1978c. "Comment to L. S. Spindler: Researching the Psychology of Culture Change and Urbanization." In G. D. Spindler, ed., *The Making of Psychological Anthropology.* Berkeley, Calif.: The University of California Press.

———, ed., 1978d. *The Making of Psychological Anthropology.* Berkeley, Calif.: The University of California Press.

———, and L. S. Spindler, 1971. *Dreamers Without Power: The Menomini Indians.* New York: Holt, Rinehart and Winston.

———, ———, 1978. *Schooling in Schönhausen Revisited: A Restudy of Cultural Transmission and Instrument Adaptation in an Urbanizing German Village.* (Mimeo.)

Spindler, L. S., 1962. *Menomini Women and Culture Change.* American Anthropological Association, Memoir 91.

———, 1970. "Menomini Witchcraft." In D. Walker, ed., *Systems of North American Witchcraft and Sorcery.* Anthropological Monographs, 1, University of Idaho.

———, 1977. *Culture Change and Modernization: Mini-Models and Case Studies.* New York: Holt, Rinehart and Winston.

———, 1978. "Researching the Psychology of Culture Change and Urbanization." In G. D. Spindler, ed., *The Making of Psychological Anthropology.* Berkeley, Calif.: University of California Press.

———, and G. D. Spindler, 1967 (orig. 1958). "Male and Female Adaptations in Culture Change: Menomini." In R. Hunt, ed., *Personalities in Cultures: Readings in Psycho-*

logical Anthropology. Garden City, N.Y.: Natural History Press.

Spiro, M. E., 1953. "Ghosts: An Anthropological Inquiry into Learning and Perception." *Journal of Abnormal and Social Psychology* 48:376–382.

———, 1954a. "Human Nature in Its Psychological Dimensions." *American Anthropologist* 56:19–30.

———, 1954b. "Is the Family Universal?" *American Anthropologist* 56:839–846.

———, 1958. *Children of the Kibbutz.* Cambridge, Mass.: Harvard University Press.

———, 1959. "Cultural Heritage, Personal Tension, and Mental Illness in a South Sea Culture." In M. K. Opler, ed., *Culture and Mental Health.* New York: Macmillan.

———, 1961. "An Overview and a Suggested Reorientation." In F. L. K. Hsu, ed., *Psychological Anthropology: Approaches to Culture and Personality.* Homewood, Ill.: Dorsey.

———, 1963. "Education in a Communal Village in Israel." In G. D. Spindler, ed., *Education and Culture: Anthropological Approaches.* New York: Holt, Rinehart and Winston.

———, 1967. *Burmese Supernaturalism.* Englewood Cliffs, N.J.: Prentice-Hall.

———, 1977. *Kinship and Marriage in Burma: A Cultural and Psychodynamic Analysis.* Berkeley, Calif.: University of California Press.

———, 1978. "Culture and Human Nature." In G. D. Spindler, ed., *The Making of Psychological Anthropology.* Berkeley, Calif.: University of California Press.

———, and R. G. D'Andrade, 1958. "A Cross-Cultural Study of Some Supernatural Beliefs." *American Anthropologist* 60:456–466.

Spitz, R. A., 1945. "Hospitalism: An Inquiry into the Genesis of a Psychiatric Condition in Early Childhood." *The Psychoanalytic Study of the Child* 1:53–74.

Stefflre, V., V. Vales, and L. Morley, 1966. "Language and Cognition in Yucatán: A Cross-Cultural Replication." *Journal of Personality and Social Psychology* 4:112–115.

Stein, H., 1977. "Review of *Salish Indian Mental Health and Culture Change: Psychohygienic and Therapeutic Aspects of the Guardian*

Spirit Ceremonial by Wolfgang C. Jilek." *American Anthropologist* 79:668–669.

Stern, W., and O. Lippmann, eds., 1912. "Vorschläge zur psychologischen Untersuchung primitiver Menschen." *Zeitschrift für angewandte Psychologie und psychologische Sammelforschung,* Beiheft 5, pt. 1.

Steward, J., ed., 1944–1950. *Handbook of South American Indians,* vols. 1–6. Bureau of American Ethnology, Bulletin 143.

———, 1948. "A Functional-Developmental Classification of American High Cultures." In W. C. Bennett, ed., *A Reappraisal of Peruvian Archaeology.* Memoir 4, Society for American Archaeology.

———, 1949. "Cultural Causality and Law: A Trial Formulation of the Development of Early Civilizations." *American Anthropologist* 51:1–27.

———, 1955. *Theory of Culture Change: The Methodology of Multilinear Evolution.* Urbana, Ill.: University of Illinois Press.

Stroup, K., n.d. *Understanding Imu.* Paper presented to a graduate seminar on ethnopsychiatry. Department of Anthropology, Ohio State University.

Sutton-Smith, B., and J. M. Roberts, 1963. "Game Involvement in Adults." *Journal of Social Psychology* 60:15–30.

Swanson, G. E., 1960. *The Birth of the Gods: The Origin of Primitive Beliefs.* Ann Arbor, Mich.: University of Michigan Press.

———, 1973. "The Search for a Guardian Spirit: A Process of Empowerment in Simpler Societies." *Ethnology* 12:359–378.

Tan, E. K., and J. E. Carr, 1977. "Psychiatric Sequelae Amok." *Culture, Medicine and Psychiatry* 1:59–68.

Tart, C. T., ed., 1972. *Altered States of Consciousness.* Garden City, N.Y.: Doubleday-Anchor Books.

Tax, S., ed., 1960. *Evolution after Darwin,* 3 vols. Chicago: University of Chicago Press.

Teja, J. S., et al., 1970. " 'Possession States' in Indian Patients." *Indian Journal of Psychiatry* 12:71–87.

Textor, R. B., 1967. *A Cross-Cultural Summary.* New Haven, Conn.: HRAF Press.

Thorpe, W. H. 1961. *Bird Song.* London: Cambridge University Press.

Thrupp, S. L., ed., 1970. *Millenial Dreams in Action: Studies in Revolutionary Religious Movements.* New York: Schocken Books.

Thurnwald, R., 1913. "Ethnopsychologische Studien an Südsee Völkern." *Zeitschrift für angewandte Psychologie und psychologische Sammelforschung,* Beiheft 6.

Tiger, L., 1969. *Men in Groups.* New York: Random House.

———, and R. Fox, 1971. *The Imperial Animal.* New York: Holt, Rinehart and Winston.

———, and J. Shepher, 1975. *Women in the Kibbutz.* New York: Harcourt, Brace, Jovanovich.

Titchener, E. B., 1916. "On Ethnological Tests of Sensation and Perception with Special Reference to Tests of Color Vision and Tactile Discrimination Described in the Reports of the Cambridge Anthropological Expedition to Torres Straits." *Proceedings of the American Philosophical Society* 55:209–236.

Toffelmeier, G., and K. Luomala, 1936. "Dreams and Dream Interpretation of the Diegueno Indians of Southern California." *Psychoanalytic Quarterly* 2:195–225.

Townsend, J. M., 1975. "Cultural Conceptions and Mental Illness: A Controlled Comparison of Germany and America." *The Journal of Nervous and Mental Disease* 160:409–421.

Triandis, H. C., R. Brislin, and J. Draguns, eds., 1979. *Handbook of Social Psychology,* 5 vols. Boston: Allyn and Bacon.

Turnbull, C. M., 1965. *Wayward Servants.* Garden City, N.Y.: Natural History Press.

Turner, V., 1964. "An Ndembu Doctor in Practice." In A. Kiev, ed., *Magic, Faith and Healing.* New York: Free Press.

Tylor, E. B., 1958 (orig. 1871). *Primitive Culture,* 2 vols. Vol. 1, *The Origins of Culture.* Vol. 2, *Religion in Primitive Culture.* New York: Harper.

Virchow, R., 1878, 1879. "Über die Nubier." *Zeitschrift für Ethnologie* 10:333–356; 11:449–456.

von Frisch, K., 1950. *Bees, Their Vision, Chemical Senses, and Language.* Ithaca, N.Y.: Cornell University Press.

Vonnegut, K. Slaughterhouse-five. New York, Delacorte.

Wagley, C., 1977. *Welcome of Tears: The Tapirapé Indians of Central Brazil.* New York: Oxford University Press.

Wallace, A. F. C., 1950. "A Possible Technique for Recognizing Psychological Characteristics of the Ancient Maya from an Analysis of Their Art." *American Imago* 7:239–258.

——, 1952. *The Modal Personality Structure of the Tuscarora Indians, as Revealed by the Rorschach Test*. Bulletin 150, Bureau of American Ethnology. Washington, D.C.: Smithsonian Institution.

——, 1958. "Dreams and the Wishes of the Soul: A Type of Psychoanalytic Theory Among the Seventeenth Century Iroquois." *American Anthropologist* 60:234–248.

——, 1959. "Cultural Determinants of Response to Hallucinatory Experiences." *A.M.A. Archives of General Psychiatry* 1:58–69.

——, 1963. "Anthropological Contributions to the Theory of Personality." In E. Norbeck, D. Price-Williams, and W. M. McCord, eds., *The Study of Personality: An Interdisciplinary Appraisal*. New York: Holt, Rinehart and Winston.

——, 1966. *Religion: An Anthropological View*. New York: Random House.

——, 1969. "The Trip." In R. E. Hicks and P. J. F. Fink, eds., *Psychedelic Drugs*. New York: Grune & Stratton.

——, 1970. *Culture and Personality*, 2nd ed. New York: Random House.

——, 1972. "Mental Illness, Biology and Culture." In F. L. K. Hsu, ed., *Psychological Anthropology*, new ed. Cambridge, Mass.: Schenkman.

Warren, N., 1972. "African Infant Precocity." *Psychological Bulletin* 78:35–67.

Washburn, S., and C. Lancaster, 1968. "The Evolution of Hunting." In R. B. Lee and I. DeVore, eds., *Man the Hunter*. Chicago: Aldine.

Wasson, G., 1961 (orig. 1959). "The Hallucinogenic Mushrooms of Mexico: An Adventure in Ethnomycological Exploration." In D. Ebin, ed., *The Drug Experience*. New York: Orion Press.

Weiner, A. B., 1976. *Women of Value, Men of Renown: New Perspectives in Trobriand Exchange*. Austin, Texas: University of Texas Press.

Werner, E. E., 1972. "Infants Around the World: Cross-Cultural Studies of Psychomotor Development from Birth to Two Years." *Journal of Cross-Cultural Psychology* 3: 111–134.

White, A., and L. S. Taylor, 1904. *Shakerism: Its Meaning and Message. Embracing an Historical Account, Statement of Belief and Spiritual Experience of the Church from the Rise to the Present Day*. Columbus, Ohio: Press of Fred J. Hear.

White, J., ed., 1972. *The Highest State of Consciousness*. New York: Anchor Books.

White, L., 1925. "Personality and Culture." *Open Court* 39:145–49.

——, 1949. *The Science of Culture*. New York: Grove.

Whiting, B. B., 1950. *Paiute Sorcery*. Viking Fund Publications in Anthropology, 15.

——, ed., 1963. *Six Cultures: Studies of Child Rearing*. New York: Wiley.

——, and J. W. M. Whiting, 1975. With R. Longavough, *Children of Six Cultures: A Psychocultural Analysis*. Cambridge, Mass.: Harvard University Press.

Whiting, J. W. M., 1964. "Effect of Climate on Certain Cultural Practices." In W. H. Goodenough, ed., *Explorations in Cultural Anthropology*. New York: McGraw-Hill.

——, et al. 1966. *Field Guide for the Study of Socialization*. New York: Wiley.

——, 1974. *A Model for Psycho-Cultural Research*. Distinguished Lecture, Annual Report 1973 American Anthropological Association.

——, and I. L. Child, 1953. *Child Training and Personality: A Cross-Cultural Study*. New Haven, Conn.: Yale University Press.

——, R. Kluckhohn, and A. Anthony, 1958. "The Function of Male Initiation Ceremonies at Puberty." In E. E. Maccoby, T. Newcomb, and E. Hartley, eds., *Readings in Social Psychology*. New York: Henry Holt.

——, and T. K. Landauer, 1968. "Infantile Immunization and Adult Status." *Child Development* 39:59–67.

——, and B. B. Whiting, 1978. "A Strategy for Psychocultural Research." In G. D. Spindler, ed., *The Making of Psychological Anthropology*. Berkeley, Calif.: University of California Press.

Whorf, B. L., 1956 (orig. 1940). "Science and Linguistics." In J. B. Carroll, ed., *Language, Thought, and Reality: Selected Writings of*

Benjamin Lee Whorf. Cambridge, Mass.: MIT Press.

Williams, J., and R. B. Scott, 1953. "Growth and Development of Negro Infants: IV. Motor Development and Its Relationship to Childrearing Practices in Two Groups of Negro Infants." *Child Development* 24: 103–121.

Wilson, E. O., 1975. *Sociobiology: The New Synthesis.* Cambridge, Mass.: Belknap.

Wilson, P. J., 1975. *Oscar: An Inquiry into the Nature of Sanity.* New York: Vintage Books.

Witkin, H. A., 1966. "Cultural Influences in the Development of Cognitive Style." In *Cross-Cultural Studies in Mental Development,* Symposium 36, 18th International Congress in Psychology, Moscow.

———, 1974. "Cognitive Styles Across Cultures." In J. W. Berry and P. Dasen, eds., *Culture and Cognition: Readings in Cross-Cultural Psychology.* London: Methuen.

———, et al., 1954. *Personality Through Perception.* New York: Harper.

———, R. B. Dyk, H. F. Paterson, D. E. Goodenough, and S. A. Karp, 1962. *Psychological Differentiation.* New York: Wiley.

Wittfogel, K., 1938. "Die Theorie der orientalischen Gesellschaft." *Zeitschrift für Sozialforschung* 7:90–122.

———, 1955. "Developmental Aspects of Hydraulic Societies." In J. H. Steward, et al., *Irrigation Civilizations: A Comparative Study.* Social Science Monographs, 1. Washington: Pan American Union.

———, 1957. *Oriental Despotism.* New Haven, Conn.: Yale University Press.

Witkowski, S. R., and C. H. Brown, 1977. "An Explanation of Color Nomenclature Universals." *American Anthropologist* 79:50–57.

Wober, M., 1974 (orig. 1966). "Sensotypes." In J. W. Berry and P. Dasen, eds., *Culture and Cognition: Readings in Cross-Cultural Psychology.* London: Methuen.

———, 1975. *Psychology in Africa.* London: International African Institute.

Wolf, A. P., 1966. "Childhood Association, Sexual Attraction, and the Incest Taboo: A Chinese Case." *American Anthropologist* 68:883–898.

Wolfenstein, M., 1963 (orig. 1954). "French Parents Take Their Children to the Park." In M. Mead and M. Wolfenstein, eds., *Childhood in Contemporary Society.* Chicago: University of Chicago Press, Phoenix Books.

Woodworth, R. S., 1905–1906. "Color Sense in Different Races of Mankind." *Proceedings of the Society for Experimental Biology and Medicine* 3:24–26.

Wright, G. O., 1954. "Projection and Displacement: A Cross-Cultural Study of Folk Tale Aggression." *Journal of Abnormal and Social Psychology.* 49:523–528.

Wundt, W., 1900–1920. *Völkerpsychologie: eine Untersuchung der Entwicklungsgesetze von Sprache, Mythus und Sitte,* vols. 1–10. Leipzig: Engelmann.

Wylie, L., 1974. *Village in the Vaucluse,* 3rd ed. Cambridge, Mass.: Harvard University Press.

Yap, P. M., 1969. "The Culture-Bound Reactive Syndromes." In W. Caudill and T. Ling, eds., *Mental Health Research in Asia and the Pacific.* Honolulu: East-West Center Press.

Young, F., 1962. "The Function of Male Initiation Ceremonies: A Cross-Cultural Test of an Alternative Hypothesis." *American Journal of Sociology* 67:379–391.

Young, V. H., 1970. "Family and Childhood in a Southern Negro Community." *American Anthropologist* 72:269–288.

Zaretsky, I. I., and M. P. Leone, eds., 1973. *Religious Movements in Contemporary America.* Princeton, N.J.: Princeton University Press.

Zempleni, A., 1966. "La Dimension Thérapeutique du Culte des Rab: Ndöp, Tuuru et Samp, Rites de Possession chez les Lébou et les Wolof." *Psychopathologie Africaine* 2: 296–439.

———, 1977. "From Symptom to Sacrifice, the Story of Khady Fall." In V. Crapanzano and V. Garrison, eds., *Case Studies in Spirit Possession.* New York: Wiley.

Name Index

Subject Index